T0211115

Communications
in Computer and Information Science

1919

Rationale

The CCIS series is devoted to the publication of proceedings of computer science conferences. Its aim is to efficiently disseminate original research results in informatics in printed and electronic form. While the focus is on publication of peer-reviewed full papers presenting mature work, inclusion of reviewed short papers reporting on work in progress is welcome, too. Besides globally relevant meetings with internationally representative program committees guaranteeing a strict peer-reviewing and paper selection process, conferences run by societies or of high regional or national relevance are also considered for publication.

Topics

The topical scope of CCIS spans the entire spectrum of informatics ranging from foundational topics in the theory of computing to information and communications science and technology and a broad variety of interdisciplinary application fields.

Information for Volume Editors and Authors

Publication in CCIS is free of charge. No royalties are paid, however, we offer registered conference participants temporary free access to the online version of the conference proceedings on SpringerLink (http://link.springer.com) by means of an http referrer from the conference website and/or a number of complimentary printed copies, as specified in the official acceptance email of the event.

CCIS proceedings can be published in time for distribution at conferences or as post-proceedings, and delivered in the form of printed books and/or electronically as USBs and/or e-content licenses for accessing proceedings at SpringerLink. Furthermore, CCIS proceedings are included in the CCIS electronic book series hosted in the SpringerLink digital library at http://link.springer.com/bookseries/7899. Conferences publishing in CCIS are allowed to use Online Conference Service (OCS) for managing the whole proceedings lifecycle (from submission and reviewing to preparing for publication) free of charge.

Publication process

The language of publication is exclusively English. Authors publishing in CCIS have to sign the Springer CCIS copyright transfer form, however, they are free to use their material published in CCIS for substantially changed, more elaborate subsequent publications elsewhere. For the preparation of the camera-ready papers/files, authors have to strictly adhere to the Springer CCIS Authors' Instructions and are strongly encouraged to use the CCIS LaTeX style files or templates.

Abstracting/Indexing

CCIS is abstracted/indexed in DBLP, Google Scholar, EI-Compendex, Mathematical Reviews, SCImago, Scopus. CCIS volumes are also submitted for the inclusion in ISI Proceedings.

How to start

To start the evaluation of your proposal for inclusion in the CCIS series, please send an e-mail to ccis@springer.com.

Fuchun Sun · Qinghu Meng · Zhumu Fu ·
Bin Fang
Editors

Cognitive Systems and Information Processing

8th International Conference, ICCSIP 2023
Luoyang, China, August 10–12, 2023
Revised Selected Papers, Part II

 Springer

Editors
Fuchun Sun
Tsinghua University
Beijing, China

Zhumu Fu
Henan University of Science and Technology
Luoyang, China

Qinghu Meng
Southern University of Science
and Technology
Shenzhen, China

Bin Fang
Tsinghua University
Beijing, China

ISSN 1865-0929 ISSN 1865-0937 (electronic)
Communications in Computer and Information Science
ISBN 978-981-99-8020-8 ISBN 978-981-99-8021-5 (eBook)
https://doi.org/10.1007/978-981-99-8021-5

This Springer imprint is published by the registered company Springer Nature Singapore Pte Ltd.
The registered company address is: 152 Beach Road, #21-01/04 Gateway East, Singapore 189721, Singapore

Paper in this product is recyclable.

Preface

This volume contains the papers from the Eighth International Conference on Cognitive Systems and Information Processing (ICCSIP 2023), which was held in Fuzhou during August 10–12, 2023. The conference was hosted by the Chinese Association for Artificial Intelligence and organized by Tsinghua University, Henan University of Science and Technology, the Cognitive Systems and Information Processing Society of the Chinese Association for Artificial Intelligence, and the Cognitive Computing and Systems Society of the Chinese Association of Automation, with Zhengzhou University of Light Industry, Zhongyuan University of Technology, Luoyang Institute of Science and Technology, and Luoyang Normal University as co-organizers.

ICCSIP is the prestigious biennial conference on Cognitive Systems and Information Processing, with past events held in Beijing (2012, 2014, 2016, 2018), Zhuhai (2020), Suzhou (2021), and Fuzhou (2022). Over the past few years, ICCSIP has matured into a well-established series of international conferences on cognitive information processing and related fields. Like its predecessors, ICCSIP 2023 provided an academic forum for the participants to share their new research findings and discuss emerging areas of research. It also established a stimulating environment for the participants to exchange ideas on future trends and opportunities in cognitive information processing research.

Currently, cognitive systems and information processing are applied in an increasing number of research domains such as cognitive sciences and technology, visual cognition and computation, big data and intelligent information processing, and bioinformatics and applications. We believe that cognitive systems and information processing will certainly exhibit greater-than-ever advances in the near future. With the aim of promoting the research and technical innovation in relevant fields domestically and internationally, the fundamental objective of ICCSIP is defined as providing a premier forum for researchers and practitioners from academia, industry, and government to share their ideas, research results, and experiences.

ICCSIP 2023 received 136 submissions, all of which were written in English. After a thorough reviewing process in which all submissions received three single-blind reviews, 52 papers were selected for presentation as full papers, resulting in an approximate acceptance rate of 38%. The accepted papers not only address challenging issues in various aspects of cognitive systems and information processing but also showcase contributions from related disciplines that illuminate the state of the art. In addition to the contributed papers, the ICCSIP 2023 technical program included seven plenary speeches by Qinghu Meng, Dewen Hu, Jianwei Zhang, Xuguang Lan, Jing Liang, Yongduan Song, and Xinyu Wu. We would like to thank the members of the Advisory Committee for their guidance, the members of the International Program Committee and additional reviewers for reviewing the papers, and members of the Publications Committee for checking the accepted papers in a short period of time.

Last but not least, we would like to thank all the speakers, authors, and reviewers as well as the participants for their great contributions that made ICCSIP 2023 successful and all the hard work worthwhile. We also thank Springer for their trust and for publishing the proceedings of ICCSIP 2023.

August 2023

Fuchun Sun
Qinghu Meng
Zhumu Fu
Bin Fang

Organization

Conference Committee

Honorary Chairs

Bo Zhang   Tsinghua University, China
Nanning Zheng   Xi'an Jiaotong University, China
Deyi Li   Chinese Association for Artificial Intelligence, China

General Chairs

Fuchun Sun   Tsinghua University, China
Qinghu Meng   Southern University of Science and Technology, China
Xinchang Pang   Henan University of Science and Technology, China
Xiao Zhang   Zhengzhou University of Light Industry, China
Boyang Qu   Zhongyuan University of Technology, China
Zhiquan Huang   Luoyang Institute of Science and Technology, China

Program Committee Chairs

Zhumu Fu   Henan University of Science and Technology, China
Qingtao Wu   Henan University of Science and Technology, China
Juwei Zhang   Henan University of Science and Technology, China

Organizing Committee Chairs

Bin Fang	Tsinghua University, China
Zhiyong Zhang	Henan University of Science and Technology, China
Yan Li	Zhongyuan University of Technology, China
Chao Wu	Luoyang Institute of Science and Technology, China
Youzhong Ma	Luoyang Normal University, China

Publicity Committee Chairs

Mingchuan Zhang	Henan University of Science and Technology, China
Miao Du	Zhengzhou University of Light Industry, China

Publications Committee Chair

Wenshao Bu	Henan University of Science and Technology, China

Finance Committee Chair

Meng Wang	Henan University of Science and Technology, China

Local Affairs Committee Chair

Jingtao Huang	Henan University of Science and Technology, China

Electronic Review Committee Chair

Qingduan Meng	Henan University of Science and Technology, China

Steering Committee

Qionghai Dai	Tsinghua University, China
Shimin Hu	Tsinghua University, China

Program Committee

Baofeng Ji	Henan University of Science and Technology, China
Yongsheng Dong	Henan University of Science and Technology, China
Xiaona Song	Henan University of Science and Technology, China
Ruijuan Zheng	Henan University of Science and Technology, China
Zhifeng Zhang	Zhengzhou University of Light Industry, China
Wenqing Chen	Luoyang Institute of Science and Technology, China
Jianhu Jiang	Luoyang Institute of Science and Technology, China
Lijun Song	Luoyang Institute of Science and Technology, China
Lifan Sun	Henan University of Science and Technology, China
Fazhan Tao	Henan University of Science and Technology, China
Pengju Si	Henan University of Science and Technology, China
Junlong Zhu	Henan University of Science and Technology, China
Lin Wang	Henan University of Science and Technology, China
Bin Song	Henan University of Science and Technology, China
Xuzhao Chai	Zhongyuan University of Technology, China
Deguang Li	Luoyang Normal University, China
Shijie Jia	Luoyang Normal University, China
Tongchi Zhou	Zhongyuan University of Technology, China
Baihao Qiao	Zhongyuan University of Technology, China
Jiaquan Shen	Luoyang Normal University, China

Contents – Part II

Robotics and Bioinformatics

Vision

Contents – Part I

Algorithm and Control

Application

Robotics and Bioinformatics

Iris Recognition Network Based on Full Coordinate Attention

Xina Liu[1], Xinying Xu[1], Jiayan Zhang[1], Pengyue Li[1(✉)], and Jijun Tang[2]

[1] College of Electrical and Power Engineering, Taiyuan University of Technology, Taiyuan 030024, China
lipengyue@tyut.edu.cn
[2] University of South Carolina, Columbia, USA

Abstract. Although deep learning methods have shown better performance than traditional algorithms in iris recognition, exploring new CNN network architectures is still valuable. In this paper, we propose a new iris recognition network architecture named FCA-Net, which leverages the full coordinate attention mechanism. Specifically, the proposed architecture introduces an attention mechanism into the ResNet Block and uses global average pooling instead of fully connected layers at the end of the network to reduce the number of parameters and prevent overfitting. Our full coordinate attention mechanism comprises two essential blocks: CH block and W block. The CH block embeds spatial horizontal coordinate information into the channel attention, capturing long-term dependency information along the spatial horizontal coordinate while preserving precise spatial vertical coordinate information, enabling the network to accurately locate the interested parts of the iris image. The W block encodes spatial vertical coordinate and generates attention through 1D convolution with adaptive kernels, without dimensionality reduction. By complementarily applying our attention mechanism to the input feature map, we enhance the representation of the regions of interest effectively. We evaluate our model on the CASIA-Iris-Thousand and JLU-7.0 datasets, and the experimental results show our method performs favorably against its counterparts.

Keywords: Iris Recognition · Attention Mechanism · Feature Extraction · Convolutional Neural Network · Deep Learning

1 Introduction

Studies have demonstrated that certain physiological information in humans can effectively represent individuals. These physiological features possess distinct characteristics, such as universality and immutability, making them highly secure and resistant to tampering or loss. Consequently, biometric technologies based on human features, including

This work was supported in part by the Research Project Supported by Shanxi Scholarship Council of China (2021-046); Natural Science Foundation of Shanxi Province (202103021224056); Shanxi Science and Technology Cooperation and Exchange Project (202104041101030); Natural Science Foundation of China, Young Scientists Fund (No. 62203319)

F. Sun et al. (Eds.): ICCSIP 2023, CCIS 1919, pp. 3–15, 2024.
https://doi.org/10.1007/978-981-99-8021-5_1

face, fingerprint, and iris, have found widespread applications in various domains, especially in major security fields. Among these biological features, iris recognition stands out due to its superior representation and heightened security.

Compared to facial and fingerprint features, iris features offer enhanced concealment, making them difficult to steal or forge. Furthermore, in comparison to gait and voice recognition, iris recognition boasts higher accuracy and uniqueness. Additionally, iris information remains relatively stable throughout personal growth and development, with significant differences in iris patterns between individuals. The collection of iris data also avoids direct contact with volunteers, adding to its advantages as a biometric technology. Considering these merits, iris recognition emerges as the most promising biometric technology. As a result, research in this field holds crucial theoretical significance and immense practical value for real-world applications.

Since it was first proposed by Burch in the nineteenth century [1], lots of studies and methods have emerged. Daugman [2] developed the first complete iris recognition system which used 2D Gabor wavelet transform. Boles *et al.* [3] used the wavelet transform zero crossings to represent the iris features, though it reduced the time cost but caused the noise retardation. Li Ma *et al.* [4] used a bank of circular symmetric filters on local iris texture information extracting and a nearest feature line method is employed in iris matching. Liu *et al.* [5] combined the local Gabor features and the key-point descriptors of SIFT to improve the characteristics of Gabor filtered image.

In recent years, due to the outstanding performance of deep learning, it has been applied in iris recognition. Shervin *et al.* [6] utilized VGG-Net as deep feature extractors for iris recognition and got promising results. Abhishek *et al.* [7] proposed a deep network as DeepIrisNet for iris representation, which can effectively model the micro-structures of iris and performed robust and discriminative. Liu *et al.* [8] applied modified FCN named as HCNNs and MFCNs to iris segmentation, both of them can automatically locate iris pixels with high accuracy. However, these methods ignore the importance of spatial positions, channels and scales and only study with position-invariant kernels.

Attention mechanism has become an efficient part in various computer version tasks [9–11]. These modules highlight the important local regions transferred by local features and filter the irrelevant counterparts, contextualized the prediction. SE-Net [12] utilized the channel relationship of CNN and proposed the *Squeeze-and-Excitation* module to compute channel-wise attention. However, SE-Net only focuses on the importance of the channel dimension, ignoring the spatial position and scale information of the feature map. CBAM [13] noticed the importance of spatial attention and applied channel and spatial modules as attention-based feature refinement, achieving good performance. However, CBAM generated channel attention by using global average pooling operation, which may ignore some local detailed information. Therefore, the performance of CBAM may be limited in some tasks that require more fine-grained attention control. GE [14] introduced two operators: gather and excite, to achieve better context exploitation of CNNs, which employed a depth-wise convolution effectively gathering features from spatial extent. Instead of employing multiple fully-connected layers as in SE, ECA-Net [15] introduced a 1D convolutional operator to model the interaction between channels. This leads to a more lightweight and computationally efficient architecture while still achieving competitive performance on various computer vision tasks. Unlike other spatial attention mechanisms that rely on pooling operations to obtain attention maps, Coordinate Attention (CA) [16] used a coordinate matrix to encode the coordinates of each spatial location in a feature map. This allows CA to capture the spatial context of each location in the feature map and to generate attention maps that are more accurate and informative than those produced by other spatial attention mechanisms.

In order to facilitate better interaction between channel and spatial information, enhance sensitivity to local features, and reduce network parameters, we propose a novel attention mechanism by combining the spatial coordinate convolution proposed by [15] and the one-dimensional channel convolution proposed by [16]. We introduce this attention mechanism into the iris feature extraction model. Considering the characteristics of preprocessed iris images, we propose a two-stage coordinate attention mechanism that can extract more expressive features and improve image classification. Experimental results demonstrate that our attention method further improves recognition accuracy.

The main contributions of this paper are as follows:

(1) We propose an iris recognition model, which utilizes ResNet-101 as the feature extraction model and introduces attention mechanism in the Block layer. In addition, we replace the fully connected layer with global average pooling at the end of the network to reduce the number of model parameters and prevent overfitting.
(2) To address the characteristics of iris feature distribution, we propose a full coordinate attention mechanism (FCA), which combines the channel and spatial coordinate attention to significantly improve iris recognition accuracy.
(3) We conduct two types of experiments, closed-set and open-set, to evaluate the performance of our proposed model. In the closed-set experiment, we ought to retrain the model every time a different dataset is used, while in the open-set experiment, we aim at testing the model's performance in practical recognition scenarios therefore we no longer retrain the model when performing recognition on new datasets. Specifically, we use the model trained in the closed-set experiment as the feature extractor in the open-set.

The rest of this paper is organized as follows. Section "Methodology" introduces the iris recognition process and the iris pre-processing steps firstly and then illustrates the details of our proposed FCA module, which is composed of the CH attention block and the W attention block. Section "Experiment" describes the experimental results of ablation studies and comparison studies. Finally, section "Conclusion" presents the conclusions of this paper.

2 Methodology

2.1 Iris Recognition Process

The specific process of the proposed iris recognition method is shown in Fig. 1, which consists of four parts: 1) iris image acquisition, i.e., collecting iris images using dedicated equipment for subsequent recognition; 2) iris image preprocessing, extracting the effective area of the collected iris image through a series of steps, and cropping it to the input size of the network model; 3) iris feature extraction, inputting the preprocessed iris feature into the deep learning network to extract the feature vector and construct the feature vector database; 4) iris feature matching, using the cosine similarity algorithm to match and recognize the extracted iris feature with the iris feature vector database, and finally obtaining the iris matching result.

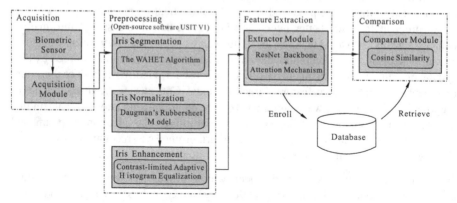

Fig. 1. Flow chart of iris recognition methods

To verify the proposed iris recognition method can achieve promising performance in both closed-set and open-set iris recognition scenarios, we define two recognition methods in Step 3 of iris feature extraction: closed-set recognition and open-set recognition.

In closed-set recognition, the last layer of the network model is used to directly recognize iris individuals. The model will be retrained every time there is a new dataset, and the result outputted by the network model can be regarded as the probability estimation of each class.

Considering the frequent registration operations in practical iris recognition applications, we define open-set recognition by using the model trained in closed-set recognition as a feature extractor. At the enrollment phase, the model is used to extract feature vectors from the enrollment image, which are then stored in the enrollment iris feature library. In the recognition stage, the model is used to extract feature vectors from the input recognition image, and the cosine similarity between this feature vector and all enrollment vectors in the feature library is calculated. The individual with the highest similarity is identified as the recognition result. This approach makes it easy to register new iris individuals without the need for model training.

2.2   Iris Pre-Processing

The open source iris recognition software USIT (University of Salzburg Iris Toolkit) Version 1 [17] is used for iris preprocessing, which is a software developed by the University of Salzburg that includes a variety of iris segmentation, feature extraction and comparison algorithms open source iris recognition software.

The software is modified on the traditional Daugman iris preprocessing method, using weighted adaptive Hough transformation and ellipse polar coordinate transformation to segment the iris image with a size of 640×480, and normalize the segmented iris

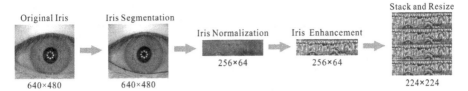

Original Iris   Iris Segmentation

Iris Normalization   Iris Enhancement   Stack and Resize

640×480   640×480   256×64   256×64   224×224

Fig. 2. Iris image preprocessing

to 256×64 size, and finally enhance the normalized image by increasing the contrast of dark and shallow areas. To match the square size required by the model, the preprocessed image needs to be stacked four times and resized to 224×224. The overall steps of iris preprocessing are shown in Fig. 2.

2.3 Attention Blocks

Considering that the stacking process of 224×224 size after iris preprocessing will lead to the redundancy of iris features, and it is observed that the normalized 256×64 iris image has fewer effective features in the vertical direction than in the horizontal direction and has an uneven spatial distribution. Therefore, we propose a FCA (full coordinate attention) module for two-stage coordinate direction feature extraction.

Taking the intermediate feature map $F \in \mathrm{R}^{C \times H \times W}$ as input, FCA sequentially derives a 2D attention map $\mathrm{M_{CH}} \in \mathrm{R}^{C \times H \times 1}$ along the channel direction and X coordinate direction and a 1D attention map $\mathrm{M_W} \in \mathrm{R}^{1 \times 1 \times W}$ along the Y coordinate direction as shown in Fig. 3. The whole attention process can be summarized as

$$F' = \mathrm{M_{CH}}(F) \otimes F + F$$
$$F'' = \mathrm{M_W}(F') \otimes F' + F' \tag{1}$$

where $\otimes$ denotes element-wise multiplication and $+$ denotes element-wise addition. In the process of multiplication and addition, the attention in each direction is attached to the corresponding dimension, which F'' represents the final output.

The detailed description of each block will be provided below.

CH Attention Block. Since channel attention focuses on "what" is in a given input image, while spatial attention is more concerned with "where", we retain some positional information while focusing on channel information and aggregate the spatial horizontal features of iris information along the channel direction and spatial vertical direction.

For an input X, inspired by [16] who used global pooling for 1D feature encoding, we use the global pooling kernels $(H, 1)$ to encode each channel along the spatial horizontal coordinate, so the output z_c^h of the c-th channel at height h is described as

$$z_c^h(h) = \frac{1}{W} \sum_{0 \leq i \leq W} x_c(h, i) \tag{2}$$

Next, we move on to the second step of transforming the encoded position information, which is attention generation. To make the attention block as simple and cost-effective as possible while fully utilizing the captured position information and effectively capturing the relationships between channels, we refer to the coordinate attention

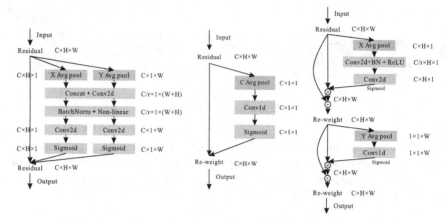

Fig. 3. Comparison of the structure of different attention modules

generation part in [16]. Then we feed the aggregated features into a 1×1 convolutional transformation function F1, obtaining

$$f^h = \delta(F_1(z^h)) \tag{3}$$

where δ is a non-linear activation function, $f^h \in R^{C/r \times (H+W)}$ is an intermediate feature maps encoding the horizontal direction and r is the reduction ratio for controlling the block size.

Another 1×1 convolution transformation F_h is used to transform f^h into a tensor with the same number of channels as the input X, yielding

$$M_{CH} = \sigma(F_h(f^h)) \tag{4}$$

where σ represents the sigmoid function.

The structure of the CH attention block is shown in Fig. 4. Unlike the channel attention that only focuses on the importance of channels, our CH attention block encodes spatial information, captures long-range dependencies along the spatial horizontal direction, and retains accurate spatial vertical position information. This enables the network to locate the regions of interest more accurately. The positional information in the other spatial direction is implemented by the W module.

W Attention Block. After encoded the channel features and spatial vertical features, we proceed to encode another spatial coordinate direction. To save computation, we no longer consider channel features here and only learn spatial horizontal attention features.

Similar to the 1D feature encoding operation of the CH module, we use global pooling kernels $(1, W)$ to encode each channel along the vertical spatial coordinate without considering channel features to save computation. The formula is as follows

$$z_c^w(h) = \frac{1}{H} \sum_{0 \leq j \leq H} x_c(j, w) \tag{5}$$

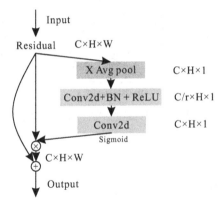

Fig. 4. The structure of the CH attention module

After obtaining the C × 1 × W features, we remove the channel dimension and send the resulting 1 × 1 × W spatial horizontal features through a 1D convolutional layer F_{1D} to generate attention weights, resulting in

$$M_W = \sigma(F_{1D}(z^w)) \tag{6}$$

Here, σ represents the sigmoid function.

The structure of the W attention module is shown in Fig. 5. In this way, our module achieves full coordinate attention encoding in three directions: channel, vertical spatial coordinate, and horizontal spatial coordinate. This allows our module to focus on the specific location of the interesting features more accurately, thereby helping the model achieve higher accuracy in recognition.

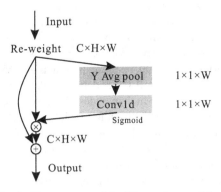

Fig. 5. The structure of the W attention module

The FCA module possesses lightweight characteristics and seamless integration capabilities. In this paper, we integrate it with ResNet, and the exact location of the module in the network is shown in Fig. 6. We apply FCA to the convolution output in each block.

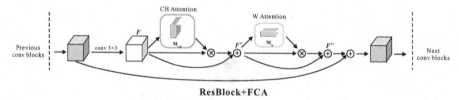

Fig. 6. FCA module integrated with a bottleneck in ResNet

3 Experiments

3.1 Datasets and Metrics

We evaluate the experimental performance of the model using the CASIA-Iris-Thousand [18] and JLU-7.0 [19] iris datasets. CASIA-Iris-Thousand is the 4th generation iris dataset released by the Institute of Automation, Chinese Academy of Sciences. All iris images are 8-bit grayscale JPEG files with a resolution of 640 × 480, as shown in Fig. 7(a). It includes 20,000 iris images from 1,000 subjects, with 10 images from each eye of each individual. Since the iris of each eye is unique, each eye is defined as a class in this experiment, and the dataset contains a total of 2,000 classes.

The CASIA-Iris-Thousand dataset is divided into two parts. One part is used for closed-set training, mainly for training a CNN network as the feature extractor. This part consists of 1500 classes, with 10 iris images per class. 7 images are used as the training set, 2 as the validation set, and 1 as the test set. The second part is used for open-set recognition and is mainly used to test the performance in practical iris recognition environments. This part consists of 500 classes, with 10 iris images per class. We use 7 images for enrollment, and 3 for testing.

The JLU dataset is developed by the Laboratory of Biometric Recognition and Information Security Technology at Jilin University, collected by self-developed devices and has been updated to its 7th generation, as shown in Fig. 7(b). The JLU-7.0 dataset consists of 65 eyes from 33 subjects, with 400 images for each eye except for the right eye of subject 11, which has only 311 images. For convenience, we duplicates the right eye of subject 11 to expand its number to 400, resulting in a dataset of 65 classes, each with 400 images, totaling 26,000 images. The JLU-7.0 dataset is also divided into two parts. One part is used for closed-set training, which includes 50 classes, each with 400 iris images. Among them, 300 images are used for training, 80 images are used for validation, and 20 images are used for testing. The other part is used for open-set recognition, which includes 15 classes, each with 400 iris images. Among them, 350 images are used for enrollment and 50 images are used for testing.

We employ commonly used machine learning evaluation metrics, Rank-1 accuracy, Rank-5 accuracy, and Cumulative Match Characteristic (CMC) curve to evaluate algorithm performance. Rank-n is defined as the probability that the top n images in the recognition result contain the correct class. Rank-1 represents the probability that the first image in the recognition result is the correct class, and Rank-5 represents the probability that the top 5 images in the recognition result contain the correct class. The CMC (Cumulative Match Characteristic) curve is a curve used to evaluate the accuracy from

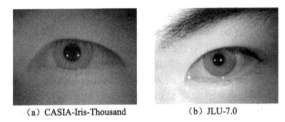

(a) CASIA-Iris-Thousand   (b) JLU-7.0

Fig. 7. Dataset images

Rank-1 to Rank-n, with the x-axis being the Rank level and the y-axis being the corresponding accuracy of the Rank level. The CMC curve not only shows the trend of recognition accuracy with the increase of Rank level but also comprehensively reflects the performance of the classifier.

3.2 Experiment Setup

We use Pytorch toolbox as our experimental framework, and the GPU used is NVIDIA GeForce RTX3090. We employ ResNet-101 as backbone model, which is optimized by Adam optimizer and uses the cross-entropy loss function, with a learning rate of 0.001. Different network models we are trained using the same parameters on the same datasets.

3.3 Ablation Studies

Importance of Full Coordinate Attention. Using ResNet-101 as the backbone network, we conduct a series of ablation experiments on the CASIA-Iris-Thousand dataset to validate the performance of the CH and W modules in the proposed attention block, by comparing them with other classic attention modules. The results are shown in Table 1.

Table 1. Ablation studies of FCA structure on CASIA-Iris-Thousand

Methods	Closed set		Open set	
	Top-1(%)	Top-5(%)	Top-1(%)	Top-5(%)
ResNet101(baseline)	94.27	98.40	97.87	98.93
+ Se	94.47	98.47	98.00	99.20
+ CBAM	92.2	97.67	97.06	99.06
+ ECA	97.27	98.93	98.67	99.20
+ CA	97.3	99	98.73	99.27
+ CH Attention	97.87	99.13	98.33	99.27
+ W Attention	97.6	99.2	98.73	**99.33**
+ FCA	**98.07**	**99.27**	**98.80**	**99.33**

It can be observed that both the CH attention block and the W attention block achieve better results than other classic modules, and the best performance is obtained when both blocks are combined, compared to the ResNet-101 backbone network. These results suggest that the proposed attention modules are more effective for iris classification.

The CMC curves of our proposed modules and other classic attention modules are plotted in Fig. 8. As is shown in Fig. 8, the proposed attention structure, whether as a single block or a combination module, achieves the best performance.

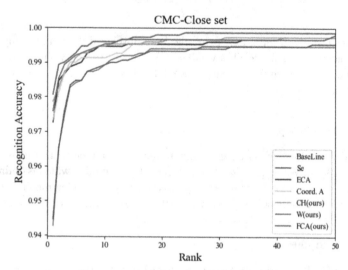

Fig. 8. CMC curves of attention modules

To better verify the performance of our model, we also conduct experiments on the JLU-7.0 dataset. Compared with other classic attention modules, our module also achieves ideal results, as shown in Table 2.

Table 2. Ablation studies of FCA structure on JLU-7.0

Methods	Closed set		Open set	
	Top-1(%)	Top-5(%)	Top-1(%)	Top-5(%)
ResNet101(baseline)	94.27	98.40	99.47	**1.00**
+ Se	98.3	99.2	99.07	**1.00**
+ CBAM	98.5	99.2	99.33	**1.00**
+ ECA	98.5	99.1	99.07	**1.00**
+ CA	98.5	**99.4**	99.2	**1.00**
+ FCA	**98.9**	**99.4**	**99.73**	**1.00**

The Impact of Module Arrangement. In this experiment, we compare three different ways of arranging the CH module and the W module: CH-W sequential concatenation, W-CH sequential concatenation, and parallel connection of the two modules. Since each module focuses on different regions, their arrangement order in the network may affect the overall performance. The results of the different arrangements of the two modules are shown in Table 3.

According to Table 3, it can be observed that the performance of the serial connection of the two modules is better than that of the parallel connection. When the CH module is placed before the W module, three indicators are the best, and only the Top-5 accuracy in closed-set recognition is suboptimal. On the other hand, when the W module is placed before the CH module, there are only two indicators obtaining the best, and the other indicators are not. Therefore, considering all aspects, we choose the CH-W serial connection structure as our FCA module.

Table 3. Ablation studies of module arrangement on CASIA-Iris-Thousand

Methods	Closed set		Open set	
	Top-1(%)	Top-5(%)	Top-1(%)	Top-5(%)
ResNet101(baseline)	94.27	98.40	97.87	98.93
+ Se	94.47	98.47	98.00	99.20
+ CBAM	92.2	97.67	97.06	99.06
+ ECA	97.27	98.93	98.67	99.20
+ CA	97.3	99	98.73	99.27
+ CH + W	**98.07**	99.27	**98.80**	**99.33**
+ W + CH	**98.07**	**99.33**	98.60	99.20
+ CH&W in parallel	97.27	99.2	98.47	**99.33**

The Impact of Module Connection. An innovation of our module lies in the connection of each module. It is not the simple element-wise multiplication as the traditional connection method but involves adding the multiplied result to the original input. Compared to the traditional single multiplication approach, this method can deepen the effect of the attention module weighting and facilitate the extraction of iris texture features without increasing excessive computational overhead. We compare this approach with traditional methods, and the experimental results are shown in Table 4.

Table 4 shows that the FCA module with multiplication and addition outperforms the traditional approach of only multiplication. This confirms the effectiveness of our proposed model design, which greatly improves the accuracy of iris recognition.

Table 4. Ablation studies of module connection on CASIA-Iris-Thousand

Methods	Closed set		Open set	
	Top-1(%)	Top-5(%)	Top-1(%)	Top-5(%)
ResNet101(baseline)	94.27	98.40	97.87	98.93
+ Se	94.47	98.47	98.00	99.20
+ CBAM	92.2	97.67	97.06	99.06
+ ECA	97.27	98.93	98.67	99.20
+ CA	97.3	99	98.73	99.27
+ FCA(*out)	97.27	99.2	98.47	99.20
+ FCA(*out + out)	**98.07**	**99.27**	**98.80**	**99.33**

4   Conclusions

This paper proposes a novel iris recognition method based on the full coordinate attention mechanism. This approach adopts ResNet-101 as the feature extraction backbone and incorporates the attention mechanism into the ResNet Block. The attention mechanism is designed based on the characteristics of the iris image and performs feature extraction in both channel and spatial coordinates, facilitating more efficient targeting of regions of interest.

Through extensive experiments, the proposed attention mechanism is shown to be highly effective in extracting essential iris features, leading to significant improvements in iris recognition accuracy. Comparative analyses against classical attention methods, such as SE-Net and ECA-Net, reveal superior performance in terms of Top-1 accuracy and Top-5 accuracy evaluation metrics.

Moreover, the practical implementation of the proposed method in iris recognition scenarios is considered. We introduce open-set recognition, an innovative approach that eliminates the need for model training. This enables a more comprehensive assessment of our proposed model performance across a broader spectrum of iris recognition scenarios.

References

1. Irsch, K., Guyton, D.: Anatomy of Eyes. Springer. 1212–1217 (2009). https://doi.org/10.1007/978-0-387-73003-5_253
2. Daugman, J.G.: High confidence visual recognition of persons by a test of statistical independence. IEEE Trans. Pattern Anal. Machine Intell. **15**, 1148–1161 (1993). https://doi.org/10.1109/34.244676
3. Boles, W.W., Boashash, B.: A human identification technique using images of the iris and wavelet transform. IEEE Trans. Signal Process. **46**, 1185–1188 (1998). https://doi.org/10.1109/78.668573
4. Li, P., Ma, H.: Iris recognition in non-ideal imaging conditions. Pattern Recogn. Lett. **33**, 1012–1018 (2012)
5. Liu, Y., He, F., Zhu, X., et al.: The improved characteristics of bionic Gabor representations by combining with SIFT key-points for iris recognition. J. Bionic Eng. **12**, 504–517 (2015)

6. Minaee, S., Abdolrashidiy, A., Wang, Y.: An experimental study of deep convolutional features for iris recognition. In: 2016 IEEE Signal Processing in Medicine and Biology Symposium (SPMB), pp. 1–6. IEEE, Philadelphia, PA, USA (2016)

7. Gangwar, A., Joshi, A.: DeepIrisNet: deep iris representation with applications in iris recognition and cross-sensor iris recognition. In: 2016 IEEE International Conference on Image Processing (ICIP), pp. 2301–2305. IEEE, Phoenix, AZ, USA (2016)

8. Liu, N., et al.: Accurate iris segmentation in non-cooperative environments using fully convolutional networks. In: 2016 International Conference on Biometrics (ICB), pp. 1–8 (2016)

9. Fu, J., et al.: Dual attention network for scene segmentation. In: Presented at the Proceedings of the IEEE/CVF Conference on Computer Vision and Pattern Recognition (2019)

10. Lu, J., et al.: Knowing when to look: adaptive attention via a visual sentinel for image captioning. In: Presented at the Proceedings of the IEEE Conference on Computer Vision and Pattern Recognition (2017)

11. Wang, F., et al.: Residual attention network for image classifications. In: Presented at the Proceedings of the IEEE Conference on Computer Vision and Pattern Recognition (2017)

12. Hu, J., Shen, L., Sun, G.: Squeeze-and-excitation networks. In: 2018 IEEE/CVF Conference on Computer Vision and Pattern Recognition, pp. 7132–7141 (2018)

13. Woo, S., et al.: CBAM: convolutional block attention module. In: Presented at the Proceedings of the European Conference on Computer Vision (ECCV) (2018)

14. Hu, J., et al.: Gather-Excite: exploiting feature context in convolutional neural networks. In: Advances in Neural Information Processing Systems. Curran Associates, Inc. (2018)

15. Wang, Q., Wu, B., Zhu, P., et al.: ECA-Net: efficient channel attention for deep convolutional neural networks. https://arxiv.org/abs/1910.03151v4

16. Hou, Q., Zhou, D., Feng, J.: Coordinate attention for efficient mobile network design. In: Presented at the Proceedings of the IEEE/CVF Conference on Computer Vision and Pattern Recognition (2021)

17. Rathgeb, C., Uhl, A., Wild, P., Hofbauer, H.: Design decisions for an iris recognition SDK. In: Bowyer, K.W., Burge, M.J. (eds.) Handbook of Iris Recognition. ACVPR, pp. 359–396. Springer, London (2016). https://doi.org/10.1007/978-1-4471-6784-6_16

18. Institute of Automation: CASIA Iris Image Database. http://biometrics.idealtest.org/

19. Laboratory of Biometric Recognition and Information Security Technology: JLU-7.0. http://jlucomputer.com/index/irislibrary/irislibrary_e.html

Obstacle Avoidance Control Method for Robotic Assembly Process Based on Lagrange PPO

Weixin Quan, Wenbo Zhu[✉], Qinghua Lu, Lufeng Luo, Kai Wang, and Meng Liu

School of Mechatronic Engineering and Automation, Foshan University, Foshan 528000, China
zhuwenbo@fosu.edu.cn

Abstract. The actual 3C assembly of robotic arms in factories often involves high-risk operations that need to be secured to prevent accidents. However, traditional reinforcement learning (RL) methods tend to pursue high rewards while ignoring behaviors that may lead to safety risks. To ensure the safety and efficiency of the industrial robot production process, we use the Lagrange Proximal Policy Optimization (L-PPO) algorithm to control the robotic arm. This method incorporates constraints into the agent learning and decision-making process, and the robotic arm considers obstacle locations and characteristics during task execution to ensure that its behavior is within safe limits. First, sensors are used to obtain information about the current state of the robotic arm and the obstacles in the environment. Then, L-PPO is used to train the robot arm's policy network. This network maps the current state to the robot arm's action space to generate the robot arm's action strategy. By interacting with the environment and collecting trajectory data, the strategy of the robotic arm is continuously improved by performing gradient updates using the L-PPO. Experimental results show that by using the L-PPO, the robotic arm is able to efficiently avoid obstacles and successfully reach the target. The method showed better performance on the obstacle avoidance task compared to traditional RL methods.

Keywords: Robotic Arm · Lagrange Proximal Policy Optimization · Obstacle Avoidance · Policy Gradient

1 Introduction

Reinforcement Learning (RL) is an important branch in the field of machine learning, where the goal is to design intelligent agent that can learn and develop optimal decision policies by interacting with their environment. A key concept in RL is the trade-off between exploration and exploitation. Exploration refers to an intelligent agent trying new actions in unknown or uncertain situations to discover potentially high-reward policy [1]. And utilization is the selection of known high-return actions based on existing knowledge and experience. In the learning process, the intelligent agent needs to balance exploration and exploitation in order to obtain the best long-term returns. RL has the ability to solve complex problems that may be challenging for traditional methods by interacting with and learning from the environment. An important feature of RL is its

F. Sun et al. (Eds.): ICCSIP 2023, CCIS 1919, pp. 16–26, 2024.
https://doi.org/10.1007/978-981-99-8021-5_2

ability to learn without artificially labelled data, gaining feedback and experience through interaction with the environment. It also gradually improves decision-making policies, which has a wide range of applications in artificial intelligence.

In summary, RL has several advantages, including adaptability, long-term reward optimization, and learning by trial and error. These features have led to a wide range of applications for RL in many fields, including robot control, autonomous driving, and financial trading [2]. As algorithms continue to improve and computing power advances, RL has enormous potential in solving complex tasks and addressing decision-making problems under uncertainty.

In addition, RL has the ability to interact with and learn from the environment, which makes it more advantageous for real-world applications. By interacting with the environment in real time, RL is able to continuously adapt its policies to changes in the environment and make accurate decisions in dynamic and complex environments.

Nowadays, RL has many application scenarios in robotics, including robot control [3–8], navigation and path planning [9–11], intelligent interaction and dialogue systems [12], autonomous driving [13, 14], medical robotics [15], and other fields. These are just some examples of application scenarios of RL in robotics. As technology continues to advance and research deepens, the application of RL in robotics will continue to expand and provide greater enhancements to the intelligence and autonomy of robots.

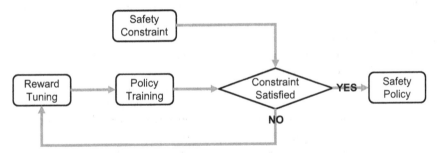

Fig. 1. In Safe RL, the algorithm design is simplified as the safety constraint will automatically be satisfied during training.

The actual 3C assembly of robotic arms in factories usually involves high-risk operations such as welding and shearing, and the robots need to ensure operational safety to prevent accidents. At the same time, robots need to collaborate with people to ensure human-machine safety. Complex environments and uncertainty require robots with the ability to recognize and respond. Robots must remain safe while complying with regulatory and safety standards under the requirements of continuous operation and efficiency. By ensuring robot safety, worker safety can be protected, accident risk can be reduced, and productivity and quality can be improved. Therefore, RL needs strong safety guarantees in migrating to real-world robot scenarios to ensure that robots can operate safely in complex, uncertain and dynamic environments. To solve this problem, we propose a safe reinforcement learning (Safe RL) method based on Lagrange proximal policy optimization to ensure the safety of the robotic arm while working. By introducing Lagrange multipliers, Lagrange PPO is able to better handle constraints while maintaining policy stability and finding a more appropriate policy during optimization (see Fig. 1). This approach provides a more flexible and reliable way of policy optimization when dealing with complex tasks and application scenarios.

The paper is structured as follows: Sect. 2 introduces existing methods for obstacle avoidance by robotic arms. In Sect. 3, the proposed method is elaborated upon. Section 4 presents the experimental verification of the method's effectiveness in obstacle avoidance and compares it with the state of the art. Finally, Sect. 5 provides the conclusions and outlines future work.

2 Related Work

Traditional methods for obstacle avoidance in robotic arms typically rely on sensor data and planning algorithms. In the context of robotic arm obstacle avoidance planning, there are several commonly used algorithms available for generating safe paths for the robotic arm, such as RRT (Rapidly-Exploring Random Trees) [16, 17], SST (Stable Sparse RRT) [18, 19], and OMPL (Open Motion Planning Library) [20], among others. These algorithms are utilized to efficiently explore the configuration space and find collision-free paths for the robotic arm to navigate through obstacles. These traditional algorithms for robotic arm obstacle avoidance can demonstrate good performance in specific scenarios and tasks. However, these methods typically require accurate sensor data, precise models and complex planning algorithms. They are limited in complex and unknown environments due to their perceptual capabilities, rigid planning and limitations, and lack of self-adaptability and learning capabilities.

Traditional RL algorithms can be adapted to the robotic arm obstacle avoidance problem by defining an appropriate state space, action space and reward function. They provide an optimization method based on a value function or a policy function that enables the robotic arm to learn the appropriate action policy for avoiding obstacles. However, RL algorithms are usually black-box models, and their decision processes and behavioral outcomes may be difficult to interpret and understand. In the robotic arm obstacle avoidance problem, safety is a key issue, and traditional RL methods have difficulty in providing an explanation of the decision and a guarantee of safety.

Model Predictive Control (MPC) [21, 22] is a model-based control method that has a wide range of applications in robotic arm safety obstacle avoidance problems. The core idea of MPC is to make predictions by building a dynamic model of the system and optimize the control policy at each time step to achieve the goal and satisfy the constraints. MPC has the flexibility, real-time and system optimization capabilities in robotic arm safety obstacle avoidance, which can generate safe and optimal path planning and dynamically adjust the control policy in the real environment. However, the performance of MPC is also limited by factors such as model accuracy and computational complexity, and needs to be properly tuned and optimized according to specific application scenarios. Meanwhile, MPC usually determines the optimal control policy by local optimization, but this may lead to getting trapped in a local optimal solution without finding the global optimal solution. This means that MPC may be limited by the local environment and cannot explore better control policies.

Although these methods can improve the safety of robots to some extent, they may have limitations and challenges in avoiding collisions with obstacles and considering production efficiency. For example, overly conservative rules may limit the flexibility and production efficiency of robots. Setting too many constraints can result in the robot being unable to complete tasks or perform inefficiently. In complex and rapidly changing environments, perceiving obstacles and responding accurately can pose challenges. The monitoring and detection systems themselves may also have certain delays and false-positive rates, which can affect the real-time safety of the robot.

In recent years, Safe RL is a new research direction in the field of RL that focuses on solving the safety problem in RL. Garcia [23] et al. proposed a definition of Safe RL as a RL process that guarantees reasonable performance and long-term rewards for satisfying specific safety constraints during the learning or deployment process. In other words, Safe RL is a RL method with constraints.

Compared to traditional RL, Safe RL introduces additional safety constraints. These safety constraints can include avoiding dangerous actions, ensuring system stability, and preventing irreversible damage with the environment. The goal of Safe RL is to achieve learning performance while ensuring the safety of the system and avoiding unacceptable risk or damage [24, 25]. To achieve safety reinforced learning, researchers have proposed a series of methods and techniques. These methods include, but are not limited to, modeling and defining safety constraints, solving safety optimization problems, safety monitoring and verification, etc. By introducing safety constraints and using appropriate algorithms and techniques, Safe RL can ensure the safety of the system and compliance with specific safety requirements during the learning and decision-making process.

Research on Safe RL also includes a class of methods based on constraint optimization. These methods are simpler, less demanding on the system, and more widely applicable than other methods. Constraint-based optimization approaches model Safe RL problems by representing safety requirements as constraints using a CMDP.

In the constraint-based optimization approach, the safety requirements are translated into constraints on the policy. In this way, the Safe RL problem can be formalized as a constrained optimization problem. During training and iteration, classical constraint optimization solution theory and methods can be applied to solve this problem.

3 Methodology

3.1 Constrained Markov Decision Process

CMDP is a formal framework for modeling Safe RL problems. Safe RL is usually formulated as a CMDP $\mathcal{M} \cup \mathcal{C}$ [26], which is extended by introducing a loss function $\mathcal{C}$ on top of the MDP. In a standard MDP $\mathcal{M}$, an additional set of constraints $\mathcal{C}$ is added. The set of constraints is $\mathcal{C} = (c_i, b_i)_{i=1}^m$, where c_i is the cost function of the safety constraint: $c_i : \mathcal{S} \times \mathcal{A} \to \mathbb{R}$ and the cost threshold is $b_i, i = 1, \cdots, m$ (see Fig. 2). Thus, a CMDP [27] is defined as the seven-tuple $\mathcal{CM} = (\mathcal{S}, \mathcal{A}, \mathcal{P}, \mathcal{P}_0, \mathcal{R}, \mathcal{C}, \zeta)$ [28]. In addition, the cumulative expected discount cost for state i under policy π_θ as,

$$C_\pi^k(i) = \sum_{n=1}^{\infty} \sum_{j,a} \zeta^{n-1} P^\pi(s_n = j, a_n = a \mid s_o = i) \mathcal{C}_k(j, a), \forall i \in \mathcal{S}, \forall k. \quad (1)$$

The solution of the CMDP is a Markov decision maximizing the policy pi under the constraint, in other words it maximizes $\langle V_\pi, \beta \rangle$ under the constraint $\langle C_\pi^k, \beta \rangle \leq E_k, \forall k$.

$$\max_\pi \sum_{n=1}^\infty \sum_{j,a} \zeta^{n-1} P^\pi (s_n = j, a_n = a) \mathcal{R}(j, a) \tag{2}$$

$$\sum_{n=1}^\infty \sum_{j,a} \zeta^{n-1} P^\pi (s_n = j, a_n = a) \mathcal{C}_k(j, a) \leq E_k, \forall k \tag{3}$$

Further, by analogy with $V_{\pi\theta}$, $Q_{\pi\theta}$, and $A_{\pi\theta}$, the reward $\mathcal{R}$ is replaced by the cost constraint c_i, which defines the value function, the action value function, and the advantage function of the cost constraint, respectively.

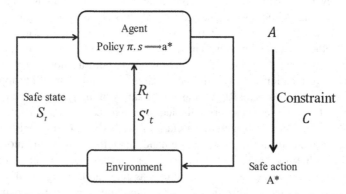

Fig. 2. The process of intelligent body-environment interaction in Safe RL.

In summary, CMDP ensures the safety of a system by introducing constraints. The goal of CMDP is to find the optimal policy while satisfying the constraints. By combining techniques such as constraint optimization, RL, and optimal control, CMDP provides an effective approach to Safe RL problems and drives its development in practical applications.

3.2 Safe RL

Traditional RL methods typically focus on maximizing long-term cumulative rewards, but in certain application scenarios, system safety is a crucial consideration. Safe RL is an extension of RL that aims to guarantee system safety during the learning and decision-making process. By introducing safety constraints and risk-avoidance policies, Safe RL ensures that the system operates within a safe range during the learning and decision-making process [31]. Its goal is to find an optimal policy that not only satisfies safety requirements but also achieves good performance.

L-PPO is a specific implementation of Safe RL that transforms a CMDP into an equivalent unconstrained problem by embedding safety constraints into the optimization problem using Lagrange relaxation techniques.

$$\max_{\pi} \min_{\eta \geq 0} \mathcal{L}(\pi, \eta) = \max_{\pi} \min_{\eta \geq 0} \langle \mathbf{V}_{\pi}, \boldsymbol{\beta} \rangle - \sum_{k} \eta_k \left(\langle \mathbf{C}_{\pi}^k, \boldsymbol{\beta} \rangle - E_k \right) \tag{4}$$

and invoke the least limit theorem.

$$\max_{\pi} \min_{\eta \geq 0} \mathcal{L}(\pi, \eta) = \min_{\eta \geq 0} \max_{\pi} \mathcal{L}(\pi, \eta) \tag{5}$$

The basic idea is to transform these constraints into penalty terms in the objective function, and to combine the constraints with the objective function by introducing Lagrange multipliers to obtain the Lagrange Function [29]:

$$L(\pi, \lambda) = J_r(\pi) - \lambda(J_c(\pi) - \alpha) \tag{6}$$

where, λ is an arbitrary real number, if the constraint is equational; $\lambda \geq 0$, if the constraint is unequal.

Lagrange dual function is an important concept used in the Lagrange multiplier method. Lagrange dual function is a function obtained by maximizing or minimizing the Lagrange function with respect to the multipliers of the constraints.

$$\min_{\lambda \geq 0} \max_{\pi} L(\pi, \lambda) = \min_{\lambda \geq 0} \max_{\pi} [J_r(\pi) - \lambda(J_c(\pi) - \alpha)] \tag{7}$$

The Lagrange method is based on the Lagrange function and uses the gradient method to update the Lagrange multiplier λ along with the update policy π [30]. The update equation is as follows:

$$\pi_{k+1} = \pi_k + \alpha_k \nabla_{\pi} (J_r(\pi) - \lambda(J_c(\pi) - \alpha)) \tag{8}$$

$$\lambda_{k+1} = [\lambda_k + \beta_k (J_c(\pi) - \alpha)]_+ \tag{9}$$

where, $\alpha_k, \beta_k \geq 0$, denote the learning rates of π and π respectively; $\lambda_0 = 0$; $[\cdot]_+ = max\{\cdot, 0\}$.

4 Experimental

4.1 Experimental Setup

The robot was simulated on Gazebo and ROS, and human avoidance experiments were designed. The positions of the start and episode targets were manually defined so that the robot collided with the human while taking the shortest path. At the same time the intelligences had to learn to avoid humans by taking longer paths or by waiting for them to leave the table. In this case, the goal of each episode is only slightly randomized so that the human never blocks the goal state. When training is performed, the human walks to the table and performs a wrenching action to achieve obstacle interference (see Fig. 3).

To prevent overfitting of the motion data, randomization was applied to the X and Y positions and start times of the human animation for each episode. In all experiments, the maximum length of each episode was set to 100 steps to give the robot enough time to move around the human to any target. An episode ends early when the robot arm collides and successfully reaches the target, so the number of RL steps varies per episode. When training the L-PPO algorithm, the distance between the robot arm and the obstacle is added as a restriction to the objective function, turning it into an unconstrained optimization problem.

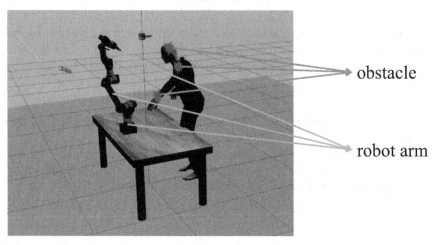

Fig. 3. Simulation setup with the robot mounted on a desk in which a human performs a task and also acts as an obstacle.

4.2 Experimental Analysis

In this paper, each experiment was timed 200 times and multiple experiments were conducted to obtain confidence regions for rewards during interaction with the environment (see Fig. 4).

At the beginning of the experiment, agent collided with humans in almost every set in the first half of the training because humans blocked the optimal path. In the sec-ond half of the training, the agent learned to avoid collisions with humans more fre-quently. The probability that the PPO algorithm eventually reaches the target is small and mostly collisions (see Fig. 5). Since the robot arm ends the current episode when it collides resulting in a high final reward value, this situation is actually not safe, in other words the agent does not learn how to avoid humans. However, the safe agent using the L-PPO algorithm learns to move around the human in order to reach the goal efficiently (see Fig. 6).

By comparing with the traditional PPO approach, the L-PPO algorithm explicitly defines safety constraints. The safety constraints of L-PPO allow the robot to consider the location and characteristics of obstacles and avoid collisions with them when performing tasks. This explicit constraint ensures that the robot's actions do not exceed the safety limits, reducing the potential risk and damage.

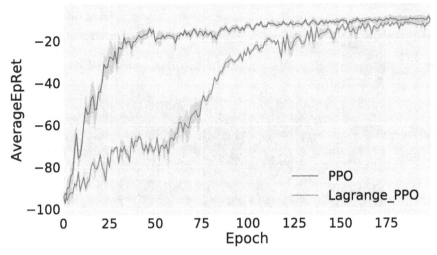

Fig. 4. In the simulation environment it is the PPO and the L-PPO that are used to control the rewards of the task.

Thus, the introduction of the L-PPO algorithm provides better safety for robot operations and finds a suitable balance between robot efficiency and safety. The development and application of this method provides more possibilities for the application of robotics in practical scenarios and further promotes the development of robotics and the expansion of application prospects.

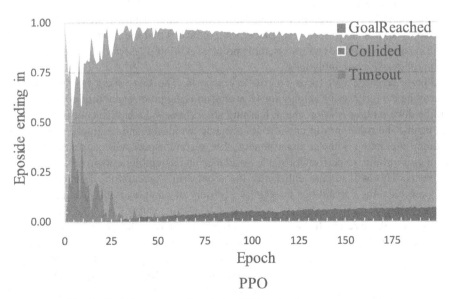

Fig. 5. Collision rate per Epoch for PPO in simulation environment.

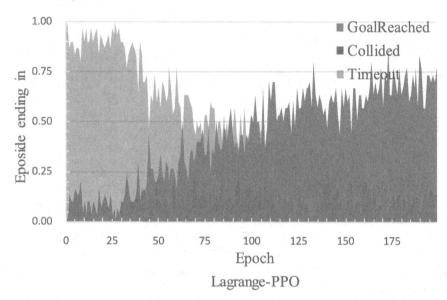

Fig. 6. Collision rate per Epoch for L-PPO in simulation environment.

5   Conclusion and Prospect

In this paper, a Lagrange Proximal Policy Optimization based obstacle avoidance control method for robot arm assembly process is proposed to realize the obstacle avoidance control of robot arm in the assembly process. Compared with traditional reinforcement learning methods, Lagrange Proximal Policy Optimization achieves significant success rate improvement in obstacle avoidance. This indicates that the method is effective in ensuring the safety of the factory assembly process, exhibits practicality, and is applicable to the robot arm's assembly tasks.

Future research will focus on two key aspects. The first aspect involves further improving the robot arm's autonomous learning and adaptation capabilities. Exploration will be done on how reinforcement learning algorithms and adaptive control strategies can enable the robot arm to enhance its obstacle avoidance and assembly capabilities through interaction with the environment. The second aspect will concentrate on the robot arm's ability to perform obstacle avoidance and assembly tasks in unknown environments. This will require enhancing the robot arm's perception, decision-making, and path planning capabilities to address a variety of complex real-world application scenarios.

Through these research extensions, we expect to improve the flexibility and robustness of the robotic arm to enable it to efficiently perform obstacle avoidance and assembly tasks in a variety of challenging environments. This is of great significance for practical applications in industrial automation and smart manufacturing, helping to improve production efficiency, reduce labor costs, and promote the widespread use of robotics in various fields.

Acknowledgment. The successful completion of this work is thanks to the support of the following projects:

A. Guangdong Key Area R&D Program: "New Generation Artificial Intelligence" Key Special Project "Multi-degree-of-Freedom Intelligent Body Complex Skills Autonomous Learning, Key Components and 3C Manufacturing Demonstration Applications" (2021B010410002).

B. Guangdong Key Area R&D Program Project: "Research and Development of Micron-level Real-time Vision Inspection Technology and System" (2020B0404030001).

C. Southern Marine Science and Engineering Guangdong Provincial Laboratory (Zhuhai) Independent Research Project: "Research and Application Demonstration of Key Technology for Cooperative Search of Small Targets in Shallow Sea Underwater" (SML2022SP101).

D. National Natural Science Foundation of China (NSFC) 2021 - Youth Program: "Research on Adaptation Problem and Update Mechanism of Online Learning of Data Stream in Visual Ash Measurement of Flotation Tail Coal" (62106048).

References

1. Kaiser, L., et al.: Model-based reinforcement learning for atari. arXiv preprint arXiv:1903. 00374(2019)
2. Naeem, M., Rizvi, S.T.H., Coronato, A.: A gentle introduction to reinforcement learning and its application in different fields. IEEE Access **8**, 209320–209344 (2020)
3. Zeng, A., et al.: Learning synergies between pushing and grasping with self-supervised deep reinforcement learning. In: 2018 IEEE/RSJ International Conference on Intelligent Robots and Systems (IROS) (2018)
4. Haarnoja, T., et al.: Composable deep reinforcement learning for robotic manipulation. In: 2018 IEEE International Conference on Robotics and Automation (ICRA). IEEE (2018)
5. Valarezo Añazco, E., Rivera Lopez, P., Park, N., et al.: Natural object manipulation using anthropomorphic robotic hand through deep reinforcement learning and deep grasping probability network. Appl. Intell. **51**(2), 1041–1055 (2021)
6. Levine, S., Finn, C., Darrell, T., et al.: End-to-end training of deep visuomotor policies. J. Mach. Learn. Res. **17**(1), 1334–1373 (2016)
7. Andrychowicz, O.M., Baker, B., Chociej, M., et al.: Learning dexterous in-hand manipulation. Int. J. Robot. Res. **39**(1), 3–20 (2020)
8. Duan, Y., et al.: Benchmarking deep reinforcement learning for continuous control. In: Proceedings of the International Conference on Machine Learning, F. PMLR (2016)
9. Liu, Z. X., Wang, Q., Yang, B.: Reinforcement learning-based path planning algorithm for mobile robots. Wireless Commun. Mob. Comput. (2022)
10. Ruqing, Z., et al.: Deep reinforcement learning based path planning for mobile robots using time-sensitive reward. In: 2022 19th International Computer Conference on Wavelet Active Media Technology and Information Processing (ICCWAMTIP), pp. 1–4. IEEE (2022)
11. Yan, T., Zhang, Y., Wang, B.: Path planning for mobile robot's continuous action space based on deep reinforcement learning. In: 2018 International Conference on Big Data and Artificial Intelligence (BDAI). IEEE (2018)
12. Brown, T., Mann, B., Ryder, N., et al.: Language models are few-shot learners. Adv. Neural. Inf. Process. Syst. **33**, 1877–1901 (2020)
13. Kiran, B.R., Sobh, I., Talpaert, V., et al.: Deep reinforcement learning for autonomous driving: a survey. IEEE Trans. Intell. Transp. Syst. **23**(6), 4909–4926 (2021)
14. Sallab, A E L., et al.: Deep reinforcement learning framework for autonomous driving. arXiv preprint arXiv:1704.02532(2017)

15. Aydın, Ö., Karaarslan, E.: OpenAI ChatGPT generated literature review: digital twin in healthcare. Available at SSRN 4308687 (2022)

16. Xinyu, W., Xiaojuan, L., Yong, G., et al.: Bidirectional potential guided RRT* for motion planning. IEEE Access **7**, 95046–95057 (2019)

17. Zhao, C., Ma, X., Mu, C.: Research on path planning of robot arm based on RRT-connect algorithm. In: 2021 33rd Chinese Control and Decision Conference (CCDC). IEEE (2021)

18. Johnson, J.J., et al.: Motion planning transformers: one model to plan them all. arXiv preprint arXiv:2106.02791 (2021)

19. Schramm, L., Boularias, A.: Learning-guided exploration for efficient sampling-based motion planning in high dimensions. In: 2022 International Conference on Robotics and Automation (ICRA), pp. 4429–4435, IEEE (2022)

20. Sucan, I.A., Moll, M., Kavraki, L.E.: The open motion planning library. IEEE Rob. Autom. Mag. **19**(4), 72–82 (2012)

21. Da Jiang, Z.C., Zhongzhen, L., Haijun, P., et al.: Reinforcement-learning-based adaptive tracking control for a space continuum robot based on reinforcement learning. J. Syst. Simul. **34**(10), 2264–2271 (2022)

22. Tang, M., et al.: Motion control of photovoltaic module dust cleaning robotic arm based on model predictive control. J. Ind. Manage. Optim. **19**(10), 7401–7422 (2023)

23. Garcia, J., Fernández, F.: A comprehensive survey on safe reinforcement learning. J. Mach. Learn. Res. **16**(1), 1437–1480 (2015)

24. Garcia, J., Fernández, F.: A comprehensive survey on safe reinforcement learning. J. Mach. Learn. Res. **16**(1), 1437–1480 (2015)

25. XU, M., et al.: Trustworthy reinforcement learning against intrinsic vulnerabilities: robustness, safety, and generalizability. arXiv preprint arXiv:2209.08025 (2022)

26. Altman, E.: Constrained Markov Decision Processes, vol. 7. CRC Press (1999)

27. Lillicrap, T.P., Hunt, J.J., Pritzel, A., et al.: Continuous control with deep reinforcement learning. arXiv preprint arXiv:1509.02971 (2015)

28. Wachi, A., Sui, Y.: Safe reinforcement learning in constrained Markov decision processes. In: International Conference on Machine Learning, pp. 9797–9806. PMLR (2020)

29. Boyd, S.P., Vandenberghe, L.: Convex optimization. Cambridge University Press, Cambridge (2004)

30. Rose, K H.: Introduction to optimization. Optimization 1.8.5: 7 (2013)

31. Thumm, J., Althoff, M.: Provably safe deep reinforcement learning for robotic manipulation in human environments. In: 2022 International Conference on Robotics and Automation (ICRA), pp. 6344–6350. IEEE (2022)

Zero-Shot Sim-To-Real Transfer of Robust and Generic Quadrotor Controller by Deep Reinforcement Learning

Meina Zhang, Mingyang Li, Kaidi Wang, Tao Yang, Yuting Feng, and Yushu Yu[✉]

Beijing Institute of Technology, Beijing 100081, China
yushu.yu@bit.edu.cn

Abstract. The goal of this paper is to develop a controller that can be trained in a simulation environment and seamlessly applied to different types of real-world quadrotors without requiring any additional adaptation or fine-tuning. First, a training environment framework for a generic quadrotor based on the high-fidelity dynamics model is designed. The input for the training environment consists of angular velocity and thrust. Next, the policy network and the detailed policy learning procedure are presented. The training process includes investigating and mitigating differences in dynamics, sensor noise, and environmental conditions between the simulation and real-world quadrotor systems. Efforts are also made to increase the continuity of the action output from the policy during training. The efficiency of the proposed approach is demonstrated through a series of real-world experiments. The trained controller exhibits remarkable robustness and versatility across different quadrotor models, successfully completing flight tasks in real-world scenarios without requiring additional training or modifications. These results highlight the potential of deep reinforcement learning for achieving zero-shot sim-to-real transfer in the domain of quadrotor control.

Keywords: Reinforcement Learning · Quadrotor Control · Sim-to-real Transfer

1 Introduction

In recent years, the field of robotics has witnessed significant advancements in autonomous aerial systems, particularly in the domain of quadrotor control [1, 2]. The ability to control quadrotors with precision and adaptability has wide-ranging applications, from aerial surveillance and inspection to package delivery and search-and-rescue missions. However, achieving effective control of quadrotors in real-world scenarios remains a challenging task. Traditional control methods often require extensive parameter tuning and fail to generalize well to different quadrotor models or handle disturbances and uncertainties present in real-world environments.

Different to conventional controllers, researchers have also started to train controllers using Reinforcement Learning (RL) to improve control accuracy and robustness, and to exploit the generalization of RL to enable the controllers to be applied to more Unmanned Aerial Vehicle (UAV) models and to achieve more complex tasks [3]. Lin et al. proposed a

F. Sun et al. (Eds.): ICCSIP 2023, CCIS 1919, pp. 27–43, 2024.
https://doi.org/10.1007/978-981-99-8021-5_3

RL controller for UAVs based on YOLO target recognition [4]. Bøhn et al. completed the training of a fixed-wing UAV RL controller using Proximal Policy Optimization (PPO) algorithm and compared it with traditional control methods [5]. Tuan et al. used policy-based imitation learning to obtain a RL controller that imitates the Model Predictive Control (MPC) algorithm [6].

In recent research, it is also a challenge that how to optimize the RL training of the controller. Song et al. trained the controller in parallel in multiple environments [7]. Park et al. introduced curriculum learning in UAV navigation [8], which was divided into two courses, unobstructed navigation and obstructed navigation. Both methods improved the training speed of RL. Chikhaoui et al. considered the limitation of UAV energy in RL, and added the influence of battery factor in the simulation environment, which made the simulation environment closer to the reality [9]. Wang et al. introduced the integral compensator in RL, and the tracking accuracy and robustness were greatly improved [10]. Wang et al. added a priori knowledge to the RL training of UAV controller to improve the reliability of RL [11].

However, the above UAV RL controller is only experimented in a simulation environment, because sim-to-real is an important difficulty in RL training of the underlying robot controller. With noticeable differences between the real-world and simulation environment, challenges such as easy actuator saturation, the need for a high simulation environment and combating model errors exist. These challenges make it difficult to apply RL in real systems.

Aimed at the above challenges of sim-to-real transfer in robot RL, some researchers have considered narrowing the gap between simulation environment and real world by finely estimating the parameters of the real system to achieve a closer simulation to reality. Antonova et al. performed precise model estimation to train robust policies for rotating objects to a desired angle [12]. However, this approach usually requires complex design and computation. Another approach to overcome the sim-to-real transfer gap problem is to learn the distribution of plant parameters iteratively. In [13], Christiano et al. learned inverse dynamics from data collected in real-world systems while exploring policies of trajectory planning from virtual systems. However, the problem with this approach is that an untrained policy must be executed directly on the robot, which may cause safety issues and cannot be applied to UAVs.

Another approach to solve the sim-to-real gap problem is domain randomization [14]. Domain randomization makes the simulation environment closer to the real environment by heavily randomizing the parameters of the training source, thus avoiding the need for extensive data collection and solving the problem that some parameters are difficult to obtain through extensive data collection. In some cases, domain randomization can even completely eliminate the need to collect data on a robot in a real environment. Domain randomization has been successfully applied to the transfer of visualization features and high-level polices. Chebotar et al. used domain randomization to train a visual target location predictor for a target grasping task [15], and the policy was trained in a simulation environment with random materials and illumination. Zhu et al. used domain randomization to train a policy to stack objects using a Baxter robot [16].

As for the problem of easy saturation of actuators in sim-to-real transfer, Convens et al. designed a restriction rule for the Proportional-Derivative (PD) control algorithm of drone control, which was superimposed on the output to limit the amplitude of the control signal [17]. Lin et al. on the other hand, added a compression function to the output of the network to limit the output value [4].

In the sim-to-real transfer study of RL UAV controllers, Hwangbo et al. used RL to train a controller that is applicable to a hummingbird quadrotor and is able to recover from a very poor initial state to a hovering equilibrium point, but this method is only applicable to the specific UAV it was trained for and has limited use scenarios [18]. Mu et al. proposed a RL UAV control method that is trained to resist time-varying, coupled uncertainties and environment disturbances [19]. In addition, Molchanov et al. used a domain randomization approach to solve the generalization problem of motor delays [20]. Huang et al. used RL controllers to enable UAVs to accomplish perching tasks [21]. However, all the current studies have only partially solved the problems in sim-to-real transfer, and the RL UAV controller can only be applied to one model with very limited application scenarios.

In summary, the previous research have shown that RL-based method can be applied to the low-level control of aerial vehicles successfully. However, RL-based control of quadrotors presents several challenging problems, including:

- Generalization of the low-level controller: The quadrotor low-level controller is typically trained based on a specific quadrotor, limiting its adaptability to other quadrotor models. Enhancing the generalization capabilities of the controller is essential to enable its effective deployment across various quadrotor platforms.
- Robustness against disturbances: Learning-based controllers trained in numerical simulations often struggle to perform well in real-world systems due to the disparities between the simulated and real environments. Improving the robustness of the learned policies against disturbances encountered in real-world scenarios is crucial to ensure reliable performance.
- Challenges in applying complex neural network controllers: Learning-based controllers implemented using neural networks are often more complex than traditional model-based controllers. Incorporating such controllers into real-world systems poses additional challenges, including addressing issues related to computational efficiency, real-time processing, and hardware constraints.

Overcoming these challenges requires dedicated research and development efforts in the field of RL-based control for quadrotors. Enhancing the generalization capabilities, improving robustness against disturbances, and addressing implementation complexities are vital steps towards achieving reliable and effective control of quadrotors using learning-based approaches.

In this paper, we aim to solving the above challenging problems in learning the low-level control of quadrotors. By training the controller in a simulated environment and seamlessly transferring it to real-world quadrotors without additional adaptation or fine-tuning, we aim to overcome the limitations of traditional control methods and enhance the versatility and performance of quadrotor systems in real-world applications. Our contribution is summarized as follows.

- We carefully design the quadrotor dynamics model for training. By employing angular velocity and thrust as input, and parametrizing the mass, the low-level control policy is trained in a baseline environment and can be transferred to different types of quadrotors.

- To enhance the adaptability of the low-level control policy from simulation to reality, we employ the domain randomization technique. This technique increases the sim-to-real transferability of the policy, which is initially trained in a numerical simulation environment but can be seamlessly applied to real-world systems with zero-shot adaptation.
- To validate the robustness and transferability of the low-level neural network control policy, we conduct a series of real-world experiments. These experiments serve as practical demonstrations of the policy's effectiveness in different scenarios, further supporting its applicability and performance in real-world settings.

This paper consists of six sections. Section 2 presents the problem statement. In Sect. 3, we design the quadrotor model used as the training environment, the RL network, and the environment framework. Section 4 provides a detailed explanation of the training process, particularly focusing on sim-to-real transfer. Finally, Sect. 5 showcases the real-world experimental tests.

2 Problem Statement

This study aims to train a policy capable of controlling various models of quadrotors with RL, the output of which is the thrust and angular velocity commands of the quadrotor. The state of quadrotor is described as a tuple (e_v, R, e_p, e_ω), where $e_p \in \mathbf{R}^3$ is the position error of the quadrotor in the world coordinate system, $e_v \in \mathbf{R}^3$ is the linear velocity error of the quadrotor in the world coordinate system, $e_\omega \in \mathbf{R}^3$ is the angular velocity error of the quadrotor in the airframe coordinate system, and $R \in \mathrm{SO}(3)$ is the rotation matrix of the quadrotor from the airframe coordinate system to the world coordinate system. To make the training better, this study uses the rotation matrix instead of Euler angles or quaternions to represent the attitude of the quadrotor. Because the unit quaternion representation encounters the unwinding problem, while Euler angles suffer from the singularity problem. The RL training goal is to minimize the parametrization of e_v, e_p, e_ω and to transform the third column of R to $[0, 0, 1]^T$ in the shortest time possible. This study also requires that the policy trained with RL is robust to enable the quadrotor to reach the target point and hover even under random initial conditions. In addition, the policy should be directly transferable to other quadrotor platforms for use.

In this study, only the quadrotor with the x-shaped model configuration is considered. Since the basic geometric relationship between the motor and quadrotor rotation axis has changed, it is not possible for a single policy to control both + and × quadrotor configurations without specifying the inputs for the current system configuration.

This study assumes that the state information of position, velocity, orientation, and angular velocity of the quadrotor can be estimated with reasonable accuracy. Similar assumptions are typical in the literature in the field of robotics. In actual flight, this state information is usually obtained by fusing onboard inertial measurements with one external localization, such as vision or GPS.

3   Training Environment Implementation

In this section, the dynamics model of a single quadrotor used to build a RL environment is described in detail. The dynamics model is also optimized to make it more suitable for RL training.

3.1   Rigid Body Dynamics of Quadrotor

In this paper, a coordinate system fixed to the fuselage is established as shown in Fig. 1, where the head is pointing to the x-axis and the perpendicular to the plane of the fuselage upward is the z-axis. In the world coordinate frame, the vertical upward direction is chosen as z-axis, north as x-axis, and west as y-axis.

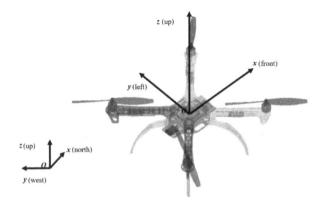

Fig. 1. Established world and body coordinate system

The dynamics model uses the Newton-Euler equation [22, 23]:

$$m \cdot \ddot{x} = mge + RF \qquad (1)$$

$$\dot{\omega} = I^{-1}(\tau - \omega \times (I\omega)) \qquad (2)$$

$$\dot{R} = \omega_\times R \qquad (3)$$

where $m \in \mathbb{R} > 0$ is the mass of the quadrotor, $x \in \mathbb{R}^3$ is the position of the quadrotor in the world coordinate system, $g = -9.81$, and $\mathbf{e} = [0, 0, 1]^T$ $[0, 0, 1]^T$ is the unit vector in the z-axis direction. $R \in SO(3)$ represents the rotation matrix of the quadrotor, $F \in \mathbb{R}^3$ is the net thrust, $\omega \in \mathbb{R}^3$ is the angular velocity in the airframe coordinate system, $I \in \mathbb{R}^{3 \times 3}$ is the inertia tensor of the aircraft, and $\tau \in \mathbb{R}^3$ is the torque in the airframe coordinate system, where $\omega_\times \in \mathbb{R}^{3 \times 3}$ is a skew-symmetric matrix associated with the rotation of ω into the world coordinate system. The torque τ is obtained as:

$$\tau = \tau_p + \tau_{th} \qquad (4)$$

where τ_{th} is the motor torque generated by the thrust [24], and τ_p is the torque along the z-axis of the quadrotor due to the difference in the rotational speed of the rotor.

$$\tau_p = r_{t2t}[+1, -1, +1, -1]^T \odot \mathbf{f} \tag{5}$$

where r_{t2t} represents the factor of torque to thrust conversion, number -1 means that the corresponding motor is rotating clockwise, $+1$ means counterclockwise. And $\mathbf{f} = [f_1, f_2, f_3, f_4]^T$ represents the vector of thrusts generated by each rotor rotation. The top view of the model is shown in Fig. 2. The motors generate thrusts f_1, f_2, f_3, and f_4 in a clockwise direction.

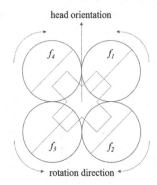

Fig. 2. Top view of the quadrotor model.

3.2   Motor Model in Simulator

In this section, the motor model is optimized. In this study, in order to apply the same policy to a variety of different motors, the motor input is normalized as $f \in [0, 1]$. $f = 0$ corresponds to no motor output and $f = 1$ full power. In traditional quadrotor control studies, it is usually assumed that the motor speed variation is almost instantaneous, so that the thrust of each motor can be considered as a directly controllable quantity.

To avoid the policy trained using a software simulation environment being too idealized, two elements are introduced in this paper to increase the realism of simulation: noise process and motor hysteresis simulation, which helps to improve the robustness and practicality of the trained neural network policy.

Motor Hysteresis Simulation

Discrete-time first-order low-pass filters are used to simulate motor hysteresis:

$$\hat{u}'_t = \frac{4dt}{T}(\hat{u}'_t - \hat{u}'_{t-1}) + \hat{u}'_{t-1} \tag{6}$$

where $\hat{u}'_t \in \mathbb{R}^4$ is the filtered and normalized angular velocity vector of the rotor, and dt represents the time duration between each input, $T \geq 4dt$ denotes the 2% settling time, given by:

$$T = dt \cdot \min\{t \in \mathbb{N} : ||\hat{u}'_{t'} - \hat{u}'_t||_\infty < 0.02, \forall t' \geq t\} \tag{7}$$

Motor Noise

Adding motor noise according to the discrete Ornstein-Uhlenbeck process:

$$\epsilon_t^u = \epsilon_{t-1}^u + \theta(\mu - \epsilon_{t-1}^u) + \sigma \mathcal{N}(0, 1) \tag{8}$$

where $\mu = 0$ is the noise mean, θ and σ are the positive factors, and $\mathcal{N}(0, 1)$ is a random variable. Then the thrust provided by each motor-propeller is calculated as follows:

$$f = f_{\max} \cdot (\hat{u}'_t + \epsilon_t^u)^2 \tag{9}$$

where the maximum thrust f_{max} is related to the thrust-to-weight ratio r_{t2w}:

$$f_{\max} = 0.25 m g r_{t2w} \tag{10}$$

where g is the gravity constant.

3.3 Environment Framework for Real Flight Test

We design the environment framework and software architecture of the actual quadrotor test. And based on these, the framework of RL network applicable to quadrotor is designed.

The RL UAV controller runs in the on-board computer Nano. The environment framework and software architecture for the real flight test are shown in Fig. 3 and Fig. 4, which are divided into 4 parts.

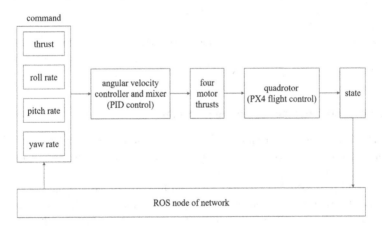

Fig. 3. Environment framework of real flight test

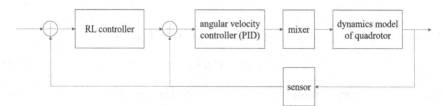

Fig. 4. Software framework of real flight test

The first part is the control commands received by the UAV, and this study uses the control commands of angular velocity and thrust to control the UAV.

The second part is the ROS control node where the neural network is located, and its input is the UAV state and target state obtained from the UAV sensors, i.e., current position, velocity, angular velocity, attitude, and target position. This node makes an error between the actual state information and the reference value and feeds the error into the RL network to obtain angular velocity and thrust control commands. These control commands are generated by the ROS control node and sent to the Pixhawk flight controller.

The third part is the angular velocity controller and mixer in the Pixhawk flight controller. The Pixhawk flight controller converts the angular velocity command into the thrust of each of the four motors through the angular velocity controller and mixer, and converts it into a PWM waveform signal to send to the motors. The angular velocity controller is designed as an optimized PID controller, which is optimized to ensure that the motor thrusts converted by the mixer are not too aggressive when the error is too large. The motor rotates according to the value of the PWM signal and the rotor provides the thrust to control the flight of the UAV.

The fourth part is the UAV sensor module, which obtains the state information of the UAV, including position and attitude, and passes the state information as part of the input to the neural network control node.

3.4 Training Environment Framework Design

Based on the actual flight environment and software architecture, an environment framework suitable for RL training is designed in this study. The framework of the whole environment during training is shown in Fig. 5.

The current position error, velocity error, attitude error, and angular velocity error of the UAV are used as observations for RL, i.e., the input of the RL controller. Four-dimensional actions are output through the neural network, which are the total thrust and the angular velocity commands of roll, pitch, and yaw. These commands are output to the angular velocity controller, which is designed in the same way as in the actual flight test, converting the commands into the thrust values of the 4 motors and inputting them into the quadrotor dynamics model to obtain the state information of the UAV. In turn, the difference is made with the target state to obtain the observation values of the target position error, velocity error, attitude error, and angular velocity error. The training data are obtained by iterating the dynamics model in the training environment.

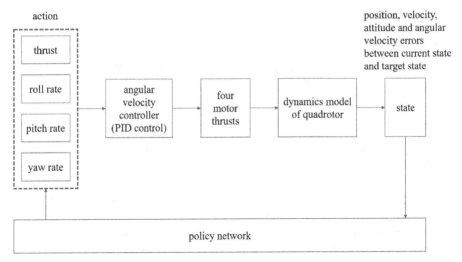

Fig. 5. Environment framework during training for RL

In this study, only the error between the current state and the target state is used as input, and not all the states of the current and target are used as input. This choice reduces the input dimension of the neural network, while still allowing the time-varying trajectory tracking function by changing the target state.

4   Control Policy Training Considering Sim-To-Real Transfer

4.1   Network of Policy

In this paper, a fully connected neural network is used as the RL training model. The neural network of the control policy contains two hidden layers, each containing 128 neurons. The hyperbolic tangent function is used as the activation function, while the linear activation function is used for the output layer.

4.2   Initial State and Target State

The policy in this study is trained using the PPO algorithm [25]. In the training process, the initial state is sampled uniformly in the following way: the initial pose is sampled randomly from a complete SO(3) space, the initial position is sampled randomly in a cube of 10 m sides around the target position, the maximum amplitude of the initial velocity is 1 m/s, and the maximum amplitude of the initial angular velocity is 2π rad/s. The target state is hovering at a random position in a cube of 10 m sides in the world coordinate system. The target position can be changed over time during training and actual flight, thus allowing the trained policy to be used as a time-varying trajectory tracking controller.

4.3 RL Cost Function

The RL cost function (Reward) is formulated as:

$$c_t = [\alpha_p\|\mathbf{e}_p\|_2 + \alpha_v\|\mathbf{e}_v\|_2 + \alpha_\omega\|\mathbf{e}_\omega\|_2 + \alpha_a\|\mathbf{a}\|_2 + \alpha_0\mathbf{R}_{0,0} + \alpha_1\mathbf{R}_{1,1} + \alpha_2\mathbf{R}_{2,2}$$
$$+ shaping(\mathbf{e}_p) + \alpha_R cos^{-1}(\frac{Tr(\mathbf{R}) - 1}{2})] \cdot dt \tag{11}$$

$$shaping(x) = x_{now} - x_{pre} \tag{12}$$

where $\alpha_p, \alpha_v, \alpha_\omega, \alpha_a, \alpha_0, \alpha_1, \alpha_2, \alpha_R$ are the weight values of the corresponding terms in the cost function, $\mathbf{R}_{0,0}, \mathbf{R}_{1,1}, \mathbf{R}_{2,2}$ are the diagonal elements of the rotation matrix $\mathbf{R}$. $cos^{-1}((Tr(\mathbf{R}) - 1)/2)$ is actually the rotation angle between the current direction and the identity rotation matrix, and $Tr(\mathbf{R})$ denotes the trace of the rotation matrix $\mathbf{R}$.

Shaping$(\mathbf{e}_p)$ is the shaping reward added to the reward design of this study for the current position and the target position. Specifically, the error between the current position and the target position of the current iteration and the error between the current position and the target position of the last iteration are added to the reward in each iteration. This allows the reward to take into account not only the current iteration but also the previous iteration, thus making the agent converge to the final position more stably, reducing the steady-state error, and accelerating the learning process.

The effect of $\alpha_p\|\mathbf{e}_p\|_2 + \alpha_v\|\mathbf{e}_v\|_2 + \alpha_\omega\|\mathbf{e}_\omega\|_2 + \alpha_0\mathbf{R}_{0,0} + \alpha_1\mathbf{R}_{1,1} + \alpha_2\mathbf{R}_{2,2} + \alpha_R cos^{-1}((Tr(\mathbf{R}) - 1)/2)$ is to make the final goal of the policy to hover at the target state. The advantage of using the diagonal elements of the rotation matrix R as reward is that it can effectively reduce the steady-state error of the final attitude. The term $\alpha_a\|\mathbf{a}\|_2$ in reward is to make the action selection gentler, which can make the RL controller more stable, and solve the problem that small UAV RL training controllers tend to saturate the actuator. The image of reward convergence in learning is shown in Fig. 6, which requires about 7000 iterations per training.

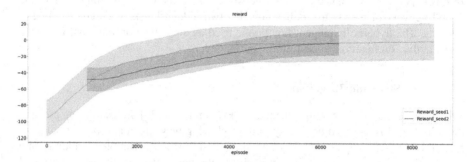

Fig. 6. Image of reward convergence

4.4 Sim-To-Real Transfer

The difficulty of applying RL controllers to real aircraft lies in the cross-domain transfer (sim-to-real), i.e., the trained network model can usually only accomplish the task of controlling the UAV in the simulation environment, because the models of actual UAVs, noise disturbances, etc. often differ significantly from those in ideal simulation environments, and it is prone to training erroneous policies that would saturate the actuator. Therefore, while RL network policies show good control effects in the simulation environment, the effect is often poor in flight tests of real UAVs or the policy can only be tested in real aircraft with the exact same model parameters as those used in RL training. To address the cross-domain transfer problem, this study tackles four aspects: adapting to real-world environment disturbances, generalizing the angular velocity controller, generalizing the UAV hardware parameters, and solving the actuator saturation problem.

Adaptation to Actual Environment Interference

There are various noises and disturbances in the actual UAV test, and this paper classifies, them into four categories: sensor noise, external interference, motor noise, and motor delay, and solve them respectively.

The actual sensor noise and motor noise values are obtained according to the real flight tests. The noises in position, direction estimation and linear velocity estimation use zero Gaussian model. Angular velocity noise measurement with gyroscope uses the method proposed by [26]. The external disturbance is approached using domain randomization at the corresponding position in the dynamics model. As for motor delay, a delay is added when assigning the respective thrust values of the 4 motors, as described in the Sect. 3.2.

Angular Velocity Controller Generalization

In actual flight tests, since the quadrotor is an under-actuated complex system, a feedforward loop needs to be added to enable the aircraft attitude to quickly track the desired attitude change, which is, the angular velocity controller. Therefore, it is necessary to imitate the actual angular velocity controller design in the RL environment and incorporate the angular velocity controller in RL training. And the values of each parameter of the angular velocity controller in the RL environment are domain randomized so that the RL trained controller can adapt to the angular velocity controller with various parameter values in the actual flight test.

Generalization of UAV Hardware Parameters

It is almost impossible for the parameters such as motor thrust, mass, inertia tensor, and arm length of an actual UAV to be exactly the same as those in the training environment. This paper deals with this in three ways:

a) Hardware-related parameters such as mass, inertia tensor, and motor thrust of a single UAV are generalized in RL training, i.e., domain randomization is used. So that the controller trained with RL can be adapted to the UAV with various parameters.

b) The thrust is normalized to adapt to various UAVs with different thrust-to-weight ratios.

c) Focusing on the stability of the instructions in RL reward function, better stability makes the RL controller more generalizable to different models of UAVs.

The above three processing points allow the RL controller to generalize to a variety of different UAV hardware parameters.

Solving the Actuator Saturation Problem

RL controllers often have the problem of over-idealized outputs leading to actual actuator saturation or discontinuous actions. This study deals with this in three ways:

a) Add a compression function to the final layer of output of the actor network to limit the range of the output, ensuring that the output values are within the appropriate range.

b) Add motor delays so that more realistic actuator models make the network output more suitable for real-world testing.

c) Substantial penalty for excessive output in the reward function.

The above three processing points solve the problem of actuator saturation due to the output of the RL controller. A comparison of the processed and unprocessed action outputs of this study is shown in Fig. 7.

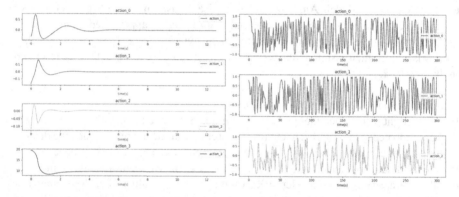

Fig. 7. Outputs of RL controller. The left one is unsaturated action output after processing and the right one is saturated action output without processing.

In summary, this section analyzes and solves the problems of cross-domain transfer in four aspects: adapting to real environment disturbances, generalizing angular velocity controllers, generalizing UAV hardware parameters, and solving actuator saturation problems. And the RL controller of this study is transferred to an actual UAV and accomplishes the flight mission.

5 Real-World Experiments

5.1 Real Flight Test on Different Quadrotors

Real-world tests of the RL controller are conducted, using the modular UAV system developed by ourselves. In order to verify the excellent generalization capability of the RL controller, this paper conducts real-world test experiments on two models, F450 and F550.

Firstly, the F450 model is used for test, and the target position is given by remote control to RL controller for fixed-point hovering. The initial target position of this test is the starting position of the UAV, and the node performs the integration operation according to the value of remote sensing signal of the remote control to obtain the target position, thus realizing the target position control by remote control. The results are shown in Fig. 8.

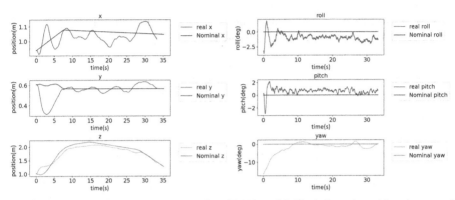

Fig. 8. Test results of hovering at target point of F450 model. The left one is position change and the right one is attitude change.

In the same test environment, the model was changed from F450 to F550 UAV for test, and the test results are shown in Fig. 9.

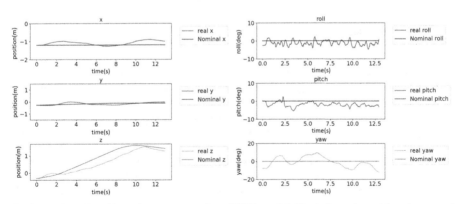

Fig. 9. Test results of hovering at target point of F550 model. The left one is position change and the right one is attitude change.

The PID parameters of the angular velocity controller of F450 and F550 models in Pixhawk flight controller are shown in Table 1.

The experiment results verify that the RL controller is able to hover the UAV stably even for different models. In contrast, the MPC controller and PID controller of the traditional control method need to re-tune the parameters to make the UAV hover stably.

Table 1. Parameters of Different Models of Pixhawk Flight Controllers

Model	Pitch_P	Roll_P	Yaw_P
F450	7.0	7.0	3.0
F550	6.5	6.5	2.8

Next, linear trajectory and circular trajectory flight tests of the RL controller are performed, and the linear trajectory results are shown in Fig. 10.

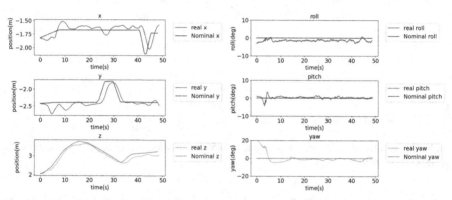

Fig. 10. Test results of linear trajectory. The left one is position change and the right one is attitude change.

The circular trajectory results are shown in Fig. 11.

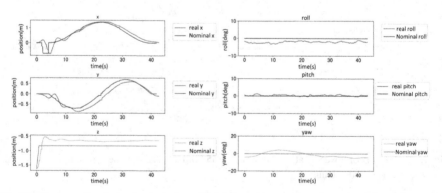

Fig. 11. Test results of circular trajectory. The left one is position change and the right one is attitude change.

The experiment results verify that the RL controller can perform the task of time-varying trajectory tracking very well.

5.2 Real Flight Robustness Test

This paper then verifies that the RL controller can enable the UAV to complete the flight mission from any initial state through two experiments.

The first experiment is to place the UAV on a slope and make it take off on the slope with a RL controller. The purpose of this experiment is to verify that the UAV can still take off and complete the mission when it is at a roll angle that is not initially 0. The experiment requires a certain performance of the UAV to ensure that the thrust of the UAV is sufficient to make the UAV take off from the slope.

The results of the slope takeoff test are shown in Fig. 12.

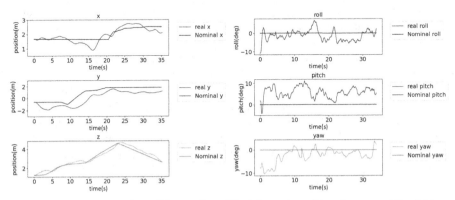

Fig. 12. Test results of taking off from a slope. The left one is position change, and the right one is attitude change.

The second set of experiments is to input a step yaw command of 180 degrees while the UAV is hovering, and the results are shown in Fig. 13.

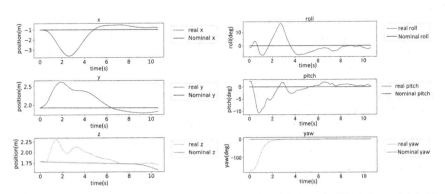

Fig. 13. Test results of inputting a step yaw command of 180 degrees. The left one is position change, and the right one is attitude change.

The above experiment results verify that the RL controller can make the quadrotor UAV complete the flight task in any initial state during the real flight.

In summary, the simulation and real environments are not exactly the same due to the existence of external disturbances and hardware performance differences. However, due to generalization, the RL controller can complete the real-world test and can be applied on different models in the real-world test without complicated parameter rectification sessions. And it can accomplish the task in complex environment with various disturbances, such as fixed-point hovering and trajectory tracking. The mission can be completed in any initial state. It exhibits excellent stability and robustness.

6 Conclusions

This paper presents the RL design methodology for a quadrotor low-level controller, which utilizes angular velocity and total thrust as control outputs. The paper successfully addresses the challenges of accurately modeling UAV dynamics and dealing with actuator saturation during cross-domain transfer when implementing the RL controller on a real aircraft. Through a series of real-world experiments involving different quadrotor models, the exceptional performance of the RL controller is demonstrated. The quadrotor under the RL controller exhibits remarkable adaptability to various models, and the ability to operate effectively even with significant initial errors. Importantly, it is worth noting that all real-world experiments were conducted without any further tuning of the policy trained in simulation environments, achieving zero-shot sim-to-real transfer in quadrotor low-level control. These findings pave the way for broader applications and advancements in autonomous aerial systems.

Acknowledgment. This work was supported by the National Natural Science Foundation of China under Grant 62173037, the National Key R. D. Program of China, and the State Key Laboratory of Robotics and Systems (HIT).

References

1. Yu, Y., Shan, D., Benderius, O., Berger, C., Kang, Y.: Formally robust and safe trajectory ssplanning and tracking for autonomous vehicles. IEEE Trans. Intell. Transp. Syst. **23**(12), 22971–22987 (2022)
2. Yushu, Y., Shi, C., Shan, D., Lippiello, V., Yang, Y.: A hierarchical control scheme for multiple aerial vehicle transportation systems with uncertainties and state/input constraints. Appl. Math. Model. **109**, 651–678 (2022)
3. Feng, Y., Shi, C., Du, J., Yu, Y., Sun, F., Song, Y.: Variable admittance interaction control of UAVs via deep reinforcement learning. In: 2023 IEEE International Conference on Robotics and Automation (ICRA), London, United Kingdom, pp. 1291–1297 (2023)
4. Lin, X.: Reinforcement learning control for small-scale unmanned aerial vehicles. Beijing University of Science and Technology (2020)
5. Bøhn, E., Coates, E.M., Moe, S., et al.: Deep reinforcement learning attitude control of fixed-wing UAVs using proximal policy optimization. In: 2019 International Conference on Unmanned Aircraft Systems (ICUAS), pp. 523-533 (2019)
6. Tuan, H.D., Nasir, A.A., Savkin, A.V., et al.: MPC-based UAV navigation for simultaneous solar-energy harvesting and two-way communications. IEEE J. Sel. Areas Commun. **39**(11), 3459–3474 (2021)

7. Song, Y., Steinweg, M., Kaufmann, E., et al.: Autonomous drone racing with deep rein-forcement learning. In: 2021 IEEE/RSJ International Conference on Intelligent Robots and Systems (IROS), pp. 1205-1212 (2021)
8. Park, J., Jang, S., Shin, Y.: Indoor path planning for an unmanned aerial vehicle via curricu-lum learning. In: 2021 21st International Conference on Control, Automation and Systems (ICCAS), pp. 529–533 (2021)
9. Chikhaoui, K., Ghazzai, H., Massoud, Y.: PPO-based reinforcement learning for UAV nav-igation in urban environments. In: 2022 IEEE 65th International Midwest Symposium on Circuits and Systems (MWSCAS), pp.1–4 (2022)
10. Wang, Y., Sun, J., He, H., et al.: Deterministic policy gradient with integral compensator for robust quadrotor control. IEEE Trans. Syst. Man Cybernet.: Syst. **50**(10), 3713–3725 (2019)
11. Wang, Z.: Distributed reinforcement learning for unmanned aerial vehicle flight control based on limited human experience. Southeast University (2020)
12. Antonova, R., Cruciani, S., Smith, C., et al.: Reinforcement learning for pivoting task. arXiv preprint arXiv:1703.00472 (2017)
13. Christiano, P., Shah, Z., Mordatch, I., et al.: Transfer from simulation to real world through learning deep inverse dynamics model. arXiv preprint arXiv:1610.03518 (2016)
14. Tobin, J., Fong., R., Ray, A., et al.: Domain randomization for transferring deep neural net-works from simulation to the real world. In: 2017 IEEE/RSJ International Conference on Intelligent Robots and Systems (IROS), pp. 23-30 (2017)
15. Chebotar, Y., Handa, A., Makoviychuk, V., et al.: Closing the sim-to-real loop: adapting simulation randomization with real world experience. In: 2019 International Conference on Robotics and Automation (ICRA), pp, 8973-8979 (2019)
16. Zhu, .S, Kimmel, A., Bekris, K.E., et al.: Fast model identification via physics engines for data-efficient policy search. arXiv preprint arXiv:1710.08893 (2017)
17. Convens, B., Merckaert, K., Nicotra, M.M., et al.: Control of fully actuated unmanned aerial vehicles with actuator saturation. IFAC-PapersOnLine **50**(1), 12715–12720 (2017)
18. Hwangbo, J., Sa, I., Siegwart, R., et al.: Control of a quadrotor with reinforcement learning. IEEE Robot. Autom. Lett. **2**(4), 2096–2103 (2017)
19. Mu, C., Zhang, Y.: Learning-based robust tracking control of quadrotor with time-varying and coupling uncertainties. IEEE Trans. Neural Netw. Learn. Syst. **31**(1), 259–273 (2019)
20. Molchanov, A., Chen,T., Hönig, W., et al.: Sim-to-(multi)-real: transfer of low-level robust control policies to multiple quadrotors. In: 2019 IEEE/RSJ International Conference on Intelligent Robots and Systems (IROS), pp. 59-66 (2019)
21. Huang, Y.T., Pi, C.H., Cheng, S.: Omnidirectional autonomous aggressive perching of unmanned aerial vehicle using reinforcement learning trajectory generation and control. In: 2022 Joint 12th International Conference on Soft Computing and Intelligent Systems and 23rd International Symposium on Advanced Intelligent Systems (SCIS&ISIS), pp. 1–6 (2022)
22. Shi, C., Yu, Y., Ma, Y., Chang, D.E.: Constrained control for systems on matrix Lie groups with uncertainties. Int. J. Robust Nonlinear Control **33**(5), 3285–3311 (2023)
23. Yu, Y., Li, P., Gong, P.: Finite-time geometric control for underactuated aerial manipulators with unknown disturbances. Int. J. Robust Nonlinear Control **30**(13), 5040–5061 (2020)
24. Martin, P., Salaün, E.: The true role of accelerometer feedback in quadrotor control. In: IEEE International Conference on Robotics and Automation (ICRA) (2010)
25. Schulman, J., Wolski, F., Dhariwal, P., et al.: Proximal policy optimization algorithms. arXiv preprint arXiv:1707.06347 (2017)
26. Furrer, F., Burri, M., Achtelik, M., Siegwart, R.: Rotors—a modular gazebo MAV simulator framework. In: Koubaa, A. (ed.) Robot Operating System (ROS), pp. 595–625. Springer International Publishing, Cham (2016). https://doi.org/10.1007/978-3-319-26054-9_23

Robot Manipulation Strategy for Explosives Disposal in Cluttered Scenes

Run Guo[1], Yi Yuan[1(✉)], Funchun Sun[2(✉)], Shuhuan Wen[1], Yang Chen[2], and Linxiang Li[1]

[1] School of Electrical Engineering, Yanshan University, Qinhuangdao, China
{yuanyi513,swen}@ysu.edu.cn
[2] Department of Computer Science and Technology, Tsinghua University, Beijing, China
fcsun@tsinghua.edu.cn

Abstract. Compared to human operator, robotic arm possesses the advantages of high accuracy and controllability in handling and manipulating hazardous materials. Due to the complexity and variability of application scenarios, such as the objects are stacked, it is a great challenge to accurately select target objects and manipulation mode in the fields of security and demolition. To address these problems, robotic arm systems require capabilities in target object detection, object relationship reasoning, and manipulation strategy selection. In this paper, we propose a framework with the abilities of reasoning about the unknown relationships between target objects and interfering objects, predicting manipulation sequences, and adopting appropriate manipulation strategies for hazardous object detection and manipulation processing. We conduct a series of experiments in indoor single-target, multi-target, and outdoor scenarios to complete the assigned tasks with improved manipulation sequences. These results serve as evidence of the effectiveness of the proposed framework.

Keywords: manipulation strategy · hazardous object detection · relationship reasoning · cluttered Scenes

1 Introduction

Robotic arms have already found wide-ranging applications for grasping moving objects in the industrial and service sectors. However, regarding security and explosive removal, the application of robotic arms still faces challenges and opportunities for further development due to the complex and varied nature of application scenarios.

In particular, hazardous objects exhibit specific properties that can lead to many interfering objects. Effectively enabling robots to accurately identify specific objects in scenarios where multiple objects are stacked remains an immense challenge. Objects in unordered stacked scenes often display irregular shapes, sizes, and positions, and can present complications such as occlusions and overlaps. It is crucial to select appropriate manipulation strategies based on acquired information to enhance manipulative performance in complex object-stacking scenes. This selection process aims to reduce the number of executions, minimize execution time, and enhance the accuracy and efficiency of execution.

Accomplishing locating and grasping target objects in such complex object-stacking scenes necessitates the robotic arm system to possess specific capabilities. These include the ability to detect objects accurately for identifying target objects, the ability to detect object relationships to understand the stacking situation and relationships between objects, and the ability to select optimal manipulation strategies for effective grasping. This paper proposes a framework for hazardous object detection and manipulation processing. Our framework involves reasoning about the unknown relationships between target objects and interfering objects in complex scenarios, predicting manipulation sequences, and executing appropriate manipulations to remove various hazardous target objects. The aim is to improve the manipulative efficiency and safety of hazardous object processing.

Our proposed framework aims to address the challenges associated with hazardous object removal manipulations in complex scenarios by integrating object detection, object relationship reasoning, and manipulation strategy selection. Through this comprehensive approach, we seek to enhance the efficiency and safety of hazardous object processing.

Fig. 1. A scene with hazardous objects and surroundings.

The structure of this paper is organized as follows. Section 2 provides an overview of the relevant literature on visual detection, object relationship reasoning, and manipulation strategy. Section 3 elaborates on the research conducted in this paper. In Sect. 4, we present the experimental design for evaluating the proposed algorithm in both indoor and outdoor environments. Finally, Section 5 presents the conclusion of this study.

2 Related Work

In complex hazardous object handling tasks, object detection algorithms are used to locate and classify hazardous objects. Relationship reasoning analyzes the connections between hazardous objects and other objects in the scene, aiding in the development of safe manipulation plans. Based on object detection and relationship reasoning, factors are considered to select the appropriate manipulation strategy. Object detection, relationship reasoning, and manipulation strategy selection play vital roles in handling hazardous objects in complex scenarios.

2.1 Object Detection

Convolutional neural networks (CNNs) provide advantages in target detection by directly processing original images without complex preprocessing. They combine feature extraction, selection, and classification, optimizing performance and efficiency. Two types of CNN-based target detection methods exist: two-stage and single-stage. Two-stage approaches generate candidate regions for classification and regression, seen in algorithms like Faster R-CNN [1]. Single-stage methods directly regress category and location information, as seen in YOLO [2], SSD [3]. Transformer models, including Vision Transformer (ViT) [4], have gained attention for their simplicity and scalability, achieving success in image classification tasks and expanding their applications in computer vision.

2.2 Object Relationship Reasoning

Deep learning advancements have led to object relationship reasoning in various fields. Dai et al. [5] introduced a visual relationship inference network, while Zhang et al. [6] proposed the Visual Manipulation Relationship Network (VMRN), enabling real-time target detection and object relationship reasoning for robots. Hu et al. [7] developed a neural message passing algorithm for propagating contextual information, addressing unrealistic spatial relationships. Mi et al. [8] incorporated prior knowledge and attention mechanisms to improve graph construction. Li et al. [9] introduced an interpretable model that aligns images and text descriptions, capturing essential objects and semantic concepts for comprehensive understanding of visual content.

2.3 Robot Manipulation Strategies

Lee et al. [10] introduced a tree search-based planning algorithm for object rearrangement and grasping in dense spaces, enhancing robot manipulation. Nam et al. [11] proposed a task-planning algorithm for object manipulation in cluttered environments, optimizing efficiency by managing picking and placing actions. Wang et al. [12] integrated new skills with skill models to achieve long-term goals in complex environments. Thakar et al. [13] determined optimal start and end positions for robotic arm movements, minimizing overall movement time. Reister et al. [14] addressed integration of navigation and manipulation in mobile manipulation tasks. Sun et al. [15] developed a mobile dual-arm robot system and achieved stable grasping of explosives with an impedance control method.

The primary contributions of this paper are as follows:

1. Proposal of a comprehensive framework for target object detection and grasping in complex stacked scenes within security environments.

2. Development of diverse manipulation strategies tailored to specific objects in complex scenes.
3. Execution of a series of actual scenario experiments to validate the proposed framework and assess its effectiveness in practical environment.

3 Proposed Framework

Our study focuses on identifying and handling hazardous substances in cluttered scenes. Objects in these scenarios suffer from occlusion, overlapping, and stacking, making detection difficult. We create complex environments with multiple objects, targeting explosives. Using visual detection and our neural network, we determine the positional relationships of the objects and achieve object grasping through step-by-step interference removal.

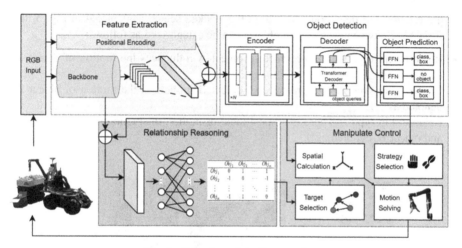

Fig. 2. Overview of the framework.

The general framework is illustrated in Fig. 2. The network architecture comprises four distinct modules: feature extraction, object detection, relationship reasoning, and manipulation control, each distinguished by different colors. The framework takes an RGB image captured by the camera as input. Initially, a traditional convolutional neural network is employed to extract features from the image, which is the foundation for subsequent stages. During object detection, the feature map is flattened, and position information is encoded and embedded into the feature map. The relational inference module takes the extracted features and the output from the target detection network as input. It performs a convolution manipulation to predict the manipulative relationship between each pair of objects detected in the object detection phase. Subsequently, the manipulation control module selects an appropriate manipulation strategy by utilizing the output results from both the target detection and manipulation relationship networks, controls the robotic arm to execute the corresponding manipulation.

3.1 Object Detection

The object detection module within the framework leverages the widely adopted Transform network-based DETR algorithm [16]. DETR employs a conventional CNN backbone network in this module to extract features from the input 2D image. Following this, the model undergoes dimensionality reduction using a 1×1 convolutional kernel. Distinct position codes are computed and concatenated individually to effectively capture position information in both the x and y dimensions. The serialized input is then propagated through the Encoder and Decoder layers. Object queries are also introduced into the Transformer Decoder to generate n decoders output embeddings. Two feedforward networks (FFNs) are employed to predict the bounding box's center coordinates, height, width, and category labels.

3.2 Object Relationship Reasoning

In the relationship detection task within the stacked scene, as depicted in Fig. 3, the relationships between each pair of objects can be categorized as follows:

- Relationship type 1: The presence of object A influences the motion of object B, denoted as 1.
- Relationship type 2: The presence of object B influences the motion of object A, denoted as -1.
- Relationship type 3: There is no positional or motion interaction between object A and object B, denoted as 0.

Fig. 3. Schematic diagram of relational reasoning. a): Pair(Bottle, Grenade) = 1, b): Pair(Bottle, Grenade) = -1, c): Pair(Bottle, Grenade) = 0.

Zhang et al. introduced the Object Pair Pooling Layer (OP^2L) in their work [6]. OP^2L serves as a layer designed explicitly for end-to-end training of the entire visual manipulation relationship network. It is inserted between the feature extractor and the manipulation relation predictor, taking object locations and shared feature maps as inputs. OP^2L identifies all feasible object pairs and utilizes their features as a small batch to train the manipulation relation reasoning network. In particular, for each object pair ($Pair(O_1, O_2)$) obtained from object detection, we can predict the object relation ($rel(O_1, O_2)$) based on the outputs of the object detection network and the convolutional features from the CNN network. Each pair of object relationship $rel(O_1, O_2) \in (-1, 0, 1)$, This approach allows the construction of an $n \times n$ adjacency matrix, facilitating the establishment of relative position relationships between every object pair.

3.3 Manipulation Control

Manipulation Target Selection
The results of relational reasoning for object detection, represented by the adjacency matrix capturing the relationships between each object and others, can be equivalently transformed into a directed graph. In this graph, the nodes correspond to each target object, the edges represent the relationships between the objects, and the end of the robot arm can be included as a node. Consequently, the problem of selecting the target object for grasping can be transformed into finding the shortest path in this directed graph, which can be addressed using Dijkstra algorithm.

Manipulation Strategy Selection
The robot must be capable of effectively responding to various types hazardous objects. Given the vast array of explosives, detecting every single variant becomes virtually impossible. Therefore, for simplification purposes, we categorize explosives into two main types: explosives and grenades. The homemade explosives are simulated, while the grenade toys are purchased online, all as depicted in the Fig. 4.

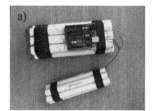 

Fig. 4. Examples of hazardous items. a): explosives, b): grenades.

First, when dealing with a single hazardous object, the appropriate manipulation must be selected based on its specific types, such as grenades or explosives. Second, in scenarios where multiple hazardous objects are present, the robot is tasked with classifying and isolating these objects within the scene. The objective is to minimize interference between each hazardous object and between hazardous objects and other interfering objects.

Spatial Calculation
Hand-eye calibration is crucial for calculating the transformation between the camera and the robotic arm, enabling accurate determination of the end-effector's position during grasping. This calibration converts the object's camera position to the required spatial coordinates for the robotic arm's end-effector. Precise measurements of relative position and orientation between the robotic arm and camera are involved in this calibration. Spatial coordinates are calculated using parameters ^{hand}P, $^{hand}_{cam}T$, and ^{cam}P: coordinates in the robotic arm's world system, conversion matrix from camera to robotic arm's world system, and coordinates in the camera's world system. The formula for spatial coordinate calculation is as follows:

$$^{hand}P = {}^{hand}_{cam}T \, {}^{cam}P \tag{1}$$

3.4 Train

We can train both networks simultaneously to maximize their synergy. Weighted loss functions are used to effectively integrate their training effects by balancing their contributions. Adjusting the weights optimizes the training process for a more balanced and effective training procedure. The overall loss function combines object detection and relational inference by weighting their respective loss functions, α is the weighting factor.

$$L = L_O + \alpha L_R \tag{2}$$

L_O represents the loss function of the object detection network and L_R represents the loss function of the relation reasoning network. The output of the DETR network includes object class detection and object bounding box detection, so

$$L_O = \sum_{i=1}^{N} L_{cls}(\widehat{c}_i, c_i) + L_{box}(\widehat{b}_i, b_i) \tag{3}$$

$L_{cls}(\widehat{c}_i, c_i)$ represents the loss for object class detection, where $\widehat{c}_i$ and c_i are respectively the ground truth and the classification results from the network, $L_{box}(\widehat{b}_i, b_i)$ represents the loss for object class detection, where $\widehat{b}_i$ and b_i are respectively the ground truth bounding box, and predicted bounding box by the network,

$$L_{cls}(\widehat{c}_i, c_i) = \begin{cases} 0, & \widehat{c}_i = c_i \\ 1, & \text{otherwise} \end{cases} \tag{4}$$

$$L_{box}(\widehat{b}_i, b_i) = \frac{\widehat{b}_i \cap b_i}{\widehat{b}_i \cup b_i} \tag{5}$$

The loss function for relation reasoning can be expressed as follows:

$$L_R = \sum_{i=0}^{N} \sum_{j=0}^{N} \log(1 + |p_{ij} - \widehat{p}_{ij}|) \tag{6}$$

where $\widehat{p}_{ij}$ and p_{ij} are respectively the true relationship of object pairs and the results from the reasoning network.

During training, the value of α is set to 1, the hardware platform employed consisted of an i9 11900K CPU, Nvidia RTX 3060 GPU with 12GB memory, and Ubuntu 18.04 operating system.

4 Experiments

4.1 Indoor Environmental Experiments

Determine the Manipulative Strategy Based on the Type of Hazardous Material
The robot must employ a suitable response strategy based on the specific type of hazardous object encountered. We conducted experiments involving explosive objects with

Fig. 5. For grenade direct grabbing manipulation (left). For explosives, first using scissors to handle the fuse, and then performing the grabbing manipulation(right).

fuses, as well as independent explosive objects placed on a table. The corresponding experimental results are depicted in Fig. 6.

Stacked Scenes with Only One Explosive, the Fewer the Number of Manipulations, the Better

In the context of a single-objective scenario, we conducted a series of comparative experiments with greedy algorithm and random algorithm to validate the efficacy of the manipulative decision network. The greedy algorithm involved selecting the nearest operable object to the target point when multiple operable objects were present. Conversely, the random algorithm randomly selected operable objects from the available options. To facilitate the experiments, we designed a scenario depicted in Fig. 6 a), wherein a yellow explosive served as the target object. The objective was to minimize the number of manipulations required to remove interfering objects and successfully grasp the target object. The experimental results are shown in Fig. 6.

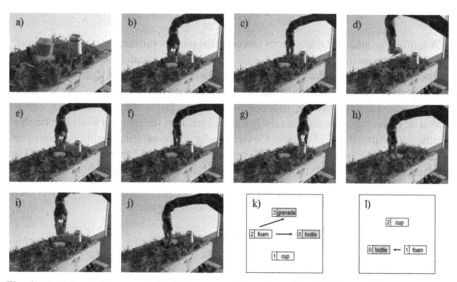

Fig. 6. Experimental scene and single target experimental results, a) is the experimental scenario, b) - d) are the greedy algorithm execution, e) - h) are the random algorithm execution, i) - j) are our proposed algorithm execution, and k) - l) are the results of reasoning about the operation-object relationship in our proposed algorithm's execution.

From the experimental process, it can be seen that when there are more interfering objects around the target object, our proposed operation strategy can complete the grasp and remove operation of the target object with the least number of operations based on the results of target detection and relationship prediction.

Multi-target

In the multi-target scenario, we encounter various challenges due to interference from multiple known or unknown objects. We address these challenges by considering three cases, as depicted in Fig. 8. Case I involves the scenario where the positions of all interferers and dangerous objects are known. Case II focuses on situations where the positions of some interferers and all dangerous objects are known, potentially with the emergence of hidden interferers during the robot's execution of the plan. Finally, Case III deals with scenarios where the positions of some interfering objects and some dangerous objects are known, with the possibility of hidden interference and target objects appearing during the robot's manipulation task.

a) case I   b) case II   c) case III

Fig. 7. Schematic diagram of multi-target scenario.

Additionally, since the robot exerts forces on the objects surrounding the manipulated object during the manipulation, the object's pose can dynamically change in all cases.

The experimental results are presented in Table 1, demonstrate that our proposed method performs better in grasping the target object with fewer manipulations when the target object is known. However, in scenarios where the target object is unknown, ensuring that all target objects are successfully grasped requires the removal of all identifiable disturbances within the field of view. Consequently, our proposed algorithm operates on the same objects as other algorithms. Nevertheless, due to the optimized manipulation sequence we introduce, our algorithm gains an advantage regarding manipulation time.

Table 1. Results of multi-target scenario

	Strategies	Number of executions	Execution time
Case I	greedy algorithm	4	2:25
	random algorithm	5	2:55
	proposed algorithm	**3**	**1:41**

(continued)

Table 1. (*continued*)

	Strategies	Number of executions	Execution time
Case II	greedy algorithm	5	2:49
	random algorithm	5	3:01
	proposed algorithm	4	**2:11**
Case III	greedy algorithm	5	2:51
	random algorithm	5	2:55
	proposed algorithm	5	**2:41**

4.2 Outdoor Environmental Experiments

In practice, the growing complexity of demolition and bomb disposal tasks necessitates the development of machines capable of continuously improving and adapting to search for and acquire explosives in complex environments effectively. We conducted experiments in a simulated outdoor setting featuring a complex scenario with stacked explosives to validate the proposed network. The experimental results, depicted in Fig. 8, are presented in three columns: the first column showcases the target detection results,

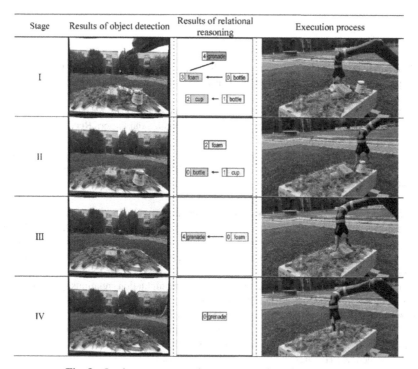

Fig. 8. Outdoor scene experiment process from Stage I to IV.

the second column displays the relationship reasoning results, and the third column illustrates the process of controlling the robotic arm to execute the manipulation.

5 Conclusion

This paper presents a framework for target object detection and grasping in complex stacked scenes within security contexts. It utilizes different manipulation strategies for target objects in diverse scenarios, considering object properties, relative positions, and other relevant factors. By combining these strategies with the robot's action capabilities, the framework enables the successful removal of dangerous objects in complex scenes. Real-world experiments are conducted to validate the effectiveness of the proposed framework and strategies. The framework's performance we proposed is evaluated in both indoor single and multi-objectives scenarios. The results demonstrate that the framework outperforms greedy and random strategies regarding the number of manipulations required to complete tasks on target objects. Additionally, the framework exhibits efficient detection and grasping of dangerous objects in outdoor scenarios, showcasing its robustness in various complex scenarios.

Acknowledgements. This work is supported by National Key Research and Development Program of China with No. 2021ZD0113804.

References

1. Ren, S., He, K., Girshick, R., et al.: Faster R-CNN: towards real-time object detection with region proposal networks[J/OL]. IEEE Trans. Pattern Anal. Mach. Intell. **39**(6), 1137–1149 (2017)
2. Redmon, J., Divvala, S., Girshick, R., et al.: You only look once: unified, real-time object detection. In: 2016 IEEE Conference on Computer Vision and Pattern Recognition (CVPR). Las Vegas, NV, USA, pp. 779–788 IEEE (2016)
3. Liu, W., Anguelov, D., Erhan, D., Szegedy, C., Reed, S., Fu, C.-Y., Berg, A.C.: SSD: Single Shot MultiBox Detector. In: Leibe, B., Matas, J., Sebe, N., Welling, M. (eds.) ECCV 2016. LNCS, vol. 9905, pp. 21–37. Springer, Cham (2016). https://doi.org/10.1007/978-3-319-464 48-0_2
4. Dosovitskiy, A., Beyer, L., Kolesnikov, A., et al.: An Image is Worth 16x16 Words: Transformers for Image Recognition at Scale[A/OL] (2021). http://arxiv.org/abs/2010.11929
5. Dai, B., Zhang, Y., Lin, D.: Detecting visual relationships with deep relational networks. In: 2017 IEEE Conference on Computer Vision and Pattern Recognition (CVPR). Honolulu, HI, pp. 3298–3308, IEEE (2017)
6. Zhang, H., Lan, X., Zhou, X., et al.: Visual manipulation relationship network for autonomous robotics. In: 2018 IEEE-RAS 18th International Conference on Humanoid Robots (Humanoids), Beijing, China, pp. 118–125 IEEE (2018)
7. Hu, Y., Chen, S., Chen, X., et al.: Neural message passing for visual relationship detection [A/OL]. arXiv (2022). http://arxiv.org/abs/2208.04165
8. Mi, L., Chen, Z.: Hierarchical graph attention network for visual relationship detection. In: 2020 IEEE/CVF Conference on Computer Vision and Pattern Recognition (CVPR). Seattle, WA, USA, pp. 13883–13892, IEEE (2020)

9. Li, K., Zhang, Y., Li, K., et al.: Image-text embedding learning via visual and textual semantic reasoning. IEEE Trans. Pattern Anal. Mach. Intell. **45**(1), 641–656 (2023). https://doi.org/10.1109/TPAMI.2022.3148470

10. Lee, J., Nam, C., Park, J., et al.: Tree search-based task and motion planning with prehensile and non-prehensile manipulation for obstacle rearrangement in clutter. In: 2021 IEEE International Conference on Robotics and Automation (ICRA). Xi'an, China, pp. 8516–8522 IEEE (2021)

11. Nam, C., Cheong, S.H., Lee, J., et al.: Fast and resilient manipulation planning for object retrieval in cluttered and confined environments. IEEE Trans. Rob. **37**(5), 14 (2021)

12. Wang, Z., Garrett, C.R., Kaelbling, L.P., et al.: Learning compositional models of robot skills for task and motion planning. arXiv (2021). http://arxiv.org/abs/2006.06444

13. Thakar, S., Rajendran, P., Kabir, A.M., et al.: Manipulator motion planning for part pickup and transport operations from a moving base. IEEE Trans. Autom. Sci. Eng. **19**(1), 191–206 (2022)

14. Reister, F., Grotz, M., Asfour, T.: Combining navigation and manipulation costs for time-efficient robot placement in mobile manipulation tasks[J]. IEEE Robot. Autom. Lett. **7**(4), 9913–9920 (2022)

15. Sun, F., Chen, Y., Wu, Y., et al.: Motion planning and cooperative manipulation for mobile robots with dual arms. IEEE Trans. Emerg. Topics Comput. Intell. **6**(6), 1345–1356 (2022)

16. Carion, N., Massa, F., Synnaeve, G., et al.: End-to-End Object Detection with Transformers [A/OL]. arXiv (2020). http://arxiv.org/abs/2005.12872

Adaptive Neural Composite Learning Finite-Time Control for a QUAV with Guaranteed Tracking Performance

Chenglin Wu[ORCID] and Shuai Song[✉][ORCID]

School of Information Engineering, Henan University of Science and Technology,
Luoyang 471023, China
songshuai_1010@163.com

Abstract. This paper discusses the neural adaptive composite learning finite-time control for a quadrotor unmanned aerial vehicle (QUAV). Based on the command filter backstepping control (CFBC) scheme, the computational complexity caused by repetitive derivation and the inverse effect of the filter error are effectively removed. Moreover, the neural networks (NNs) are employed to identify the nonlinear coupling terms in the controlled vehicle, and the prediction error is introduced to adjust the composite learning law of neural weights, which improves the learning ability of NNs. Then, an adaptive neural composite learning finite-time prescribed performance controller is designed to achieve the convergence constraint on the tracking error, which makes the tracking error always in the planned steady-state region, and all variables of the closed-loop system are practical finite-time bounded. Finally, simulation results are shown to demonstrate the validity of the proposed method.

Keywords: Composite learning control · Finite-time control · Prescribed performance function · Quadrotor unmanned aerial vehicle

1 Introduction

The quadrotor unmanned aerial vehicle (QUAV), with its high degree of maneuverability and integrated information technology, plays an important role in military and civilian fields. However, it is difficult to design an ideal control algorithm to achieve the anticipated control performance, because it suffers from strong nonlinearities, multi-state coupling, and external disturbances. To solve this problem, intelligent control algorithms integrating neural networks (NNs) and fuzzy logic systems (FLSs) have been widely reported for QUAV, in which the nonlinear coupling terms are approximately modeled [1–4], for instance, in [1], a fuzzy backstepping control method was reported for the QUAV with

This work was supported in part by the National Natural Science Foundation of China under Grants 62203153, and in part by the Natural Science Fund for Young Scholars of Henan Province under Grant 222300420151.

unmeasurable state. [4] studied the adaptive neural fractional-order control for QUAV. However, the above-mentioned NN control schemes focus only on the stability analysis of the closed-loop system (CLS) without sufficient regard for the purpose of the approximation strategy. Fortunately, composite learning control constructs the prediction error through series-parallel estimation models (SPEM) to further enhance the approximation ability of NNs [5–7], for instance, [7] studied an adaptive composite neural dynamic surface control for robotic manipulators, where the prediction error and the tracking error are co-engaged to update the neural weights to improve the estimation accuracy. Although the above control schemes in [5,7,8] enhance the control accuracy by improving the learning capability of the neural network and eliminating the computational explosion problem caused by the repeated derivation, they fail to weaken the adverse response of the filter error. The command-filtered backstepping control (CFBC) strategy avoids the complex calculation and attenuates the influence of filter errors by introducing the error compensation function (ECF) [9]. Nevertheless, the above results in [5,7–9] only achieve the asymptotic stability of CLS, which is not compatible with the fast response and high steady-state accuracy required by the QUAV operation.

Finite-time control (FTC) has been widely investigated for its advantages of high accuracy, anti-disturbance, and fast convergence [10–13]. Among them, [12] developed an adaptive CBFC method for the QUAV. In [13], an adaptive composite finite-time control method was studied and applied for the QUAV. Despite the above FTC methods ensuring that all states of CLS are finite-time bounded, the transient and steady-state responses fail to receive attention, simultaneously. Prescribed performance control (PPC), due to its ability to plan the convergence behavior of the tracking error, has been widely applied for QUAV [14–16]. It is worth emphasizing that the above exponential performance function-based control methods appropriately improve the tracking performance, but the time for the tracking error to reach the desired steady-state value cannot be expressed quantitatively. Therefore, it is interesting to design an ideal control scheme to achieve the performance constraints at a pre-specified time for the QUAV.

Inspired by the aforesaid insights, the adaptive neural composite learning finite-time prescribed performance tracking control is investigated for the QUAV. The major contributions are outlined as follows:

(i) Different from DSC results in [7,8] and PPC results in [14–16], the adaptive CFB finite-time prescribed performance control method is developed with the aid of the novel prescribed performance function and CFBC strategy, which not only achieves the desired tracking performance targets in finite time but also circumvents complex computational problems and weakens the effects of filter error.

(ii) In contrast to the traditional fuzzy or neural approximation methods aiming to focus on Liapunov stability [8,9,11,12,14–16], the prediction error is obtained by SPEM together with tracking error to update the composite learning law of weights to improve the approximation accuracy of the nonlinear coupled term of the controlled vehicle, which in turn adjusts the tracking performance.

2   Problem Statements and Preliminaries

2.1   Model Description

Consider the dynamic system of QUAV as [17]:

$$
\begin{cases}
\ddot{\phi} = \dfrac{\mathcal{P}}{\Upsilon_x} u_\phi + \dot{\theta}\dot{\psi}\dfrac{\Upsilon_y - \Upsilon_z}{\Upsilon_x} - \dfrac{\Lambda_\phi \mathcal{P}}{\Upsilon_x}\dot{\phi} + w_\phi \\[2mm]
\ddot{\theta} = \dfrac{\mathcal{P}}{\Upsilon_y} u_\theta + \dot{\phi}\dot{\psi}\dfrac{\Upsilon_z - \Upsilon_x}{\Upsilon_y} - \dfrac{\Lambda_\theta \mathcal{P}}{\Upsilon_y}\dot{\theta} + w_\theta \\[2mm]
\ddot{\psi} = \dfrac{\mathcal{P}}{\Upsilon_z} u_\psi + \dot{\phi}\dot{\theta}\dfrac{\Upsilon_x - \Upsilon_y}{\Upsilon_z} - \dfrac{\Lambda_\psi \mathcal{P}}{\Upsilon_z}\dot{\psi} + w_\psi \\[2mm]
\ddot{z} = \dfrac{u_p}{\Xi}\mathbb{C}_\phi\mathbb{C}_\theta - \mathrm{g} - \dfrac{\Lambda_z}{\Xi}\dot{z} + w_z \\[2mm]
\ddot{x} = \dfrac{u_p}{\Xi}(\mathbb{C}_\phi\mathbb{S}_\theta\mathbb{C}_\psi + \mathbb{S}_\phi\mathbb{S}_\psi) - \dfrac{\Lambda_x}{\Xi}\dot{x} + w_x \\[2mm]
\ddot{y} = \dfrac{u_p}{\Xi}(\mathbb{C}_\phi\mathbb{S}_\theta\mathbb{S}_\psi - \mathbb{S}_\phi\mathbb{C}_\psi) - \dfrac{\Lambda_y}{\Xi}\dot{y} + w_y
\end{cases}
\tag{1}
$$

where ϕ, θ, and ψ stand for the roll, pitch, and yaw angles; x, y, and z are three positions; $\mathcal{P}$ is between the mass center and the rotor center of the QUAV; Υ_z, Υ_x, and Υ_y represent the rotary inertia; u_ϕ, u_θ, and u_ψ indicate control inputs; u_p denotes the total lift force; Ξ and g are the mass and the gravitational acceleration; $\mathbb{S}_\star$ and $\mathbb{C}_\star$ stand for $\sin(\star)$ and $\cos(\star)$. For $j = \phi, \theta, \psi, z, x, y$, Λ_j is the drag coefficients, w_i denotes the unknown bounded disturbances satisfying $|w_i| \le w_i^*$ with $w_i^* > 0$.

For the brief expression, the dynamic model (1) can be represented as:

$$
\ddot{\zeta}_i = \mathcal{L}_i\tau_i + \Gamma_i + w_i, i = 1, 2, \ldots, 6,
\tag{2}
$$

where $(\zeta_1, \zeta_2, \zeta_3, \zeta_4, \zeta_5, \zeta_6) = (\phi, \theta, \psi, z, x, y)$, $(\mathcal{L}_1, \mathcal{L}_2, \mathcal{L}_3) = (\mathcal{P}/\Upsilon_x, \mathcal{P}/\Upsilon_y, \mathcal{P}/\Upsilon_z)$, $(\mathcal{L}_4, \mathcal{L}_5, \mathcal{L}_6) = (1/\Xi, 1/\Xi, 1/\Xi)$, $(\tau_1, \tau_2, \tau_3) = (u_\phi, u_\theta, u_\psi)$, $(\tau_4, \tau_5, \tau_6) = (u_p\mathbb{C}_\phi\mathbb{C}_\theta - \Xi\mathrm{g}, u_p(\mathbb{C}_\phi\mathbb{S}_\theta\mathbb{C}_\psi + \mathbb{S}_\phi\mathbb{S}_\psi), u_p(\mathbb{C}_\phi\mathbb{S}_\theta\mathbb{S}_\psi - \mathbb{S}_\phi\mathbb{C}_\psi))$, $(\Gamma_1, \Gamma_2, \Gamma_3) = (\dot{\theta}\dot{\psi}(\Upsilon_y - \Upsilon_z)/\Upsilon_x - \Lambda_\phi\mathcal{P}\dot{\phi}/\Upsilon_x, \dot{\psi}\dot{\phi}(\Upsilon_z - \Upsilon_x)/\Upsilon_y - \Lambda_\theta\mathcal{P}\dot{\theta}/\Upsilon_y, \dot{\phi}\dot{\theta}(\Upsilon_x - \Upsilon_y)/\Upsilon_z - \Lambda_\psi\mathcal{P}\dot{\psi}/\Upsilon_z)$, $(\Gamma_4, \Gamma_5, \Gamma_6) = (-\Lambda_z\dot{z}/\Xi, -\Lambda_x\dot{x}/\Xi, -\Lambda_y\dot{y}/\Xi)$, $(w_1, w_2, w_3, w_4, w_5, w_6) = (w_\phi, w_\theta, w_\psi, w_z, w_x, w_y)$.

Control Objective: This brief investigates an adaptive neural composite learning finite-time trajectory tracking control method for a QUAV to enable all states of CLS to achieve finite-time convergence, where the tracking error evolves into a preassigned area in a given finite time interval and never violates the allowed region.

Assumption 1. The reference trajectories ζ_{id} and $\dot{\zeta}_{id}(i = 3, 4, 5, 6)$ are continues and bounded.

2.2 Finite-Time Prescribed Performance Function

Define the tracking error as $e_{i1} = \zeta_i - \zeta_{id}$. By constructing the inequality relationship $-\varphi_i(t) < e_{i1} < \varphi_i(t)$ to achieve the convergence constraint on e_{i1}. $\varphi_i(t)$ represents a monotone decreasing finite-time prescribed performance function (FTPPF) described as [18,19]:

$$\varphi_i(t) = \begin{cases} \left(\varphi_{i0} - \dfrac{t}{T_f^i}\right) e^{\left(1 - \frac{T_f^i}{T_f^i - t}\right)} + \varphi_{T_f^i}, & t \in [0, T_f^i) \\ \varphi_{T_f^i}, & t \in [T_f^i, +\infty) \end{cases} \tag{3}$$

in which φ_{i0} and $\varphi_{T_f^i}$ are positive design parameters.

Construct the transformation function as:

$$e_{i1}(t) = \varphi_i(t)\Pi_i(\xi_i(t)), \tag{4}$$

with

$$\Pi_i(\xi_i(t)) = \frac{e^{\xi_i(t)} - e^{-\xi_i(t)}}{e^{\xi_i(t)} + e^{-\xi_i(t)}}, \tag{5}$$

where $\xi_i(t)$ is a transformed error.

Furthermore, $\dot{\xi}_i(t)$ can be calculated as:

$$\dot{\xi}_i(t) = \frac{\dot{e}_{i1}(t) - \dot{\varphi}_i(t)\Pi_i(\xi_i(t))}{\varphi_i(t)\frac{\partial \Pi_i(\xi_i(t))}{\partial \xi_i(t)}} = \mathcal{C}_i + \hbar_i \dot{e}_{i1}, \tag{6}$$

where $\mathcal{C}_i = -\frac{\dot{\varphi}_i(t)\Pi_i(\xi_i(t))}{\varphi_i(t)\frac{\partial \Pi_i(\xi_i(t))}{\partial \xi_i(t)}}$, $\hbar_i = \frac{1}{\varphi_i(t)\frac{\partial \Pi_i(\xi_i(t))}{\partial \xi_i(t)}}$.

2.3 RBFNNs

Given that RBFNNs possess universal estimation capabilities to identify unknown nonlinear terms in the controlled vehicle. Thus, there is a continuous function $f_i(\nu_i) : \mathbf{R}^k \to \mathbf{R}$ on a compact set $\Omega_{\nu_i} \in \mathbf{R}^k$ can be estimated through an RBFNN satisfying

$$f_i(\nu_i) = \vartheta_i^{\mathrm{T}} S_i(\nu_i) + \delta_i(\nu_i), \quad \forall \nu_i \in \Omega_{\nu_i}$$

where $\delta_i(\nu_i)$ is the approximation error satisfying $|\delta_i(\nu_i)| \leq \delta_i^*$, $\vartheta_i = [\vartheta_{i1}, \vartheta_{i2}, \ldots, \vartheta_{il}]^{\mathrm{T}} \in \mathbf{R}^l$ is the ideal weights vector, which is represented as:

$$\vartheta_i = \arg \min_{\vartheta_i \in \mathbf{R}^l} \left\{ \sup_{\nu_i \in \Omega_{\nu_i}} |f_i(\nu_i) - \vartheta_i^{\mathrm{T}} S_i(\nu_i)| \right\},$$

and $S_i(\nu_i) = [S_{i1}(\nu_i), S_{i2}(\nu_i), \ldots, \phi_{il}(\nu_i)]^{\mathrm{T}} \in \mathbf{R}^l$ donates the basis function vector with $S_{ij}(\nu_i)$ being chosen as:

$$S_{ij}(\nu_i) = \exp\left[-\frac{(\nu_i - b_{ij})^{\mathrm{T}}(\nu_i - b_{ij})}{a_i^{\mathrm{T}} a_i}\right], j = 1, \cdots, l,$$

where a_i and b_{ij} stand for the width of the Gaussian function and the centre of the receptive field, respectively.

Lemma 1 [20]. *For the system $\dot{\chi}(t) = \mathcal{F}(\chi(t))$. If there is a continuous positive-definite Lyapunov function $V(\chi) : \mathbf{R}^n \to \mathbf{R}$ and scalars $\varpi_1 > 0$, $\varpi_2 > 0$, $0 < q < 1$, $0 < p < 1$, and $0 < \ell < \infty$ such that $\dot{V}(\chi) + \varpi_1 V(\chi) + \varpi_2 V^q(\chi) \leq \aleph$ holds, then the system $\dot{\chi} = \mathcal{F}(\chi(t))$ is practical finite-time stable, and the setting time t_r can be calculated as:*

$$t_r \leq \max\left\{t_0 + \frac{1}{p\varpi_1(1-q)} \ln \frac{p\varpi_1 V^{1-q}(t_0) + \varpi_2}{\varpi_2},\right.$$
$$\left. t_0 + \frac{1}{\varpi_1(1-q)} \ln \frac{\varpi_1 V^{1-q}(t_0) + p\varpi_2}{p\varpi_2}\right\}.$$

Lemma 2 [22]. *For positive parameter ρ and $\mathfrak{W} \in \mathbf{R}$, one has*

$$0 \leq |\mathfrak{W}| \leq \frac{\mathfrak{W}^2}{\sqrt{\mathfrak{W}^2 + \rho^2}} \leq \rho.$$

Lemma 3 [21]. *For any positive constants $\mathfrak{R}_1$, $\mathfrak{R}_2$, and $\mathfrak{S}$, the following inequality holds*

$$|\mathfrak{p}_1|^{\mathfrak{R}_1}|\mathfrak{p}_2|^{\mathfrak{R}_2} \leq \frac{\mathfrak{R}_1 \mathfrak{S}}{\mathfrak{R}_1 + \mathfrak{R}_2}|\mathfrak{p}_1|^{\mathfrak{R}_1+\mathfrak{R}_2} + \frac{\mathfrak{R}_2 \mathfrak{S}^{-\frac{\mathfrak{R}_1}{\mathfrak{R}_2}}}{\mathfrak{R}_1 + \mathfrak{R}_2}|\mathfrak{p}_2|^{\mathfrak{R}_1+\mathfrak{R}_2},$$

where $\mathfrak{p}_1$ and $\mathfrak{p}_2$ are any variables.

Lemma 4 [20]. *For $\mathcal{Q}_i \in \mathbf{R}, i = 1, \ldots, n, 0 < \jmath < 1$, we can obtain*

$$\left(\sum_{i=1}^n |\mathcal{Q}_i|\right)^{\jmath} \leq \sum_{i=1}^n |\mathcal{Q}_i|^{\jmath} \leq n^{1-\jmath}\left(\sum_{i=1}^n |\mathcal{Q}_i|\right)^{\jmath}.$$

3   Main Result

In this section, an adaptive neural composite learning finite-time controller is designed for the attitude and position subsystem of the QUAV. Firstly, the state transformation is defined as:

$$\begin{cases} \chi_{i,1} = z_{i,1} - \eta_{i,1}, \\ \chi_{i,2} = z_{i,2} - \eta_{i,2}, \\ z_{i,2} = \dot{\zeta}_i - \gamma_{i,c}, \end{cases} \tag{7}$$

where $z_{i,1} = \xi_i$. $\eta_{i,1}$ and $\eta_{i,2}$ are the error compensation signals, expressed as:

$$\begin{cases} \dot{\eta}_{i,1} = -k_1^i \eta_{i,1} - \bar{k}_1^i \eta_{i,1}^q + \hbar_i(\eta_{i,2} + \alpha_i^*), \\ \dot{\eta}_{i,2} = -k_2^i \eta_{i,2} - \bar{k}_2^i \eta_{i,2}^q - \hbar_i \eta_{i,1}, \ i = 1, 2, \dots, 6, \end{cases} \tag{8}$$

where $1/2 < q = q_1/q_2 < 1$, q_1 and q_2 are odd positive integers, and k_1^i, $\bar{k}_1^i$, k_2^i and $\bar{k}_2^i$ are positive design constants. $\alpha_i^* = \gamma_{i,c} - \gamma_{i,1}$ stands for the filer error, $\gamma_{i,c}$ and $\gamma_{i,1}$ represent the output and the input signal of the finite-time command filter, described as follows:

$$\begin{cases} \dot{\mathfrak{R}}_{i,1} = \Psi_{i,1}, \\ \Psi_{i,1} = -R_{i,1} |\mathfrak{R}_{i,1} - \gamma_{i,1}|^{\frac{1}{2}} sign(\mathfrak{R}_{i,1} - \gamma_{i,1}) + \mathfrak{R}_{i,2}, \\ \dot{\mathfrak{R}}_{i,2} = -R_{i,2} sign(\mathfrak{R}_{i,2} - \dot{\mathfrak{R}}_{i,1}), \end{cases} \tag{9}$$

where $\gamma_{i,c}(t) = \mathfrak{R}_{i,1}(t)$, $\dot{\gamma}_{i,c}(t) = \Psi_{i,1}(t)$. $R_{i,1} > 0$ and $R_{i,2} > 0$ are design parameters.

The adaptive law $\hat{\vartheta}_{i,1}(i = 1, 2, \dots, 6)$ is designed as:

$$\dot{\hat{\vartheta}}_{i,1} = \mu_{i,1}(\chi_{i,1} S_{i,1}(\nu_{i,1}) - \bar{\mu}_{i,1} \hat{\vartheta}_{i,1}), \tag{10}$$

where $\tilde{\vartheta}_{i,1} = \vartheta_{i,1} - \hat{\vartheta}_{i,1}$, $\hat{\vartheta}_{i,1}$ is the estimate of $\vartheta_{i,1}$, $\mu_{i,1}$ and $\bar{\mu}_{i,1}$ are design parameters.

Design the virtual control function $\gamma_{i,1}(i = 1, 2, \dots, 6)$ as:

$$\gamma_{i,1} = -\frac{\chi_{i,1} \bar{\gamma}_{i,1}^2}{\sqrt{\chi_{i,1}^2 \bar{\gamma}_{i,1}^2 + \triangle_{i,1}^2}}, \tag{11}$$

with

$$\bar{\gamma}_{i,1} = \frac{1}{\hbar_i} \left(k_1^i z_{i,1} + \check{k}_1^i \chi_{i,1}^q + \hat{\vartheta}_{i,1}^{\mathrm{T}} S_{i,1}(\nu_{i,1}) \right) + \dot{\zeta}_{id}, \tag{12}$$

where $\triangle_{i,1}$, k_1^i, and $\check{k}_1^i$ are positive constants.

By introducing the prediction error $\Psi_{i,2} = \zeta_i - \hat{\zeta}_i$ to improve the approximation accuracy of the RBFNN and thus the control performance of the controlled vehicle, where $\hat{\zeta}_i$ is obtained from the SPEM:

$$\dot{\hat{\zeta}}_i = \hat{\vartheta}_{i,2}^{\mathrm{T}} S_{i,2}(\nu_{i,2}) + \mathcal{L}_i \tau_i + \bar{l}_{i,2} \Psi_{i,2} + \check{l}_{i,2} \Psi_{i,2}^q. \tag{13}$$

Furthermore, one has

$$\dot{\Psi}_{i,2} = \tilde{\vartheta}_{i,2}^{\mathrm{T}} S_{i,2}(\nu_{i,2}) + w_i - \bar{l}_{i,2} \Psi_{i,2} - \check{l}_{i,2} \Psi_{i,2}^q, \tag{14}$$

where $\bar{l}_{i,2}$ and $\check{l}_{i,2}$ are positive design parameters.

The composite learning law of $\hat{\vartheta}_{2,i}(i = 1, 2, \dots, 6)$ is designed as:

$$\dot{\hat{\vartheta}}_{i,2} = \mu_{i,2}[(\chi_{i,2} + l_{i,2} \Psi_{i,2}) S_{i,2}(\nu_{i,2}) - \bar{\mu}_{i,2} \hat{\vartheta}_{i,2}], \tag{15}$$

where $l_{i,2}$, $\mu_{i,2}$, and $\bar{\mu}_{i,2}$ are positive design parameters.

Design the actual control law $\tau_i (i = 1, 2, \ldots, 6)$ as:

$$\tau_i = -\frac{1}{\mathcal{L}_i} \left(k_2^i z_{i,2} + \check{k}_2^i \chi_{i,2}^q + \chi_{i,2} + \hbar_i z_{i,1} + \hat{\vartheta}_{i,2}^{\mathrm{T}} S_{i,2}(\nu_{i,2}) - \dot{\gamma}_{i,c} \right), \qquad (16)$$

where k_2^i and $\check{k}_2^i$ are positive parameters to be designed.

3.1 Adaptive Composite Learning Finite-Time Controller Design

Step $i, 1$. Based on (7), the derivative of $\chi_{i,1}$ can be calculated as:

$$\dot{\chi}_{i,1} = C_i + \hbar_i \left(z_{i,2} + \alpha_i^* + \gamma_{i,1} - \dot{\zeta}_{id} \right) - \dot{\eta}_{i,1}. \qquad (17)$$

Select the Lyapunov function as follows:

$$V_{i,1} = \frac{1}{2} \chi_{i,1}^2 + \frac{1}{2} \eta_{i,1}^2 + \frac{1}{2} \tilde{\vartheta}_{i,1}^{\mathrm{T}} \mu_{i,1}^{-1} \tilde{\vartheta}_{i,1}, \qquad (18)$$

where $\mu_{i,1}$ is a positive constant.

Taking the derivative of $V_{i,1}$ yields

$$\dot{V}_{i,1} \le \chi_{i,1} \hbar_i (z_{i,2} + \alpha_i^* + \gamma_{i,1} - \dot{\eta}_{i,1}) + \chi_{i,1} f_{i,1}$$
$$+ \eta_{i,1} \dot{\eta}_{i,1} - \tilde{\vartheta}_{i,1}^{\mathrm{T}} \mu_{i,1}^{-1} \dot{\hat{\vartheta}}_{i,1}, \qquad (19)$$

where $f_{i,1} = C_i$, and an RBFNN $\vartheta_{i,1}^{\mathrm{T}} S_{i,1}(\nu_{i,1})$ is employed to approximate $f_{i,1}$ such that $f_{i,1} = \vartheta_{i,1}^{\mathrm{T}} S_{i,1}(\nu_{i,1}) + \delta_{i,1}(\nu_{i,1})$, where $\nu_{i,1} = [\varphi_i, \dot{\varphi}_i, \xi_i, \zeta_i]^{\mathrm{T}}$, $i = 1, 2, \ldots, 6$, and $\delta_{i,1}(\nu_{i,1})$ is the approximate error satisfying $|\delta_{i,1}(\nu_{i,1})| \le \delta_{i,1}^*$.

Consider the following fact:

$$\chi_{i,1} \delta_{i,1} \le \frac{1}{2} \chi_{i,1}^2 + \frac{1}{2} \delta_{i,1}^{*2}. \qquad (20)$$

Substituting (8), (10), (11), and (20) into (19), one has

$$\dot{V}_{i,1} \le - \left(k_1^i - \frac{1}{2} \right) \chi_{i,1}^2 - \check{k}_1^i \chi_{i,1}^{1+q} + \bar{k}_1^i \chi_{i,1} \eta_{i,1}^q + \hbar_i \eta_{i,1} \eta_{i,2} + \hbar_i \chi_{i,1} \chi_{i,2}$$
$$- k_1^i \eta_{i,1}^2 - \bar{k}_1^i \eta_{i,1}^{1+q} + \hbar_i \eta_{i,1} \alpha_i^* + \frac{\bar{\mu}_{i,1}}{\mu_{i,1}} \tilde{\vartheta}_{i,1}^{\mathrm{T}} \hat{\vartheta}_{i,1} + \aleph_{i,1}, \qquad (21)$$

where $\aleph_{i,1} = \hbar_i \triangle_{i,1} + \delta_{i,1}^{*2}/2$.

Step $i, 2$. Along with (2) and (7), the derivative of $\chi_{i,2}$ can be represented as:

$$\dot{\chi}_{i,2} = \mathcal{L}_i \tau_i + \Gamma_i + w_i - \dot{\gamma}_{i,c} - \dot{\eta}_{i,2}. \qquad (22)$$

Choose the following Lyapunov function:

$$V_i = V_{i,1} + \frac{1}{2} \chi_{i,2}^2 + \frac{1}{2} \eta_{i,2}^2 + \frac{1}{2} l_{i,2} \Psi_{i,2}^2 + \frac{1}{2} \tilde{\vartheta}_{i,2}^{\mathrm{T}} \mu_{i,2}^{-1} \tilde{\vartheta}_{i,2}, \qquad (23)$$

where $l_{i,2}$ and $\mu_{i,2}$ are positive design parameters.

Calculating $\dot{V}_i$, one has

$$\dot{V}_i \leq \dot{V}_{i,1} + \chi_{i,2}\left(\mathcal{L}_i \tau_i + \Gamma_i + w_i - \dot{\gamma}_{i,c} - \dot{\eta}_{i,2}\right)$$
$$+ \eta_{i,2}\dot{\eta}_{i,2} + l_{i,2}\Psi_{i,2}\dot{\Psi}_{i,2} - \tilde{\vartheta}_{i,2}^{\mathrm{T}}\mu_{i,2}^{-1}\dot{\hat{\vartheta}}_{i,2}. \tag{24}$$

Since there are nonlinear coupling factors in the controlled vehicle, an RBFNN $\vartheta_{i,2}^{\mathrm{T}}S_{i,2}(\nu_{i,2})$ is used to estimate $f_{i,2} = \Gamma_i$ such that $f_{i,2} = \vartheta_{i,2}^{\mathrm{T}}S_{i,2}(\nu_{i,2}) + \delta_{i,2}(\nu_{i,2})$, where $\nu_{i,2} = [\dot{\phi}, \dot{\theta}, \dot{\psi}]^{\mathrm{T}}$ with $i = 1,2,3$ and $\nu_{i,2} = [\zeta_i, \dot{\zeta}_i]^{\mathrm{T}}$ with $i = 4,5,6$. $\delta_{i,2}(\nu_{i,2})$ stands for the approximate error satisfying $|\delta_{i,2}(\nu_{i,2})| \leq \delta_{i,2}^*$.

With Young's inequality, we get

$$\chi_{i,2}\delta_{i,2} \leq \frac{1}{2}\chi_{i,2}^2 + \frac{1}{2}\delta_{i,2}^{*2}, \tag{25}$$

$$\chi_{i,2}w_i \leq \frac{1}{2}\chi_{i,2}^2 + \frac{1}{2}w_i^{*2}, \tag{26}$$

$$\tilde{\vartheta}_{i,1}^{\mathrm{T}}\hat{\vartheta}_{i,1} \leq \frac{1}{2}\vartheta_{i,1}^{\mathrm{T}}\vartheta_{i,1} - \frac{1}{2}\tilde{\vartheta}_{i,1}^{\mathrm{T}}\tilde{\vartheta}_{i,1}, \tag{27}$$

$$\tilde{\vartheta}_{i,2}^{\mathrm{T}}\hat{\vartheta}_{i,2} \leq \frac{1}{2}\vartheta_{i,2}^{\mathrm{T}}\vartheta_{i,2} - \frac{1}{2}\tilde{\vartheta}_{i,2}^{\mathrm{T}}\tilde{\vartheta}_{i,2}. \tag{28}$$

In light of [20], it can be concluded that $|\alpha_i^*| \leq \mathcal{J}_i$ can be attained in finite time T_*, thus the following inequality holds:

$$\hbar_i \eta_{i,1}\alpha_i^* \leq \frac{1}{2}\hbar_i^2\mathcal{J}_i^2 + \frac{1}{2}\eta_{i,1}^2, \tag{29}$$

where $\mathcal{J}_i$ is an unknown parameter.

Taking the help of Young's inequality, we can obtain

$$l_{i,2}w_i\Psi_{i,2} \leq \frac{1}{2}l_{i,2}w_i^{*2} + \frac{1}{2}l_{i,2}\Psi_{i,2}^2. \tag{30}$$

Based on Lemma 3, in which $r = 1,2$, one has

$$\bar{k}_r^i\chi_{i,r}\eta_{i,r}^q \leq \frac{\bar{k}_r^i}{1+q}|\chi_{i,r}|^{1+q} + \frac{q\bar{k}_r^i}{1+q}|\eta_{i,r}|^{1+q}, \tag{31}$$

$$\left(\frac{1}{2}\tilde{\vartheta}_{i,r}^{\mathrm{T}}\mu_{i,r}^{-1}\tilde{\vartheta}_{i,r}\right)^{\frac{1+q}{2}} \leq \frac{1}{4}\tilde{\vartheta}_{i,r}^{\mathrm{T}}\mu_{i,r}^{-1}\tilde{\vartheta}_{i,r} + \frac{1-q}{2}(1+q)^{\frac{1+q}{1-q}}. \tag{32}$$

Taking (25)–(32) into (24), we have

$$\dot{V}_i \leq -\left(k_1^i - \frac{1}{2}\right)\chi_{i,1}^2 - \left(k_1^i - \frac{1}{2}\right)\eta_{i,1}^2 - \left(\check{k}_1^i - \frac{\bar{k}_1^i}{1+q}\right)\chi_{i,1}^{1+q} - \left(\bar{k}_1^i - \frac{q\bar{k}_1^i}{1+q}\right)\eta_{i,1}^{1+q}$$

$$- k_2^i\chi_{i,2}^2 - k_2^i\eta_{i,2}^2 - \left(\check{k}_2^i - \frac{\bar{k}_2^i}{1+q}\right)\chi_{i,2}^{1+q} - \left(\check{k}_2^i - \frac{q\bar{k}_2^i}{1+q}\right)\eta_{i,2}^{1+q} - \frac{\bar{\mu}_{i,1}}{4\mu_{i,1}}\tilde{\vartheta}_{i,1}^{\mathrm{T}}\tilde{\vartheta}_{i,1}$$

$$- \frac{\bar{\mu}_{i,2}}{4\mu_{i,2}}\tilde{\vartheta}_{i,2}^{\mathrm{T}}\tilde{\vartheta}_{i,2} - \bar{\mu}_{i,1}\left(\frac{1}{2}\tilde{\vartheta}_{i,1}^{\mathrm{T}}\mu_{i,1}^{-1}\tilde{\vartheta}_{i,1}\right)^{\frac{1+q}{2}} - l_{i,2}(\bar{l}_{i,2} - \frac{1}{2})\Psi_{i,2}^2 - l_{i,2}\check{l}_{i,2}\Psi_{i,2}^{1+q}$$

$$- \bar{\mu}_{i,2}\left(\frac{1}{2}\tilde{\vartheta}_{i,2}^{\mathrm{T}}\mu_{i,2}^{-1}\tilde{\vartheta}_{i,2}\right)^{\frac{1+q}{2}} + \bar{\aleph}_{i,2}, \tag{33}$$

where $\bar{\aleph}_{i,2} = \aleph_{i,1} + \delta_{i,2}^{*2}/2 + w_i^{*2}/2 + \frac{\bar{\mu}_{i,1}}{2\mu_{i,1}}\vartheta_{i,1}^{\mathrm{T}}\vartheta_{i,1} + \frac{\bar{\mu}_{i,2}}{2\mu_{i,2}}\vartheta_{i,2}^{\mathrm{T}}\vartheta_{i,2} + \bar{\mu}_{i,1}\frac{1-q}{2}(1+$
$q)^{\frac{1+q}{1-q}} + \bar{\mu}_{i,2}\frac{1-q}{2}(1+q)^{\frac{1+q}{1-q}} + \frac{l_{i,2}}{2}w_i^{*2} + \frac{1}{2}\hbar_i^2 \mathcal{J}_i^2$.

3.2 Stability Analysis

Theorem 1. *Consider the simplified QUAV (1), the first-order command filter (9), error compensation signal (8), adaptive law (10), the composite learning law (15), the virtual control law (16) and actual control law (10), under the Assumptions 1, then all states of the CLS are practical finite-time bounded, and the tracking errors of the position and attitude subsystem converge to a preassigned area within a given finite time interval.*

Proof. Select the entire Lyapunov function candidate as $V = \sum\limits_{i=1}^{6} V_i$. Based on Lemma 4 and (33), the time derivative of V is calculated as:

$$\dot{V} \leq -\varpi_1 V - \varpi_2 V^{\frac{1+q}{2}} + \aleph, \tag{34}$$

where $\varpi_1 = \min\left\{2(k_1^i - \frac{1}{2}), 2k_2^i, k_2^i, \frac{\bar{\mu}_{i,1}}{2}, \frac{\bar{\mu}_{i,2}}{2}, 2(\bar{l}_{i,2} - \frac{1}{2})\right\}$, $\varpi_2 = \min\left\{2^{\frac{1+q}{2}}(\check{k}_1^i\right.$
$-\frac{\check{k}_1^i}{1+q}), 2^{\frac{1+q}{2}}\bar{k}_1^i(1 - \frac{q}{1+q}), 2^{\frac{1+q}{2}}(\check{k}_2^i - \frac{\check{k}_2^i}{1+q}), 2^{\frac{1+q}{2}}\bar{k}_2^i(1 - \frac{q}{1+q}), \bar{\mu}_{i,2}, \check{l}_{i,2}(\frac{2}{l_{i,2}})^{\frac{1+q}{2}}\right\}$,
and $\aleph = \sum\limits_{i=1}^{6} \bar{\aleph}_{i,2}$.

According to Lemma 1 and (34), if $\varpi_1 > 0$, $\varpi_2 > 0$, $0 < \aleph < \infty$, and $0 < (1+q)/2 < 1$ are satisfied, it follows that $\chi_{i,1}$ and $\eta_{i,1}$ will converge to the following region

$$|\chi_{i,1}| \leq \min\left\{\sqrt{\frac{2\aleph}{\varpi_1(1-p)}}, \sqrt{2\left(\frac{\aleph}{\varpi_2(1-p)}\right)^{\frac{2}{1+q}}}\right\},$$

$$|\eta_{i,1}| \leq \min\left\{\sqrt{\frac{2\aleph}{\varpi_1(1-p)}}, \sqrt{2\left(\frac{\aleph}{\varpi_2(1-p)}\right)^{\frac{2}{1+q}}}\right\},$$

where $0 < p < 1$.

The setting time t_r can be calculated as:

$$t_r \leq \max\left\{\frac{1}{p\varpi_1(1 - \frac{1+q}{2})}\ln\frac{p\varpi_1 V^{1-\frac{1+q}{2}}(0) + \varpi_2}{\varpi_2},\right.$$
$$\left.\frac{1}{\varpi_1(1 - \frac{1+q}{2})}\ln\frac{\varpi_1 V^{1-\frac{1+q}{2}}(0) + p\varpi_2}{p\varpi_2}\right\}.$$

From the above stability analysis, it can be obtained that all states of CLS are finite-time bounded, then, the boundedness of $\xi_i(t)$ can be obtained. Further, the tracking error e_{i1} will decay into the pre-specified set $\Omega_{e_{i1}} = \{e_{i1} \in \mathbf{R}| - \varphi_i(t) < e_{i,1} < \varphi_i(t)\}$ in a predefined finite time, which means the desired tracking performance is achieved. ∎

Table 1. Model Parameters

Symbol	value	Unit	Symbol	value	Unit
Ξ	2	kg	g	9.8	m/s^2
$\mathcal{P}$	0.325	m	Λ_x	0.6	kg/s
Λ_y	0.6	kg/s	Λ_z	0.6	kg/s
Λ_ϕ	0.6	kg/rad	Λ_θ	0.6	kg/rad
Λ_ψ	0.6	kg/rad	Υ_x	8.2×10^{-2}	$kg \cdot m^2$
Υ_y	8.2×10^{-2}	$kg \cdot m^2$	Υ_z	1.49×10^{-1}	$kg \cdot m^2$

4 Simulation Result

To demonstrate the validity of the developed control algorithm, a simulation example is presented. The model parameters of the QUAV are shown in Table 1. The reference trajectories are set as $[\zeta_{3d}, \zeta_{4d}, \zeta_{5d}, \zeta_{6d}] = [0.3, \frac{t}{8}, \sin(\frac{\pi t}{5}), \cos(\frac{\pi t}{5})]$. The initial values are selected as $[\phi(0), \theta(0), \psi(0), z(0), x(0), y(0)] = [0, 0, 0, 0, 0.5, 0.5]$. The external disturbances are chosen as $w_\phi = 0.1\cos(\frac{\pi t}{8})$, $w_\theta = 0.1\sin(\frac{\pi t}{10})$, $w_\psi = 0.1\cos(\frac{\pi t}{15})$, $w_z = 0.1\cos(\frac{\pi t}{10})$, $w_x = 0.1\sin(\frac{\pi t}{8})$, and $w_y = 0.1\cos(\frac{\pi t}{9})$. The control parameters are set as $q = \frac{3}{5}, k_1^i = k_2^i = 5$, $\bar{k}_1^i = \check{k}_1^i = 3$, $\bar{k}_2^i = \check{k}_2^i = 2$, $\mu_{i,1} = \mu_{i,2} = 1$, $\triangle_{i,1} = 0.1$, $\bar{\mu}_{i,1} = 0.02$, $\bar{\mu}_{i,2} = 1$, and $l_{i,2} = \bar{l}_{i,2} = \check{l}_{i,2} = 1$. The parameters of FTPPF and the finite-time command filter are specified as $\varphi_{i0} = 2$, $\varphi_{T_f^i} = 0.1$, $T_f^i = 1$, $R_{i,1} = 30$, and $R_{i,1} = 20$.

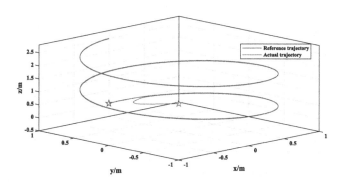

Fig. 1. The Curves of the reference and the actual trajectory in 3-D space

The simulation results are displayed in Figs. 1, 2, 3, 4 and 5. Figure 1 depicts the reference trajectory and actual trajectory curves in 3-dimensional space. Figure 2 and Fig. 3 plot the reference and actual trajectories of the state variables in the attitude subsystem and the position subsystem, respectively, and it can be observed that each variable effectively and quickly follows the reference trajectory. Figure 4 and Fig. 5 draw the tracking error curves for the attitude

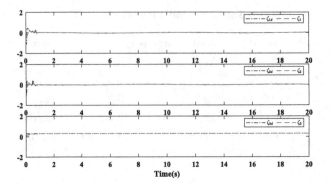

Fig. 2. The Curves of attitude subsystem states and desired signals.

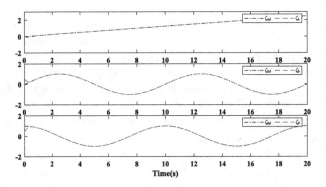

Fig. 3. The Curves of position subsystem states and desired signals.

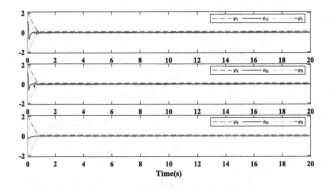

Fig. 4. The Curves of the tracking errors $e_{i1}, (i = 1, 2, 3)$.

and position subsystems, and we can intuitively conclude that the tracking error converges rapidly to a given performance region at a given finite time $T_f^i = 1$, and never crosses out of that region. The simulation results prove the proposed scheme's validity, and the desired tracking performance targets are achieved.

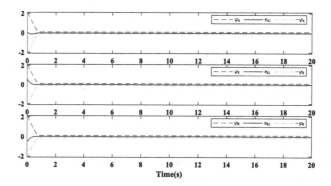

Fig. 5. The Curves of the tracking errors $e_{i1}, (i = 4, 5, 6)$.

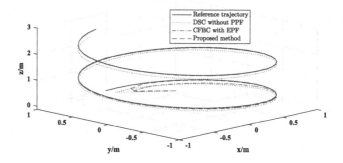

Fig. 6. Comparison result.

Table 2. Comparison of the Quantitative Performance

Performance Index	Items	DSC without PPF	CFBC with EPF	Proposed Method
$\text{IAE} = \int_0^t |e_{i1}(\tau)| d\tau$	e_{11}	0.4946	0.4041	**0.426**
	e_{21}	0.6193	0.436	0.4175
	e_{31}	0.1183	0.1278	0.06519
	e_{41}	2.827	0.778	0.3469
	e_{51}	1.73	0.2787	0.1645
	e_{61}	1.775	0.285	0.1715
$\text{ITAE} = \int_0^t t|e_{i1}(\tau)| d\tau$	e_{11}	2.409	2.578	2.693
	e_{21}	3.978	3.096	2.942
	e_{31}	0.715	0.2299	0.1164
	e_{41}	28.89	4.107	2.932
	e_{51}	17.13	1.065	0.7924
	e_{61}	17.42	1.09	0.8077

To show the advantages of the proposed control scheme, the DSC method without PPF and CFBC method with the exponential performance function (EPF) $h(t) = (h_0 - h_\infty)e^{-lt} + h_\infty$ are selected for comparison, where $h_0 = 2$, $h_\infty = 0.1$, and $l = 0.5$. The initial conditions, the disturbance parameters, and the controller parameters are selected consistently to ensure that the comparison experiments are reasonable, and the simulation result is shown in Fig. 6. Performance metrics, IAE and ITAE, are employed to quantitatively compare the tracking performance of different control methods, as shown in Table 2. It can be seen that the developed method achieves better tracking performance over the DSC without the PPF method and the CFBC with the EPF method in terms of steady-state error and response time.

5   Conclusion

This article has discussed the adaptive neural composite learning finite-time control for a QUAV. With the support of prescribed performance control and CFB control methods, a command-filtered-based finite-time prescribed performance trajectory tracking control scheme has been constructed. The approximate accuracy of NNs has been improved by introducing the prediction error combined with tracking errors to update the weights of NNs. Simulation results have demonstrated that the proposed control algorithm ensures all states of the CLS are finite-time bounded, and the tracking error converges to a preassigned region in finite time and always stays in it.

References

1. Yacef, F., Bouhali, O., Hamerlain, M., Rizoug, N.: Observer-based adaptive fuzzy backstepping tracking control of quadrotor unmanned aerial vehicle powered by Li-ion battery. J. Intell. Rob. Syst. **84**, 179–197 (2016)
2. Xie, W., Cabecinhas, D., Cunha, R., Silvestre, C.: Adaptive backstepping control of a quadcopter with uncertain vehicle mass, moment of inertia, and disturbances. IEEE Trans. Ind. Electron. **69**(1), 549–559 (2022)
3. Zhang, X., Wang, Y., Zhu, G., Chen, X., Li, Z., Wang, C., Su, C.: Compound adaptive fuzzy quantized control for quadrotor and its experimental verification. IEEE Trans. Cybern. **51**(3), 1121–1133 (2021)
4. Guettal, L., Chelihi, A., Ajgou, R., Touba, M.M.: Robust tracking control for quadrotor with unknown nonlinear dynamics using adaptive neural network based fractional-order backstepping control. J. Franklin Inst. **359**(14), 7337–7364 (2022)
5. Liu, S., Wang, H., Li, T.: Adaptive composite dynamic surface neural control for nonlinear fractional-order systems subject to delayed input. ISA Trans. **134**, 122–133 (2023)
6. Zhu, G., Ma, Y., Li, Z., Malekian, R., Sotelo, M.: Dynamic event-triggered adaptive neural output feedback control for MSVs using composite learning. IEEE Trans. Intell. Transp. Syst. **24**(1), 787–800 (2023)
7. Peng, J., Ding, S., Dubay, R.: Adaptive composite neural network disturbance observer-based dynamic surface control for electrically driven robotic manipulators. Neural Comput. Appl. **33**, 6197–6211 (2021)

8. Hua, C., Chen, J., Guan, X.: Dynamic surface based tracking control of uncertain quadrotor unmanned aerial vehicles with multiple state variable constraints. IET Control Theory Appl. **13**(4), 526–533 (2019)

9. Liu, K., Wang, R.: Antisaturation command filtered backstepping control-based disturbance rejection for a quadarotor UAV. IEEE Trans. Circuits Syst. II Express Briefs **68**(12), 3577–3581 (2021)

10. Sun, P., Song, X., Song, S., Stojanovic, V.: Composite adaptive finite-time fuzzy control for switched nonlinear systems with preassigned performance. Int. J. Adapt. Control Signal Process. **37**(3), 771–789 (2023)

11. Song, S., Park, J.H., Zhang, B., Song, X.: Adaptive NN finite-time resilient control for nonlinear time-delay systems with unknown false data injection and actuator faults. IEEE Trans. Neural Netw. Learn. Syst. **33**(10), 5416–5428 (2022)

12. Yang, W., Cui, G., Ma, Q., Ma, J., Tao, C.: Finite-time adaptive event-triggered command filtered backstepping control for a QUAV. Appl. Math. Comput. **423**, 126898 (2022)

13. Xu, B.: Composite learning finite-time control with application to quadrotors. IEEE Trans. Syst. Man Cybern. Syst. **48**(10), 1806–1815 (2018)

14. Hua, C., Chen, J., Guan, X.: Adaptive prescribed performance control of QUAVs with unknown time-varying payload and wind gust disturbance. J. Franklin Inst. **355**(14), 6323–6338 (2018)

15. Chen, Q., Ye, Y., Hu, Z., Na, J., Wang, S.: Finite-time approximation-free attitude control of quadrotors: theory and experiments. IEEE Trans. Aerosp. Electron. Syst. **57**(3), 1780–1792 (2021)

16. Zhao, X., Tian, B., You, M., Ma, L.: Adaptive distributed sliding mode control for multiple unmanned aerial vehicles with prescribed performance. IEEE Trans. Veh. Technol. **71**(11), 11480–11490 (2022)

17. Cui, G., Yang, W., Yu, J., Li, Z., Tao, C.: Fixed-time prescribed performance adaptive trajectory tracking control for a QUAV. IEEE Trans. Circuits Syst. II Express Briefs **69**(2), 494–498 (2022)

18. Liu, Y., Liu, X., Jing, Y.: Adaptive neural networks finite-time tracking control for non-strict feedback systems via prescribed performance. Inf. Sci. **468**, 29–46 (2018)

19. Song, X., Wu, C., Stojanovic, V., Song, S.: 1 bit encoding-decoding-based event-triggered fixed-time adaptive control for unmanned surface vehicle with guaranteed tracking performance. Control. Eng. Pract. **135**, 105513 (2023)

20. Yu, J., Shi, P., Zhao, L.: Finite-time command filtered backstepping control for a class of nonlinear systems. Automatica **92**, 173–180 (2018)

21. Qian, C., Lin, W.: Non-Lipschitz continuous stabilizers for nonlinear systems with uncontrollable unstable linearization. Syst. Control Lett. **42**(3), 185–200 (2001)

22. Chen, M., Wang, H., Liu, X.: Adaptive fuzzy practical fixed-time tracking control of nonlinear systems. IEEE Trans. Fuzzy Syst. **29**(3), 664–673 (2021)

Multimodal Wearable Device Signal Based Epilepsy Detection with Multi-scale Convolutional Neural Network

Yangbin Ge[1,2], Dinghan Hu[1,2], Xiaonan Cui[1,2], Tiejia Jiang[3], Feng Gao[3], Tao Jiang[4,5], Pierre-Paul Vidal[1,6], and Jiuwen Cao[1,2(✉)]

[1] Machine Learning and I-health International Cooperation Base of Zhejiang Province, Hangzhou Dianzi University, Hangzhou 310018, China
{ggyb,jwcao}@hdu.edu.cn
[2] Artificial Intelligence Institute, Hangzhou Dianzi University, Hangzhou 310018, Zhejiang, China
[3] Department of Neurology, Children's Hospital, Zhejiang University School of Medicine, Hangzhou 310018, China
[4] Department of Neurosurgery, The First Affiliated Hospital of Anhui Medical University, Hefei 230002, China
[5] Department of Neurosurgery, Anhui Public Health Clinical Center, Hefei 230002, China
[6] Plateforme d'Etude de la Sensorimotricité (PES), BioMedTech Facilities, Université Paris Cité, Paris 75270, France

Abstract. Seizure detection based on wearable devices has gradually become a popular research direction. The ability of wearable devices to capture signals is also improving, and a variety of physiological signals can be collected. However, current models for wearable devices focus on single-scale analysis and cannot adapt to current multi-modal signals. In this paper, an attention module-based convolutional neural network multi-scale model based on a novel wearable device is proposed to recognize epileptic seizures. The network extracts feature at different scales from multimodal physiological signals, supplemented by an attention module to retain valuable information. Experiments on multimodal physiological data from 13 typical epilepsy patients demonstrated that the proposed model achieves 93.5% sensitivity and 97.3% specificity.

Keywords: Convolutional neural network · Wearable device · Seizure · Multimodal signal · Multi-scale

This work was supported by the National Key Research and Development of China (2021YFE0100100), the National Natural Science Foundation of China (U1909209), the National Key Research and Development Program of China (2021YFE0205400), the Natural Science Key Foundation of Zhejiang Province (LZ22F030002), and the Research Funding of Education of Zhejiang Province (Y202249784).

1   Introduction

Recently, research on seizure detection based on wearable devices has attracted widespread attention, stemming from the many advantages of wearable devices. Firstly, immediate intervention for seizures can be taken to effectively avoid accidental injuries, such as state epileptic seizures and sudden unexpectable death in epilepsy (SUDEP) [1]. Another significant advantage is that wearable devices offer great convenience compared to instruments such as electroencephalography (EEG) monitoring, and do not cause psychological burden to patients. Moreover, wearable devices can collect various types of physiological signals, such as electrocardiography (ECG), electrodermal activity (EDA), electromyography (EMG), acceleration (ACC), EEG, temperature (TEM), Heart Rate (HR), blood volume pulse (BVP), photoplethysmography signal (PPG), which have been shown to be effective in seizure monitoring [2].

Early research on wearable devices mainly focused on thresholding algorithms, which are commonly used for single-modality epilepsy detection. In [3], EMG signals are used for generalized tonic-clonic seizures (GTCS) detection, and competitive sensitivity is achieved by monitoring zero crossing number time-domain features. Statistical analysis of EMG signals is performed in [4] to detect epilepsy with a sensitivity of 80%. However, thresholding and statistical analysis algorithms are susceptible to interference from daily activities.

Later, the application of machine learning in wearable device-based seizure detection can fuse multimodal signals, resulting in higher seizure detection accuracy. In [5], ACC and EDA signals are used for GTCS detection. The time-frequency and nonlinear features are extracted to represent the signal, and the support vector machine (SVM) is used for classification to obtain a sensitivity of 94.55%. In recent years, PPG signals have also been applied to motor epilepsy detection. In [6], the gradient tree is adopted to improve the performance, and the sensitivity of 75% and the false alarm rate of 0.56 are achieved. However, traditional machine learning takes a lot of time on feature extraction, and misjudgment will occur for some complex fragments.

Benefiting from its ability in complex signal representation, deep learning has been widely studied in epilepsy analysis. In [7], a convolutional neural network (CNN) is utilized to characterize multimodal signals (ACC, EDA, and BVP) and performed seizure detection. However, Ref. [7] only compares the sensitivity of epilepsy detection under different modal signals without a unified analysis, resulting in underutilization of feature information. In addition, wearable devices have also been studied in seizure prediction. In [8], Meisel et al. perform seizure prediction on EDA, TEM, BVP, and ACC signals, and compare the predictive effects of CNN and Long Short-Term Memory (LSTM) networks. Further, PPG signal is added in [9], and LSTM networks achieves a sensitivity of 75%. However, the above methods are generally direct applications of deep learning models, and do not dynamically capture feature information of various modal signals.

To make full use of multimodal signals, we propose a multi-scale convolutional neural network (MSCNN) based on attention modules to detect seizures. The flowchart of MSCNN is shown in Fig. 1. MSCNN can jointly process multimodal signals and capture multimodal signal features from multi-scale resolutions. In addition, the attention module can better preserve effective information at different resolutions. This paper is organized as follows: Sect. 2 describes the dataset, the proposed MSCNN model for seizure detection, and model parameter settings. Section 3 describes the performance indicators of the characterization model, the experimental results and analysis of the proposed method and the comparison results with the mainstream methods. Section 4 is the conclusion of this paper.

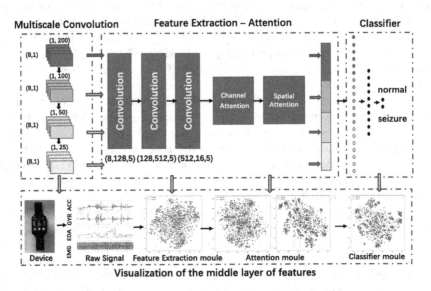

Fig. 1. The proposed seizure detection algorithm. In the visualization part of the middle layer, the red dots represent seizures, and the blue dots represent normal. Each picture represents the effect produced after passing through the different module. Firstly, the samples after passing through the multi-scale module are in a disordered state. Through the attention mechanism module, the occurrence samples are located in the periphery, and the normal samples are concentrated in the middle part. In the final classifier module, the occurrence samples are concentrated in the middle side. (Color figure online)

2   Methodology

This section describes the datasets used in the paper. Then the specific architecture of MSCNN is introduced. The settings of specific experimental parameters are given.

2.1   Data Acquisition

The multimodal data used in this paper comes from the Children's Hospital, Zhejiang University School of Medicine (CHZU) and is collected by the wearable device 'Real-Brainhealth'. The CHZU database contains ACC, GYR, EDA,

Table 1. Specifications of CHZU Dataset (h: hour)

Patient ID	Age	Gender	No. of seizures	Record duration(h)
1	6Y2M	F	2	8
2	7Y8M	F	7	6.25
3	7Y3M	M	5	7.26
4	1Y4M	F	1	8.54
5	2Y11M	F	1	5.1
6	7Y6M	F	7	13.11
7	5M	F	1	5.18
8	1Y2M	F	2	5.16
9	2Y9M	F	4	7.4
10	7Y7M	M	0	13
11	10Y11M	M	0	12
12	10Y6M	F	0	14
13	9Y8M	M	0	15
#13 Patients	5Y3M	/	27	120

and EMG signals with sampling frequencies of 50 Hz, 50 Hz, 4 Hz, and 200 Hz, respectively. As shown in Table 1, 13 patients (4 males and 9 females) with a history of benign epileptic seizures are taken part in data recording. The age range is 7~10 years old for males and 1.2~10 years old for females. The average recording time is 9.2 h. In this paper, different preprocessing operations are used for multimode signals. For ACC, GYR and other acceleration signals, median filter is used to eliminate noise and the band-pass filter is implemented to retain the main signal. For EDA signal, because of the lower sampling frequency, median filter is used to remove some shock signals. The comb filter removes power frequency interference of EMG signals, and then the bandpass filter is used to remove noise. Further, we segment the samples using a window length of 1 s. The low-frequency data is upsampled to 200 Hz. The number of channels of the multimodal input is 8, and the length is 200.

2.2 Proposed MSCNN Based Seizure Detection

As shown in Fig. 1, the proposed model mainly consists of three modules, which are multi-scale convolution, attention module based feature extraction, and classifier module.

Multiscale. Several studies have demonstrated the effectiveness of examining EEG at multiple scales. In addition, different modal signals are affected by the signal type and sampling frequency, and their characteristics cannot be measured by a unified scale. Therefore, it is meaningful to perform multiscale analysis on multi-modal signals. In this module, the shape of original input is $(C, 1, T)$, where C is the number of channels and T is the length of the sample. Each layer performs a depthwise convolution on each channel with kernel size $(1, 2)$, stride 2, and no padding. With this setting, the input size of k-th layer is $(C, 1, \frac{T}{2^{k-1}})$. This paper sets the maximum number of layers to 4 layers. By changing its scale, it is possible to ensure that each modality signal is not disturbed by other signals, while preserving information at different scales.

Feature Extraction. The module is divided into two parts, the first is the convolution block for feature extraction. And the second is a spatio-temporal attention mechanism for feature selection. In the convolution block, there are three different convolution kernels, each followed by dropout, LeaklyRelu and MaxPool1d layers. This layer utilizes convolution kernels of different sizes to extract effective information from the outputs of multi-scale modules. The specfic implementations of the three convolutional layers are conv1D (8, 128, 5), conv1D (128, 512, 5), and conv1D (512, 16, 5). The feature map learned from each scale is $M \in \mathbb{R}^{L*d}$, and three convolution operations are performed $F = conv3(conv2(conv1(M)))$. After each convolution operation, the maximum pooling layer is used to compress the global spatial information.

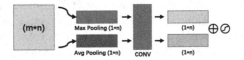

Fig. 2. Channel Attention module.

The spatio-temporal attention mechanism module is further performed on multi-scale features. The attention mechanism can extract the knowledge of each channel by strengthening the learning ability of the network, which has been proved by many studies [10–12]. In this study, we extend the spatio-temporal attention module to multi-scale network structures to learn correlation features between different modal signals. The attention mechanism module is built by the Convolutional Block Attention Module (CBAM). For the Channel Attention module, as shown in Fig. 2, the average pooling F_{avg}^c and maximum pooling F_{max}^c operations are first performed on the features extracted by the previous module to aggregate multimodal information. Convolution operations are then performed on the outputs of the maximum pooling and average pooling respectively. Finally, after applying the shared network to each descriptor, element-wise summation is used to combine the output feature vectors. The channel attention formula is calculated as follows:

$$M_c(F) = \sigma(conv(AvgPool(F)) + conv(MaxPool(F)))$$
$$= \sigma(W_1(W_0(F_{avg}^c)) + W_1(W_0(F_{max}^c))), \tag{1}$$

where σ represents the sigmoid function, W_0 is Conv1d $(C, R, 1)$, and W_1 is Conv1d $(R, C, 1)$. Note that the parameters of the shared convolutional layer for the input are W_0 and W_1, and the ReLU activation function is followed by W_0.

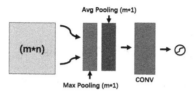

Fig. 3. Spatial Attention Module.

For the Spatial Attention Module, as Fig. 3 shows, we use two pooling operations $F_{avg}^{'s}$ and $F_{max}^{'s}$ to integrate different modal information. Its outputs are then linearly concatenated to form a 2D spatial attention map. In short, spatial attention is computed as follows:

$$M_s(F^{'}) = \sigma(W_2([AvgPool(F^{'}); MaxPool(F^{'})]))$$
$$= \sigma(W_2([F_{avg}^{'s}; F_{max}^{'s}])), \tag{2}$$

where σ represents the sigmoid function, and W_2 is the convolution module of Conv1d $(2, R, 7)$. In summary, the overall attention mechanism process can be summarized as

$$F^{'} = M_c(F) \otimes F, \tag{3}$$

$$F^{''} = M_s(F^{'}) \otimes F^{'}, \tag{4}$$

where $\otimes$ denotes element-wise multiplication. $F^{''}$ is the final output. Finally, the feature of the three scales are linearly combined to form a feature vector with a length of 512.

Classifer. In this module, there are mainly three fully connected layers with sizes of 512, 64, and 32, respectively. And focal loss is adopted to optimize the proposed model, which is expressed as

$$FL(p_t) = -\alpha(1 - p_t)^\gamma log(p_t). \tag{5}$$

By calculating the similarity between two sets of prediction probability values, focal loss can avoid problems caused by imbalanced datasets and solve the samples that are difficult to distinguish.

2.3 Parameter Setting

The proposed method is implemented using the PyTorch v1.8.0 framework. The training process is implemented on an NVIDIA RTX3080ti with 12 GB of memory. At each iteration of training, the loss function is optimized by using an Adam optimizer with a learning rate of 0.001. And the batch size is set to 16 for all experiments.

3 Experimental Result and Analysis

This section first presents the evaluation indicators of the algorithm. Then the proposed algorithm is compared with mainstream methods, and ablation experiments are carried out for each module. Finally, the classification effect of the model is tested by the actual signal. In Subsects. 3.2 and 3.3, the signals are divided into small samples for the classification experiments, aiming to obtain the performance of the model. In Subsect. 3.4, the continuous signals are adopted to verified the effectiveness of the proposed algorithm, aiming to observe the accuracy of capturing a continuous episode signal.

3.1 Experimental Evaluation

The accuracy, sensitivity and specificity are used as the performance indicators. Accuracy is the percentage of signal segments that are computed correctly, as in

$$Accuracy = \frac{TP + TN}{TP + FP + TN + FN}, \tag{6}$$

where *TP, TN, FP,* and *FN* denote true positives, true negatives, false positives, and false negatives.

Sensitivity provides the true positive rate of the relevance class (seizure), and specificity indicates the true negative rate of the nonrelevance class (nonseizure). They are calculated as

$$Sensitivity = \frac{TP}{TP + FN}, \tag{7}$$

$$Specificity = \frac{TN}{TN + FP}. \tag{8}$$

3.2 Comparison with Mainstream Methods

We compare the performance of MSCNN with two mainstream methods. The first approach is manual feature extraction combined with traditional classifiers. The time domain, frequency domain and nonlinear features of multi-modal signals are analyzed, and the cosine KNN method is used for classification. The other is currently the mainstream CNN model for wearable devices. As shown in Table 2, all results are obtained by 5-fold cross-validation. Obviously, MSCNN has better performance compared with other methods. Specifically, MSCNN has higher sensitivity of 93.5% than that of the handcrafted feature-based methods. Meanwhile, the detection speed of the proposed model is faster. Compared with the method proposed in [7], both sensitivity and specificity are significantly improved. The proposed method achieves the highest accuracy of 96.7%, the highest sensitivity of 93.5% and the hisghest specificity of 97.3%, which provides 3.7%, 4.2% and 2.9% increments over the method in [7] on accuracy, sensitivity and specificity, respectively.

Table 2. Comparison between the proposed method and mainsteam methods on the CHZU dataset. For each institution, the best values are highlighted in bold.

Method	Accuracy	Sensitivity	Specifity
Manual feature extraction	93.3%	88.2%	95.4%
Tang et al. [7]	93.0%	89.3%	94.4%
Proposed	**96.7%**	**93.5%**	**97.3%**

3.3 Ablation Study

To investigate the contribution of each module to the effective performance of MSCNN, we conducted an ablation study on the CHZU dataset. CNN is used as the basic model, attention modules and multi-scale modules are stacked sequentially. Among them, CNN combined with the attention module is recorded as CNN-ST. The experimental results are shown in the Table 3. The proposed MSCNN method provides 2.5%, 0.3% and 3.1% increments over CNN on accuracy, sensitivity and specificity, and 0.9%, 0.6% and 1.1% increments over CNN-ST on accuracy, sensitivity and specificity, respectively.

Table 3. Ablation study of the designed variant models to verify the effectiveness of different modules of MSCNN.

	CNN	CNN-ST	MSCNN
Accuracy	94.2%	95.8%	**96.7%**
Sensitivity	93.2%	92.9%	**93.5%**
Specivity	94.2%	96.2%	**97.3%**

As observed, the addition of the spatio-temporal attention mechanism module can effectively improve the specificity and reduce its false alarm rate, but it will have a certain impact on the sensitivity. Specifically, the introduction of multi-scale modules has significantly improved various indicators, especially compared to CNN networks. Ablation experiment verifies that the modules in our model are effective for epilepsy detection. It also fully demonstrates that MSCNN is beneficial to capture valuable multi-scale features of different modal signals.

3.4 Epilepsy Detection Results

The proposed model has shown good performance on sliced data, and the real effect of the model is further tested from the actual input. Therefore, we use 27 continuous episodes in the CHZU dataset as input to test the model.

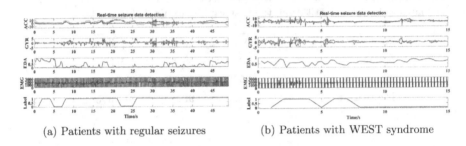

(a) Patients with regular seizures   (b) Patients with WEST syndrome

Fig. 4. Visualization of different modal signals and prediction results in consecutive seizures.

First, Fig. 4 shows the result of epilepsy detection of a continuous signal. The abscissa is time, and the ordinate is label, where 1 is seizure and 0 is normal. Seizures cannot be completely detected, and there are some missed detections. This is because the body movements reflected in epilepsy are intermittent. Therefore, in the research, it often leads to a period of ictal EEG signals continuously calibrated by neurologists, and the multimodal signals corresponding to wearable devices do not always have seizures.

The ictal signals presented in Fig. 4(a) and 4(b) are from common epilepsy patient and West syndrome patient, respectively. From Fig. 4(a), it can be seen that its real seizure is in good agreement with the model detection results. In

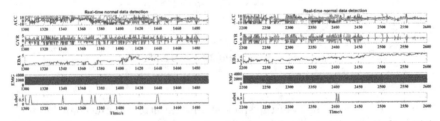

(a) normal fragment with complex activity (b) normal fragment without complex activity

Fig. 5. Visualization of different modal signals and predictive results of patients' daily activities.

addition, by observing different modal signals, it is found that acceleration signals can better characterize epilepsy than skin electrophoresis. For Fig. 4(b), the seizure characteristics of patients with West syndrome are quite different from those of common epilepsy. There are long periods of quiescence, thus not all seizures can be detected by multimodal signal.

Further, we take the multimodal signals of patients' daily activities as input to detect the false positive rate of actual seizures. As shown in Fig. 5, it can be found through experiments that some misjudged action occurs when patients have many complex movements. This is consistent with previous studies [13]. It is worth noting that in Fig. 5, besides limb movement, the mutation of skin electricity is also an important factor for the false positives of the two normal samples.

4   Conclusions

In this paper, a multi-scale convolutional neural network model based on attention modules for wearable device epilepsy detection is proposed. The multi-scale module can learn different scale features of multi-modal signals and effectively fuse information. And the attention mechanism module can further select feature information to obtain differentiated multi-modal signals and multi-scale features. In addition, focal loss well alleviates the troubles caused by unbalanced datasets and indistinguishable samples. Finally, the proposed algorithm achieves a sensitivity of 93.5% and specificity of 97.3% on the CHZU dataset.

Ethical Statement. This study has been approved by the fourth Affiliated Hospital of Anhui Medical University registered in Chinese Clinical Trail Registry (PJ-YX2021-019). All patients gave their informed consent prior to their inclusion in the study.

References

1. Sveinsson, O., Andersson, T., Mattsson, P., Carlsson, S., Tomson, T.: Clinical risk factors in SUDEP: a nationwide population-based case-control study. Neurology **94**(4), e419–e429 (2019)
2. Onorati, F., et al.: Multi-center clinical assessment of improved wearable multi-modal convulsive seizure detectors (2017)
3. Conradsen, I., Beniczky, S., Hoppe, K., Wolf, P., Sorensen, H.B.D.: Automated algorithm for generalized tonic-clonic epileptic seizure onset detection based on sEMG zero-crossing rate. IEEE Trans. Biomed. Eng. **59**(2), 579–585 (2011)
4. Baumgartner, C., Whitmire, L.E., Voyles, S.R., Cardenas, D.P.: Using sEMG to identify seizure semiology of motor seizures. Seizure **86**, 52–59 (2020)
5. Poh, M.-Z., et al.: Convulsive seizure detection using a wrist-worn electrodermal activity and accelerometry biosensor. Epilepsia **53**(5), e93–e97 (2012)
6. Böttcher, S., et al.: Intra- and inter-subject perspectives on the detection of focal onset motor seizures in epilepsy patients. Sensors **22**(9), 3318 (2022)
7. Tang, J., et al.: Seizure detection using wearable sensors and machine learning: setting a benchmark. Epilepsia **62**(8), 1807–1819 (2021)

8. Meisel, C., El Atrache, R., Jackson, M., Schubach, S., Ufongene, C., Loddenkemper, T.: Machine learning from wristband sensor data for wearable, noninvasive seizure forecasting. Epilepsia **61**(12), 2653–2666 (2020)
9. Nasseri, M., et al.: Non-invasive wearable seizure detection using long-short-term memory networks with transfer learning. J. Neural Eng. **18**(5), 056017 (2021)
10. Yuanchen, W., Zhou, Y., Zeng, W., Qian, Q., Song, M.: An attention-based 3D CNN with multi-scale integration block for Alzheimer's disease classification. IEEE J. Biomed. Health Inform. **26**(11), 5665–5673 (2022)
11. Chen, J., Chen, Y., Li, W., Ning, G., Tong, M., Hilton, A.: Channel and spatial attention based deep object co-segmentation. Knowl.-Based Syst. **211**, 106550 (2021)
12. Feng, Y., et al.: 3D residual-attention-deep-network-based childhood epilepsy syndrome classification. Knowl.-Based Syst. **248**, 108856 (2022)
13. Milosevic, M., et al.: Automated detection of tonic-clonic seizures using 3-D accelerometry and surface electromyography in pediatric patients. IEEE J. Biomed. Health Inform. **20**(5), 1333–1341 (2015)

Improving EEG-Based Continuous Grip Force Decoding in Grasp-Lift Tasks by Considering Grip Force Levels

Sikai Wu, Zeqi Ye, Xingxing Chu, Gai Lu, Yang Yu, and Ling-Li Zeng[✉]

College of Intelligence Science and Technology, National University of Defense Technology, Changsha, Hunan, China
{yezeqigfkd,zengphd}@nudt.edu.cn

Abstract. Electroencephalography(EEG)-based brain-computer interfaces(BCIs) for motor control can restore or enhance users' motor ability. Grasp-lift is one of the critical hand movements in daily life. Continuous decoding of grip force in grasp-lift tasks is significant in developing natural motor control BCIs. According to different grasping target objects, the hand takes different grip force levels in grasp-lift tasks. However, it remains unclear whether the performance of continuous grip force decoding in grasp-lift tasks can be improved if considering grip force levels. To address this issue, we define low, medium and high grip force levels based on object weights in grasp-lift tasks. Then we develop corresponding force-specific decoders named EEGForceNET based on CNN+LSTM to decode continuous grip force using low delta frequency band (0-1 Hz) EEG signals. After that, we conduct pseudo-online experiments on WAY-EEG-GAL dataset to evaluate the decoding performance of force-specific models. Finally, with the improved force-specific models, the average Pearson correlation coefficient(PCC) between reconstructed and recorded grip force trajectories is increased by approximately 0.137. The results suggest that the performance of continuous grip force decoding can be improved by differentiating different grip force levels and that the CNN+LSTM model can be used to decode continuous grip force in motor control BCIs.

Keywords: Brain-Computer Interface · Electroencephalography · Grasp-Lift Task · Grip Force · Continuous Decoding

1 Introduction

In recent years, non-invasive BCIs have emerged as promising solutions for motor control. Specifically, non-invasive BCIs, which use EEG signals to decode users' intentions, are widely adopted due to their more convenience, lower risk and lower cost than other non-invasive BCI paradigms. The motor-BCIs can detect brain activity associated with users' motor intentions, imagination or execution.

© The Author(s), under exclusive license to Springer Nature Singapore Pte Ltd. 2024
F. Sun et al. (Eds.): ICCSIP 2023, CCIS 1919, pp. 81–91, 2024.
https://doi.org/10.1007/978-981-99-8021-5_7

Thus, motor-BCIs can be applied to control wheelchairs [11,19], robotic arms [15,22,25] and exoskeletons [8,20] to restore or enhance the motor ability of users.

Previous studies for motor control BCI mainly focus on motor classification [4,9,12,24], enabling discrete control of external devices. However, continuous control of external devices requires decoding continuous motion parameters. Bradnerry et al. [3] first employ EEG data to decode hand position, velocity, and acceleration when the subjects touch the target. The study demonstrates that the non-invasive BCI has the capability to decode continuous kinematic parameters. After that, decoding continuous kinematic parameters from non-invasive brain signals has gained extensive interest.

Since the signal-to-noise ratio and spatial resolution of non-invasive EEG signals are lower than invasive methods. The selection of suitable features plays a crucial role in decoding performance. Agasge et al. [1] demonstrate that EEG signals can effectively predict hand position and other parameters, with a correlation coefficient exceeding 0.7 between the reconstructed position and actual trajectory. The high performance of the decoder is mainly attributed to the effective feature extraction. Specifically, They select low-frequency band EEG features for decoding.

Grasp-lift is one of the critical hand movements in daily life and grip force is a crucial continuous parameter of grasping. Invasive BCI studies have suggested that decoding grip force from neural activity can be applied to provide more natural and generalizable BCI systems [2,5,6,16]. Towards achieving continuous grip force decoding, Paek et al. [18] first investigate the feasibility of utilizing EEG signals to decode continuous grip force. Decoders employing low-frequency band EEG signals exhibit favorable performance in decoding continuous grip force. Specifically, amplitude features extracted from EEG signals in the low delta band (0-1 Hz) demonstrate the strongest correlation with grip force trajectory. By employing a linear regression decoder, they achieve a correlation coefficient of 0.42 in isometric force production tasks.

However, linear models may not capture the inherent nonlinear components of EEG signals. Deep learning has emerged as a popular nonlinear modeling technique that shows promise for decoding complex and variable continuous kinematic parameters in BCI. Ortega et al. [17] conduct a study where they combine EEG and functional near-infrared spectroscopy (fNIRS) signal features to decode continuous grip force. In their study, subjects are required to generate hand-specific force profiles. The best decoding performance is achieved by self-attention+CNN networks. The average Spearman's correlation coefficient(SCC) between the actual and reconstructed force trajectories achieves 0.676/0.689(left/right hands) and 0.597/0.594 for decoding using the EEG signal alone. The results highlight the potential of nonlinear methods, such as deep learning models, in improving the decoding accuracy for continuous grip force from EEG signals.

In general, methods for decoding continuous kinematic parameters such as grip force based on EEG signals have developed rapidly in recent years. However, there are still some questions that have not been investigated. In daily life, the target object of grasp-lift tasks often varies, resulting in corresponding changes in grip force levels. Many studies have suggested the amplitude features of low-frequency EEG signals can be used to decode continuous grip force. However, it is still unclear whether this feature can distinguish the grip force levels and whether the decoding performance can be improved by considering the grip force level.

In this study, we found that variations in grip force levels have a significant impact on decoding performance. Therefore, we define low, medium and high grip force levels based on object weights. Then, we develop corresponding force-specific decoders based on CNN+LSTM architecture to decode continuous grip force in grasp-lift tasks. We conduct pseudo-online experiments for force-specific models on the WAY-EEG-GAL dataset to confirm whether the models can be performed online. We use PCC between reconstructed grip force trajectories and recorded grip force trajectories as an evaluation metric. With the improved force-specific models, the average PCC is increased by 0.137 compared to the direct model, which decodes continuous grip force without considering grip force levels.

The main contributions of this study are as follows:

1. We find it difficult for the decoder to distinguish different grip force levels using amplitude features of low-frequency band EEG signals. Therefore, We propose a feasible approach to define the grip force levels of tasks based on object weights. The performance of continuous grip force decoding in grasp-lift tasks can be improved by about 0.137 if considering grip force levels.
2. We develop EEGForceNET based on CNN+LSTM for continuous grip force decoding. It shows a good performance in continuous grip force decoding.

2   Materials and Method

2.1   WAY-EEG-GAL Dataset

The WAY-EEG-GAL dataset is utilized for decoding continuous grip force from EEG in grasp-lift tasks [14]. In the dataset, 12 subjects perform grasp-lift tasks under varying object weights (165g, 330g or 660g) and frictions (sandpaper, suede or silk). The dataset consists of 3936 grasp-lift trials, with each subject performing nine experiments and each containing approximately 36 trials. EEG data are recorded at a sampling rate of 500 Hz using a 32-channel ActiCap during each experiment, while grip force data are recorded by pressure sensors at the same sampling rate.

The experiments in this dataset can be classified into three categories: weight experiments (involving trials with different object weights), friction experiments (involving trials with different frictions) and mixed experiments (involving trials with both different target object weights and frictions). In this study, we pick 2240 trials from weight experiments to decode continuous grip force.

Each trial begins when the LED is turned on. Subjects reach for the object and grasp it between their forefinger and thumb, lift it to a specified position and hold it stable for 2 s. After the LED is turned off, they return the object to its initial position and rest their hand on the resting area.

2.2 Grip Force Level Analysis

In this study, we define low, medium and high force levels for trials with 165g, 330g and 660g object weights, respectively.

To analyze the difference in grip force level between trials with different target weights, we calculate the Time Averaged Grip Force (TAGF) by dividing the sum of grip force values by the time of the grasp-lift period. The mean TAGF values for all subjects increased $64.09 \pm 13.70\%$ between 330 g and 165 g object weight and $91.60 \pm 12.5\%$ between 660 g and 330 g object weight.

For example, Fig. 1 displays the force levels used by subject 1 in grasp-lift tasks with different object weights. Trials with the same object weight have relatively concentrated distributions of TAGF values. In contrast, trials with different object weights have significantly different distributions of TAGF values. Additionally, the differences in grip force level mainly exist in grip force maintenance and reduction stages during grasp-lift movement.

2.3 Data Preprocessing

This study uses two preprocessing pipelines for EEG signals and grip force data. All data preprocessing is implemented by Python and toolbox MNE.

For the EEG signals preprocessing, we first re-reference EEG data to the whole-brain average to remove spatial noise. Next, the data are band-pass filtered using a zero-phase FIR filter into 0.02-40 Hz to remove baseline drift. Then, the data are downsampled to 100 Hz to reduce computational costs. After that, the movement artifacts are removed using independent component analysis. Previous studies suggest that low-frequency components of EEG [7,10,21], particularly delta band(0-1 Hz) components, can effectively decode continuous grip force [18]. Thus, the data are further low-pass filtered using a zero-phase FIR filter with a cutoff frequency of 1 Hz. Finally, EEG data are standardized by min-max normalization for each channel.

For the grip force data preprocessing, a zero-phase FIR filter with a cutoff frequency of 10 Hz is used to smooth the data. Then, the data are downsampled to a sampling rate of 100 Hz to match the sampling rate with the EEG data.

2.4 Decode Continuous Grip Force

Figure 2 illustrates the process flow of force-specific models for continuous grip force decoding. For each trial, a 300 ms time sliding window (30 sample points) with a 290 ms overlap is used to split EEG segments, resulting in data of size $N \times (32 * 30)$, where $N = T-30-1$ represents the number of EEG data segments in a single trial. Then, the continuous grip force decoding can be expressed as $f_t = \theta(X_{t-300ms}, X_{t-290ms}, ..., X_t)$, where f_t represents grip force at time t, X_t represents an array of delta band EEG data at time t.

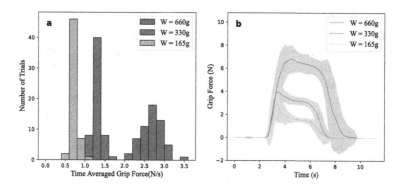

Fig. 1. The grip force levels analysis for subject 1. a, The histogram of TAGF values between different object weights for subject 1. b, Mean grip force trajectories between different object weights for subject 1. The colored shaded areas present the mean confidence interval ($alpha = 0.05$).

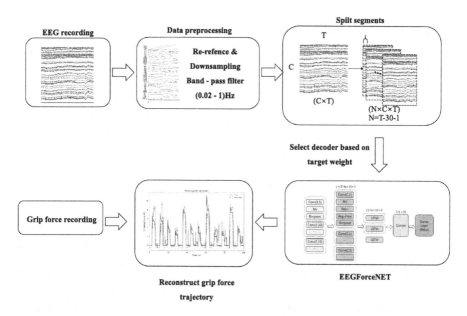

Fig. 2. Flowchart of the force-specific models' framework.

The EEGForceNet is developed based on CNN+LSTM to decode continuous grip force, as shown in Fig. 3. To extract temporal features from the input feature map, we employ three parallel convolutions along the temporal dimension with zero-padding. The three convolution kernel sizes used are (1,5), (1,10) and(1,15), and the number of filters is 5. This allows for extracting temporal features at different granularities, offering a more comprehensive representation of the input.

Compared to fixed-size convolutional kernels, varying kernel sizes offer enhanced temporal feature extraction capability.

The resulting feature maps from the three parallel convolutions are then passed through a deepwise convolutional layer with a kernel size of 32 and the number of filters is 2. This layer aggregates information across different feature channels to further enhance the representation. Next, an average pooling layer with a kernel size of 4 is applied to reduce the dimensionality of the features. This step helps in reducing computational complexity.

Exploiting the temporal structure improves grip force decoding, based on previous invasive Brain-Computer Interface (BCI) studies. Therefore, an LSTM layer is added after the CNN component [16,23]. The output of the LSTM layer is concatenated and passed through a dense layer with the ReLU activation function, resulting in the decoding grip force value. The adaptive moment estimation (Adam) optimization algorithm and mean squared error (MSE) loss function are employed for model training.

2.5   Pseudo-Online Experiment

To confirm whether the models can be performed online. We conduct pseudo-online experiments to confirm whether the models can be performed online.

In WAY-EEG-GAL dataset, each subject completes five weight experiments. EEG and grip force data from four of the five experiments are used as a training set, and the data from the remaining experiment are used as a test set. Five rounds of testing are conducted for each subject, with data from a different experiment used as the test set in each round.

Three force-specific models are trained using data from trials with corresponding force levels in the training set. We also train the direct model, which is trained directly using data from all trials in the training set without considering differences between trails in grip force levels.

In the pseudo-online experiments, we first select the force-specific model based on object weights for each trial. Then force-specific and direct models decode the grip force values from EEG signals every 10ms. After decoding, the grip force trajectories are reconstructed by concatenating the decoding grip force value in time order. We apply the one-way analysis of variance (ANOVA) with Tukey's honestly significant difference for the statistical test of decoding results.

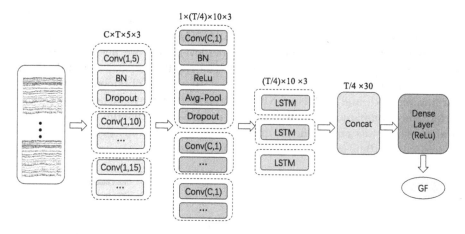

Fig. 3. GripForceNet based on CNN+LSTM architecture for continuous grip force decoding.

3   Result

To investigate the ability of the direct model to differentiate grip force levels. The TAGF of the reconstructed grip trajectories by the direct model is calculated. The mean TAGF values across all subjects are 2.51 ± 0.67, 2.53 ± 0.63, and 2.60 ± 0.63 for tasks with low, medium and high grip force levels, respectively. However, no significant differences exist between the TAGF values, indicating the difficulty of distinguishing grip force levels using low-frequency EEG signal features.

To compare the decoding performance of force-specific decoder and direct decoder, the PCC between the actual and reconstructed grip force trajectories is used to evaluate the decoding performance. Figure 3 illustrates the decoding performance between the force-specific and direct models. The mean PCC across all subjects is 0.697 ± 0.088 for the force-specific models and 0.560 ± 0.116 for the direct models. The results show that the average PCC is increased by about 0.137 with force-specific models. PCC is significantly higher ($p < 1e - 7$) for force-specific models than for direct models.

To investigate the reasons for the improved performance of the force-specific models, we compare the PCC of reconstructed grip trajectories under the three grip force level tasks. The results indicated that only Subject 2 and Subject 11 showed significant differences between the low and high grip force level tasks ($p < 0.01$). The decoding performance at different grip force levels is not significantly different for most subjects. We present a part of the reconstructed and the actual force trajectories for subject 1 in Fig. 4. As shown in this figure, the direct model can decode the shape of grip force trajectories. However, the model is difficult to differentiate trials with different grip force levels. In contrast, the force-specific model better differentiates between different grip force levels. Thus, the force-specific models show improved decoding performance in grasp-lift tasks.

To further verify the effectiveness of the proposed method, we also compare
the model with some other models on the WAT-GAL-EEG dataset. Each model
is specifically trained for different grip force levels, and we perform extensive
debugging to optimize their performance. The results are shown in Table 1, it
can be seen that the highest decoding performance is obtained by the deep
learning method, and EEGForceNET obtains approximate or better decoding
performance compared to cnnatt [18] with fewer network parameters. After verification, there was no significant difference in decoding time between different
models(with a 10ms average delay on our computer).

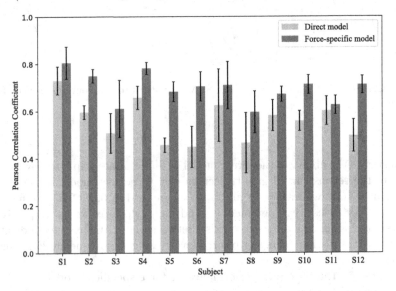

Fig. 4. PCC analysis for reconstructed grip force trajectory.

Table 1. PCC PCC Analysis of Different Model

Subject	mLR	EEGNET [13]	CNNATT [18]	EEGForceNet
S1	0.734 ± 0.077	0.766 ± 0.082	$\mathbf{0.827 \pm 0.068}$	0.805 ± 0.068
S2	0.609 ± 0.044	$0.727 \pm \pm 0.016$	0.722 ± 0.021	$\mathbf{0.749 \pm 0.028}$
S3	0.623 ± 0.062	$\mathbf{0.631 \pm 0.063}$	0.598 ± 0.062	0.611 ± 0.021
S4	0.751 ± 0.024	0.759 ± 0.013	$\mathbf{0.815 \pm 0.020}$	0.782 ± 0.026
S5	0.645 ± 0.068	0.655 ± 0.036	0.658 ± 0.049	$\mathbf{0.682 \pm 0.042}$
S6	0.646 ± 0.067	0.666 ± 0.071	0.678 ± 0.066	$\mathbf{0.704 \pm 0.066}$
S7	0.671 ± 0.131	0.694 ± 0.094	$\mathbf{0.718 \pm 0.125}$	0.710 ± 0.096
S8	0.563 ± 0.174	0.544 ± 0.145	0.543 ± 0.126	$\mathbf{0.596 \pm 0.098}$
S9	0.673 ± 0.050	0.662 ± 0.027	0.658 ± 0.041	$\mathbf{0.671 \pm 0.088}$
S10	0.653 ± 0.042	0.694 ± 0.040	$\mathbf{0.740 \pm 0.036}$	0.712 ± 0.032
S11	0.623 ± 0.060	0.615 ± 0.048	0.591 ± 0.049	$\mathbf{0.625 \pm 0.041}$
S12	0.537 ± 0.023	0.674 ± 0.046	0.696 ± 0.051	$\mathbf{0.711 \pm 0.038}$
Average	0.644 ± 0.099	0.674 ± 0.090	0.687 ± 0.107	$\mathbf{0.697 \pm 0.088}$

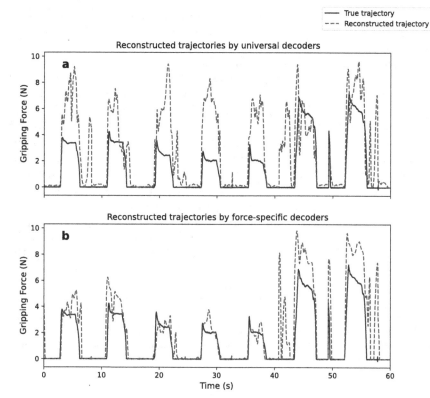

Fig. 5. Reconstructed grip force trajectories of seven trials for subject 1 using force-specific and direct decoders (Two trials with medium grip force level, three trials with low grip force level and two trials with high grip force level). a, Reconstructed grip force trajectories by force-specific models. b, Reconstructed grip force trajectories by direct model.

4 Conclusion and Discussion

Previous studies have shown that amplitude features of low-frequency band EEG signals can be used to decode continuous kinematic parameters like grip force. In this study, we find it difficult to distinguish the variation of grip force levels using low-frequency band EEG signals. To circumvent the problem of insufficient ability to decode force levels, we distinguish between the three types of grip force levels as low, medium and high. This setup is mainly due to the experimental setup of the dataset used in this paper. As shown in Fig. 1, the grip experiments conducted for the three categories of target objects with different weights have consistency in grip force levels at the same weight and differences at different target weights, therefore, the category of grip force levels is set to 3. The result of this study suggests that if the grip force levels are distinguished before decoding, better decoding performance can be obtained.

In addition, we develop a decoder named EEGForceNET. This model achieves good performance on the WAY-EEG-GAL dataset and is an effective method that can be used for continuous grip force decoding.

If we aim to deploy this method in real-world scenarios, it is necessary to classify the grip force level during the reaching target phase, where the actual grip force has not yet been generated. Subsequently, the continuous decoding of the grip force can be conducted in the subsequent grasping process.

Since the experimental setup of the dataset used in this study has target objects of different weights suspended under the tabletop, The weight of the target object can only be ascertained when the subject lifts it, and the information obtained during the reaching phase is same across tasks with different target weights. Therefore, we try to differentiate the grip force levels using EEG signals in the reaching phase and do not get a good performance.

To address this limitation, our future research will design proper grip experiments and focus on the classification of different grip force levels based on EEG signals in the early stages of grasp-lift tasks automatically. By optimizing the experimental setup and incorporating advanced analysis techniques, we aim to deploy this method in real-world scenarios.

Acknowledgements. This work is supported by the STI 2030-Major Projects (2022ZD0208903), the National Natural Science Foundation of China (62006239, 61722313, and 62036013), the Fok Ying Tung Education Foundation (161057) and the Defense Industrial Technology Development Program (JCKY2020550B003).

References

1. Agashe, H.A., Paek, A.Y., Zhang, Y., Contreras-Vidal, J.L.: Global cortical activity predicts shape of hand during grasping. Front. Neurosci. **9**, 121 (2015)
2. Bansal, A., Truccolo, W., Vargas-Irwin, C., Donoghue, J.: Decoding 3D reach and grasp from hybrid signals in motor and premotor cortices: spikes, multiunit activity, and local field potentials. J. Neurophysiol. **107**, 1337–1355 (2012)
3. Bradberry, T.J., Gentili, R.J., Contreras-Vidal, J.L.: Decoding three-dimensional hand kinematics from electroencephalographic signals. In: 2009 Annual International Conference of the IEEE Engineering in Medicine and Biology Society, pp. 5010–5013. IEEE (2009)
4. Bressan, G., Cisotto, G., Müller-Putz, G.R., Wriessnegger, S.C.: Deep learning-based classification of fine hand movements from low frequency EEG. Future Internet **13**(5), 103 (2021)
5. Carmena, J.M., et al.: Learning to control a brain-machine interface for reaching and grasping by primates. PLoS Biol. **1**, e42 (2003)
6. Flint, R.D., et al.: Extracting kinetic information from human motor cortical signals. NeuroImage **101**, 695–703 (2014)
7. Fu, Y., Xu, B., Li, Y., Wang, Y., Yu, Z., Li, H.: Single-trial decoding of imagined grip force parameters involving the right or left hand based on movement-related cortical potentials. Chin. Sci. Bull. **59**, 1907–1916 (2014)
8. Gordleeva, S.Y., et al.: Real-time EEG-EMG human-machine interface-based control system for a lower-limb exoskeleton. IEEE Access **8**, 84070–84081 (2020)

9. Hualiang, L., et al.: A novel noninvasive brain-computer interface by imagining isometric force levels. Cogn. Neurodyn. **17**, 1–9 (2022)
10. Iyengar, V., Santos, M.J., Ko, M., Aruin, A.S.: Grip force control in individuals with multiple sclerosis. Neurorehabil. Neural Repair **23**, 855–861 (2009)
11. Jiang, L., et al.: SmartRolling: a human-machine interface for wheelchair control using EEG and smart sensing techniques. Inf. Process. Manage. **60**, 103262 (2023)
12. Kwon, H.G., Kim, J.S., Lee, M.Y.: Brain activation induced by different strengths of hand grasp: a functional magnetic resonance imaging study. Neural Regen. Res. **15**, 875–879 (2020)
13. Lawhern, V.J., Solon, A.J., Waytowich, N.R., Gordon, S.M., Hung, C.P., Lance, B.J.: EEGNet: a compact convolutional neural network for EEG-based brain-computer interfaces. J. Neural Eng. **15**(5), 056013 (2018)
14. Luciw, M.D., Jarocka, E., Edin, B.B.: Multi-channel EEG recordings during 3,936 grasp and lift trials with varying weight and friction. Sci. Data **1**, 140047 (2014)
15. Nandikolla, V., Portilla, D.A.M.: Teleoperation robot control of a hybrid EEG-based BCI arm manipulator using ROS. J. Robot. **2022** (2022)
16. Naufel, S., Glaser, J.I., Kording, K.P., Perreault, E.J., Miller, L.E.: A muscle-activity-dependent gain between motor cortex and EMG. J. Neurophysiol. **121**, 61–73 (2019)
17. Ortega, P., Faisal, A.A.: Deep learning multimodal fNIRS and EEG signals for bimanual grip force decoding. J. Neural Eng. **18** (2021)
18. Paek, A.Y., Gailey, A., Parikh, P.J., Santello, M., Contreras-Vidal, J.L.: Regression-based reconstruction of human grip force trajectories with noninvasive scalp electroencephalography. J. Neural Eng. **16**(6), 066030 (2019). https://doi.org/10.1088/1741-2552/ab4063
19. Pawuś, D., Paszkiel, S.: BCI wheelchair control using expert system classifying EEG signals based on power spectrum estimation and nervous tics detection. Appl. Sci. **12**, 10385 (2022)
20. Roy, G., Bhoi, A.K., Das, S., Bhaumik, S.: Cross-correlated spectral entropy-based classification of EEG motor imagery signal for triggering lower limb exoskeleton. Signal Image Video Process. **16**, 1831–1839 (2022)
21. Song, T., Shu, Z., Yang, Y., Han, J., Yu, N.: An effective connectivity analysis method to explore visual-motor coordination during a grip task. In: 2021 IEEE 11th Annual International Conference on CYBER Technology in Automation, Control, and Intelligent Systems (CYBER), pp. 31–36 (2021)
22. Staffa, M., Giordano, M., Ficuciello, F.: A WiSARD network approach for a BCI-based robotic prosthetic control. Int. J. Soc. Robot. **12**, 749–764 (2020)
23. Sussillo, D., et al.: A recurrent neural network for closed-loop intracortical brain-machine interface decoders. J. Neural Eng. **9**, 026027 (2012)
24. Wang, K., et al.: An EEG study on hand force imagery for brain-computer interfaces. In: 2017 8th International IEEE/EMBS Conference on Neural Engineering (NER) (2017)
25. Zhang, S., Chen, Y., Zhang, L., Gao, X., Chen, X.: Study on robot grasping system of SSVEP-BCI based on augmented reality stimulus. Tsinghua Sci. Technol. **28**, 322–329 (2023)

3D Path Planning and Tracking of Quadrotors Based on Improved Whale Optimization Algorithm

Jingrun Liang[1,2](✉) [ID], Lisang Liu[1,2](✉) [ID], and Wei Chen[1,2] [ID]

[1] School of Electronic, Electrical Engineering and Physics, Fujian University of Technology, Fuzhou 350118, China
`liangjingrun@smail.fjut.edu.cn, liulisang@fjut.edu.cn`
[2] Fujian Province Industrial Integrated Automation Industry Technology Development Base, Fuzhou 350118, China

Abstract. Aiming at the shortcomings of standard whale optimization algorithm (WOA) in three-dimensional (3D) path planning of quadrotors, such as long path length, high time-consumption and path roughness, an improved whale optimization algorithm called SAMWOA is proposed in this paper. Firstly, Singer chaotic mapping strategy is introduced to enrich the diversity of whale population and improve the quality of initial solution of the algorithm. Secondly, an adaptive cognitive factor is proposed to improve the position updating method of the whale leader and balance the exploration and development ability. Then, the wavelet mutation mechanism is used to disturb the current optimal solution position of the whale population, so that the algorithm can jump out of the local optimum. Moreover, the cubic spline interpolation method is utilized to smooth the path planned by the proposed SAMWOA. Finally, the proposed SAMWOA is applied to the 3D path planning and tracking of the quadrotor. The simulation results show that, compared with the WOA, the path length, steering cost and time-consuming planned by the proposed SAMWOA is reduced by 25.78%, 37.5% and 42.21%, respectively. The proposed SAMWOA not only solves the issues of the WOA, but also can plan and track the 3D path and avoid obstacles in real time, which is advanced and robust.

Keywords: Singer Chaotic Mapping · Adaptive Cognitive Factor · Wavelet Mutation Mechanism · Whale Optimization Algorithm · Cubic Spline Interpolation · Path Planning and Tracking

1 Introduction

Path planning is one of the key technologies for autonomous navigation and control of UAV, and its purpose is to plan an optimal collision-free path from the starting point to the end point [1]. The quadrotor as a kind of UAV, its 3D path planning and tracking has attracted extensive attention from scholars [2]. In order to carry out the payload hold-release mission by avoiding obstacles, Belge et al. [3] proposed a meta-heuristic

F. Sun et al. (Eds.): ICCSIP 2023, CCIS 1919, pp. 92–105, 2024.
https://doi.org/10.1007/978-981-99-8021-5_8

algorithm which mixed Harris Hawk Optimization Algorithm (HHO) and Grey Wolf Optimization Algorithm (GWO) for the optimal path planning and tracking of UAV, and quickly generated a safe UAV path without falling into local minimum, and consumed less energy and time. Liu et al. [4] proposed an improved sparrow search algorithm (SSA) based on multi-strategies for path planning of the mobile robot, and combined it with dynamic window approach (DWA) to realize obstacle avoidance of the mobile robot in real-time. To reduce both flight time and memory consumption of the covered path planning, Paolo et al. [5] proposed a method of generating and smoothing the navigation path of UAVs, which can generate waypoints for arbitrary enclosed polygon area. Liu X. et al. [6] proposed an evolutionary algorithm based on improved t-distribution for path planning of UAV, which improved the search efficiency of path tracking. Lee et al. [7] proposed a path tracking algorithm, which guided the heading or yaw rate of the vehicle to minimize the path tracking error, and the spatial parameters were used to specify the convergence shape of the flight path. Liao et al. [8] proposed a transition path algorithm to generate waypoints that meet the flight capability of UAV, and developed a circular path algorithm to monitor the relative position between the target and the UAV. Abolfazl et al. [9] proposed an error-based constrained model predictive control (MPC) method to deal with the path tracking problem of quadrotor. It was constructed by Laguerre function, which can be used to stabilize quadrotor and reduce the computational burden significantly. Rubí et al. [10] proposed a solution to the path tracking problem of quadrotor based on deep reinforcement learning framework, which computed the optimal velocity according to the path shape, and the experimental results are verified on the RotorS platform. Qian et al. [11] proposed a path tracking controller based on Uncertainty Interference Estimator (UDE) for quadrotor with cable suspension payload. The attitude controller was decoupled by using the reduced-order theory, so that the quadrotor could be stabilized on the desired path under different wind disturbances. Moussa et al. [12] proposed a fractional-order (FO) improved super-torsion proportional integral differential sliding film control (STPIDSMC) and designed the FOPIDSM surface, which can ensure the quadrotor to track the pre-planned route stably. Xu et al. [13] proposed a control scheme based on Gaussian information for attitude control of quadrotor, and proved the convergence and robustness of the proposed algorithm by Lyapunov theory. To solve the tracking control problem of unmanned surface vehicles (USVs) with disturbance, Zheng [14] proposed a control algorithm based on barrier Lyapunov function, which made the ship following the desired geometric path, and satisfying the tracking error. Liang et al. [15] proposed an improved white shark optimization algorithm for global dynamic optimal path planning of USV, and combined it with the DWA method to realize the obstacle ship avoidance in real-time, and its dynamic collision avoidance behavior conforms to the COLREGs. Wang et al. [16] proposed an integrated path planning and trajectory tracking control framework for a quadrotor, which employed the pure-pursuit path method and adaptive sliding mode trajectory tracking controller to realize the stable path tracking of UAV. Xu C. et al. [17] proposed a chaotic feedback adaptive whale optimization algorithm (CFAWOA), which used the Sine chaotic mapping to generate the initial population, added a feedback stage in the later iteration, and introduced adaptive inertia weight into the whale individual position updating formula to improve its optimization performance.

These researchers have provided commendable work, but there are still some problems, such as unaffordable cost of the path length, steering times and time-consuming and the rough path. Whale Optimization Algorithm (WOA) is a swarm intelligence algorithm proposed by Mirjalili et al. [18] in 2016, which has the advantages of simple parameters, convenient calculation process and strong global search ability [19]. However, WOA still has some shortcomings, such as uneven population distribution, low initial solution quality and easy to fall into local optimum [20]. Therefore, in view of the issues of WOA, an improved WOA based on Singer chaotic mapping strategy, adaptive cognitive factor, wavelet mutation mechanism and cubic spline interpolation method is proposed, which is called the SAMWOA, and it has been verified in 3D path planning and tracking of a quadrotor.

The main contributions of this paper are as follows:

1. In order to solve the problem of uneven whale population distribution in WOA, Singer chaotic mapping strategy is used to initialize whale population and improve its diversity.
2. Aiming at the whale leader position is not always close to the target prey in WOA, the adaptive cognitive factor is used to improve the location update method of whale leader to balance the exploration and development capabilities.
3. As the WOA falling into local optimum easily in the bubble net predation stage, wavelet mutation mechanism is utilized to disturb the current optimal solution position of the whale population and improve the ability of jumping out the local optimum.
4. An innovative algorithm called SAMWOA is proposed and integrated with the cubic spline interpolation method to the 3D path planning and tracking of the quadrotor.

The rest of this paper is arranged as follows: Sect. 2 introduces the standard WOA. Then, a novel innovative algorithm called SAMWOA based on advanced strategies is proposed in Sect. 3. The Sect. 4 presents the simulation experiment results of the proposed SAMWOA for 3D path planning and tracking of a quadrotor, including the comparison with other algorithms. Section 5 summarizes the research and highlights the future work.

2 Standard Whale Optimization Algorithm (WOA)

The standard WOA mainly includes three stages: hunting prey stage, surrounding prey stage and bubble net predation stage.

2.1 Hunting Prey Stage

In the hunting prey stage, whales search for prey in a random way in the ocean. Assuming that the whale is represented by x, then the whale population can be represented by the following matrix:

$$X = \begin{bmatrix} x_1^1 x_2^1 \cdots x_d^1 \\ x_1^2 x_2^2 \cdots x_d^2 \\ \vdots \\ x_1^n x_2^n \cdots x_d^n \end{bmatrix} \tag{1}$$

where, X represents the whale population. n represents the size of whale population and d represents the input dimension of the problem.

In the process of randomly searching for prey, whales often update the position of the next generation according to their mutual information exchange, which broadens the search scope and determines the position of the target prey easily. The location updating method of whale searching for prey is controlled by parameters A. When $|A| > 1$ and $p \leq 0.5$, whales randomly select and move to other whale individuals. The position updating method of the whales in the hunting prey stage is expressed as follows:

$$\begin{cases} x(t+1) = x_{rand} - A \cdot D_{rand} \\ D_{rand} = |c \cdot x_{rand} - x(t)| \\ A = 2 \cdot a \cdot r - a \\ c = 2 \cdot r \end{cases} \tag{2}$$

where t represents the current iteration. $x(t)$ represents the current whale individual position at t iteration. $x(t+1)$ represents the new whale individual position at $t+1$ iteration. x_{rand} represents the position of randomly selected whale individuals at t iteration. $r \in (0, 1)$ is a random number. T represents the maximum number of iterations, and the control parameter $a = 2 - 2 \cdot \frac{t}{T}$. With the increase of iterations, a decreases monotonously, so as the A. When $|A| \leq 1$, the algorithm changes from the hunting prey stage to the surrounding prey stage.

2.2 Surrounding Prey Stage

In the surrounding prey stage, whales spiral upward to approach and surround the target prey. As the iterations increasing, the parameter A decreases monotonously. At the initial stage of surrounding the prey, since the exact position of the target prey is unknown, the fitness value of the current whale individuals closest to the target prey will be assumed to be the optimal solution in the current whale population, and other whale individuals in the current whale population will update their positions according to the current optimal solution, and continue to surround and approach the target prey, which is expressed as follows:

$$\begin{cases} x(t+1) = x'(t) - A \cdot D_1 \\ D_1 = |c \cdot x'(t) - x(t)| \end{cases} \tag{3}$$

where $x'(t)$ represents the position of the optimal solution in the current whale population. D_1 stands for the distance between $x'(t)$ and the current whale individual $x(t)$. $A \cdot D_1$ is called the surrounding step size. With the iterative updating of control parameters A and D_1, the position of the new whale individual $x(t+1)$ is also iteratively updated by $x'(t)$ and $x(t)$, gradually encircling the prey and approaching the global optimal solution.

2.3 Bubble Net Predation Stage

In the bubble net predation stage, whales move to the target prey while shrinking the encirclement along the spiral path, and adopt the attack strategy of bubble net to approach the target prey to the sea surface, so as to prey conveniently. In the process, the whale population contracts and surrounds the target prey, calculates the position between the whale population and the target prey, and realizes the spiral upward movement of the whale population to the target prey, which is expressed by the following formula:

$$\begin{cases} x(t+1) = D_2 \cdot e^{bl} \cdot \cos(2\pi l) + x'(t) \\ \quad D_2 = |x'(t) - x(t)| \end{cases} \tag{4}$$

where b represents the coefficient of the spiral equation. D_2 represents the distance between the current whale individual and the optimal solution position in the current whale population. $l \in [-1, 1]$ represents a random number.

The whales often adopt the synchronous hunting method of spiral surrounding prey and bubble net attacking prey in the bubble net predation stage. To simulate this process, a random probability is set to switch the two hunting methods randomly, and different strategies are used to update the position of the whale individuals. The surround predation mechanism of WOA in the bubble net predation stage is expressed as follows:

$$x(t+1) = \begin{cases} D_2 \cdot e^{bl} \cdot \cos(2\pi l) + x'(t), \ p \geq 0.5 \\ \quad x'(t) - A \cdot D_1, \quad\quad p < 0.5 \end{cases} \tag{5}$$

where $p \in [0, 1]$ represents the random probability. Other variables have been explained in formula (3) and formula (4) and will not be repeated here. As can be seen that when $p \geq 0.5$, whales attack the prey in the form of spiral bubble nets. Otherwise, when $p < 0.5$, the prey near the current optimal solution position is gradually rounded up by the whale individuals.

3 Improved Whale Optimization Algorithm (SAMWOA)

3.1 Singer Chaotic Mapping

In the standard WOA, since the whale population is generated randomly, the whale population distribution is sparse and uneven, and the diversity of the whale population is poor, which will make it difficult for whales to lock the current prey position in the hunting prey stage and decelerate the convergence speed of the algorithm. Chaos phenomenon is often produced by the deterministic nonlinear systems and used to generate rich random values in a specific range. Compared with the Gussian chaotic mapping and Bernoulli chaotic mapping, Singer chaotic mapping provides more uniform and rich distribution of random numbers, and has the characteristics of regularity, randomness and ergodicity. Thus, aiming at the poor diversity of the initial whale population in the standard WOA, the Singer chaotic mapping strategy is utilized to initialize the whale population, which uniforms the whale population distribution and improves the quality of the initial solution. The mathematical model of the Singer chaotic mapping strategy is expressed as follows [21]:

$$x_{t+1} = \mu(7.68x_t - 23.31x_t^2 + 28.75x_t^3 - 13.302875x_t^4) \tag{6}$$

where $\mu \in [0.9, 1.08]$ represents a random number.

After the initial whale population is generated by the Singer chaotic mapping, the Singer whale population and the random whale population are combined together, and the fitness values of the two sets of whale individuals are compared one by one by using elite greedy strategy. The whale individuals with lower fitness values will be retained as the next generation whale individuals. At the time, the optimized initial whale population will be closer to the current optimal solution than those of the Singer whale population and the random whale population, which greatly improves the quality of the initial solution and accelerates the convergence speed of the algorithm.

3.2 Adaptive Cognitive Factor

In the bubble net predation stage of the standard WOA, as the leader position is not always close to the target prey, which will lead to the decline of the search ability and the insufficient spatial search scope in the later iterations, and the global exploration ability and local development ability could not be balanced. Therefore, to solve the problem, an adaptive cognitive factor is proposed in this paper to help the whale leader getting closer to the target prey, which enhances the global search ability at the beginning of iterations and focus on the local development ability at the later iterations. The adaptive cognitive factor is expressed as follows:

$$\omega = 0.4 + \frac{1}{0.2 + e^{-(5t/T)^4}} \tag{7}$$

where ω stands for the adaptive cognitive factor. Other variables have been explained in formula (2) and will not be repeated here. The improved whales position updating formula using the adaptive cognitive factor is expressed as follows:

$$x(t+1) = \begin{cases} \omega \cdot D_2 \cdot e^{bl} \cdot \cos(2\pi l) + x'(t), & p \geq 0.5 \\ (1-\omega) \cdot x'(t) - A \cdot D_1, & p < 0.5 \end{cases} \tag{8}$$

The variables in the formula have been explained in formula (5) and formula (7), so they are not repeated here.

3.3 Wavelet Mutation Mechanism

In the standard WOA, whales use the spiral bubble nets to attack the target prey, and the whale population may fall into local optimum in the process. The wavelet function is a single-frequency complex sine exponential function under Gaussian envelope, which has the characteristics of limited length, alternating positive and negative fluctuations and zero average value. The wavelet function is expressed as follows [22]:

$$\sigma = \frac{1}{\sqrt{2}} \psi\left(\frac{\varphi_i}{a_1}\right) \tag{9}$$

where σ represents the expansion parameter. $\psi(x)$ stands for the Morlet wavelet function, which is defined as follows:

$$\psi(x) = e^{-\frac{x^2}{2}} \cos(5x) \tag{10}$$

where $x = \frac{\varphi_i}{a_1}$. Since the energy of Morlet wavelet function is almost concentrated in the interval $[-2.5, 2.5]$, and σ can be randomly generated from the interval $[-2.5a_1, 2.5a_1]$. a_1 represents a monotonically increasing function, which increases from 1 to g with the increase of algorithm iterations, which is expressed as follows:

$$a_1 = e^{-\ln(g)\cdot(1-\frac{t^3}{T^3})+\ln(g)} \tag{11}$$

where $g = 20000$. It can be seen that a_1 changes with the increase of iterations, which can help whale population jumping out the local optimum. The position of the whale individuals updating by the wavelet mutation mechanism is expressed as follows:

$$x'(t+1) = \sigma \cdot x(t+1) \tag{12}$$

where $x(t+1)$ is the position of the new whale individual. $x'(t+1)$ is the position of the new whale individual after the wavelet mutation mechanism disturbance.

3.4 Cubic Spline Interpolation

Cubic spline interpolation method adopts piecewise interpolation to construct multiple interpolation point intervals based on cubic polynomials, which can help tortuous paths form a smooth curve. Thus, in order to avoid the missing details of trajectory and ensure that the quadrotor tracks the path planned by the proposed SAMWOA steadily, cubic spline interpolation method is used to interpolate the planned path of a quadrotor, which improves the smoothness. Let the path be divided into $n + 1$ nodes in the interval $[a, b]$, which can be expressed as follows:

$$a = x_0 < x_1 < ... < x_n = b \tag{13}$$

Then, the cubic spline function can be expressed by following formula [23]:

$$s(x) = a_i'x^3 + b_i'x^2 + c_i'x + d_i' \tag{14}$$

where a_i', b_i', c_i', d_i' are the coefficients. $i = 0, 1, ..., n$. It can be inferred that the cubic spline function $s(x)$ has the reciprocal of the first order and the second order in the interval $[a, b]$, and it is a polynomial with a degree not greater than three in each subinterval $[a, b]$.

4 Simulation Results and Analysis

4.1 Environment Map Modeling

To better simulate the actual flight state of the quadrotor, two 3D environment maps are established in Fig. 1. The size of the environment map 1 is 20 m × 20 m × 10 m, and the starting point is (10,2,3) and the end point is (10,18,3). The size of the environment map 2 is 40 m × 40 m × 10 m, and the starting point is (20,2,5) and the end point is (20,38,5). The red blocks represent the obstacles. The blue triangle represents the starting point and the green star represents the end point. As can be seen from the figure, the environment map 2 is more complicated than that of environment map 1.

Moreover, the simulation experiment platform is a notebook computer with Intel(R) Core(TM) i7–5500 processor, clocked at 2.4 GHz, 8 GB memory, Windows 7 operating system with the software MATLAB 2017b.

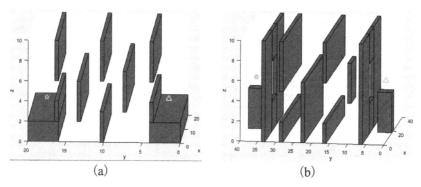

Fig. 1. The established environment maps: (a) environment map 1; (b) environment map 2

4.2   3D Path Planning Experiment

In the simulation experiment of 3D path planning, the size of whale population is set to 30. The maximum iterations of the algorithm is uniformly set to 100. The standard WOA, the CFAWOA in Ref. [17] and the proposed SAMWOA are simulated in environment map 1, and the experimental results are shown in Fig. 2.

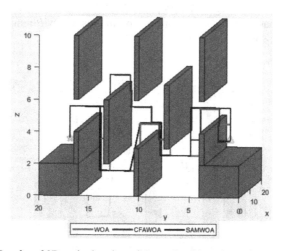

Fig. 2. Results of 3D path planning of three algorithms in environment map 1

It can be seen from the figure that the proposed SAMWOA is superior to the WOA and the CFAWOA when the path length and steering times are considered as the measurement standards. In terms of the path length, the order from small to large is SAMWOA < WOA < CFAWOA. In terms of the steering times, the order from small to large is also SAMWOA < WOA < CFAWOA. In order to observe the performance of the three algorithms more intuitively, the fitness convergence curves of the three algorithms in environment map 1 are shown in Fig. 3.

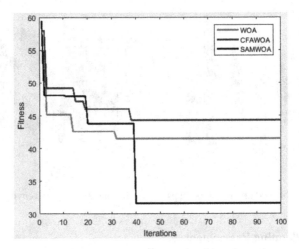

Fig. 3. Results of convergence curve of three algorithms in environment map 1

As can be seen from the figure, the order of convergence accuracy from high to low is SAMWOA > WOA > CFAWOA. Thus, in terms of the convergence accuracy, the proposed SAMWOA is far exceeding the standard WOA and the CFAWOA.

To verify the performance of the proposed SAMWOA widely, three algorithms are applied to the 3D path planning simulation experiments in environment map 2, and the experimental results are shown in Fig. 4.

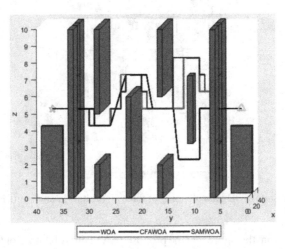

Fig. 4. Results of 3D path planning of three algorithms in environment map 2

Similarly, when considering the path length and steering times as the test criteria of the algorithm, compared with the standard WOA and the CFAWOA, the proposed SAMWOA has shorter path length and smaller steering times. From the perspective of path length, the sequence from small to large is SAMWOA < WOA < CFAWOA. From the perspective of steering times, the sequence from small to large is also SAMWOA < WOA < CFAWOA. For the convenient comparison, the fitness convergence curves of the three algorithms in environment map 2 are drawn in Fig. 5.

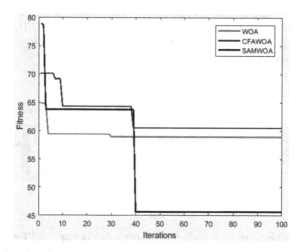

Fig. 5. Results of convergence curve of three algorithms in environment map 2

As can be seen from the figure, the proposed SAMWOA is stable after about 40 iterations. In terms of convergence accuracy, the proposed SAMWOA far exceeds that of the standard WOA and the CFAWOA. Therefore, in both environment map 1 and environment map 2, compared with the standard WOA and the CFAWOA, the proposed SAMWOA has the shortest path length and the least number of turns.

When summarizing the performance of the three algorithms in digital form, the performance metrics of the three algorithms in environment map 1 and environment map 2 are summarized in Table 1.

Table 1. Results of performance metrics comparison of three algorithms

Performance metrics	Environment map 1			Environment map 2		
	WOA	CFAWOA	SAMWOA	WOA	CFAWOA	SAMWOA
Path length(m)	41.50	44.30	31.63	58.90	60.50	45.68
Steering times	16	26	10	14	26	10
Time-cost(s)	34.80	24.24	20.11	37.58	36.52	34.44

4.3 3D Path Tracking Experiment

In the 3D path planning experiment, the proposed SAMWOA is proved to have a good competitive advantage in solving the 3D path planning problem of quadrotor. Then, on the basis of the above simulation experiments, the quadrotor is used to track the path planned by the proposed SAMWOA to further verify its effectiveness. The simulation parameters of the quadrotor are designed according to the KMel Nano Plus quadrotor, and the trajectory tracking control model is the PID controller. Firstly, the 3D path tracking experiment of quadrotor is carried out in environment map 1. The solid black line represents the 3D path pre-planned by the proposed SAMWOA. The red connecting line represents the tracking trajectory of the quadrotor. The dark green cylinder represents a quadrotor. The experimental results are shown in Fig. 6.

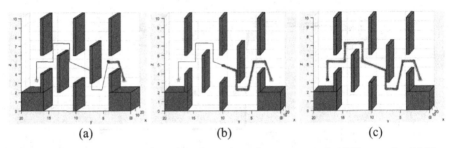

(a)   (b)   (c)

Fig. 6. Results of 3D path tracking of quadrotor in environment map 1: (a) Time = 4 s; (b) Time = 12 s; (c) Time = 23 s.

It can be seen from the figure that the tracking trajectory of the quadrotor is basically coincident with the 3D path planned by the proposed SAMWOA, which shows that the 3D path planned by proposed SAMWOA is smooth and trackable, and there is no state in which the quadrotor is in extreme motion. Thus, the proposed SAMWOA can plan the 3D path suitable for the actual flight of a quadrotor in environment map 1. The flight state of the quadrotor tracking the path in environment map 1 is shown in Fig. 7.

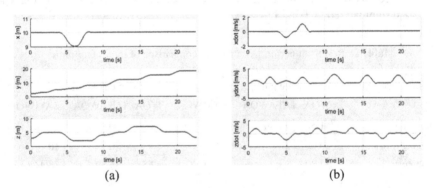

(a)   (b)

Fig. 7. Change of convergence curve in environment map 1: (a) the motion positions of the quadrotor; (b) the motion velocities of the quadrotor.

As can be seen from the figure, the fluctuation amplitude of the motion positions of the quadrotor is relatively peaceful, which shows that there is no extreme motion in the 3D path planned by the proposed SAMWOA. The motion velocities fluctuation of quadrotor is not violent, which shows that the 3D path planned by the proposed SAMWOA is relatively smooth.

After completing the 3D path tracking experiment in environment map 1, then the 3D path tracking experiment in environment map 2 is carried out. Similarly, the solid black line represents the 3D path planned by the proposed SAMWOA. The red connecting line represents the tracking trajectory of the quadrotor. The dark green cylinder represents a quadrotor, and the experimental results are shown in Fig. 8.

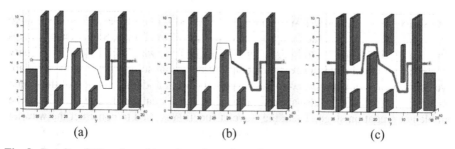

Fig. 8. Results of 3D path tracking of quadrotor in environment map 2: (a) Time = 4 s; (b) Time = 12 s; (c) Time = 23 s.

It can be seen from the figure that the quadrotor can basically track and control along the 3D pre-planned path. Although the x-position of the quadrotor fluctuates slightly, there is no excessive deviation, which can be basically ignored, indicating that the 3D path planned by the proposed SAMWOA is reliable. Therefore, whether in environment map 1 or environment map 2, the proposed SAMWOA can plan the 3D path suitable for the actual flight of a quadrotor. The flight state of the quadrotor tracking the path in environment map 2 is shown in Fig. 9.

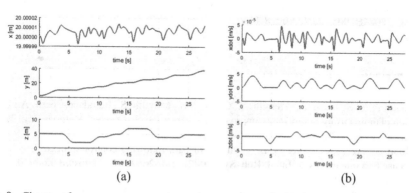

Fig. 9. Change of convergence curve in environment map 2: (a) the motion positions of the quadrotor; (b) the motion velocities of the quadrotor.

As can be seen from the figure, in terms of motion positions, the x-position of the quadrotor fluctuates slightly, and the y-position and the z-position are relatively stable.

In terms of motion velocities, the x-velocity of the quadrotor is small. The y-velocity and the z-velocity is relatively stable. Therefore, both in environment map 1 and environment map 2, when considering the degree of variation of the motion positions and the motion velocities as the measurement criteria, the 3D path planned by the proposed SAMWOA is optimal and smooth, which can be tracked and controlled by the quadrotor, which is robust and reliable.

5 Conclusion

In this paper, a novel improved WOA named SAMWOA is innovatively proposed to solve the 3D path planning and tracking problem of the quadrotor. Firstly, Singer chaotic mapping strategy is introduced to initialize whale population, which increases the diversity of whale population and improves the quality of the initial solution. Secondly, an adaptive cognitive factor is proposed to improve the position updating method of the whale leader so as to balance the global exploration ability and local development ability in the bubble net predation stage. Then, the wavelet function is used to construct the wavelet mutation mechanism to realize the disturbance of the current optimal solution of whale population, so that the algorithm can jump out of the local optimal value. Moreover, cubic spline interpolation method is utilized to reduce the path points and improve its smoothness. Finally, the proposed SAMWOA is verified in the 3D path planning and tracking experiment of a quadrotor. When considering the path length, steering times and time-cost as the measurement criteria, the experimental simulation results show that the proposed SAMWOA is outperformed the standard WOA and the CFAWOA, which not only overcomes the shortcomings of the standard WOA, but also can avoid static obstacles and track the planned path. The proposed SAMWOA is only evaluated on the simulation platform of a quadrotor, and the future research will be recommended to focus on the practical engineering application of a quadrotor to further verify its effectiveness.

Acknowledgment. The work was jointly supported by Natural Science Foundation of Fujian Province (2022H6005 and 2020J01878).

References

1. Saadi, A.A., Soukane, A., Meraihi, Y., Gabis, A.B., Mirjalili, S., Ramdane-Cherif, A.: UAV path planning using optimization approaches: a survey. Arch. Comput. Methods Eng. **29**(6), 4233–4284 (2022). https://doi.org/10.1007/s11831-022-09742-7
2. Rubí, B., Pérez, R., Morcego, B.: A survey of path following control strategies for UAVs focused on quadrotors. J. Intell. Rob. Syst. **98**(2), 241–265 (2019). https://doi.org/10.1007/s10846-019-01085-z
3. Belge, E., Altan, A., Hacıoğlu, R.: Metaheuristic optimization-based path planning and tracking of quadcopter for payload hold-release mission. Electronics **11**(8), 1208 (2022). https://doi.org/10.3390/electronics11081208
4. Liu, L., Liang, J., Guo, K., Ke, C., He, D., Chen, J.: Dynamic path planning of mobile robot based on improved sparrow search algorithm. Biomimetics **8**(2), 182 (2023). https://doi.org/10.3390/biomimetics8020182

5. Tripicchio, P., Unetti, M., D'Avella, S., Avizzano, C.A.: Smooth coverage path planning for UAVs with model predictive control trajectory tracking. Electronics **12**(10), 2310 (2023). https://doi.org/10.3390/electronics12102310

6. Xiaolei, L., Xiaojiang, D., Xiaosong, Z., Qingxin, Z., Mohsen, G.: Evolution-algorithm-based unmanned aerial vehicles path planning in complex environment. Comput. Electr. Eng. **80**, 106493 (2019). https://doi.org/10.1016/j.compeleceng.2019.106493

7. Dongwoo, L., Seungkeun, K., Jinyoung, S.: Formation flight of unmanned aerial vehicles using track guidance. Aerosp. Sci. Technol. **76**, 412–420 (2018). https://doi.org/10.1016/j.ast.2018.01.026

8. Liao, S.L., Zhu, R.M., Wu, N.Q., Shaikh, T.A., Sharaf, M., Mostafa, A.M.: Path planning for moving target tracking by fixed-wing UAV. Defence Technol. **16**(4), 811–824 (2020)

9. Eskandarpour, A., Sharf, I.: A constrained error-based MPC for path following of quadrotor with stability analysis. Nonlinear Dyn. **99**(2), 899–918 (2019). https://doi.org/10.1007/s11071-019-04859-0

10. Rubí, B., Morcego, B., Pérez, R.: Deep reinforcement learning for quadrotor path following with adaptive velocity. Auton. Robot. **45**(1), 119–134 (2020). https://doi.org/10.1007/s10514-020-09951-8

11. Qian, L., Liu, H.H.T.: Path-following control of a quadrotor UAV with a cable-suspended payload under wind disturbances. IEEE Trans. Industr. Electron. **67**(3), 2021–2029 (2020)

12. Labbadi, M., Boukal, Y., Cherkaoui, M.: Path following control of quadrotor UAV with continuous fractional-order super twisting sliding mode. J. Intell. Rob. Syst. **100**(3–4), 1429–1451 (2020). https://doi.org/10.1007/s10846-020-01256-3

13. Xu, Q., Wang, Z., Zhen, Z.: Information fusion estimation-based path following control of quadrotor UAVs subjected to Gaussian random disturbance. ISA Trans. **99**, 84–94 (2020)

14. Zheng, Z.: Moving path following control for a surface vessel with error constraint. Automatica **118**, 109040 (2020). https://doi.org/10.1016/j.automatica.2020.109040

15. Liang, J., Liu, L.: Optimal path planning method for unmanned surface vehicles based on improved shark-inspired algorithm. J. Marine Sci. Eng. **11**(7), 1386 (2023). https://doi.org/10.3390/jmse11071386

16. Wang, B., Zhang, Y., Zhang, W.: Integrated path planning and trajectory tracking control for quadrotor UAVs with obstacle avoidance in the presence of environmental and systematic uncertainties: Theory and experiment. Aerosp. Sci. Technol. **120**, 107277 (2022)

17. Tu, C., Chen, G., Liu, C.: Research on chaos feedback adaptive whale optimization algorithm. Stat. Decision **35**(07), 17–20 (2019). https://doi.org/10.13546/j.cnki.tjyjc.2019.07.004

18. Mirjalili, S., Lewis, A.: The whale optimization algorithm. Adv. Eng. Softw. **95**, 51–67 (2016)

19. Li, M., Xu, G., Lai, Q., Chen, J.: A chaotic strategy-based quadratic opposition-based learning adaptive variable-speed whale optimization algorithm. Math. Comput. Simul **193**, 71–99 (2022)

20. Deng, H., Liu, L., Fang, J., Qu, B., Huang, Q.: A novel improved whale optimization algorithm for optimization problems with multi-strategy and hybrid algorithm. Math. Comput. Simul **205**, 794–817 (2023)

21. Tubishat, M., et al.: Improved sine cosine algorithm with simulated annealing and singer chaotic map for Hadith classification. Neural Comput. Appl. **34**(2), 1385–1406 (2021). https://doi.org/10.1007/s00521-021-06448-y

22. Liao, Y., Zhao, W., Wang, L.: Improved manta ray foraging optimization for parameters identification of magnetorheological dampers. Mathematics **9**(18), 2230 (2021). https://doi.org/10.3390/math9182230

23. Gan, W., Lixia, Su., Chu, Z.: Trajectory planning of autonomous underwater vehicles based on gauss pseudospectral method. Sensors **23**(4), 2350 (2023). https://doi.org/10.3390/s23042350

Multimodal Pneumatic Control System for Soft Robot

Changsheng Chen, Di'en Wu[✉], Wenqing Chai, Guoquan Yang,
and Haiming Huang[✉]

College of Electronics and Information Engineering,
Shenzhen University, Shenzhen 518060, People's Republic of China
wudien2021@email.szu.edu.cn, haimhuang@szu.edu.cn

Abstract. In order to satisfy the requirements of output channels, drive modes and pressure detection for the complex motion of soft pneumatic robots, a multimodal pneumatic control system is proposed to solve the problem of pneumatic control and condition detection for multi-chamber soft robot of different shapes. The pneumatic control unit of the system consists of hybrid valve which composed of proportional valve and solenoid valve. In the hybrid valve, the positive proportional valve is connected with the positive air pressure source, and the negative proportional valve is connected with the negative air pressure source, then two solenoid valves are connected in series to switch the air pressure on and off. This enables the controllable output of positive and negative air pressure to control soft robots of different structures. In detection, the solenoid valve is used to achieve pressure detection of the pneumatic control process and the working state detection of the soft robot. Based on the principle of pneumatic control and detection, positive pressure output and detection mode, negative pressure output and detection mode, positive pressure cutoff and chamber pressure detection mode, and negative pressure cutoff and chamber pressure detection mode are realized, and a control of multi-chamber soft robot through channel expansion. The experimental results show that the positive pressure output and detection mode, negative pressure output and detection mode and the negative pressure cutoff and chamber pressure detection mode can adjust the bending attitude of the variable stiffness four-chamber soft robot from 0° to 360° and the maximum stiffness change of 1.47N. Combining positive pressure output and detection mode, negative pressure output and detection mode and positive pressure cutoff and chamber pressure detection mode, as well as 12-channel pressure control and 0−60 kPa chamber pressure detection, the operation control of the six-finger soft gripper and finger damage detection are realized. The multimodal pneumatic control system can adapt to control and detection of various types of soft robots through channel expansion.

Keywords: air pressure control and detection · multi-mode air pressure output · soft robot · hybrid valve

This work was supported by the Natural Science Foundation of the Guangdong Province, China (2021A1515011582); National Natural Science Foundation of China (62173233); Science, Technology and Innovation Commission Foundation of Shenzhen Municipality (JCYJ20210324094401005).

1   Introduction

Soft robots are mostly made of silicone, sponge, hydrogel and other flexible materials, which have the advantages of flexibility, safety and adaptability. These unique capabilities have led to varieties of potential applications in the area of industrial automation, medical treatment, rescue robots [1–3]. The soft robot is driven by smart memory alloy, pneumatic [4, 5], hydraulic [6, 7], tendons [8]. Among them, pneumatic drive is an important method for soft robot because of its good performances in rapid response, easy control and high safety [9].

In order to satisfy the driving requirements of soft robots, Hashem et al. [10] designed a pneumatic control unit that can switch between positive and negative pressure to control soft actuators. However, the system consists of few channels and is difficult to adapt to multiple types of soft robot. Zhang et al. [11] developed the pneumatic control system. The solenoid valve is used to control the on-off between the air pump and the robot, so as to control the wormlike soft robot to crawl in the pipeline. Liao et al. [12] adjusted the air pressure in the chamber of the snake-like soft robot through the solenoid valve and the air pump, so that the snake-like soft robot could climbed on the external surface of the rod, pipe, and rope. However, they can only realize separate positive pressure or negative pressure control, and the application is limited. Huang et al. [13] designed pneumatic control system to drive multimodal soft robot by air pump, solenoid valve and throttle valve. Lee et al. [14] referred to the fish heart structure and proposed a new soft air valve recirculation system, which has the advantages of high efficiency, low error and low noise, but they do not have the detection ability to sense the working state of the robot.

Pneumatic soft robot which can realize complex motion needs more functions of its pneumatic control system. Fei et al. [15] realized the clamping, wrapping, supporting and twisting of different objects by pneumatic grippers through the 20-channel positive pressure control system. Liu et al. [16, 17] designed a 12-channel air pressure control system with positive and negative air pressure to satisfy the air pressure control requirements of origami rehabilitation gloves and four-joint soft robotic arms. Tawk et al. [18] proposed a tactile sensor based on air pressure detection, which can be embedded in soft pneumatic robots such as soft gloves, soft fingers and multi-chamber pneumatic actuators. Zhou et al. [19] designed a bending sensor based on air pressure detection and embedded it into the five-finger robot hand joint to detect the finger bending angle so as to recognize the gestures. Alifdhyatra et al. [20] designed a pneumatic control system to realize closed-loop control of soft robots through pressure sensors.

In order to satisfy the requirements of complex motion and perception of soft robots with different structures, the pressure control system needs to have multi-channel, multi-mode and pressure detection functions. Therefore, we propose a hybrid valve unit composed of proportional valve and solenoid valve to realize positive pressure output and detection, negative pressure output and detection, positive pressure cutoff and chamber pressure detection, and negative pressure cutoff and chamber pressure detection. The multi-mode pneumatic control system can control and detect the heterogeneous multi-chamber soft robot by means of channel extension.

2   Method and Martials

2.1 System Design

The multimodal pneumatic control system consists of two parts:

Hybrid valve unit. The hybrid valve unit realizes the soft robot pressure control according to the control signal. The air pressure sensor uploads the feedback signal to the control circuit to detect the air pressure of the soft robot.

Control circuit. According to the command of the computer, the output signal of the control circuit is adjusted to realize the output pressure control of the hybrid valve unit. The control circuit receives and processes the feedback signal of the air pressure sensor and uploads the pressure signal.

As shown in Fig. 1, the air pressure control and detection between the hybrid valve units in the multimodal pneumatic control system are independent of each other, and the control requirements of different pneumatic soft robots are satisfied through channel expansion. The hybrid valve unit is composed of negative proportional valve, positive pressure proportional valve, 3-way 2-state solenoid valve, 2-way 2-state solenoid valve and air pressure sensor. The positive proportional valve is connected to the positive air source, and the negative proportional valve is connected to the negative air source. The

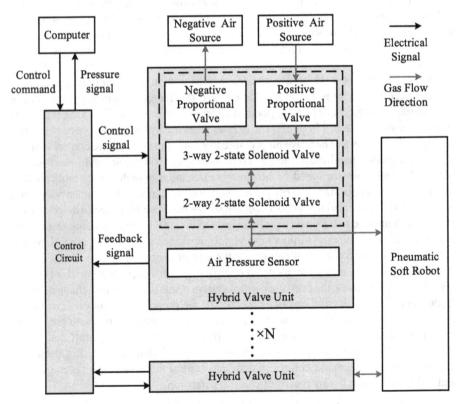

Fig. 1. Principle of the multimodal pneumatic control system

output of the positive proportional valve and the output of the negative proportional valve are respectively connected to the 3-way 2-state solenoid valve. In addition, 2-way 2-state solenoid valve input is connected with the 3-way 2-state solenoid valve, and the output is connected with the air pressure sensor and the pneumatic soft robot. The positive proportional valve and negative proportional valve adjust the input pressure of the air source. The positive pressure adjustment range is 0– 0.65 MPa, and the negative pressure adjustment range is −0.1–0 MPa. The 3-way 2-state solenoid valve switches the positive and negative air pressure output, and the 2-way 2-state solenoid valve controls the unit output air pressure on and off. The air pressure sensor detects the output air pressure and the chamber air pressure of the soft robot.

Figure 2 show shows the principle of the control circuit. The microcontroller of the multimodal pneumatic control system communicates with the computer through USB-CAN conversion module, and the signal is encoded and decoded according to the communication protocol. The I/O signal is output by microcontroller, and is amplified from 0–3.3 V to 0–24 V through the voltage signal amplifier module to realize the status control of the solenoid valve. The microcontroller controls the analog signal output by the DAC chip through the SPI bus, and amplifies the analog signal voltage to 0–10 V through the voltage amplifier circuit, so as to adjust the output pressure of the proportional valve. The feedback signal of the air pressure sensor is received by the microcontroller through the ADC interface, converts into the pressure signal, and finally uploads to computer.

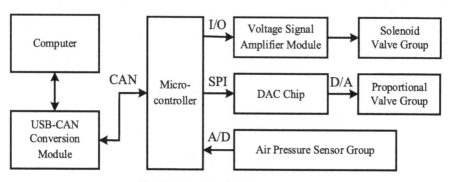

Fig. 2. Principle of the control circuit

2.2 Multi-mode Pressure Control Method

The four modes of the hybrid valve unit include positive pressure output and detection, negative pressure output and detection, positive pressure cutoff and chamber pressure detection, and negative pressure cutoff and chamber pressure detection. According to the requirements of pneumatic soft robot for pressure control and detection, the hybrid valve unit can be switched between four modes as required.

In positive pressure output and detection mode and negative pressure output and detection mode, the output pressure of the hybrid valve unit is consistent with the output pressure of the proportional valve in the unit. The output pressure of the proportional valve can be expressed by the following formula:

$$P_{out} = \begin{cases} P_{set}, & |P_{in}| > |P_{set}| \\ P_{in}, & |P_{in}| < |P_{set}| \end{cases} \tag{1}$$

where P_{out} is the output pressure of the proportional valve, P_{in} is the input pressure of the proportional valve, and P_{set} is the preset pressure of the proportional valve. Moreover, the positive pressure proportional valve provides input pressure by the positive pressure air source, and the negative pressure proportional valve provides input pressure by the negative pressure air source. The preset pressure P_{set} of the positive pressure and negative pressure proportional valve can be expressed by the following formula:

$$P_{set} = k_1 \times \frac{P_{max} - P_{min}}{U_{max} - U_{min}} \times U_{in} \tag{2}$$

where k_1 is the linear coefficient of the proportional valve, P_{max} and P_{min} are the maximum and minimum adjustable pressure of the proportional valve respectively, U_{max} and U_{min} are the maximum and minimum effective input voltage of the proportional valve respectively, and U_{in} is the input voltage of the proportional valve.

After the proportional valve outputs the air pressure, the solenoid valve selects the mode of the hybrid valve unit according to the I/O signal. In the solenoid valve, the 3-way 2-state solenoid valve selects the positive and negative pressure output mode, and the 2-way 2-state solenoid valve controls the output pressure on and off.

Figure 3 (a) shows the positive pressure output and detection mode. The 3-way 2-state solenoid valve inlet port (P1) and outlet port (A1) conduction, and the 2-way 2-state solenoid valve conduction. At this time, the hybrid valve unit outputs positive pressure. Figure 3 (b) shows the negative pressure output and detection mode. The 3-way 2-state solenoid valve exhaust ports (O1) and outlet port (A1) conduction, and the 2-way 2-state solenoid valve conduction. At this time, the hybrid valve unit outputs negative pressure. Both modes detect the output pressure of the working process through the pressure sensor.

Figure 3 (c) shows the positive pressure cutoff and chamber pressure detection mode. This mode keeps the status of the 3-way 2-state solenoid valve in the positive pressure output and detection mode, and converts the 2-way 2-state solenoid valve from on-state to off-state. At this time, the positive pressure output of the hybrid valve unit is cut off, and the pressure sensor only detects the air pressure in the chamber of the pneumatic soft robot. Figure 3 (d) shows the negative pressure cutoff and chamber pressure detection mode. This mode keeps the status of the 3-way 2-state solenoid valve in the negative pressure output and detection mode, and converts the 2-way 2-state solenoid valve from on-state to off state. At this time, the negative pressure output of the hybrid valve unit is cut off, and the pressure sensor only detects the air pressure in the chamber of the pneumatic soft robot.

The hybrid valve unit realizes the pressure detection through the pressure sensor, and the detected pressure can be expressed as.

$$P_{sense} = k_2 \times \frac{U_{out} - U'_{min}}{U'_{max} - U'_{min}} \times P_{range} \tag{3}$$

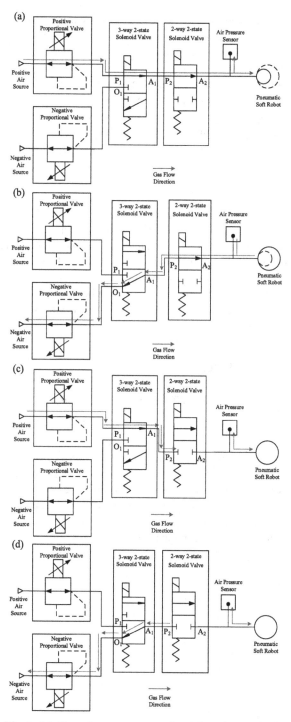

Fig. 3. Multi-mode pressure control and detection methods.

where P_{sense} is the detected air pressure; k_2 is the linear coefficient of the pressure sensor; U_{out} is the output voltage of the pressure sensor; U'_{max} and U'_{min} are the maximum output voltage and minimum output voltage of the pressure sensor; P_{range} is the pressure detection range of the pressure sensor.

When the pressure sensor is connected to the proportional valve, the detected pressure is equal to the output pressure of the proportional valve, and the working state detection of the pneumatic soft robot can be realized. When the air pressure sensor is disconnected from the proportional valve, the air pressure sensor detects the air pressure in the chamber of the pneumatic soft robot, according to the ideal air pressure formula.

$$P = \frac{nrt}{v} \tag{4}$$

where P is the air pressure in the chamber of the pneumatic soft robot, n is the gas moles, r is the gas constant, t is the thermodynamic temperature, and v is the volume of gas. The gas molar number n, gas constant r and thermodynamic temperature t of the gas in the chamber of the pneumatic soft robot are constant under the positive pressure cutoff and chamber pressure detection modes and the negative pressure cutoff and chamber pressure detection modes. Pneumatic soft robot chamber pressure P and gas volume v are inversely proportional to each other. Therefore, the working state of the pneumatic soft robot can be detected.

3   Experiments and Discussion

3.1   Prototype Production and Performance Experiment

Figure 4 shows the prototype of a multimodal pneumatic control system with 12 pressure output channels. The prototype performs module assembly and channel expansion according to the requirements of the pneumatic soft robot in the experiment. In the performance experiment, by detecting the synchronous output pressure of 5 channels, the pressure curve is shown in Fig. 5. The output pressure of the system maintains a stable pressure output of −80 kPa to 80 kPa within 3000 s. The output error of negative pressure is ±1 kPa, and that of positive pressure is ±2kPa. Thus, it is verified that the mode conversion process has little influence on the output pressure.

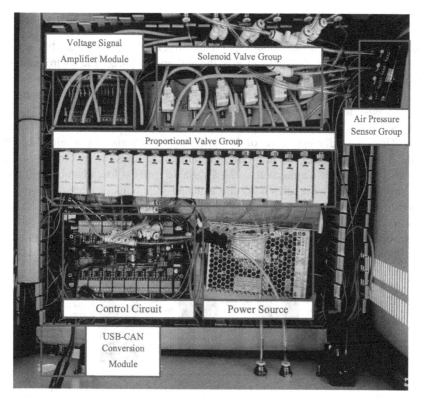

Fig. 4. Multimodal pneumatic control system prototype

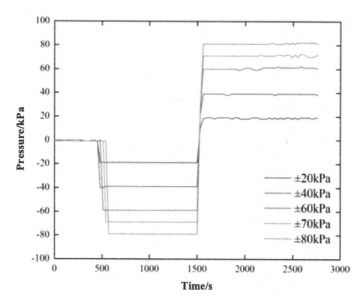

Fig. 5. Performance of multi-mode pressure control system

3.2 Application Verification of Variable Stiffness Four-Chamber Soft Robot

Through the bending attitude adjustment and stiffness change of a variable stiffness four-chamber soft robot, the application of the multimodal pneumatic control system is verified. The variable stiffness four-chamber soft robot body is made of silicone, and the stiffness change is realized by particle jamming. The production process is shown in Fig. 6 (a). First, the configured silicone is injected into the 3D printed assembly mold, and is left to stand. After the silicone is cured, the mold is released to obtain an elastic matrix. Then, the radial expansion of the elastic matrix is limited by winding the fiber, and the jamming particles are filled into the variable stiffness layer. Finally, silicone seals the top of the elastic matrix to make a variable stiffness four-chamber soft robot. As shown in Fig. 6 (b), the robot is 85 mm high and 35 mm in diameter. It is composed of four driving chambers and one variable stiffness layer. The air pressure in the inner chambers is controlled to adjust the bending attitude of the robot. The bending stiffness of the robot can be realized by controlling the pressure of the variable stiffness layer.

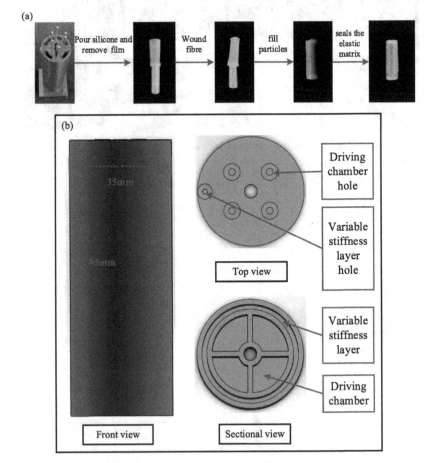

Fig. 6. Fabrication and construction of variable stiffness four-chamber soft robot

Figure 7 (a) shows the orientation angle experiment of variable stiffness four-chamber soft robot. During the experiment, the driving chamber 1, 2, 3, and 4 were in one-to-one correspondence with the four directional Angle positions of 180°, 270°, 0°, and 90° of the experimental platform. The figure shows that the variable stiffness four-chamber soft robot bends to 315° when the pressure of driving chamber 1 and driving chamber 4 are 45 kPa. When the pressure of the driving chamber 1 is 45 kPa, the robot bends to 0°. When the pressure of driving chamber 1 and driving chamber 2 is 45 kPa, the robot is bent to 45°.

Figure 7 (b) shows the relationship between the bending direction angle of variable stiffness four-chamber soft robot. The air pressure of single driving chamber 1, 2, 3, or 4 is controlled, and the robot is bent to 0°, 90°, 180°, and 270°, respectively. The variable stiffness four-chamber soft robot can bend in 30°, 60°, 120° and other directions when the air pressure difference between adjacent driving chambers is 10 kPa. The experimental

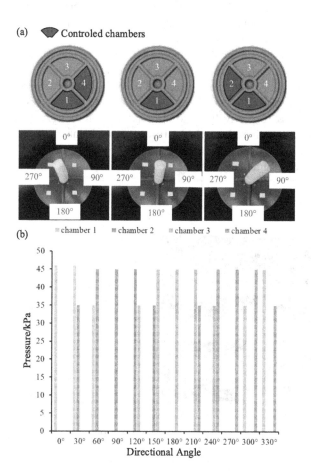

Fig. 7. Bending direction angle experiment of variable stiffness four-chamber soft robot

results show that the 0°–360° bending attitude adjustment of the variable stiffness four-chamber soft robot can be realized by controlling the air pressure of the two adjacent driving chambers.

Figure 8 (a) shows the variable stiffness experimental platform of the variable stiffness four-chamber soft robot, which is composed of a slideway, a dynamometer and a support frame. Among them, the variable stiffness four-chamber soft robot is vertically fixed under the support frame, the support frame is fixed with the slideway 1 by screws, the dynamometer is placed on the slideway 3, and the top is close to the end of the robot. During the experiment, the hybrid valve unit controls the pressure of the four driving chamber to increase synchronously through the positive pressure output and detection mode, which makes the variable stiffness four-chamber soft robot extend. The variable stiffness layer adjusts the robot stiffness through the negative pressure output and detection mode of the hybrid valve. When the negative pressure output is stable, it switches to the negative pressure cutoff and chamber pressure detection mode to maintain the bending stiffness of the robot. The bending resistance is measured by pushing the end of the robot 10 mm with a dynamometer.

The experimental results are shown in Fig. 8 (b). The pressure of the variable stiffness layer of the variable stiffness four-chamber soft robot is −80kPa, and the maximum bending force of 1.47N is reached when the robot is extended by 5 mm. When the pressure of the variable stiffness layer is unchanged, the bending resistance decreases to 1.32N and 1.07N respectively at 10 mm and 15 mm elongation. Therefore, with the increase of the length of the variable stiffness four-chamber soft robot, the bending resistance decreases gradually. In three different elongation states, the bending resistance of the robot decreases gradually with the increase of the pressure of the variable stiffness layer.

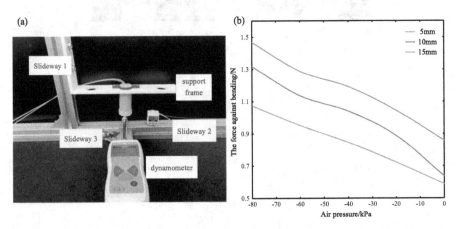

Fig. 8. Variable stiffness performance of variable stiffness four-chamber soft robot

The experiments of the variable stiffness four-chamber soft robot show that the multimodal pneumatic control system can realize the bending attitude adjustment from 0° to 360° and the stiffness change in different elongation states of the variable stiffness four-chamber soft robot through three modes: positive pressure output and detection, negative pressure output and detection, and negative pressure cutoff and chamber pressure detection.

3.3 Application Verification of Six-Finger Soft Gripper

The multimodal pneumatic control system is verified by the operation control of the six-finger soft gripper and the detection of the finger state. As shown in Fig. 9 (a), the six-finger soft gripper consists of a gripper frame and. Among them, the finger composition and movement mode are shown in Fig. 9 (b), and the finger is composed of the finger frame, the driving module (A) and the perception module (S). The driving module is made by sponge, cardboard and polymer film, and the sensing module is made by polymer film. The finger perception module is located between the drive modules A1 and A2, and A3 is placed inside the finger frame. When module A is positive pressure, the volume increases and the finger elongate. When module A is negative pressure, the volume decreases and the finger shrink. In the initial state of the six-finger soft gripper, each finger module A is in the negative pressure contraction state, and the air pressure in the chamber of module S is 0 kPa. During the grasping process, the pressure in the S chamber reaches 30 kPa by the positive pressure output and detection mode of the hybrid valve unit. After the air pressure is stabilized, the hybrid valve unit switches to the positive pressure cutoff and chamber pressure detection mode to detect the air pressure

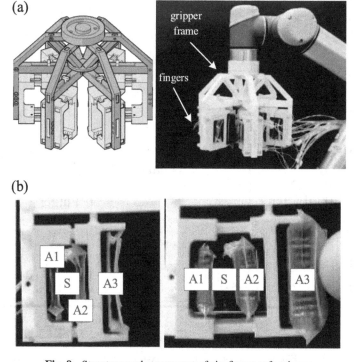

Fig. 9. Structure and movement of six-finger soft gripper

change of the module S. Through the positive pressure output and detection mode of the hybrid valve unit, the module A is extended, and the gripper grabs the object. Finally, through the negative pressure output and detection mode, the finger is restored to the initial state and the captured object is released.

In the experiment, the grasping process was repeated three times. The first time all finger modules were normal; The second time modules A1, A2 and A3 of finger 1 are damaged; The third time only module S of finger 1 is damaged. During the experiment, the pressure curve of the finger sensing module S is shown in Fig. 10. When the six-finger soft gripper grabs objects in normal state, the air pressure of sensing module S is at least 36 kPa and at most 51 kPa, all of which are greater than 30 kPa. When module A of finger 1 is damaged, the pressure of its module S remains at 30 kPa. When the module S of finger 1 is damaged, the detected air pressure of the module S is near 0 kPa, which is far less than 30 kPa. Therefore, the damage status of each module A and module S can be judged by the pressure range of the module S.

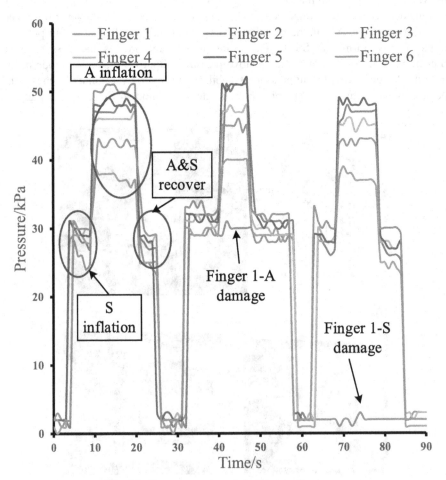

Fig. 10. Damage sensing of six-finger soft gripper

4   Conclusion

The multimodal pneumatic control system is consisted of hybrid valve which composed of proportional valve and solenoid valve. The independent switching of four modes of hybrid valve is realized by integrating the principle of air pressure control and detection. The system prototype was fabricated by channel expansion, and the application verification was completed by controlling the variable stiffness four-chamber soft robot and the six-finger soft gripper.

The traditional pneumatic control system is difficult to meet the needs of a variety of pneumatic soft robots. The multimodal air pressure control system has the advantages of multi-mode, multi-channel and air pressure detection at the same time, and realizes the bending attitude adjustment of the variable stiffness four-chamber soft robot from $0°$ to $360°$, and the maximum stiffness change of 1.47N. And the operation control of the six-finger soft gripper and the detection of the finger state. Thus, the compatibility of the multi-mode pneumatic control system for different pneumatic soft robots is verified.

In the next step, the multimodal air pressure control system will be expanded in the output speed, precise control and detection accuracy of air pressure, so that the multimodal air pressure control system can be applied to worm robot, origami robot, growing robot and other pneumatic soft robots. And through the system network, the multi-body control of pneumatic soft robot is realized.

References

1. Wang, H., Peng, X., Lin, B.: Research development of soft robots. J. South China Univ. Technol. (Natural Science Edition) **48**(2), 94–106 (2020)
2. Sitti, M.: Miniature soft robots-road to the clinic. Nat. Rev. Mater. **3**(6), 74–75 (2018)
3. Xie, Z., Domel, A.G., An, N., et al.: Octopus arm-inspired tapered soft actuators with suckers for improved grasping. Soft Rob. **7**(5), 639–648 (2020)
4. Azami, O., Morisaki, D., Miyazaki, T., et al.: Development of the extension type pneumatic soft actuator with built-in displacement sensor. Sens. Actuators, A **300**, 111623 (2019)
5. Batsuren, K., Yun, D.: Soft robotic gripper with chambered fingers for performing in-hand manipulation. Appl. Sci. **9**(15), 2967 (2019)
6. Tiwari, R., Meller, M.A., Wajcs, K.B., et al.: Hydraulic artificial muscles. J. Intell. Mater. Syst. Struct. **23**(3), 301–312 (2012)
7. Ishida, M., Drotman, D., Shih, B., et al.: Morphing structure for changing hydrodynamic characteristics of a soft underwater walking robot. IEEE Robot. Autom. Lett. **4**(4), 4163–4169 (2019)
8. Wang, P., Tang, Z., Xin, W., et al.: Design and experimental characterization of a push-pull flexible rod-driven soft-bodied robot. IEEE Robot. Autom. Lett. **7**(4), 8933–8940 (2022)
9. Zhao, Y., Zhao, H., Tan, D.: Review of fluid driving methods in soft robot. Chinese Hydraulics Pneumatics **45**(4), 135–145 (2021)
10. Hashem, R., Stommel, M., Cheng, L.K., et al.: Design and characterization of a bellows-driven soft pneumatic actuator. IEEE/ASME Trans. Mech. **26**(5), 2327–2338 (2020)
11. Zhang, B., Fan, Y., Yang, P., et al.: Worm-like soft robot for complicated tubular environments. Soft Rob. **6**(3), 399–413 (2019)
12. Liao, B., Zang, H., Chen, M., et al.: Soft rod-climbing robot inspired by winding locomotion of snake. Soft Rob. **7**(4), 500–511 (2020)

13. Huang, W., Xu, Z., Xiao, J., et al.: Multimodal soft robot for complex environments using bionic omnidirectional bending actuator. IEEE Access **8**, 193827–193844 (2020)
14. Lee, S., Lee, D., Shin, D.: An air recirculation system based on bioinspired soft re-air valve for highly efficient pneumatic actuation. Soft Rob. **8**(5), 564–576 (2021)
15. Fei, Y., Wang, J., Pang, W.: A novel fabric-based versatile and stiffness-tunable soft gripper integrating soft pneumatic fingers and wrist. Soft Rob. **6**(1), 1–20 (2019)
16. Liu, S., Fang, Z., Liu, J., et al.: A compact soft robotic wrist brace with origami actuators. Front. Robot. AI **34** (2021)
17. Liu, S., Liu, J., Zou, K., et al.: A six degrees-of-freedom soft robotic joint with tilt-arranged origami actuator. J. Mech. Robot. **14**(6), 060912 (2022)
18. Tawk, C., in het Panhuis, M., Spinks, G.M., et al.: Soft pneumatic sensing chambers for generic and interactive human–machine interfaces. Adv. Intell. Syst. **1**(1), 1900002 (2019)
19. Zhou, H., Tawk, C., Alici, G.: A 3D printed soft robotic hand with embedded soft sensors for direct transition between hand gestures and improved grasping quality and diversity. IEEE Trans. Neural Syst. Rehabil. Eng. **30**, 550–558 (2022)
20. Alifdhyatra A F, Sunarya B A Y, Hidayat E M I, et al. Development of pneumatic networks soft robot with anti-windup PID control. In: 2022 IEEE 13th Control and System Graduate Research Colloquium (ICSGRC), pp. 25–30, IEEE (2022)

Enhancing Robot Manipulation Skill Learning with Multi-task Capability Based on Transformer and Token Reduction

Renjie Han[1], Naijun Liu[2], Chang Liu[1], Tianyu Gou[1], and Fuchun Sun[2(✉)]

[1] ShenZhen University, Shenzhen, China
[2] Tsinghua University, Beijing, China
fcsun@tsinghua.edu.cn

Abstract. Learning skills from videos based on language instructions is an innate ability for humans. However, robots face significant challenge in establishing connections between language instructions and visual observations, exhibiting precise control, and retaining memory of previous actions. Additionally, multi-task learning is difficult due to potential interference between tasks. To address these issues, we propose an algorithm called CSATO, based on Transformer network architecture for robot skill learning from videos and achieving multi-task learning with given instructions. Our algorithm consists of a visual-language fusion network, a token reduction network, and a Transformer decoder network, which is trained by predicting actions for corresponding states. The fusion network facilitates the integration of information from different modalities, while the token reduction network reduces the number of tokens passed to the Transformer using channel and spatial attention mechanisms. Finally, the Transformer comprehensively models the relationships among instructions, current and historical visual observations, and generate autoregressive action predictions. To improve multi-task learning performance, learnable offsets parameters are introduced for each task in the final action prediction stage. The effectiveness of our approach is demonstrated through sereral continuous manipulation task, exhibiting the effectiveness of the proposed algorithm.

Keywords: Skill learning · Transformer · Learning from demonstrations · Multi-task learning

1 Introduction

Humans possess the innate ability to learn effortlessly from watching videos. They can understand the actions depicted in the videos, alongside their inherent language comprehension abilities. Subsequently, humans can generalize the acquired skills to previously unseen tasks and execute them based on natural language instructions. However, this poses a significant challenge for robots. Robots need to establish a connection between language and visual observations, exhibit precise control, and retain the memory of previous actions. Thus, a key challenge in robotics lies in facilitating robots to comprehend language instructions and execute the corresponding actions accurately.

Significant progress has been achieved in the fields of language [2,4,19,30], vision [5,10,23], and multimodal [8,20,26,29] general representation. Through pre-trained models, it is now possible to directly obtain high-quality representations from these modalities. Recent works [9,17,21,24] have made progress in addressing the aforementioned challenge. For instance, Lynch et al. [24] introduced a simple learning algorithm for combining freeform text conditioning with multitask imitation learning. BC-Z [17] explores the generalization of visual-based robotic manipulation systems to new tasks using pre-trained language models. Hiveformer [9] and InstructRL [21] utilize Transformer-based architectures for modeling instructions, current observations, and previously executed actions. However, several challenges still remain unexplored. One crucial challenge arises from the quadratic growth in computational complexity of Transformer models due to the fully connected attention mechanism. Although Tokenlearner [33] proposes a method to reduce the number of tokens without significant degradation in overall performance. It solely focuses on spatial reduction and overlooks inter-channel features.

Another challenge in multi-task learning arises when training multiple tasks simultaneously. When hard parameter sharing [13,25] mechanism is employed between tasks, it can lead to a phenomenon known as the "seesaw phenomenon" [37], where some sub-tasks perform well while others perform poorly or even exhibit overall poor performance. Sharing layers for different tasks can result in mutual exclusion effects between tasks. For example, in the case of the push button task, the gripper needs to closely approach the table to touch the button to complete the task. In contrast, for the put money task (see Fig. 1), the gripper only needs to be in the air to accomplish the task. This discrepancy poses additional challenges during training, especially when dealing with a large number of tasks.

To address these challenges, we introduce CSATO(Transformer-Based architecture With Channel Spatial Attention And Task Level Offset), a simple yet effective approach based on a multimodal Transformer. First, we process the language input using a pre-trained Text-To-Text Transfer Transformer(T5) model [30], employing a tokenizer and embedding techniques. Next, we extract state features from the current and historical visual observations using MBConv [36], while utilizing FiLM [27] method to focus attention on important features. Consequently, this process generates a sequence of vision-language tokens, similar to the vision-language tokens in Vision Transformer(ViT) [5]. Then, a channel-spatial attention network is applied to select tokens, effectively reducing the number of tokens. Subsequently, the token sequence is passed to the Transformer to model the instructions, current visual observations, and historical visual observations. The final output consists of two parts: one part directly predicts robot end effector rotation and gripper state using an MLP, while the other part predicts robot end effector position using a UNet [32] decoder. Task-specific position offsets are added based on the task.

We conducted experiments on RLBench [16] to evaluate our approach(see Fig. 1), including single-task learning and multi-task learning with ten tasks. Our algorithm achieved favorable performance in these settings, demonstrating the effectiveness of our proposed algorithm. Furthermore, we conducted ablation experiments to test the effectiveness of each component in our proposed algorithm.

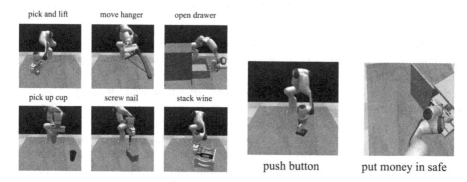

Fig. 1. left: Examples of RLBench tasks. **Right**: Comparison of push button and put money in safe gripper positions. Compared to put money in safe task, the gripper position in the push button task is closer to the desktop.

To summarize, our contributions are as follows:

1) We propose CSALearner, which reduces the number of tokens while selecting features using channel attention and spatial attention mechanisms.
2) To address the mutual interference among tasks in multi-task learning, we introduce a learnable parameter vector as an offset for each task when employing hard parameter sharing.
3) We conducted experiments on the RLBench [16] simulation platform to validate our approach, testing both single-task and multi-task success rates. The results demonstrate the effectiveness of our algorithm.

2   Related Work

Learning from Demonstrations. Recent research has focused on learning robotic manipulation skills from demonstrations, utilizing video inputs and language instructions to predict the next actions of robots. Many works [1,9,17,21,31,34,35] have explored this area. Hiveformer [9] and InstructRL [21] model multi-view images, language instructions, and historical images on the RLBench [16] simulation platform to learn the underlying relationships and directly predict the next actions. Peract [34] voxelizes the workspace and trains models to predict 3D voxels for the next end effector position in a 3D world. Gato [31] adopts the concept of representing everything as tokens, aiming to build a universal model that can transform various sensor information into tokens for learning. RT-1 [1] utilizes demonstration videos of real-world robot manipulations and employs multimodal fusion networks to predict actions for completing manipulation tasks and improving generalization performance to new scenes. In our work, we train our policies using demonstrations from videos and conduct experiments on RLBench [16], which includes challenging manipulation tasks.

Transformer. Since the introduction of the Transformer architecture [38], there has been rapid development in various domains, including natural language processing and computer vision. In subsequent advancements, the Transformer architecture has been applied in the context of supervised learning and reinforcement learning in robotics, as seen in works such as Decision Transformer [3]. VIMA [18] and PaLM-E [6], which utilize the Transformer to build multimodal agents. VIMA [18] directly takes in multimodal prompts and generates autoregressive actions to control robots conditioned on multimodal prompts. PaLM-E [6] takes multimodal sentences as input, intertwining visual, continuous state estimation, and text encoding to perform various specific tasks, including sequential robot operation planning and visual question answering. Our model also leverages this architecture in its design.

Convolutional Attention. Attention mechanisms in computer vision refer to methods that allow focusing on important regions of an image while disregarding irrelevant regions. Attention mechanisms dynamically select crucial information from image inputs by adaptively focusing on relevant details. Generally, attention mechanisms are categorized into Channel Attention [7,11,28,39], Spatial Attention [14], and Pixel Attention [12,40]. Additionally, modules like CBAM [41] and AA-Net [7] integrate multiple attention mechanisms. Since Tokenlearner [33] overlooks inter-channel features, we incorporate Channel Attention Mechanism to our model to address this limitation.

3   Problem Definition

Our goal is to develop an algorithm for learning robot manipulation skills. This algorithm can be trained with a large amount of expert video data on robot manipulation tasks from RLBench [16]. We follow the problem formulation of Hiveformer [9] and train a robot policy model, denoted as $\pi\left(a_{t+1} \mid l, \{o_i\}_{i=1}^{t}, \{a_i\}_{i=1}^{t}\right)$, which predicts the next action given a natural language instruction l, visual observations $\{o_i\}_{i=1}^{t}$, and previous actions $\{a_i\}_{i=1}^{t}$, where t is the current time step. Due to the sequences of expert trajectories typically long, we employ the keyframe method [15]. For demonstration data, we only select key frames that are crucial for completing the manipulation tasks, which are typically the turning points in the motion trajectory, where the joint velocity of the end effector of the robotic arm approaches zero or when there is a opening or closing change. We use an inverse dynamics-based controller to find trajectories between macro steps which reduces the length of an episode sequence from hundreds of small steps to a maximum of 10 macro steps.

Observation Space. Each observation, denoted as o_t, includes an RGB image I_t and a point cloud P_t derived from the depth map. Here, the RGB images $\{I_t^k\}_{k=1}^K$ are captured from K different camera viewpoints, with each image having a size of $128 \times 128 \times 3$. We use $K = 3$ camera viewpoints, namely the robot's wrist, left shoulder, and right shoulder. The point cloud data $\{P_t^k\}_{k=1}^K$ is also acquired from the same three viewpoints.

Action Space. Following the standard setup in RLBench [15], each action $a_{t+1} = (p_{t+1}, q_{t+1}, g_{t+1})$ consists of the three-dimensional position of the end effector $p_{t+1} = (x_{t+1}, y_{t+1}, z_{t+1})$, the quaternion representing the orientation $q_{t+1} = (q_{t+1}^0, q_{t+1}^1, q_{t+1}^2, q_{t+1}^3)$, and the gripper opening g_{t+1}. A successful grasping is achieved when the robot reaches the object's position and the gripper closes. Given an action, RLBench plans and executes this action using a motion planner.

4   Method

We propose an algorithm for robot manipulation skill learning called CSATO (see Fig. 2). It consists of four modules: VL fusion, CSALearner, Transformer, and Action prediction. The VL fusion module encodes the language input l to generate embeddings $\{l_j\}_{j=1}^n$, which highlight important positions and guide feature extraction from the input images $\{o_i\}_{i=1}^t$. This process results in the generation of visual-language tokens, which facilitate the fusion of visual and textual modalities. Next, the CSALearner module employs channel-wise spatial attention to reduce the number of tokens passed to the Transformer module. The Transformer learns the relationships between instructions, current observations, and historical images. Finally, the action prediction module predicts the next step position p_t, rotation q_t, and gripper g_t.

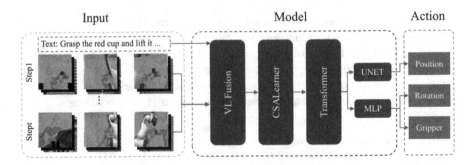

Fig. 2. CSATO consists of several components: VLFusion, CSALearner, Transformer, and action prediction. It takes language instructions and multi-view images as inputs. The VLFusion module performs fusion between different modalities by combining language and visual information. Then, the CSALearner module reduces the number of tokens using channel spatial attention mechanisms. The resulting representation sequence and historical action information are learned by the Transformer module, which predicts the next action.

4.1 Background

In the visual-language fusion architecture of RT-1 [1], a combination of FiLM [27] and MBConv [36] is employed. The basic idea of FiLM is to modulate the feature maps of a neural network using a conditioning parameter vector. This parameter vector can be adjusted based on different input data, allowing the model to adapt its behavior in different contexts and achieve more flexible feature learning. The instruction embeddings serve as the input to the FiLM layer, which then adjusts the image encoder.

Typically, inserting a FiLM layer into the internals of a pre-trained network can disrupt intermediate activations and negate the benefits of using pre-trained weights. To overcome this issue, RT-1 initializes the weights of the dense layers responsible for generating FiLM affine transformations to zero, allowing the FiLM layer to initially act as an identity and preserve the functionality of pre-trained weights.

Specifically, FiLM learns two functions, denoted as f_c and h_c, and outputs $\gamma_{t,c}$ and $\beta_{t,c}$:

$$\gamma_{t,c} = f_c(l), \quad \beta_{t,c} = h_c(l) \tag{1}$$

$$\text{FiLM}\left(\hat{F}_t \mid \gamma_{t,c}, \beta_{t,c}\right) = \gamma_{t,c}\hat{F}_t + \beta_{t,c} \tag{2}$$

where $\hat{F}_t = MBConv(F_t)$ and $F_t = (F_t^1, ..., F_t^K)$.

4.2 VL Fusion

We tokenize the instructions, visual images, and actions into a sequence of tokens (see Fig. 3).

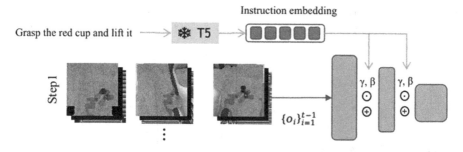

Fig. 3. The instructions are encoded using a pre-trained T5 model. FiLM is used to modulate the extraction of image features based on the encoded instructions.

Encoding Instructions. For encoding the instructions, we employ the T5 [30] model due to its excellent performance in natural language processing tasks as well as its availability as a pre-trained language model [4,29,30]. This process generates embeddings $\{l_j\}_{j=1}^{n} \in \mathbb{R}^d$, where n represents the length of language tokens, and d denotes the dimensionality of the embeddings.

Observations. The observation $\{o_i\}_{i=1}^{t}$ is composed of RGB images I_t^k, point clouds P_t^k, and proprioception A_t^k, where k represents different camera viewpoints. In this module, we only utilize I_t^k and A_t^k, while P_t^k is used in the final action prediction. The binary attention map $A_t^k \in \{0,1\}^{H \times W}$ is employed to encode the position of the gripper p_t. The gripper's location is represented by a value of 1, while other positions are assigned a value of 0. We fuse I_t^k and A_t^k along the channel dimension to obtain a feature map $F_t^k \in \mathbb{R}^{H \times W \times C}$ that includes the current gripper information, where $C = 4$ represents the number of channels in the feature map.

Encoding Observations. The FiLM [27] layer through learning, adaptively applies affine transformations to influence the output of the network, thereby enabling more flexible feature learning. The instruction embeddings serve as the input to the FiLM layer, which adjusts the image encoder. By performing multiple convolution operations and FiLM modulation, the resulting output is a sequence of vision-language tokens S_t, where $S_t = (S_t^1, ..., S_t^K)$.

4.3   CSALearner

Due to the quadratic growth of computational complexity with respect to the length of the input sequence in Transformer's fully connected attention mechanism, Tokenlearner [33] neglects inter-channel features. To address this, we introduce a channel attention mechanism inspired by SENet [11]. The goal is to weigh the features from different channels, allowing the model to automatically focus on the most important features for the current task. This approach enables the model to adaptively emphasize or suppress the importance of features selectively across different image blocks. CSALearner (see Fig. 4). incorporates this channel attention mechanism.

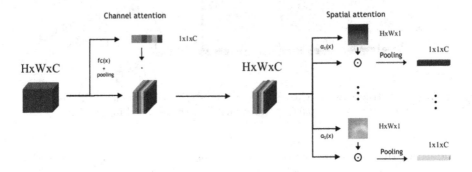

Fig. 4. In CSALearner, attention weights are first obtained for each channel to compute channel-wise attention, thereby enhancing the channel features. Then, in order to reduce the number of tokens, spatial attention weights are calculated to perform spatial attention. The resulting weights are multiplied with the channel features and then pooled to obtain the reduced tokens.

The input vision-language tokens sequence $S_t \in \mathbb{R}^{K \times H \times W \times C}$ undergoes pooling and fully connected layers to obtain the weights $W_t \in \mathbb{R}^{K \times 1 \times 1 \times C}$ for each channel. These weights are used to weight the features from different channels, adaptively selecting relevant features:

$$\hat{S}_t = W_t \cdot S_t = \mathrm{Fc}(\mathrm{meanpool}(S_t)) \cdot S_t \tag{3}$$

Next, spatial attention is calculated for the token sequence. However, instead of learning a single set of spatial attention weights, here we learn m sets of weights, representing the number of tokens to be learned (in this case, $m = 16$). This allows the attention maps to focus on different areas and reduces the number of tokens from $H \times W$ to m:

$$\tilde{S}_t = A_i(\hat{S}_t) = \rho(\hat{S}_t \odot A_{iw}) = \rho(\hat{S}_t \odot \gamma(\alpha_i(\hat{S}_t))) \tag{4}$$

where A_{iw} represents the i-th spatial attention weight matrix. Finally, we obtain $\tilde{S}_t \in \mathbb{R}^{K \times m \times C}$. This reduces the number of tokens to m and passes them to the subsequent Transformer layers.

4.4   Transformer

Given the processed token sequence $\tilde{S}_t$ from the previous module and the concatenated history images $C = \{S_i\}_{i=1}^{t}$, we then apply positional encoding to each sequence. The Transformer [38] learns the relationship between the representation of the sequence and the historical action information through attention mechanisms:

$$\text{Attn}(Q, K, V) = \text{Softmax}\left(\frac{W_Q Q (W_K K)^T}{\sqrt{d}}\right) W_V V \tag{5}$$

$$\hat{C} = \text{SA}(C) \tag{6}$$

To prevent the model from accessing future information beyond the current position before action prediction, we utilize a Transformer Decoder structure. Specifically, since we predict the next action based on historical information and the current observation, each target position can only rely on its preceding positions and cannot utilize information from subsequent positions.

4.5   Action Prediction

We utilize the Transformer's output embeddings $\hat{C} = \{C_i\}_{i=1}^{t}$ to predict the next action $a_{t+1} = [p_{t+1}; q_{t+1}; g_{t+1}]$ for current time step t. First, $\hat{C}_t$ is passed through mean pooling and then mapped to $\tilde{C}_t \in \mathbb{R}^{K \times h \times w \times C}$. Subsequently, it is concatenated using a UNet network to form the feature map $H_t \in \mathbb{R}^{K \times H \times W \times C}$. However, for certain RLBench tasks that require precise localization, unlike the rotation q_{t+1} and gripper opening g_{t+1}, the position p_{t+1} is predicted using a separate module that leverages the point cloud P_t.

Position. To predict the next position, we utilize the feature map H_t and the point cloud information P_t. Firstly, we compute the attention map $A_t^k \in \mathbb{R}^{H \times W \times 1}$ for each viewpoint by performing mean pooling on the feature map. This attention map represents the model's learned probability distribution over the regions to focus on for the next step. Then, we multiply the point cloud representation P_t element-wise with A_t, followed by pooling to obtain the output 3D vector p_{t+1}^p.

Additionally, in our experiments, we observed that for multi-task learning, if the tasks differ significantly, the model may struggle to perform well in predicting actions. To address this, Hiveformer [9] introduces an auxiliary task to predict the task category by applying softmax to the language embedding. The resulting task probabilities are multiplied by learnable embeddings to obtain offsets. However, since the magnitudes of the losses for different tasks may vary, simply adding the losses together could lead to one task dominating or biasing the multi-task learning. Therefore, instead of using the task prediction approach, we directly provide a set of learnable parameters for each task $O \in \mathbb{R}^{T \times 3}$, which act as offsets p_{t+1}^o that can be updated along with the network.

Finally, we combine the predicted next position p_{t+1}^p with the task-specific offset p_{t+1}^o. The final predicted next position is given by $p_{t+1} = p_{t+1}^p + p_{t+1}^o$.

Rotation and Gripper. For predicting the rotation q_{t+1} and gripper opening g_{t+1}, we directly employ two linear layers for simplicity. This yields a 5-dimensional vector $[q_{t+1}; g_{t+1}]$. The first four dimensions are interpreted as a quaternion q_{t+1}, while the last dimension represents the gripper opening g_{t+1}.

4.6   Training and Inference

Each demonstration We employ the behavioral cloning method to train models in the RLBench [16] environment. We collect 100 expert demonstrations for each task, and each demonstration δ is compressed to T macro-steps using keyframe techniques (T may vary for each task). The demonstration consists of observations$\{o_i\}_{i=1}^{T}$, instructions$\{l_j\}_{j=1}^{n}$, and actions$\{a_i^*\}_{i=1}^{T}$. We minimize the loss function $\mathcal{L}$ on the batch of demonstrations B, using mean squared error (MSE) loss for the actions:

$$\mathcal{L} = \frac{1}{|B|} \sum_{\delta \in B} \left[\sum_{t \leq T} \text{MSE} \left(a_t, a_t^* \right) \right] \tag{7}$$

5   Experiments

In this section, we evaluated the performance of our algorithm in the RLBench [16] simulation environment, specifically focusing on single-task performance, multi-task performance, and conducting ablation experiments. We compared our results with the Auto-λ [22] method and reproduced results of Hiveformer [9]. During the reproduction process, we noticed that some of our results were lower than the reported values in the original paper, despite using the same hyperparameter settings. We suspect that this discrepancy might be due to differences in the datasets or the GPUs used by the models. We conducted our experiments using an NVIDIA 3090 GPU, while they used NVIDIA Tesla V100.

Single-task Performance. In the single-task evaluation, we conducted tests on a total of 10 tasks, collecting 100 demonstration data points for each task variation for training. The test success rates are shown in Table 1. As seen from the results, our algorithm achieved high success rates in the single-task evaluation.

Table 1. Single-task performance

	Pick & Lift	Pick-Up Cup	Push Button	Put Knife	Put Money	Reach Target	Slide Block	Stack Wine	Take Money	Take Umbrella	Avg.
Auto-λ [22]	82.0	72.0	95.0	36.0	31.0	100.0	36.0	23.0	38.0	37.0	55.0
Hiveformer [9]	92.0	77.0	100.0	70.0	95.0	100.0	95.0	82.0	90.0	88.0	88.9
Ours	94.0	72.0	100.0	80.0	96.0	100.0	93.0	90.0	90.0	92.0	90.7

Multi-task Performance. In the multi-task setting, we utilized 10 tasks, each with a single variation consisting of 100 demonstrations. During training, all tasks were trained together, and then the model was tested for success rates on individual tasks. The results are presented in Table 2. From the results, it can be observed that our average success rate is approximately 7% higher than the results reproduced Hiveformer [9].

Table 2. Multi-task performance

	Pick & Lift	Pick-Up Cup	Push Button	Put Knife	Put Money	Reach Target	Slide Block	Stack Wine	Take Money	Take Umbrella	Avg.
Auto-λ [22]	87.0	78.0	95.0	31.0	62.0	100.0	77.0	19.0	64.0	80.0	69.3
Hiveformer [9]	88.0	76.0	86.0	62.0	81.0	100.0	60.0	70.0	64.0	80.0	76.7
Ours	90.0	84.0	97.0	70.0	83.0	100.0	55.0	85.0	78.0	97.0	83.9

Performance of Different Token Numbers. We also tested the impact of CSALearner on the number of tokens by conducting experiments with 16 tokens and 8 tokens. The experimental results are shown in the Fig. 5. It can be observed that reducing the number of tokens to 8 did not significantly decrease most of the success rates. Therefore, during training, it is possible to choose different token numbers based on the specific circumstances.

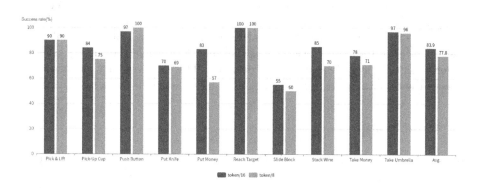

Fig. 5. The impact of different token numbers on the success rate.

Ablations Experiments. We investigated the impact of different modules on our algorithm by conducting three multi-task experiments: without using language(w/o inst), without using CSALearner(w/o CSALearner), and without using task offset(w/o Offset). The results are shown in Fig. 6.

Firstly, in the experiment without using language, we aimed to verify the effectiveness of the visual fusion module. It can be observed that without the language modality and relying solely on visual information for prediction, the performance decreased by approximately 7%.

Next, we evaluated the proposed CSALearner module. Without using this module, some tasks still maintained a relatively high success rate, but others experienced a significant drop. This indicates that the CSALearner module not only reduces the number of tokens but also filters out less important tokens, retaining only the ones that contribute more to task completion.

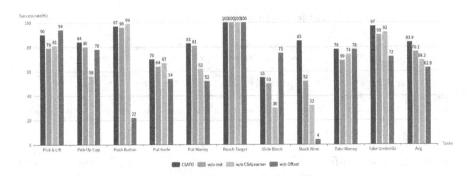

Fig. 6. The impact of different modules on our algorithm are nvestigated through three multi-task experiments: without using language, without using CSALearner, and without using task offset.

Lastly, the offset module was introduced for multi-task learning. Without using this module, the tasks of pushing a button and stack wine were almost impossible to accomplish. However, after incorporating the offset module, the success rates of these two tasks reached around 90%, while the success rates of other tasks only experienced a slight decrease. This demonstrates the effectiveness of the offset module in improving task performance in multi-task learning.

6   Conclusion

In this paper, we introduced CSATO, a multi-task approach that enables learning of robotic manipulation skills from demonstration videos. Given a language instruction and visual observations, our algorithm can predict the next action to be performed. We conducted experiments on the RLBench simulation environment to evaluate the performance in single-task and multi-task settings. The results demonstrate the effectiveness of our approach.

Furthermore, there are opportunities for further exploration in multi-task learning, such as leveraging the attention mechanism of Transformer as gates for parameter sharing between tasks. In future work, it would be interesting to conduct experiments on real robots and even explore applications in real-world 3C scenarios.

Acknowledgments. This work was funded by the "New generation artificial Intelligence" key field research and development plan of Guangdong Province (2021B0101410002). Meanwhile, this work was jointly supported by National Science and Technology Major Project of the Ministry of Science and Technology of China (No.2018AAA0102900).

References

1. Brohan, A., et al.: Rt-1: robotics transformer for real-world control at scale. arXiv preprint arXiv:2212.06817 (2022)
2. Brown, T., et al.: Language models are few-shot learners. Adv. Neural. Inf. Process. Syst. **33**, 1877–1901 (2020)
3. Chen, L., et al.: Decision transformer: reinforcement learning via sequence modeling. Adv. Neural. Inf. Process. Syst. **34**, 15084–15097 (2021)
4. Devlin, J., Chang, M.W., Lee, K., Toutanova, K.: Bert: pre-training of deep bidirectional transformers for language understanding. arXiv preprint arXiv:1810.04805 (2018)
5. Dosovitskiy, A., et al.: An image is worth 16×16 words: transformers for image recognition at scale. arXiv preprint arXiv:2010.11929 (2020)
6. Driess, D., et al.: Palm-e: an embodied multimodal language model. arXiv preprint arXiv:2303.03378 (2023)
7. Gao, Z., Xie, J., Wang, Q., Li, P.: Global second-order pooling convolutional networks. In: Proceedings of the IEEE/CVF Conference on Computer Vision and Pattern Recognition, pp. 3024–3033 (2019)
8. Geng, X., Liu, H., Lee, L., Schuurams, D., Levine, S., Abbeel, P.: Multimodal masked autoencoders learn transferable representations. arXiv preprint arXiv:2205.14204 (2022)
9. Guhur, P.L., Chen, S., Pinel, R.G., Tapaswi, M., Laptev, I., Schmid, C.: Instruction-driven history-aware policies for robotic manipulations. In: Conference on Robot Learning, pp. 175–187. PMLR (2023)
10. He, K., Chen, X., Xie, S., Li, Y., Dollár, P., Girshick, R.: Masked autoencoders are scalable vision learners. In: Proceedings of the IEEE/CVF Conference on Computer Vision and Pattern Recognition, pp. 16000–16009 (2022)
11. Hu, J., Shen, L., Sun, G.: Squeeze-and-excitation networks. In: Proceedings of the IEEE Conference on Computer Vision and Pattern Recognition, pp. 7132–7141 (2018)
12. Huang, Z., Wang, X., Huang, L., Huang, C., Wei, Y., Liu, W.: Ccnet: criss-cross attention for semantic segmentation. In: Proceedings of the IEEE/CVF International Conference on Computer Vision, pp. 603–612 (2019)
13. Jacobs, R.A., Jordan, M.I., Nowlan, S.J., Hinton, G.E.: Adaptive mixtures of local experts. Neural Comput. **3**(1), 79–87 (1991)
14. Jaderberg, M., Simonyan, K., Zisserman, A., et al.: Spatial transformer networks. Adv. Neural Inf. Process. Syst. **28** (2015)
15. James, S., Davison, A.J.: Q-attention: enabling efficient learning for vision-based robotic manipulation. IEEE Rob. Autom. Lett. **7**(2), 1612–1619 (2022)
16. James, S., Ma, Z., Arrojo, D.R., Davison, A.J.: Rlbench: the robot learning benchmark & learning environment. IEEE Rob. Autom. Lett. **5**(2), 3019–3026 (2020)
17. Jang, E., et al.: Bc-z: zero-shot task generalization with robotic imitation learning. In: Conference on Robot Learning, pp. 991–1002. PMLR (2022)
18. Jiang, Y., et al.: Vima: general robot manipulation with multimodal prompts. arXiv preprint arXiv:2210.03094 (2022)
19. Lan, Z., Chen, M., Goodman, S., Gimpel, K., Sharma, P., Soricut, R.: Albert: a lite bert for self-supervised learning of language representations. arXiv preprint arXiv:1909.11942 (2019)
20. Li, J., Li, D., Xiong, C., Hoi, S.: Blip: bootstrapping language-image pre-training for unified vision-language understanding and generation. In: International Conference on Machine Learning, pp. 12888–12900. PMLR (2022)

21. Liu, H., Lee, L., Lee, K., Abbeel, P.: Instruction-following agents with jointly pre-trained vision-language models. arXiv preprint arXiv:2210.13431 (2022)

22. Liu, S., James, S., Davison, A.J., Johns, E.: Auto-lambda: disentangling dynamic task relationships. arXiv preprint arXiv:2202.03091 (2022)

23. Liu, Z., et al.: Swin transformer: hierarchical vision transformer using shifted windows. In: Proceedings of the IEEE/CVF International Conference on Computer Vision, pp. 10012–10022 (2021)

24. Lynch, C., Sermanet, P.: Language conditioned imitation learning over unstructured data. arXiv preprint arXiv:2005.07648 (2020)

25. Ma, J., Zhao, Z., Yi, X., Chen, J., Hong, L., Chi, E.H.: Modeling task relationships in multi-task learning with multi-gate mixture-of-experts. In: Proceedings of the 24th ACM SIGKDD International Conference on Knowledge Discovery & Data Mining, pp. 1930–1939 (2018)

26. Nair, S., Rajeswaran, A., Kumar, V., Finn, C., Gupta, A.: R3m: a universal visual representation for robot manipulation. arXiv preprint arXiv:2203.12601 (2022)

27. Perez, E., Strub, F., De Vries, H., Dumoulin, V., Courville, A.: Film: visual reasoning with a general conditioning layer. In: Proceedings of the AAAI Conference on Artificial Intelligence, vol. 32 (2018)

28. Qin, Z., Zhang, P., Wu, F., Li, X.: Fcanet: frequency channel attention networks. In: Proceedings of the IEEE/CVF International Conference on Computer Vision, pp. 783–792 (2021)

29. Radford, A., et al.: Learning transferable visual models from natural language supervision. In: International Conference on Machine Learning, pp. 8748–8763. PMLR (2021)

30. Raffel, C., et al.: Exploring the limits of transfer learning with a unified text-to-text transformer. J. Mach. Learn. Res. **21**(1), 5485–5551 (2020)

31. Reed, S., et al.: A generalist agent. arXiv preprint arXiv:2205.06175 (2022)

32. Ronneberger, O., Fischer, P., Brox, T.: U-net: convolutional networks for biomedical image segmentation. In: Navab, N., Hornegger, J., Wells, W.M., Frangi, A.F. (eds.) MICCAI 2015. LNCS, vol. 9351, pp. 234–241. Springer, Cham (2015). https://doi.org/10.1007/978-3-319-24574-4_28

33. Ryoo, M.S., Piergiovanni, A., Arnab, A., Dehghani, M., Angelova, A.: Tokenlearner: what can 8 learned tokens do for images and videos? arXiv preprint arXiv:2106.11297 (2021)

34. Shridhar, M., Manuelli, L., Fox, D.: Perceiver-actor: a multi-task transformer for robotic manipulation. In: Conference on Robot Learning, pp. 785–799. PMLR (2023)

35. Stone, A., et al.: Open-world object manipulation using pre-trained vision-language models. arXiv preprint arXiv:2303.00905 (2023)

36. Tan, M., Le, Q.: Efficientnet: rethinking model scaling for convolutional neural networks. In: International Conference on Machine Learning, pp. 6105–6114. PMLR (2019)

37. Tang, H., Liu, J., Zhao, M., Gong, X.: Progressive layered extraction (PLE): a novel multi-task learning (MTL) model for personalized recommendations. In: Proceedings of the 14th ACM Conference on Recommender Systems, pp. 269–278 (2020)

38. Vaswani, A., et al.: Attention is all you need. Adv. Neural Inf. Process. Syst. **30** (2017)

39. Wang, Q., Wu, B., Zhu, P., Li, P., Zuo, W., Hu, Q.: Eca-net: efficient channel attention for deep convolutional neural networks. In: Proceedings of the IEEE/CVF Conference on Computer Vision and Pattern Recognition, pp. 11534–11542 (2020)

40. Wang, X., Girshick, R., Gupta, A., He, K.: Non-local neural networks. In: Proceedings of the IEEE Conference on Computer Vision and Pattern Recognition, pp. 7794–7803 (2018)
41. Woo, S., Park, J., Lee, J.Y., Kweon, I.S.: CBAM: convolutional block attention module. In: Proceedings of the European Conference on Computer Vision (ECCV), pp. 3–19 (2018)

Vision

Exploring Model Depth Adaptation in Image Super-Resolution for Efficient Inference

Ke Wang[1], Gang Xie[1,2], Zhe Zhang[1,2(✉)], Xinying Xu[1],
and Lan Cheng[1]

[1] Taiyuan University of Technology, Taiyuan, China
wangke0407@link.tyut.edu.cn, xiegang@tyust.edu.cn,
{zhangzhe,xuxinying,chenglan}@tyut.edu.cn
[2] Taiyuan University of Science and Technology, Taiyuan, China

Abstract. In the field of single-image super-resolution, different images have varying levels of difficulty in restoration. The restoration for images with a significant proportion of smooth regions is easier than images with complex textures or edge areas. This implies that the restoration for easy images requires fewer computational resources, whereas the restoration for difficult images requires more. Based on this, we have designed Model Depth Adaptation SR (MDASR) network, which can adaptively adjust the capacity of the model based on the difficulty level of the input image restoration. Specifically, we have employed a dynamic structural neural network that incorporates a gating mechanism to adaptively decide whether to execute or skip the current layer based on the current input, thereby achieving adaptive modeling in deep dimension. The experimental results demonstrate that our network significantly reduces FLOPS and achieves the best LPIPS performance on all the test datasets.

Keywords: SR · Dynamic Network · CNN

1 Introduction

Single image super-resolution (SISR) aims to recover a high-resolution (HR) image from a single low resolution (LR) image. Due to the powerful feature learning ability and strong adaptability of convolutional neural networks, CNN-based SR methods have made significant progress compared to traditional ones.

Since SRCNN [1] first introduced convolutional neural networks into the SR field, extensive research has been conducted on using deeper networks for image SR. The structure of SRCNN is relatively simple, consisting of only three convolutional layers. Subsequently, VDSR [2] proposed a network with 20 layers.

This work was supported by the National Natural Science Foundation of China (62073232), the Natural Science Foundation of Shanxi Province (202103021224056), Shanxi Scholarship Council of China (2021-046), the Foundation of Shanxi Key Laboratory of Advanced Control and Intelligent Information System (ACEI202101).

F. Sun et al. (Eds.): ICCSIP 2023, CCIS 1919, pp. 139–150, 2024.
https://doi.org/10.1007/978-981-99-8021-5_11

EDSR [3] introduced a wider and deeper network, extended the network depth to 60 layers, while RDN [4] and RCAN [5] increased the depth to over 100 and 400 layers, respectively. Although increasing the network depth can significantly improve the restoration performance of the network, it also brings higher computational costs, which severely limits the practical application of SR models on lightweight devices. To address this problem, several efforts have been made to reduce model size through model distillation [6–8] and network pruning [9,10].

As an alternative to CNN, Transformer [11] designs a self-attention mechanism to capture global interactions between contexts and has shown promising performance in SISR. SwinIR [12] was the first to introduce Transformer to SISR. Subsequent works, such as HTCAN [13] and ESRT [14], proposed a lightweight super-resolution network that combines CNN and Transformer.

However, these methods still involve redundant computations, because they did not consider the different amounts of computational resources required by the SR network when facing different LR images. Due to the intricate dimension changes in intermediate features within the Transformer [11] architecture, adapting its depth within the network becomes challenging. For CNN based models, ClassSR [15] changes the model capacity by introducing networks with different channel numbers, but it only has three specific capacities, which limits its adaptability. SMSR [16] transforms standard convolution kernels into sparse convolution kernels using spatial masks to reduce convolution operations on non-important pixels in spatial domain. It also achieves channel adaptability based on the related channel mask. However, it does not consider adaptability in terms of network depth. Inspired by SMSR, we consider the adaptability of adjusting the model capacity based on the difficulty level of image restoration. Specifically, we adaptively adjust the depth of the model based on the difficulty of LR image.

2   Adaptive Model Depth Adjustment

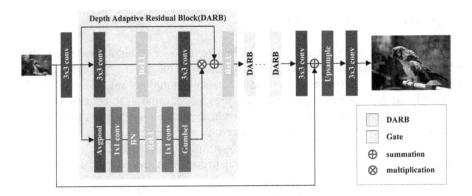

Fig. 1. An overview of our MDASR network.

2.1 MDASR Network

The overall structure of the proposed network is illustrated in Fig. 1. The main body of the network consists of 16 Deep Adaptive Residual Blocks (DARB) designed by us. Each DARB includes layers to be executed on the feature maps and a gating structure. At the end of MDASR, there are also two convolutional layers and an up-sampling module.

2.2 Depth Adaptive Residual Blocks

Figure. 2 illustrates the structural differences between the traditional residual block [17,18] and the DARB module. Let f_l be the function computed by the lth layer, $\mathbf{x}_{l-1}$ be the input LR image, and $\mathbf{x}_l$ be the output of the lth layer. In this way, such a network can be defined as follows

$$\mathbf{x}_l = \mathbf{x}_{l-1} + f_l\left(\mathbf{x}_{l-1}\right) \tag{1}$$

We have added a gating structure to the original residual block, enabling the DARB module to execute or skip certain layers. Specifically, in the gating structure, we perform calculations on the output of the previous layer to obtain two scores representing whether to execute or skip the current layer. We then determine whether to execute or skip the current layer based on the magnitudes of these two scores. As shown in Fig. 3, during training, the output of a gate

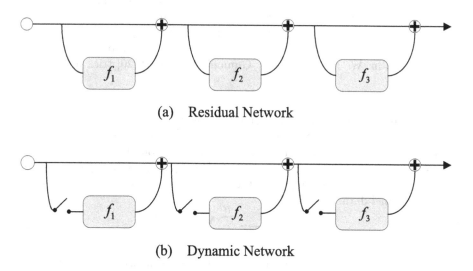

(a) Residual Network

(b) Dynamic Network

Fig. 2. Comparison of the structure between classical residual blocks and dynamic depth residual blocks.

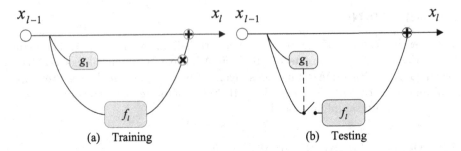

Fig. 3. (a) The gating structure during training, where the network's output is multiplied with the output of the gating structure. (b) The gating structure during testing, where the current layer is executed or skipped based on the output of the gating structure.

is multiplied with the output of its respective layer. During testing, the gate outputs a binary result of either 1 or 0, determining whether to execute or skip the current layer.

Here, g_l is a gate switch that can determine whether to execute the current residual block based on the output of the last residual block. Therefore, the gate switch has two discrete states: 0 represents 'off' and 1 represents 'on'.

To achieve the desired performance, the gating structure needs to address two issues. Firstly, the gating structure needs to calculate two scores based on the output of the previous layer x_{l-1}, where these two scores represent whether to execute or skip the current layer f_l. Secondly, gate switches need to make discrete decisions during testing, while in training, they need to provide gradient information for estimating the correlation between layers to ensure gradient backpropagation. We achieve this by Gumbel-softmax [19,20] trick and related techniques.

Calculating Two Scores. Corresponding to the two problems to be addressed, our gating structure consists of two parts. The gate's first component aims to calculate two scores based on the output of the previous layer x_{l-1}, which is a tensor of size $R^{W \times H \times C}$. Firstly, as shown in Eq. 1, we apply global average pooling to compresses the input features along the spatial dimension into a $R^{1 \times 1 \times C}$ channel data.

$$z_c = \frac{1}{H \times W} \sum_{i=1}^{H} \sum_{j=1}^{W} x_{i,j,c} \qquad (2)$$

Then, we apply fully connected layer, BatchNorm [21], ReLU [22], and another fully connected layer sequentially to z_c. This combination allows us to compute a vector $\alpha = \{\alpha_0, \alpha_1\}$, α_0 corresponds to skipping the current layer, and α_1 corresponds to executing the current layer. The vector is computed as follows

$$\alpha = FC_2 \sigma(FC_1 \mathbf{z}) \qquad (3)$$

where σ refers to the ReLU activation function, $FC_1 \in R^{d \times C}$, $FC_2 \in R^{2 \times d}$ and d refers to the dimension of the specific fully connected layer.

Gumbel Sampling. After obtaining two scores representing whether to execute or skip a layer, we need to make a discrete decision based on the magnitudes of α_0 and α_1. A natural idea is to select the larger one from α_0 and α_1 then make our decision based on its corresponding class. However, this brings obvious problems: first, due to the constraint of the L_1 loss and VGG loss, the network will easily converge towards the direction of fully executing all layers; second, this method of directly selecting the maximum value is not differentiable, so it cannot guarantee the gradient's backpropagation during the training process. We employ Gumbel-Softmax and its related techniques to address this issue.

According to the Gumbel-Softmax method, we can sample from α_0 and α_1, and the sampled results g_0 and g_1 will be proportional to the magnitudes of the original α_0 and α_1, respectively. Therefore, comparing g_0 and g_1 also allows us to compare the magnitudes of α_0 and α_1. Additionally, Gumbel-Softmax is differentiable, ensuring that gradients can be properly backpropagated to the parameters that need to be updated in the gate during training. The sampling formula can be represented as follows

$$g_i = softmax\left(\left(G_i + \alpha_i\right)\right)/\tau\right) = \frac{\exp\left(G_i + \alpha_i\right)/\tau}{\sum\left(G_j + \alpha_i\right)\right)/\tau} \tag{4}$$

where $i = 0, 1$, $G_i \sim Gumbel(0,1)$, every G_i is an independently and identically distributed variable sampled from the standard Gumbel distribution. In the above equation, τ acts as a temperature coefficient controlling the degree of approximation between the current sampling method and discrete sampling. When $\tau \to 0$, the computation of softmax can smoothly approach argmax, resulting in a sampled vector that is close to one-hot. When $\tau \to \infty$, the sampled vector becomes uniform. In the above equation, since softmax is differentiable and the noise G_i is independent, gradients can be propagated to the parameter α_i.

In the training phase, the g_i generated by our gating structure consists of g_0 and g_1, where their sum is equal to 1. In fact, to represent the impact of executing the current layer on the result, we only multiply g_1 with the output obtained from the current layer, where g_1 is a number ranging from 0 to 1. During training, the computation graph can be represented as follows

$$x_l = x_{l-1} + g_l(x_{l-1}) \cdot f_l\left(x_{l-1}\right), g_l(x_{l-1}) \in (0,1) \tag{5}$$

During testing, we use argmax to replace the softmax function for sampling. The argmax function compares the magnitudes of g_0 and g_1, resulting in the output of the gate structure taking either 0 or 1, thereby determining whether to skip or execute the current layer. The sampling process during testing phase can be represented as follows

$$g_i = argmax\left(\left(G_i + \alpha_i\right)\right)/\tau\right) \tag{6}$$

During testing, the computational graph of a residual block containing gate switches can be represented as

$$\mathbf{x_l} = \mathbf{x}_{l-1} + g_l(\mathbf{x}_{l-1}) \cdot f_l(\mathbf{x}_{l-1}), g_l(\mathbf{x}_{l-1}) \in \{0,1\} \tag{7}$$

2.3 Training Loss

We construct our loss function from three aspects: we employ L_1 loss to ensure the restoration accuracy of the network, VGG [23] loss to constrain the perceptual quality of the restoration, and L_{ACT} to maintain a certain level of sparsity in the network.

Activation Loss. To enable the network to learn whether to execute the current layer during the training process, we restrict the frequency at which each layer can be used. Specifically, we introduce a new loss term that encourages each layer in the network to be executed at a specific target rate t_l. More specifically, let L denote the set of layers in the network, and let each layer have a specific target rate t_l which ranges from 0 to 1. To ensure that each layer is equally to be executed or skipped, we set t_l to a uniform value of 0.5. For a specific training instance i in the current batch of training images B, the output of the gate computed for the ith training instance in the lth layer is denoted as $g_{l,i}$. Our loss function is defined as follows

$$L_{ACT} = \frac{1}{|L|} \frac{1}{|B|} \sum_{l \in L} \sum_{i \in B} sigmoid\{\lambda \cdot [(g_{l,i} - t_l) - s]\}, g_{l,i} \in (0,1) \tag{8}$$

where the parameter t_l controls the desired target rate for $g_{l,i}$, and λ is a scaling factor while s is a distance shift factor.

As we aim to adapt the network structure while minimizing computational costs, which means skipping layers as much as possible, a natural idea is to minimize the loss function when $g_{l,i}$ approaches t_l from the smaller side of t_l, and increase the value of the loss function when $g_{l,i}$ approaches t_l from the larger side of t_l. The sigmoid function satisfies our requirements within a certain range, so we choose it as the basic framework for this activation loss term. Assuming the current value is t_l, since the range of $g_{l,i}$ is (0,1), the range of $(g_{l,i} - t_l)$ is $(-t_l, 1 - t_l)$. We can expand the current range to the desired range through scaling and shifting. Specifically, we achieve this by using the scaling factor λ and the shift factor s.

Total Loss. To compare the restoration performance of the network under two scenarios: fully executing all layers and skipping certain layers, we added two new loss terms based on L_1 and VGG loss. These two loss terms are used to constrain the results of the network when it fully executes all layers. To distinguish them from the loss in the skip case, we named them D_L1 and D_VGG, respectively. By combining these three different types of losses, we can achieve network lightweight while maintaining the recovery effect. The final form of the loss function is as follows

$$L_{loss} = \lambda_1 L_1 + \lambda_2 L_{VGG} + \lambda_5 L_{ACT} + \lambda_4 L_{D\_L_1} + \lambda_5 L_{D\_VGG} \qquad (9)$$

3   Experiments

3.1   Settings

Datasets. DIV2K [24] dataset is a high-quality image dataset for single image super-resolution. The DIV2K [24] dataset consists of 800 training images, 100 validation images, and 100 testing images. Since the testing set lacks ground truth, we use the validation set to evaluate and compare the performance of our models. We also compare the performance on four standard benchmark datasets: ADE20K [25], Set5 [26], B100 [27], OST300 [28].

Implementation Details. During training, we set patch size of 96×96 and 192×192 for scaling factor of $\times 2$ and $\times 4$, respectively. Before feeding into our model, we pre-process all the images by subtracting the mean RGB value of the DIV2K dataset. At the end of the model, we will add the mean RGB value of the DIV2K [24] dataset to counterbalance the previous step's influence.

We set $B = 16, C = 64, L = 16$ for our network. We train our model with Adam optimizer [29] with $\beta_1 = 0.9$ and $\beta_2 = 0.999$ for optimization. The initial learning rate was set to 2×10^{-4} and reduced to half after every 2×10^5 minibatch updates. The training was stopped after 500 epochs. The overall loss for training is defined as Eq. 8, where L_{ACT} is defined in Eq. 7. We set $\lambda_1 = 1, \lambda_2 = 5, \lambda_3 = 8, \lambda_4 = 1, \lambda_5 = 5$ empirically. We trained our model on 1 NVIDIA 3090 GPU.

Evaluation on DIV2K and Benchmark Datasets. We tested our model on images 801–900 from the DIV2K [24] dataset. We used the common evaluation metrics of PSNR and SSIM. Additionally, to measure the subjective evaluation of the restored images, we also presented the results of the LPIPS [30] evaluation metric. We compared our model with other classical models, including Bicubic, SRCNN [1], and EDSR [3]. We compared the parameter count and FLOPs of different models at scaling factors of $\times 2$ and $\times 4$. To compare the effect of skipping certain layers in our model, we referred to the model that executes all layers as "Ours_D" and observed the results for comparison.

Quantitative Results. Table 1 presents the quantitative results. As shown in Table 1, compared to EDSR [3], our network has a minimal increase in the number of parameters due to the addition of the gating structure. Specifically, our network has an increase of 2K and 3K parameters for $\times 2$ and $\times 4$ SR, respectively. This increase in parameter count is negligible compared to the overall model parameters.

Fig. 4. Comparative results achieved for ×4 SR on DIV2K.

Table 1. Comparative results achieved for × 2/4 SR

Model	Scale	Params	FLOPs	Set5 PSNR/SSIM/LPIPS	BSD100 PSNR/SSIM/LPIPS	OST300 PSNR/SSIM/LPIPS	DIV2K PSNR/SSIM/LPIPS
Bicubic	×2	_	_	33.65/0.965/0.127	29.55/0.906/0.251	29.27/0.903/0.252	32.41/0.940/0.183
SRCNN [1]	×2	57K	52.88	36.65/0.977/0.064	31.35/0.932/0.174	30.74/0.929/0.182	34.68/0.958/0.115
EDSR [3]	×2	137K	1282.35	37.87/0.980/0.057	32.13/0.940/0.148	31.48/0.939/0.150	36.05/0.967/0.090
Ours_D	×2	139K	1283.29	37.06/0.978/0.040	31.67/0.936/0.122	31.05/0.934/0.123	35.28/0.963/0.068
Ours	×2	139K	391.60	35.35/0.973/0.034	30.55/0.925/0.112	30.09/0.923/0.116	33.50/0.953/0.067
Bicubic	×4	_	_	28.37/0.908/0.335	25.98/0.800/0.524	24.37/0.785/0.518	28.11/0.853/0.409
SRCNN [1]	×4	57K	13.22	30.01/0.929/0.214	26.70/0.820/0.426	26.39/0.816/0.423	29.35/0.876/0.307
EDSR [3]	×4	151K	461.50	31.96/0.949/0.173	27.57/0.843/0.372	27.05/0.837/0.371	30.42/0.897/0.270
Ours_D	×4	154K	461.74	30.98/0.940/0.124	27.00/0.829/0.289	26.52/0.823/0.287	29.61/0.883/0.204
Ours	×4	154K	281.96	30.06/0.930/0.118	26.48/0.817/0.289	26.13/0.812/0.287	28.86/0.870/0.206

In Table 1, FLOPs is computed based on HR images with a resolution of 2560×1440. Since Ours_D model is a fully dense model, it executes all layers during the testing phase, resulting in no reduction in FLOPs. However, our adaptive model (Ours), compared to EDSR [3], achieves an average reduction of 69.5% (391.60 vs. 1282.35) and 38.9% (281.96 vs. 461.50) in FLOPs during testing for the ×2 and ×4 upscaling factors, respectively. In terms of PSNR/SSIM/LPIPS, EDSR achieves good PSNR performance due to its use of only L_1 loss. However, both our models, Ours_D and Ours, balance image restoration quality and subjective evaluation metrics, resulting in slight decreases in PSNR and SSIM. However, Ours achieve the best LPIPS performance on almost all datasets (except for the results on DIV2K [24] dataset at ×4 scaling factor, where model Ours_D behaves better). Furthermore, by comparing the super-resolution results under two scenarios of Ours_D and Ours, we observe that model Ours achieves better LPIPS scores while experiencing slight decreases in PSNR and SSIM. This indicates that our network can ensure subjective evaluation quality of the super-resolution results while significantly reducing FLOPs. Furthermore, by adjusting the corresponding factor λ_1 to λ_5, our adaptive network can emphasize network computational complexity, accuracy, and subjective evaluation metrics to meet the requirements of practical scenarios.

Qualitative Results. Figure. 4 compares the qualitative results of different methods at ×4 scaling factor. In Fig. 4(a), the restoration result by EDSR [3] appears to be blurrier, and there is a clear distinction between the sculpture and the stone gate. In contrast, in our SR results (Ours_D and Ours), the textures of the sculpture and the stone gate are clearer, and the connection between them is more natural, which better aligns with human subjective evaluation standards. This observation also holds for the results in Fig. 4(b), where our results are more consistent with the texture and material of the objects in ground truth (GT). In Fig. 4(c), the SR results obtained by EDSR [3] render the vegetation portion as a simple green area and it loses a significant amount of architectural texture details. As a result, the overall image appears extremely unnatural. In contrast, our results add more shape to the vegetation portion, and our restored

SR results contain more texture details for the architectural part. Therefore, our results appear more natural. In Fig. 4(d), the results obtained by EDSR [3] lose a significant amount of texture details and appear unnatural. Our model, on the other hand, better restores the texture details and achieves a more realistic subjective effect.

In general, EDSR [3] tends to restore regions with similar pixel values to smoother results, resulting in the loss of texture information. Although this approach may achieve better results in terms of PSNR, it also leads to noticeable differences between different regions in the SR results. In contrast, our model, in both fully executed and skipped layers scenarios, can better restore texture details and overall yields results that align more closely with subjective evaluation criteria. This demonstrates the effectiveness of our model.

4   Conclusion

In this work, we demonstrate how our network in the field of SISR can adaptively adjust its structure based on the current image. Specifically, we introduce a gating mechanism to control the network's depth during execution. Extensive experiments on DIV2K [24] and other benchmark datasets show that our network can significantly reduce computational complexity while maintaining good restoration quality, which opens up possibilities for the application of SR networks on lightweight devices.

This work paves the way for future research. Currently, our network proves that different images have varying levels of restoration difficulty, but this adaptation is done at the image-level. In reality, different regions within the same image also possess distinct restoration difficulties. Therefore, our approach can also be extended to spatial-level adaptation. Future work will explore this aspect further.

References

1. Dong, C., Loy, C.C., He, K., Tang, X.: Learning a deep convolutional network for image super-resolution. In: Fleet, D., Pajdla, T., Schiele, B., Tuytelaars, T. (eds.) ECCV 2014. LNCS, vol. 8692, pp. 184–199. Springer, Cham (2014). https://doi.org/10.1007/978-3-319-10593-2_13
2. Kim, J., Lee, J.K., Lee, K.M.: Accurate image super-resolution using very deep convolutional networks. In: 2016 IEEE Conference on Computer Vision and Pattern Recognition (CVPR), pp. 1646–1654 (2016)
3. Lim, B., Son, S., Kim, H., Nah, S., Lee, K.M.: Enhanced deep residual networks for single image super-resolution. In: 2017 IEEE Conference on Computer Vision and Pattern Recognition Workshops (CVPRW), pp. 1132–1140 (2017)
4. Zhang, Y., Tian, Y., Kong, Y., Zhong, B., Fu, Y.: Residual dense network for image super-resolution. In: 2018 IEEE/CVF Conference on Computer Vision and Pattern Recognition, pp. 2472–2481 (2018)

5. Zhang, Y., Li, K., Li, K., Wang, L., Zhong, B., Fu, Y.: Image super-resolution using very deep residual channel attention networks. In: Ferrari, V., Hebert, M., Sminchisescu, C., Weiss, Y. (eds.) ECCV 2018. LNCS, vol. 11211, pp. 294–310. Springer, Cham (2018). https://doi.org/10.1007/978-3-030-01234-2_18

6. Hui, Z., Wang, X., Gao, X.: Fast and accurate single image super-resolution via information distillation network. In: 2018 IEEE/CVF Conference on Computer Vision and Pat-tern Recognition, pp. 723–731 (2018)

7. Lee, W., Lee, J., Kim, D., Ham, B.: Learning with privileged information for efficient image super-resolution. In: Vedaldi, A., Bischof, H., Brox, T., Frahm, J.-M. (eds.) ECCV 2020. LNCS, vol. 12369, pp. 465–482. Springer, Cham (2020). https://doi.org/10.1007/978-3-030-58586-0_28

8. Han, S., Pool, J., Tran, J., Dally, W.: Learning both weights and connections for efficient neural network. In: Advances in Neural Information Processing Systems. Curran Associates, Inc. (2015)

9. Liu, Z., Li, J., Shen, Z., Huang, G., Yan, S., Zhang, C.: learning efficient convolutional networks through network slimming. In: 2017 IEEE International Conference on Computer Vision (ICCV), pp. 2755–2763 (2017)

10. Luo, J.-H., Wu, J., Lin, W.: ThiNet: a filter level pruning method for deep neural network compression. In: 2017 IEEE International Conference on Computer Vision (ICCV), pp. 5068–5076 (2017)

11. Vaswani, A., et al.: Attention is all you need. In: Advances in Neural Information Processing Systems. Curran Associates, Inc. (2017)

12. Liang, J., Cao, J., Sun, G., Zhang, K., Van Gool, L., Timofte, R.: SwinIR: image restoration using swin transformer. In: 2021 IEEE/CVF International Conference on Computer Vision Workshops (ICCVW), pp. 1833–1844. IEEE, Montreal, BC, Canada (2021). https://doi.org/10.1109/ICCVW54120.2021.00210

13. Fang, J., Lin, H., Chen, X., Zeng, K.: A hybrid network of CNN and transformer for lightweight image super-resolution. In: 2022 IEEE/CVF Conference on Computer Vision and Pattern Recognition Workshops (CVPRW), pp. 1102–1111. IEEE, New Orleans, LA, USA (2022). https://doi.org/10.1109/CVPRW56347.2022.00119

14. Lu, Z., Li, J., Liu, H., Huang, C., Zhang, L., Zeng, T.: transformer for single image super-resolution. In: Presented at the 2022 IEEE/CVF Conference on Computer Vision and Pattern Recognition Workshops (CVPRW) June 1 (2022). https://doi.org/10.1109/CVPRW56347.2022.00061

15. Kong, X., Zhao, H., Qiao, Y., Dong, C.: ClassSR: a general framework to accelerate super-resolution networks by data characteristic. In: 2021 IEEE/CVF Conference on Computer Vision and Pattern Recognition (CVPR), pp. 12011–12020 (2021)

16. Wang, L., et al.: Exploring sparsity in image super-resolution for efficient inference. In: 2021 IEEE/CVF Conference on Computer Vision and Pattern Recognition (CVPR), pp. 4915–4924 (2021)

17. He, K., Zhang, X., Ren, S., Sun, J.: Deep residual learning for image recognition. In: 2016 IEEE Conference on Computer Vision and Pattern Recognition (CVPR), pp. 770–778 (2016)

18. Veit, A., Wilber, M.J., Belongie, S.: Residual networks behave like ensembles of relatively shallow networks. In: Advances in Neural Information Processing Systems. Curran Associates, Inc. (2016)

19. Maddison, C.J., Mnih, A., Teh, Y.W.: The concrete distribution: a continuous relaxation of discrete random variables. http://arxiv.org/abs/1611.00712 (2017)

20. Jang, E., Gu, S., Poole, B.: Categorical reparameterization with gumbel-softmax. http://arxiv.org/abs/1611.01144 (2017)

21. Hu, J., Shen, L., Sun, G.: Squeeze-and-excitation networks. In: 2018 IEEE/CVF Conference on Computer Vision and Pattern Recognition, pp. 7132–7141 (2018)
22. Glorot, X., Bordes, A., Bengio, Y.: Deep sparse rectifier neural networks. In: Proceedings of the Fourteenth International Conference on Artificial Intelligence and Statistics, pp. 315–323. JMLR Workshop and Conference Proceedings (2011)
23. Johnson, J., Alahi, A., Fei-Fei, L.: Perceptual losses for real-time style transfer and super-resolution. In: Leibe, B., Matas, J., Sebe, N., Welling, M. (eds.) Computer Vision - ECCV 2016, pp. 694–711. Springer International Publishing, Cham (2016). https://doi.org/10.1007/978-3-319-46475-6_43
24. Agustsson, E., Timofte, R.: NTIRE 2017 challenge on single image super-resolution: dataset and study. In: 2017 IEEE Conference on Computer Vision and Pattern Recognition Workshops (CVPRW), pp. 1122–1131 (2017)
25. Zhou, B., et al.: Semantic understanding of scenes through the ADE20K dataset. Int. J. Comput. Vis. **127**, 302–321 (2019)
26. Bevilacqua, M., Roumy, A., Guillemot, C., Morel, M.A.: Low-complexity single-image super-resolution based on nonnegative neighbor embedding. In: Proceedings of the British Machine Vision Conference 2012, pp. 135.1-135.10. British Machine Vision Association, Surrey (2012)
27. Martin, D., Fowlkes, C., Tal, D., Malik, J.: A database of human segmented natural images and its application to evaluating segmentation algorithms and measuring ecological statistics. In: Proceedings Eighth IEEE International Conference on Computer Vision, ICCV 2001, vol. 2, pp. 416–423 (2001)
28. Wang, X., Yu, K., Dong, C., Change Loy, C.: Recovering realistic texture in image super-resolution by deep spatial feature transform. In: 2018 IEEE/CVF Conference on Computer Vision and Pattern Recognition, pp. 606–615 (2018)
29. Kingma, D.P., Ba, J.: Adam: a method for stochastic optimization. http://arxiv.org/abs/1412.6980 (2017)
30. Zhang, R., Isola, P., Efros, A.A., Shechtman, E., Wang, O.: The unreasonable effectiveness of deep features as a perceptual metric. In: 2018 IEEE/CVF Conference on Computer Vision and Pattern Recognition, pp. 586–595 (2018)

RGB to $L^*a^*b^*$ Color Prediction Model Based on Color Cards

Yong Zhang[1], Jie Zou[2], Chao Ma[1], Yunpeng Gu[1], and Jianwei Ma[1(✉)]

[1] College of Information Engineering, Henan University of Science and Technology,
Luoyang 471000, China
lymjw@163.com

[2] Science and Technology on Electro-Optic Control Laboratory AVIC Optronics,
Luoyang 471000, China

Abstract. Color is a critical characteristic indicating the traits of an object and is widely used in computer vision technology. In order to ensure uniformity and device independence of color in image processing, standardized and normative color management are needed. $L^*a^*b^*$ color space is a device-independent expression of color values because it is uniform and independent of hardware devices. Therefore, in this paper, we compare four prediction models from RGB to $L^*a^*b^*$. The experimental platform was built to acquire digital images with Pantone color cards as sample data and extract RGB value. The real $L^*a^*b^*$ value is measured by colorimeter. And preprocess the original RGB value and $L^*a^*b^*$ value data, and establish four prediction models: linear, quadratic polynomial, neural network and extreme learning machine, by comparing preprocessed data with real data. Using four evaluation metrics (MAE, MSE, RMSE and R^2), and scatter fit plots were used to compare results. The results show that the model based on extreme learning machine has the highest prediction accuracy, with MAE reaching 0.021, 0.017 and 0.010, MSE 0.0006, 0.0005 and 0.0001, RMSE 0.026, 0.021 and 0.031, R^2 0.96, 0.97 and 0.96, respectively. Indicates that the extreme learning machine has good potential for application.

Keywords: Color prediction · RGB · $L^*a^*b^*$ · Pantone color card · Extreme learning machine

1 Introduction

In various industries, color is an important attribute related to product quality and producers [1, 2]. Color is frequently used for quality control in many fields, such as the food industry [3, 4], agriculture [5], medicine [6, 7], oil-based liquids [8, 9], and water [10, 11]. Similarly, color also reflects the state, chemical composition [12], and properties of materials and products [2].

Traditionally, the main method used is human eye recognition, and it is difficult to ensure consistent product quality because different people have different evaluations

This work is support by Aeronautical Science Foundation of China (Grant No. 20200051042003).

of product quality due to their own psychological, experiential, and other conditions. In order to improve the efficiency of color detection and a more accurate quantitative description of color, a large number of colorimeters have been put into use, such as densitometers, photoelectric integral colorimeters, spectrophotometers, etc. These colorimeters are portable and easy to operate and have high accuracy in color measurement. CS Schelkopf et al. presented a comparison of two colorimeters for objective evaluation of fresh beef color. The correlation between Nix and Hunterlab was 0.80 to 0.85 in terms of L, a, and b values. Consistency analysis showed that Nix and Hunterlab colorimeters had a good agreement in all color parameters. Therefore, the Nix colorimeter may be an alternative to the Hunterlab colorimeter [13]. Saúl Dussán-Sarria et al. developed and evaluated a prototype for fresh vegetable color measurement, converting the measurements to the $L^*a^*b^*$ system. Measurements were compared to PANTONE color cards using the prototype and a Konica Minolta CR-400 colorimeter, and the mean error was determined. The results showed that the colorimetric prototype is a suitable alternative technique for the color measurement of fresh vegetables, with an average error of 15.57% and 27.45% with the colorimeter, respectively [14]. However, these instruments can only detect the local color condition of the product surface and cannot achieve the complete surface color measurement of the product.

With the research and development of science and technology, machine vision techniques [15] have started to be widely used in industrial applications, and in recent years, computer vision has been used to objectively measure the color of different materials because they have some distinct advantages over traditional colorimeters, i.e., they can analyze each pixel of the entire surface of food and quantify surface features and defects. CN Nguyen et al. developed a real-time CVS for measuring food color, using the RGB-Lab color space transformation model and cross-validation to evaluate the effect of training data and regularization on higher-order regression models. The high accuracy of the test confirms the benefits of proper training data preparation and regularization. The model performed better than those reported in the literature [16]. Heng et al. evaluated the performance of the LCTF hyperspectral imaging system for fabric color measurement and proposed a radial basis function neural network model to calibrate the color agreement between the LCTF hyperspectral imaging system and Datacolor 650, which can fully utilize the reflectance information of the entire waveband, and the LCTF hyperspectral spectral imaging system can accurately measure fabric color with good repeatability and reproducibility [17]. However, any discussion in the literature about color measurement using deep learning method has been lacking.

In recent years, many studies have advanced the development of neural network theory by combining neural networks with other techniques to form extended models. Su et al. proposed a wavelet neural network model based on the optimization of the cuckoo search algorithm for converting from CMYK to $L^*a^*b^*$ color space and reducing image chromatic aberration. The model is built on the basis of a wavelet neural network, and the CS algorithm is used to optimize the WNN model parameters. The accuracy and stability of the obtained L, a, and b values of $L^*a^*b^*$ are higher than those of conventional neural networks [18]. Su et al. used an improved high-precision deep belief network algorithm to convert CMYK to $L^*a^*b^*$ color space and optimized it using a particle swarm optimization algorithm. This method has the highest accuracy and is suitable for color management needs in digital printing [19]. Heng et al. developed a new method to test the color of cashmere and compare it with standards, including RGB, XYZ, and Lab color features. Experiments showed that the color measurement method has high accuracy in RGB and XYZ space. In addition, an accurate fiber map can be obtained by the light refractive index conversion model, and this curve is an essential indicator for cashmere length determination [20]. A new color measurement system for cashmere was proposed by Zhang et al. Twenty-nine cashmere samples of different colors were selected as standard samples, and the color conversion model was calibrated. The correlation coefficients of L, a, and b values between the two systems were 0.99, 0.96, and 0.93, respectively. In addition, the category of cashmere can be determined by this method because of the high accuracy and representativeness of the new method [21].

In this work, we evaluated four different machine learning models-linear model, quadratic polynomial model, neural network model, and extreme learning machine model to predict Pantone color card $L^*a^*b^*$ values. Pantone swatch images are captured using the same illumination conditions and the same camera, and the RGB values of the digital images of the swatches are extracted. The experimental results show that the extreme learning machine model has higher prediction accuracy, and better results in RGB value to $L^*a^*b^*$ value conversion compared with the linear model, quadratic polynomial model, and neural network model.

2   Equipment and Materials

The images used in this paper were taken with a Hikvision MV-CH120-10GC color industrial camera with 12-megapixel resolution, Sony's IMX304 CMOS chip, and an 8 mm industrial camera fisheye lens. The various parameters of the camera are shown in Table 1.

Table 1. Camera settings.

Parameters	Value
Target size	1.1
Resolution	4096 × 3000
Frame Rate	9.4 fps
Exposure time	Ultra Small Exposure Mode: 1 μs–14 μs Normal exposure mode: 15 μs–10 s
Gain	0 dB–20 dB
Signal-to-Noise Ratio	40.2 dB

The illumination system uses a D65 standard light source with a color temperature of 6500K, which is placed around the sample so that the light hits the surface of the sample evenly from all angles. In order to present colors better, the device is placed in a closed box to prevent external light from entering, thereby minimizing background light.

The Pantone Colors-RGB Coated, which is widely used in Japan and abroad, was used as a sample for image acquisition. As shown in Fig. 1(a), a total of 1137 colors of Pantone color cards were used, and the average Lab value of each color in the color cards was extracted by a color difference meter to be used for color measurement. The colorimeter is LS173 handheld, as shown in Fig. 1(b).

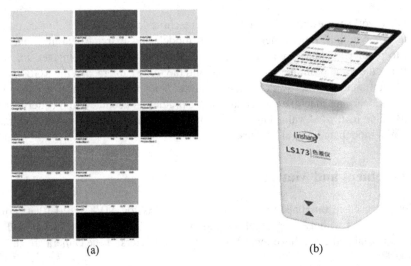

(a)   (b)

Fig. 1. (a) Pantone international color card; (b) LS173 handheld colorimeter.

The camera was placed vertically during the shooting, with the camera lens 45 cm away from the sample, and the industrial camera was connected to a computer with LAPTOP-7KENS8EV, processor AMD Ryzen 5 5600H with Radeon Graphics 3.30 GHz, via GigE data interface. The images were acquired using the software MVS V4.0.1 (Windows), a machine vision industrial camera client developed by HIKROBOT, and these images were used for RGB value extraction at the highest resolution (4096 × 3000) (Fig. 2).

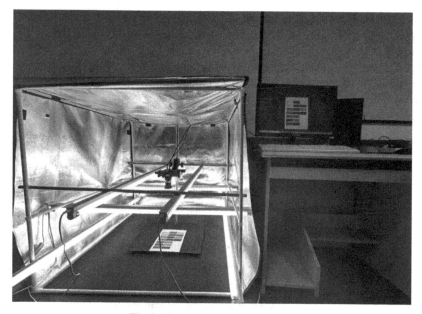

Fig. 2. Image acquisition platform.

3   Model Construction

In order to compare the relative performance in determining color values, linear models, quadratic polynomial models, neural network models, and extreme learning machine models were used to transform RGB to make predictions. The RGB to L^*, a^*, b^* transformation used to predict RGB consists of two parts (see Fig. 3 and the nomenclature in Table 2).

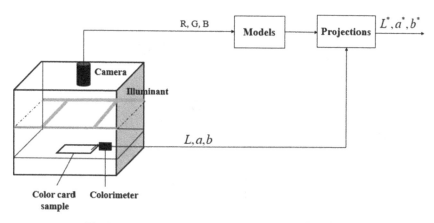

Fig. 3. Flow chart of RGB to L^*, a^*, b^* value prediction.

Model building: The model has $\theta_1, \theta_2, \cdots \theta_m$ parameters whose inputs are the RGB variables obtained from the color digital images of the color card samples, and the outputs are the L^*, a^*, b^* variables estimated from the model.

Prediction: By using the colorimeter, the parameter $\theta_1, \theta_2, \cdots \theta_m$ is estimated for the model based on the prediction between the model output L^*, a^*, b^* and the true L, a, and b variables.

Table 2. Values of each variable.

Variables	Description
L	Chromaticity meter measured values
a	Chromaticity meter measured values
b	Chromaticity meter measured values
L^*	The values obtained by the model
a^*	The values obtained by the model
b^*	The values obtained by the model
R	Value of digital image measurement
G	Value of digital image measurement
B	Value of digital image measurement

3.1 Linear Models

The linear model is a simple model of RGB to L^*, a^*, b^* transformations. In this model, these L^*, a^*, b^* parameters are linear functions of the R, G, and B variables.

$$
\begin{bmatrix} L_i^* \\ a_i^* \\ b_i^* \end{bmatrix} = \begin{bmatrix} M_{11} & M_{12} & M_{13} \\ M_{21} & M_{22} & M_{23} \\ M_{31} & M_{32} & M_{33} \end{bmatrix} \begin{bmatrix} R \\ G \\ B \end{bmatrix} \tag{1}
$$

Parameter vectors of the model:

$$
\theta = \begin{bmatrix} M_{11} & M_{12} & M_{13} \end{bmatrix}^T \tag{2}
$$

Input matrix with N measurements of R, G, B:

$$
X = \begin{bmatrix} R_1 & G_1 & B_1 \\ \vdots & \vdots & \vdots \\ R_N & G_N & B_N \end{bmatrix} \tag{3}
$$

The output vector has N measurements of L^*:

$$
y = \begin{bmatrix} L_1^* & \cdots & L_N^* \end{bmatrix}^T \tag{4}
$$

From the least squares method, we obtain the following:

$$\hat{y} = X\theta \text{ Among them } \theta = \left[X^T X\right]^{-1} X^T y \tag{5}$$

3.2 Quadratic Model

The quadratic model takes into account the effect of squaring the R, G, and B variables on the prediction of L^*, a^*, b^* values.

$$
\begin{bmatrix} L_i^* \\ a_i^* \\ b_i^* \end{bmatrix} = \begin{bmatrix} M_{11} \; M_{12} \; M_{13} \; M_{14} \; M_{15} \; M_{16} \; M_{17} \; M_{18} \; M_{19} \\ M_{21} \; M_{22} \; M_{23} \; M_{24} \; M_{25} \; M_{26} \; M_{27} \; M_{28} \; M_{29} \\ M_{31} \; M_{32} \; M_{33} \; M_{34} \; M_{35} \; M_{36} \; M_{37} \; M_{38} \; M_{39} \end{bmatrix} \begin{bmatrix} R \\ G \\ B \\ RG \\ RB \\ GB \\ R^2 \\ G^2 \\ B^2 \end{bmatrix} \tag{6}
$$

The estimation of the parameters of the matrix M is performed in the same way as in the previous model, although the variables are quadratic, The model is linear in the parameters, and the first row requires the following definition:
Parameter vector of the model:

$$\theta = \left[M_{11} \; M_{12} \cdots M_{19}\right]^T \tag{7}$$

Input matrix of N measurements with (R, G, B):

$$
X = \begin{bmatrix} R_1 \; G_1 \; B_1 \; R_1G_1 \; R_1B_1 \; G_1B_1 \; R^2 \; G^2 \; B^2 \\ \vdots \; \vdots \; \vdots \; \vdots \; \vdots \; \vdots \; \vdots \; \vdots \; \vdots \\ R_N \; G_N \; B_N \; R_NG_N \; R_NB_N \; G_NB_N \; R_N^2 \; G_N^2 \; B_N^2 \end{bmatrix} \tag{8}
$$

And an output vector with N measurements L^* as defined in the above equation. The estimation L^* is also defined using the above equation.

3.3 Neural Network Model

The neural network is a multilayer feedforward neural network, and its optimization algorithm in the training process uses the output layer error by backpropagation, which generally has a 3-layer structure: input layer, hidden layer, and output layer. As shown in Fig. 4.

And MLPRegressor algorithm is a regression analysis method based on Multilayer Perceptron (MLP) in the principle of neural network. The algorithm can learn the complex nonlinear mapping relationship from input to output, so it can be applied to regression analysis with nonlinear relationships.

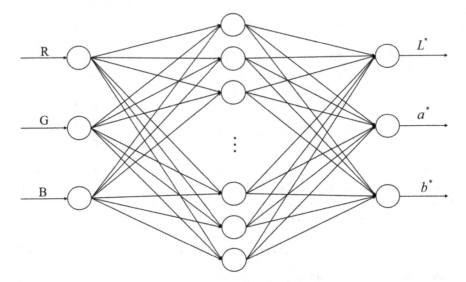

Fig. 4. Neural network architecture.

3.4 Extreme Learning Machine

ELM is a single-layer feedforward neural network, which was proposed by G.B. Huang et al. in 2004 [22, 23]. The input weights and biases of the hidden layer of ELM can be generated randomly, and the only thing that needs to be determined is the output weights of the hidden layer. Compared with traditional feedforward neural networks, ELM is very efficient in operation and has superior generalization performance.

The structure of ELM with i input layer neurons, n hidden layer neurons, and j output layer neurons can be represented as shown in Fig. 5. For N discrete training samples $\{x_i, t_i\}_{i=1}^{N}$ with input data $x_i = [x_{i1}, x_{i2}, \cdots, x_{in}]^T \in R^n$ and target output data $t_i = [t_{i1}, t_{i2}, \cdots, t_{im}]^T \in R^m$. The ELM can be trained to obtain the following model:

$$y_i = \sum_{j=1}^{L} \beta_j g(\omega_j \cdot x_i + b_j) \tag{9}$$

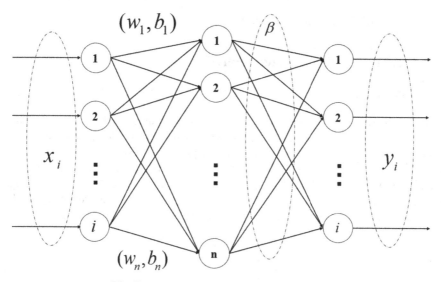

Fig. 5. Structure of extreme learning machine.

where: $y_i = [y_{i1}, y_{i2}, \cdots, y_{im}]^T$ is the input x_i of the i training sample processed by ELM; $\beta_j = [\beta_{j1}, \beta_{j2}, \cdots, \beta_{jm}]^T$ is the output weight of the j hidden layer neuron; $g(\cdot)$ is the activation function; $\omega_j = [\omega_{j1}, \omega_{j2}, \cdots, \omega_{jn}]^T$ is the input weight of the j th hidden layer neuron; $\omega_j \cdot x_i$ is the inner product of ω_j and x_i; b_j is the bias of the j th hidden layer neuron.

Since ELM can approximate the training sample with a minimal error, the target output of the training sample can be expressed as:

$$t_i = \sum_{j=1}^{L} \beta_j g(\omega_j \cdot x_i + b_j) \tag{10}$$

The corresponding matrix form is:

$$T = H\beta \tag{11}$$

where: T is the target output matrix, H is the hidden output matrix, and β is the hidden output weight matrix.

When the input weights and biases of the hidden layer are generated, H it is a constant matrix. Therefore, the solution β can be considered as the problem of solving the least squares solution of a linear system, i.e., the optimal value β to find so that the cost function (the mode of the difference between the ELM model output and the target output) is minimized.

$$\|H\beta^* - T\| = \min_{\beta}\|H\beta - T\| \tag{12}$$

From the theory of line generation and matrix theory, the least-squares solution β^* of β can be expressed as:

$$\beta^* = H^\dagger T \tag{13}$$

where: $H^\dagger$ is the Moore-Penrose generalized inverse of H.

4 Experimental Results and Analysis

4.1 Evaluation Indexes

In order to better describe the prediction performance of the model, the mean absolute error (MAE), mean square error (MSE), root mean square error (RMSE), and coefficient of determination (R^2) and are used to analyze the prediction results. Among them, MSE is used to reflect the degree of difference between the predicted quantity and the actual value; R^2 is used to judge the degree of fit of the regression equation, and its value range is [0, 1], the larger the R^2 is, the better the model fit is; MAE reflects the average of the absolute value of the error between the predicted value and the actual value.

$$MAE_{L,a,b} = \frac{1}{n} \sum_{i=1}^{n} |y_i - y_i^*| \tag{14}$$

$$MSE_{L,a,b} = \frac{1}{n} \sum_{i}^{n} (y_i - y_i^*)^2 \tag{15}$$

$$RMSE_{L,a,b} = \sqrt{\frac{\sum_{i=1}^{n} (y_i - y_i^*)^2}{n}} \tag{16}$$

$$R_{L,a,b}^2 = 1 - \frac{\sum_{i=1}^{n} (y_i - y_i^*)^2}{\sum_{i=1}^{n} (y_i - \bar{y}_i)^2} \tag{17}$$

where: n is the number of predicted samples; y_i and y_i^* are the actual and predicted values of samples at a time i, respectively; and $\bar{y}_i$ is the mean value of the actual samples.

4.2 Data Acquisition and Pre-processing

To extract the RGB values in the digital images, 1137 colors from the Pantone Colors-RGB Coated color chart were selected. In each color region, the average value of Lab colors was measured using a chromaticity instrument. 1137 colors were distributed on 55 swatch sheets and captured one by one by the built experimental platform, and the captured images are shown in Fig. 6(a). The color card images captured by the experimental platform were used to measure the R, G, and B color values in the corresponding regions using a Python program, as shown in Fig. 6(b), and the average value of each color value in the selected regions was calculated. The RGB values and Lab values are shown in Table 3.

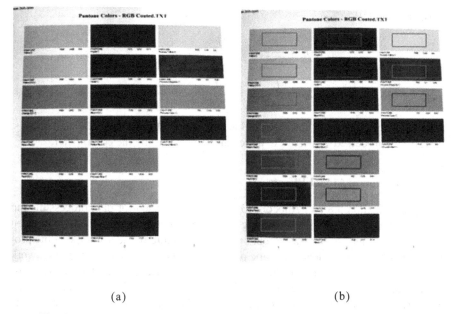

(a)   (b)

Fig. 6. Color card diagram. (a) Acquired image; (b) Extracted RGB color values.

Table 3. Acquired RGB values and Lab values.

No.	R	G	B	L	a	b
1	228.74	178.59	3.59	79.29	4.04	64.04
2	236.56	177.67	8.32	78.44	5.27	61.18
3	229.89	77.86	25.13	64.61	31.19	38.04
4	213.48	43.13	40.48	57.52	41.94	23.17
5	196.98	36.13	45.38	55.21	41.8	15.72
⋮	⋮	⋮	⋮	⋮	⋮	⋮
1133	116.36	93.8	103.54	60.05	5.17	−4.75
1134	108.91	105.43	135.52	60.68	0.92	−11.22
1135	79.9	117	154.82	60.7	−10.97	−14.92
1136	99.51	138.15	142.57	64.21	−13.15	−6.78
1137	108.13	138.44	108.56	63.64	−13.56	3.57

Due to the large type and quantity of collected data, any abnormal data caused by errors in these collected data will adversely affect the accuracy of the prediction model setup, which will lead to more significant errors in the prediction results and eventually make the model less reliable. Therefore, it is necessary to pre-process the data as shown in Eqs. (18) and (19):

$$r = \frac{R}{255}, g = \frac{G}{255}, b = \frac{B}{255} \tag{18}$$

$$L_1 = \frac{L}{100}, a_1 = \frac{a}{128}, b_1 = \frac{b}{128} \tag{19}$$

where: r, g, b are processed values; R, G, B are the values of extracted color card images; L_1, a_1, b_1 are processed values; L, a, b are values measured by the colorimeter.

4.3 Comparison of Model Effects

In this paper, Python 3.8 and Anoconda3 platform were used for data processing and modeling based on Windows 11 operating system. Simulation studies of the established models were conducted. In order to obtain a clearer picture of the accuracy of the proposed methods, linear models, quadratic polynomial regression models, neural network models, and extreme learning machine models were compared during the experiments. The 1137 data sets were divided into two groups, 920 of which were selected as the training set of the prediction network model and 217 of which were selected as the test set of the prediction model. Through the training and testing of different prediction models, the prediction results of the four models for L^*, a^*, b^* values were obtained.

To verify the validity and reliability of our collected color cards for L^*, a^*, b^* value prediction, the evaluation metrics of several models are shown in the table. As can be seen from the table, by comparing the four models, each index of the linear and quadratic polynomial models of the traditional method is at a disadvantage compared with the deep learning method. And the prediction model of the extreme learning machine has a better prediction for L^*, a^* and b^*. The MAE is 0.021, 0.017 and 0.010, MSE is 0.0006, 0.0005 and 0.0001, RMSE is 0.026, 0.021 and 0.031, R^2 reaches 0.96, 0.97 and 0.96, respectively (Tables 4, 5 and 6).

Table 4. Comparison results of different models for L^* evaluation indexes.

L^*	MAE	MSE	RMSE	R^2
Linear model	0.025	0.001	0.031	0.94
Quadratic polynomial model	0.026	0.001	0.032	0.93
Neural network models	0.023	0.0008	0.029	0.95
ELM model	**0.021**	**0.0006**	**0.026**	**0.96**

Table 5. Comparison results of different models for a^* evaluation index.

a^*	MAE	MSE	RMSE	R^2
Linear model	0.025	0.001	0.033	0.94
Quadratic polynomial model	0.024	0.001	0.033	0.93
Neural network models	0.021	0.001	0.031	0.94
ELM model	**0.017**	**0.0005**	**0.021**	**0.97**

Table 6. Comparison results of different models for b^* evaluation indexes.

b^*	MAE	MSE	RMSE	R^2
Linear model	0.039	0.0026	0.051	0.89
Quadratic polynomial model	0.038	0.0024	0.049	0.88
Neural network models	0.041	0.0024	0.050	0.91
ELM model	**0.010**	**0.0001**	**0.031**	**0.96**

The scatter plot of the predicted versus actual values of the four models is given in Fig. 7. Among them, according to the R^2 representing the goodness of fit of the predicted value to the actual value, among the four models, the R^2 of the extreme learning machine model is close to 1 in the gradient of the regression line of, and the model has a better prediction effect. The fitting effects of the other three models are the neural network model, linear model, and quadratic polynomial model, in that order.

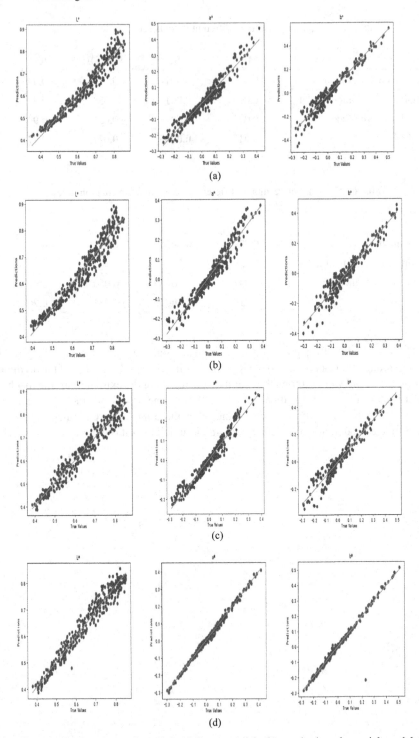

Fig. 7. Scatter fit plots for each model. (a) linear model; (b) quadratic polynomial model; (c) neural network model; (d) extreme learning machine model.

5   Conclusion

In this study, under controlled conditions (illumination, distance between camera and color card, camera angle, and light source), Using the image acquisition system built by the experimental platform, the conversion prediction of digital images to $L^*a^*b^*$ color values was established by extracting the RGB values of color cards. The experimental results show that the extreme learning machine model has more robust performance and higher prediction accuracy than the linear model, quadratic polynomial model, and neural network model. The model can meet the prediction requirements of RGB to $L^*a^*b^*$ color conversion and has good application value.

References

1. Mahanta, D.K., Laskar, S.: Electrical insulating liquid: a review. J. Adv. Dielectr. **7**(04), 1730001 (2017)
2. Lukinac, J., Mastanjević, K., Mastanjević, K., et al.: Computer vision method in beer quality evaluation—a review. Beverages **5**(2), 38 (2019)
3. Wu, D., Sun, D.W.: Colour measurements by computer vision for food quality control–a review. Trends Food Sci. Technol. **29**(1), 5–20 (2013)
4. Samiullah, S., Roberts, J.R., Chousalkar, K.: Eggshell color in brown-egg laying hens—a review. Poult. Sci. **94**(10), 2566–2575 (2015)
5. Costa, J.J.F., Giasson, E., da Silva, E.B., et al.: Use of color parameters in the grouping of soil samples produces more accurate predictions of soil texture and soil organic carbon. Comput. Electron. Agric. **177**, 105710 (2020)
6. Chu, S.J., Trushkowsky, R.D., Paravina, R.D.: Dental color matching instruments and systems. Review of clinical and research aspects. J. Dentist. **38**, e2–e16 (2010)
7. Hu, C., Mei, H., Guo, H., et al.: Color analysis of textile fibers by microspectrophotometry. Forensic Chem. **18**, 100221 (2020)
8. Leong, Y.S., Ker, P.J., Jamaludin, M.Z., et al.: UV-Vis spectroscopy: a new approach for assessing the color index of transformer insulating oil. Sensors **18**(7), 2175 (2018)
9. Ma, J., Ruan, S., Hu, J., et al.: The intrinsic relationship between color variation and performances of the deteriorated aviation lubrication oil. J. Ind. Eng. Chem. **92**, 88–95 (2020)
10. Duarte, D.P., Nogueira, R.N., Bilro, L.: Low-cost color assessment of turbid liquids using supervised learning data analysis–proof of concept. Sens. Actuators, A **305**, 111936 (2020)
11. Zobkov, M.B., Zobkova, M.V.: New spectroscopic method for accurate color determination in natural water with the high agreement with visual methods. Water Res. **177**, 115773 (2020)
12. N'cho, J.S., Fofana, I., Hadjadj, Y., et al.: Review of physicochemical-based diagnostic techniques for assessing insulation condition in aged transformers. Energies **9**(5), 367 (2016)
13. Schelkopf, C.S., Rice, E.A., Swenson, J.K., et al.: Nix Pro Color Sensor provides comparable color measurements to the HunterLab colorimeter for fresh beef. J. Food Sci. Technol. **58**, 3661–3665 (2021)
14. Dussán-Sarria, S., Garzón-García, A.M., Melo-Sevilla, R.E.: Desarrollo y evaluación de un prototipo de medición de color en vegetales frescos. Información tecnológica **31**(1), 253–260 (2020)
15. Zhang, S., Guo, Y.: Measurement of gem colour using a computer vision system: a case study with Jadeite-Jade. Minerals **11**(8), 791 (2021)
16. Nguyen, C.N., Vo, V.T., Ha, N.C.: Developing a computer vision system for real-time color measurement–a case study with color characterization of roasted rice. J. Food Eng. **316**, 110821 (2022)

17. Heng, C., Shen, H., Wang, F., et al.: Calibrated color measurement of cashmere using a novel computer vision system. Measurement **185**, 109991 (2021)
18. Su, Z., Yang, J., Li, P., et al.: Colour space conversion model from CMYK to CIELab based on CS-WNN. Color. Technol. **137**(3), 272–279 (2021)
19. Su, Z., Yang, J., Li, P., Jing, J., Zhang, H.: A precise method of color space conversion in the digital printing process based on PSO-DBN. Text. Res. J. **92**(9–10), 1673–1681 (2022). https://doi.org/10.1177/00405175211067287
20. Heng, C., Shen, H., Wang, F.: A novel digital imaging method for measuring cashmere color and its application. Text. Res. J. **91**(21–22), 2528–2539 (2021)
21. Zhang, J., Liu, Y., Zhang, X., et al.: Evaluation and consistency calibration of hyperspectral imaging system based on liquid crystal tunable filter for fabric color measurement. Color. Res. Appl. **47**(2), 401–415 (2022)
22. Huang, G.B., Zhu, Q.Y., Siew, C.K.: Extreme learning machine: a new learning scheme of feedforward neural networks. In: 2004 IEEE International Joint Conference on Neural Networks (IEEE Cat. No. 04CH37541), vol. 2, pp. 985–990. IEEE (2004). Author, F.: Article title. Journal 2(5), 99–110 (2016)
23. Author, F.: Article title. Journal 2(5), 99–110 (2016)

A Diverse Environment Coal Gangue Image Segmentation Model Combining Improved U-Net and Semi-supervised Automatic Annotation

Xiuhua Liu[1], Wenbo Zhu[1(✉)], Zhengjun Zhu[2], Lufeng Luo[1], Yunzhi Zhang[1], and Qinghua Lu[1]

[1] School of Mechatronic Engineering and Automation, Foshan University, Foshan 528000, China
zhuwenbo@fosu.edu.cn

[2] China Coal Technology Engineering Group Tangshan Research Institute, Tangshan 063000, China

Abstract. The problem of uneven illumination in the coal gangue image and the existence of fine coal gangue reduces the accuracy of the coal gangue location, which also makes it difficult to the annotation of the coal gangue images. In this paper, we propose an improved U-Net gangue segmentation algorithm to achieve gangue sorting and automatic image annotation under diversified environments. Specifically, to solve the problem that some fine coal and gangue fragments are difficult to be recognized, the InceptionV1 module is introduced instead of some of these convolutional blocks. Secondly, to solve the visual blur caused by light changes in industrial sites, the CPAM attention module is added to the fusion part of U-Net. Finally, to alleviate the difficulty of coal gangue image annotation, a semi-supervised human-in-the-loop automatic annotation framework is constructed, and a statistical method based on classification probability is proposed to automatically screen the questionable labels. The experimental results show that the proposed improved segmentation model exhibits good performance in the coal gangue sorting task with MIoU values of 80.23% and MPA values of 86.16%, which have higher accuracy compared to the original model. In addition, the statistical method proposed in this study can effectively screen out the incorrect and correct labeled data, thus enabling automatic annotation and screening.

Keywords: Semantic Segmentation · Coal Gangue Sorting · Automatic Annotation

1 Introduction

The distinction between coal gangue and coal still relies on workers' visual observation and tapping touch, but most of the coal gangue and coal with similar shape characteristics are difficult to distinguish. In addition, when working in diverse environments, the problem of uneven illumination and the presence of fine gangue can lead to sorting errors

F. Sun et al. (Eds.): ICCSIP 2023, CCIS 1919, pp. 167–179, 2024.
https://doi.org/10.1007/978-981-99-8021-5_13

and reduced sorting efficiency, thereby increasing the risk of safety hazards [1]. To cope with the impact of diverse environments, some traditional coal gangue sorting methods are being proposed and have improved the efficiency of sorting to some extent. Yang [2] constructed a system based on different impact contacts and used a support vector machine approach for identification. Hu [3] used a Bayesian algorithm to classify the generated multispectral images, which guarantees a certain accuracy but still has some shortcomings compared to deep learning algorithms. These methods have achieved some results, but still cannot solve the problem of accuracy degradation. Replacing traditional sorting methods with deep learning algorithms is important for solving diverse environmental problems and intelligent sorting of coal gangue [4]. In addition, the annotation of coal gangue images becomes difficult due to the diverse environment, and although most of the image annotation tasks can be accomplished by existing annotation tools, they also consume a large number of labor costs. To solve these problems, researchers have proposed some automatic annotation methods. Mahajan [5] proposed an end-to-end machine learning model that uses a limited number of features to predict lane-changing actions in unlabeled data, an approach that enables the annotation of small batches of data but cannot be applied to multi-feature targets. He [6] proposed a new two-stage neural embedding framework that has a redundant perceptual graph-based ranking process but cannot annotate objects with large feature differences. Balzategui [7] designed an anomaly detection model based on generative adversarial networks (GAN) that can detect and localize anomalous patterns inside solar cells from the beginning, but the model was trained using only defect-free samples and without any manual annotation, which is prone to labeling errors.

Combining the shortcomings and advantages of the above paper, in this paper, we first solve the problem that some fine coal and gangue fragments are difficult to be identified by introducing the InceptionV1 module. Secondly, the CPAM attention module is added in the feature fusion part to reduce the loss of segmentation errors caused by different lighting variations in industrial sites and improve the accuracy of segmentation. Finally, a semi-supervised human-in-the-loop automatic annotation framework is constructed based on the improved network model, and a statistical method based on classification probability is proposed to realize automatic annotation and to be able to automatically screen questionable labels.

2 Related Work

Uneven illumination and the presence of fine gangue reduce the accuracy of gangue localization and the difficulty of gangue image annotation are two important challenges for the development of intelligent gangue sorting. Some deep learning algorithms that can cope with diverse environments and improve the accuracy of coal gangue sorting have already achieved some success. Pan [8] used SE and SPP modules to improve the YOLOv3 model, enhance the accuracy of the network, and improve the speed of coal gangue identification. Xu [9] proposed an improved microminiature detection algorithm that can achieve reduced computational effort while guaranteeing a certain level of accuracy in response to the inconvenient deployment of high-performance and energy-consuming hardware devices required for deep learning in industrial sites. Song [10] used the improved effect of data enhancement and feature weighting fusion to improve the detection of coal gangue by YOLOv5, but the gangue could still not be accurately identified under illumination changes. The difficulty and huge cost of gangue image annotation have restricted the development of gangue segmentation algorithms, and some automatic annotation methods for specific objects have been generated. Chen [11] proposed a deep neural network (DNN) to annotate project targets and developed a dictionary-based multi-label classification (MLC) method to annotate projects for classifying description documents of river restoration projects, which worked well but could not be applied to the field of coal gangue sorting. Liu [12] proposed a spatially indexed hybrid atlas forest model based on an automatic annotation method in which the atlas is arbitrarily selected as the reference image in the proposed framework, which achieves randomness but does not apply to two similar objects, gangue, and coal.

Compared with existing deep learning-based coal gangue sorting algorithms, our method has three unique features.

(1) Solve the problem that some fine coal and gangue fragments are difficult to be identified.
(2) Solve the visual blurring problem caused by lighting changes at industrial sites.
(3) Alleviate the difficulty of coal and gangue image labeling by constructing a semi-supervised human-in-the-loop automatic annotation framework and proposing a statistical method based on classification probability to automatically screen problematic labels.

3 Deep Learning Semantic Segmentation Model

Semantic segmentation models are the core and foundation of this paper. The current deep-learning models widely used for semantic segmentation include PSP Net [13], Seg Net [14], DeepLabV1 [15], DeepLabV2 [16], DeepLabV3 [17], DeepLabV3+ [18], and U-Net [19]. U-Net is widely used in medical image segmentation. Since the characteristics of the gangue images with insignificant sample feature differences and dense targets are similar to those of medical image samples, U-Net is chosen as the basis of the gangue segmentation network model in this paper.

A significant advantage of U-Net is that in the enhanced feature extraction network part, each feature layer is fused with the feature layer in the backbone network, and such an operation can effectively preserve the feature information of the image. Therefore, referring to the framework of the original U-Net, as shown in Fig. 1, the part of its backbone network is modified in this paper. The backbone feature extraction part of the original U-Net is composed of a large number of convolutional layers and maximum pooling layers, and its overall structure is similar to that of VGG16. Based on this, the InceptionV1 module is added to the backbone network in this paper. The InceptionV1 module is derived from Googlenet, and the method of convolution and re-aggregation of images at multiple scales allows the network to more fully extract information from gangue images, thus enabling the localization of tiny targets. In addition, to address the shortcomings exhibited by the original network in extracting image information with uneven illumination, this paper adds the attention mechanism CPAM in the upsampling part, which can extract regional features by considering the correlation between gangue and coal, capturing the information that is easily lost in the case of uneven illumination, enhancing the ability of the network to extract information and improving the segmentation accuracy of the gangue sorting network.

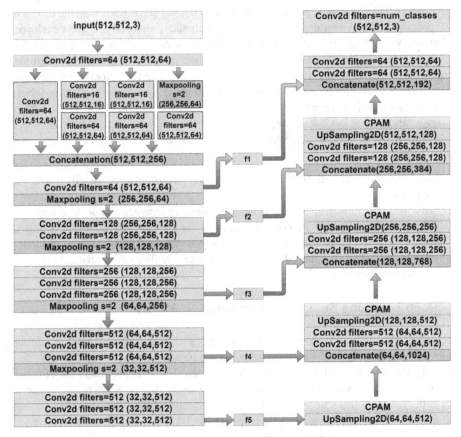

Fig. 1. Structure diagram of the improved U-Net.

4　Realization Methods of Human-in-the-Loop and Active Sensing

The overall framework for human-in-the-loop and active sensing is shown in Fig. 2. This framework consists of three parts: pre-training of the human-in-the-loop network, automatic labeling and screening of the active sensing, and manual correction. First, the improved network is trained using a small amount of accurately labeled training data to achieve pre-training of the human-in-the-loop network. Then, a large amount of unlabeled data is passed into the network to enable automatic screening. Finally, the screened mislabels are manually corrected and passed into the network as new data for further training, making the network segmentation more efficient and automatic labeling more effective.

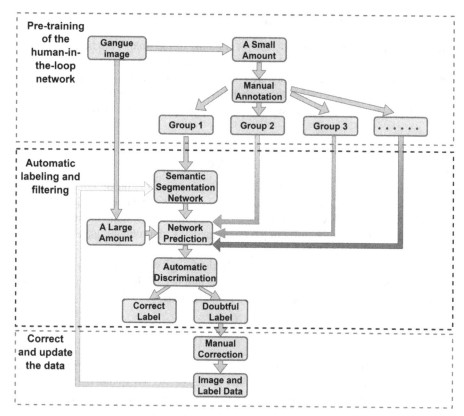

Fig. 2. General framework.

4.1 Pre-training of the Human-in-the-Loop Network

For the network to have good prediction and to be able to obtain the discriminatory criteria between incorrect and correct labels, pre-training of the human-in-the-loop network is performed. Manually label 1000 images collected from the gangue sorting site and divide the 1000 data into five groups, one group of 200. First, after the first set of images is passed into the improved U-Net model for training, the second set of images is fed into the model for prediction to obtain the predicted images, where red is the coal block and green is the coal gangue. After the prediction is completed, the predicted images are compared with the real images to filter out the erroneous images. The number of pixel points with category probability values between 0.45 and 0.55 in each incorrect image is counted, and the ratio of these numbers to the number of all pixel points in the whole image is calculated. Then all the corrected images of the second group are passed into the network as new data to continue the training. The remaining three sets of images are processed through the same process to obtain four groups of pixel ratios.

4.2 Automatic Annotation and Filtering

As image segmentation is to classify the pixel points of the image, the network model will judge the category of each pixel point of the gangue image to get the corresponding probability value, where the category are coal, gangue, and background. The Softmax function is used to judge whether the probability value is between 0.45 and 0.55. The probability value of a possible classification of a certain pixel point can be expressed as:

$$Softmax(Z_i) = \frac{e^{Z_i}}{\sum_{C=1}^{C} e^{Z_C}} \tag{1}$$

where Z_i represents the output value of a node. C represents the number of output nodes and the number of categories classified. Z_C represents the C-dimensional vector. The Softmax function allows converting the output value of the multiclassification to a probability distribution in the range of [0, 1] summed to 1, thus obtaining the probability value of the classification of the pixel.

Counting the number of all pixel points in the image with probability values distributed between 0.45 and 0.55, the ratio of the number of these pixel points to the number of total pixel points is calculated and expressed as:

$$X = \frac{B}{A} \times 100\% \tag{2}$$

where A represents the total number of all pixel points in the image. B represents the total number of pixel points for all probability values between 0.45 and 0.55.

Iterative updating of the model enables the pixel ratio to drop to a stable threshold. When the pixel ratio of the automatically annotated predicted images exceeds the set threshold, the network screens out these erroneous images and corrects itself, thus enabling automatic annotation and screening by active sensing.

4.3 Correct and Update the Data

The corrected error prediction labels are passed into the model for a new round of training. With the addition of new data, the model can be trained to obtain a good deep learning model to be applied to the coal gangue sorting process at the coal mining site and to achieve automatic labeling and screening of large amounts of data to improve production efficiency and reduce the human burden. Compared to traditional manual labeling, the automatic labeling method reduces the error of manual labeling and the cost of manual labeling. This method not only automatically screens the incorrectly predicted labels but also improves the generality of the network. Therefore, this human-in-the-loop and active-aware approach solves the problem of labeling and screening in data labeling, reduces the pressure of manual labeling while improving the sorting efficiency of coal mining sites, and ultimately promotes industrial transformation and upgrading.

5   Test Results and Analysis

The gangue images used in this study are from the coal mine industrial sites. To validate the method in this paper, an industrial camera is set up on the sorting device at the coal mining site for data acquisition, and a light source device is used to provide a uniform and stable illumination environment. The obtained gangue images are shown in Fig. 3. It can be seen that the difference between coal and gangue is not significant under the light source irradiation at the coal mine site, which increases the difficulty of sorting. A total of 20,000 images were taken for this experiment, of which 1,000 manually labeled images were used for pre-training the model. The other images were used to verify the human-in-the-loop and active-sensing coal gangue sorting and automatic labeling methods.

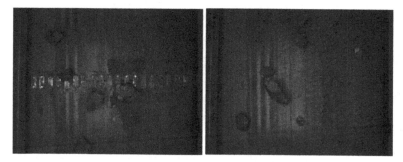

Fig. 3. Coal gangue image.

5.1   Performance Evaluation Index of the Model

Two commonly used evaluation metrics in the field of semantic segmentation are Mean Pixel Accuracy (MPA) and Mean Intersection over Union (MIoU). MPA means that the proportion of pixels correctly classified for each class is calculated separately and then averaged cumulatively. MIoU is calculated for each class separately, and the IoUs of all the classes are summed to find the average value, where IoU refers to the intersection of the genuine and predicted values of the pixel divided by the union of the genuine and predicted values of the pixel. The equations for MPA and MIoU are:

$$MPA = sum(Pi) / T \tag{3}$$

$$MIoU = \left(\frac{TP}{TP + FP + FN} + \frac{TN}{TN + FN + FP} \right) / 2 \tag{4}$$

where P_i represents the proportion of correctly classified pixels in each category. T represents the total number of categories. TP represents the number of pixels of the correct coal predicted out of the total number of genuine pixels of all coals. FP represents the number of pixels predicted to become coal out of the total number of genuine pixels of all coal gangue. FN represents the number of pixels predicted to be gangue out of the total number of genuine pixels of all coals. TN represents the number of pixels of the correct gangue is predicted from the total number of genuine pixels of all gangue.

5.2 Training and Validation of Different Segmentation Models

This paper compares different models for coal gangue image segmentation and finds U-Net to be the most suitable base model. The training images are all manually labeled 1000 coal gangue images of size 1440 × 1080. The optimizer used in this experiment is Adam. In the actual training, the batch size parameter is 8 and the number of iterations is set to 500. The experimental results of different models on test data are compared in Table 1. U-Net outperforms the other models on all index data.

Table 1. Test results of different models.

Model	MIoU/%	MPA/%	Coal IoU/%	Stone IoU/%
U-Net	**74.36**	**80.66**	**58.45**	**64.74**
PSP Net	57.83	70.47	35.12	45.34
Seg Net	60.61	70.55	54.48	57.63
DeepLabV1	71.33	74.82	50.63	60.91
DeepLabV2	72.81	73.65	58.02	61.22
DeepLabV3	72.77	78.58	56.97	62.88
DeepLabV3+	73.49	78.06	52.73	63.83

5.3 Model Improvement for Uneven Illumination and Fine Coal Gangue

The article adds the InceptionV1 module to the U-Net model to improve fine-grained gangue detection and CPAM [20] to address the difficulty of uneven illumination. The experimental results indicate that the improved U-Net model performs best among all evaluation indicators. The experimental results are summarized in Table 2.

Table 2. Performance comparison of different network models.

Model	MIoU/%	MPA/%	Coal IoU/%	Stone IoU/%
U-Net+InceptionV1+CPAM	**80.23**	**86.18**	**63.24**	**71.86**
U-Net+InceptionV1	76.33	83.64	61.75	68.41
U-Net+InceptionV1+SENet	77.34	85.77	62.01	68.68

(*continued*)

Table 2. (*continued*)

Model	MIoU/%	MPA/%	Coal IoU/%	Stone IoU/%
U-Net+InceptionV1+ECA	76.52	84.73	62.51	68.54
U-Net+InceptionV1+CA	76.41	82.22	61.81	68.72
U-Net+InceptionV1+CBAM	77.20	84.51	62.86	69.34
U-Net+VGG16	76.42	84.70	60.12	69.41
U-Net+VGG16+SENet	76.56	85.23	60.84	69.11
U-Net+VGG16+ECA	77.70	86.10	62.55	70.32
U-Net+VGG16+CA	75.50	84.89	60.01	66.77
U-Net+VGG16+CBAM	78.24	85.63	62.74	69.56
U-Net+VGG16+CPAM	77.86	85.55	61.76	68.84

Identification and Positioning of Fine Coal Gangue. As shown in Fig. 4, comparing the model with VGG16 as the backbone network, the prediction results after adding the InceptionV1 module can see that the inclusion of the InceptionV1 module can identify the fine gangue in the image more accurately, which proves that the unique convolution and pooling operation of the InceptionV1 module can locate the fine gangue in the image and enhance the extraction of image pixel information, thus enabling more accurate discrimination. All green parts in the figure are coal gangue and red parts are coal.

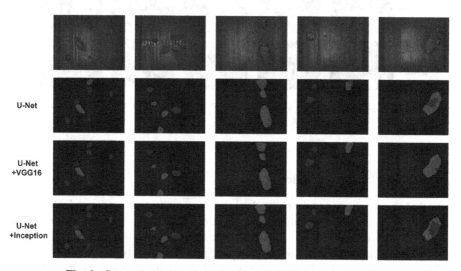

Fig. 4. Comparison of prediction images of different network models.

Prediction of Images with Excessive Brightness Illumination and Excessive Darkness Illumination. As shown in Figs. 5 and 6, the prediction results of the network models incorporating CPAM, SE Net [21], ECA [22], CA [23], and CBAM [24] for gangue images under excessive brightness illumination and excessive dark illumination, respectively. It can be seen that by considering the correlation between gangue and coal, the CPAM module can sufficiently extract the regional features and capture the information that is easily lost in the case of uneven illumination, thus effectively solving the problem of low segmentation accuracy due to over-bright illumination and over-dark illumination. All green parts in the figure are coal gangue and red parts are coal.

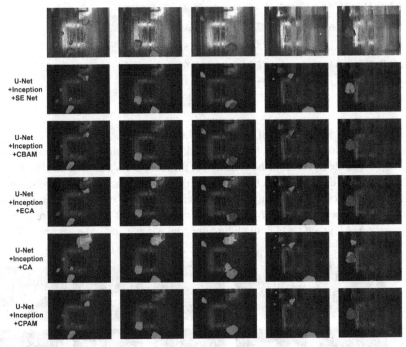

Fig. 5. Image prediction of coal gangue under excessive brightness illumination.

5.4 Setting of Pixel Ratio Index

Since the pre-training part of the network has been manually annotated with 1000 labels, the pixel ratio results obtained after comparing the four sets of predicted labels with the genuine labels are shown in Fig. 7. After the second set of images was predicted, it was found by observation that when the ratio of pixel points with probability values of 0.45–0.55 to all pixel points in an image exceeded 10.41%, that image needed to be corrected. The ratio gradually decreases in the third, fourth, and fifth groups, which indicates that the iterative update of the network makes the ratio gradually stable and allows automatic screening.

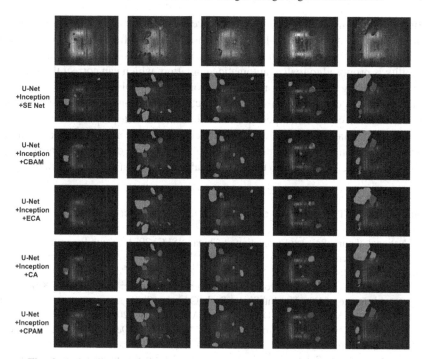

U-Net +Inception +SE Net

U-Net +Inception +CBAM

U-Net +Inception +ECA

U-Net +Inception +CA

U-Net +Inception +CPAM

Fig. 6. Image prediction of coal gangue under excessive darkness illumination.

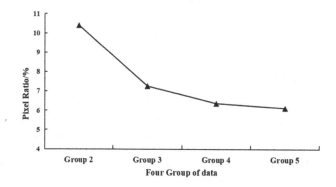

Fig. 7. Results of the pixel ratio.

6 Conclusion

Aiming at the problems of low segmentation accuracy and difficult annotation of training data by the traditional supervised deep learning gangue segmentation algorithm, this paper proposes a coal gangue sorting method based on improved U-Net. Firstly, we solve the problem that some fine coal and gangue fragments are difficult to be recognized by introducing the InceptionV1 module. Secondly, the CPAM attention module is added in the feature fusion part to reduce the loss of segmentation errors caused by different lighting variations in industrial sites and improve the accuracy of segmentation. Finally, a semi-supervised human-in-the-loop automatic annotation framework is constructed based on the improved network model, and a statistical method based on classification probability is proposed to realize automatic annotation, which can correct the incorrect labels after filtering them out automatically according to the pixel ratio, and achieve the annotation process of human-in-the-loop and active perception to reduce the enormous manual annotation costs. The experimental results show that the proposed improved segmentation model has higher accuracy, can effectively extract image information under uneven illumination, and can identify fine gangue. In addition, due to the iterative updating of the network, the pixel ratio tends to be stable, which can effectively annotate and filter.

Acknowledgment. The successful completion of this work is thanks to the support of the following projects:

A. National Natural Science Foundation of China (NSFC) 2021 - Youth Program: "Research on Adaptation Problem and Update Mechanism of Online Learning of Data Stream in Visual Ash Measurement of Flotation Tail Coal" (62106048).

B. Guangdong Key Area R&D Program: "New Generation Artificial Intelligence" Key Special Project "Multi-degree-of-Freedom Intelligent Body Complex Skills Autonomous Learning, Key Components and 3C Manufacturing Demonstration Applications" (2021B010410002).

C. Guangdong Key Area R&D Program Project: "Research and Development of Micron-level Real-time Vision Inspection Technology and System" (2020B0404030001).

D. Southern Marine Science and Engineering Guangdong Provincial Laboratory (Zhuhai) Independent Research Project: "Research and Application Demonstration of Key Technology for Cooperative Search of Small Targets in Shallow Sea Underwater" (SML2022SP101).

References

1. Song, M., Wang, J., Zhao, J., Balezentis, T., Shen, Z.: Production and safety efficiency evaluation in Chinese coal mines: accident deaths as undesirable output. Ann. Oper. Res. **291**(1), 827–845 (2020)
2. Yang, Y., Zeng, Q.: Multipoint acceleration information acquisition of the impact experiments between coal gangue and the metal plate and coal gangue recognition based on SVM and Serial Splicing Data. Arab. J. Sci. Eng. **46**(3), 2749–2768 (2021)
3. Hu, F., Zhou, M., Yan, P., Liang, Z., Li, M.: A Bayesian optimal convolutional neural network approach for classification of coal and gangue with multispectral imaging. Opt. Lasers Eng. **156**, 107081 (2022)
4. Plessis, J.J.L.: Active explosion barrier performance against methane and coal dust explosions. Int. J. Coal Sci. Technol. **2**(4), 261–268 (2015). https://doi.org/10.1007/s40789-015-0097-7
5. Mahajan, V., Katrakazas, C., Antoniou, C.: Prediction of lane-changing maneuvers with automatic labeling and deep learning. Transp. Res. Rec. **2674**(7), 336–347 (2020)
6. He, D., Ren, Y., Khattak, A.M., Liu, X., Tao, S.: Automatic topic labeling using graph-based pre-trained neural embedding. Neurocomputing **463**, 596–608 (2021)
7. Balzategui, J., Eciolaza, L., MaestroWatson, D.: Anomaly detection and automatic labeling for solar cell quality inspection based on Generative Adversarial Network. Sensors **21**(13), 4361 (2021)
8. Pan, H., Shi, Y., Lei, X., Wang, Z., Xin, F.: Fast identification model for coal and gangue based on the improved tiny YOLO v3. J. Real-Time Image Proc. **19**(3), 687–701 (2022)

9. Xu, S., Zhou, Y., Huang, Y., Han, T.: YOLOv4-tiny-based coal gangue image recognition and FPGA implementation. Micromachines **13**(11), 1983 (2022)
10. Song, Q., Liu, Z., Jiang, H.: Coal gangue detection method based on improved YOLOv5. In: 3rd International Conference on Big Data, Artificial Intelligence and Internet of Things Engineering, pp. 466–469 (2022)
11. Chen, L., Wang, Y., Mo, S.: Automatic labeling of river restoration project documents based on project objectives and restoration methods. Expert Syst. Appl. **197**, 116754 (2022)
12. Liu, H., Xu, L., Song, E., Jin, R., Hung, C.C.: Automatic labeling of brain tissues in MR images through spatial indexes based hybrid atlas forest. IET Image Proc. **14**(12), 2728–2736 (2020)
13. Zhao, H., Shi, J., Qi, X., Wang, X., Jia, J.: Pyramid scene parsing network. In: Proceedings of the IEEE Conference on Computer Vision and Pattern Recognition, pp. 6230–6239 (2017)
14. Badrinarayanan, V., Kendall, A., Cipolla, R.: SegNet: a deep convolutional encoder-decoder architecture for image segmentation. IEEE Trans. Pattern Anal. Mach. Intell. **39**, 2481–2495 (2017)
15. Chen, L.C., Papandreou, G., Kokkinos, I., Murphy, K., Yuille, A.L.: Semantic image segmentation with deep convolutional nets and fully connected CRFs. arXiv preprint arXiv:1412.7062 (2014)
16. Chen, L.C., Papandreou, G., Kokkinos, I., Murphy, K., Yuille, A.L.: DeepLab: semantic image segmentation with deep convolutional nets, atrous convolution, and fully connected CRFs. IEEE Trans. Pattern Anal. Mach. Intell. **40**, 834–848 (2018)
17. Chen, L.C., Papandreou, G., Schroff, F., Adam, H.: Rethinking atrous convolution for semantic image segmentation. arXiv preprint arXiv:1706.05587 (2017)
18. Chen, L.-C., Zhu, Y., Papandreou, G., Schroff, F., Adam, H.: Encoder-Decoder with atrous separable convolution for semantic image segmentation. In: Ferrari, V., Hebert, M., Sminchisescu, C., Weiss, Y. (eds.) ECCV 2018. LNCS, vol. 11211, pp. 833–851. Springer, Cham (2018). https://doi.org/10.1007/978-3-030-01234-2_49
19. Ronneberger, O., Fischer, P., Brox, T.: U-Net: convolutional networks for biomedical image segmentation. In: Navab, N., Hornegger, J., Wells, W.M., Frangi, A.F. (eds.) MICCAI 2015. LNCS, vol. 9351, pp. 234–241. Springer, Cham (2015). https://doi.org/10.1007/978-3-319-24574-4_28
20. Zhu, W., Wang, Q., Luo, L., Zhang, Y., Lu, Q.: CPAM: cross patch attention module for complex texture tile block defect detection. Appl. Sci. **12**(23), 11959 (2022)
21. Hu, J., Shen, L., Sun, G.: Squeeze-and-excitation networks. In: Proceedings of the IEEE Conference on Computer Vision and Pattern Recognition, pp. 7132–7141 (2018)
22. Wang, Q., Wu, B., Zhu, P., Li, P., Zuo, W.: ECA-Net: efficient channel attention for deep convolutional neural networks. In: Proceedings of the IEEE/CVF Conference on Computer Vision and Pattern Recognition, pp. 11534–11542 (2020)
23. Hou, Q., Zhou, D., Feng, J.: Coordinate attention for efficient mobile network design. In: Proceedings of the IEEE/CVF Conference on Computer Vision and Pattern Recognition, pp. 13713–13722 (2021)
24. Woo, S., Park, J., Lee, J.-Y., Kweon, I.S.: CBAM: convolutional block attention module. In: Ferrari, V., Hebert, M., Sminchisescu, C., Weiss, Y. (eds.) ECCV 2018. LNCS, vol. 11211, pp. 3–19. Springer, Cham (2018). https://doi.org/10.1007/978-3-030-01234-2_1

RB-LIO: A SLAM Solution Applied to Large-Scale Dynamic Scenes with Multiple Moving Objects

Yanzhou Zhang and Liwei Zhang[✉]

School of Mechanical Engineering and Automation, Fuzhou University, Fuzhou 350116, China
lw.zhang@fzu.edu.cn

Abstract. Simultaneous Localization And Mapping (SLAM) is a critical technology for autonomous driving in urban environments. However, in environments with many moving objects, currently available LiDAR-based SLAM methods cannot effectively detect loops as they assume a static environment, resulting in unreliable trajectories. Therefore, in this paper, we propose RB-LIO, a LiDAR SLAM system based on the LIO-SAM framework. The proposed system utilizes a dynamic object segmentation module to mitigate the influence of moving objects with tight-coupled LiDAR inertial odometry. It also corrects the complete 6-DoF loop closure with BoW3D and performs pose graph optimization using GTSAM-ISAM2. We tested RB-LIO on public datasets (KITTI and MulRan) and self-collected datasets and compared it with state-of-the-art SLAM systems such as A-LOAM, LeGO-LOAM, LINS, LIO-SAM, and Fast-LIO2. The experimental results indicate that RB-LIO achieves more than 40% improvement in accuracy and a significant improvement of map quality.

Keywords: Lidar-inertial Odometry · Dynamic Object Segmentation · Loop Closure Detection

1 Introduction

Fundamental technologies for modern autonomous driving include robust and precise state estimation, localization, and mapping. Simultaneous Localization And Mapping (SLAM) is widely used in mobile robotics to construct dense 3D maps in unknown environments. The commonly used SLAM methods are based on either vision or LiDAR. Vision-based SLAM [1, 2], which often utilizes monocular or binocular cameras, extracts feature points by moving its own position and estimates the features using triangulation. However, this method is susceptible to varying lighting and weather conditions as well as motion blur [3], which reduces the method's robustness. Alternatively, 3D LiDAR is widely utilized as a sensor in SLAM due to its high resistance to interference, high resolution, and optimal functionality at night. Additionally, the latest commercial LiDAR has reduced its cost and size, making it more widely used in various applications.

In recent decades, numerous excellent LiDAR-based SLAM methods have been proposed, such as A low-drift and real-time lidar and mapping (LOAM) [4]. This method

© The Author(s), under exclusive license to Springer Nature Singapore Pte Ltd. 2024
F. Sun et al. (Eds.): ICCSIP 2023, CCIS 1919, pp. 180–192, 2024.
https://doi.org/10.1007/978-981-99-8021-5_14

utilizes point cloud edges and plane features for point cloud registration. Lightweight and ground-optimized lidar odometry on variable terrain (LeGO-LOAM) [5] extracts ground point clouds and performs ground point segmentation. LINS [6] combines LeGO-LOAM with an IMU sensor to provide lidar-inertial odometry. Tightly coupled lidar inertial odometry via smoothing and mapping (LIO-SAM) [7] and Fast direct lidar-inertial odometry (FAST-LIO2) [8] use factor graph optimization to achieve high accuracy and low drift motion estimation based on LOAM. However, these mainstream SLAM systems assume a static environment. In dynamic environments such as urban road scenes and other scenarios with vehicles and pedestrians, moving objects can place many feature points on them. As a result, the accuracy and reliability of SLAM systems are seriously impacted. Therefore, solving SLAM problems in dynamic environments is essential for ensuring safe and reliable autonomous driving.

Currently, SLAM solutions for dynamic environments are classified into real-time filtering and post-processing approaches. For instance, Suma + + (utilizing semantic segmentation) [9] removes dynamic objects. However, it is challenging to generalize semantic information from one scene to another. In contrast, Remove-first tightly-coupled lidar-inertial odometry in high dynamic environments (RF-LIO) [10] extracts dynamic objects from submaps. Post-processing dynamic point clouds methods such as ERASOR [11] and Remove, then Revert [12] are more comprehensive in filtering dynamic objects. However, these methods lack real-time filtering of dynamic objects during the SLAM mapping process.

To improve the accuracy of SLAM mapping, in addition to improving the accuracy of front-end point cloud processing, location recognition in back-end systems is also important. Loop closure detection is required when the mobile robot arrives at a previously visited location. Although distance-based associations can also be used for small-scale loop closure detection, it can cause significant attitude drift in outdoor autonomous driving environments, therefore a robust and accurate loop closure detection module is needed. Although the Scan Context [13] is widely used as the most classic LiDAR loop detection module in many open source algorithms, there are still some shortcomings, such as lacking of rotation invariance, requiring brute force matching, and lacking feature extraction, only using maximum height while ignoring many point cloud information.

This paper presents an optimized RB-LIO system that addresses the issues of dynamic target removal and loopback constraints using Bag-of-Words. The front-end point cloud processing employs Principal Component Analysis (PCA) and region growing to segment dynamic and static object point clouds, eliminating the former to improve scan matching accuracy. In the back-end loop closure detection optimization, 3D features of the LiDAR point cloud are extracted using LinK3D. Moreover, BoW3D [14] is deployed to construct 3D features by frequently updating and retrieving the bag of words. The loop closure constraints are added in real-time during the SLAM process to enhance the mapping solutions. The experimental results demonstrate a significant improvement in SLAM mapping as a result of the proposed approach.

In summary, the primary contributions of this paper are as follows: (1) The proposal of a dynamic point cloud filtering method based on Principal Component Analysis (PCA) that can be implemented in real-time during the SLAM mapping process; (2) The application of Bag-of-Words 3D (BoW3D) to the LIO system back-end optimization to provide accurate loop closure constraints for real-time SLAM mapping; (3) Experimental results demonstrate that the proposed method effectively eliminates map "ghosting" while enhancing the accuracy of 3D LiDAR SLAM.

2 Related Work

In urban traffic, dynamic targets such as vehicles and pedestrians can be found everywhere. However, most SLAM systems' front-end processing is based on the assumption of point cloud stability. To overcome this challenge, distinguishing between dynamic and static target point clouds is crucial. Currently, mainstream methods for this purpose fall into the following categories:

1. Statistical methods: Matching adjacent frames and then applying algorithms such as RANSAC [15] or ICP [16] to remove point clouds inconsistent with the matching relationship has been the typical approach to identifying dynamic point clouds. However, the effectiveness of this method declines when there are too many dynamic point clouds.
2. Ray casting-based methods: These methods for identifying dynamic voxels utilize voxel ray casting [17, 18] to differentiate dynamic voxels based on whether they are penetrated or hit by rays. But, scanning all the voxels on each beam through this method requires excessive computational power, and the accuracy of voxel size is significantly influenced.
3. Visibility-based methods: Visual visibility-based methods [10, 12] are more efficient in computational terms compared to ray-casting-based counterparts. The underlying principle is that in the presence of dynamic objects in an environment, static background points in the distance are masked by closer dynamic objects. However, such an approach is sensitive to point cloud distortion, and spurious identification of ground points could be a possibility.
4. Deep-learning-based methods: This method [19] often heavily relies on dataset calibration and requires a dataset for network training. Although this approach has achieved good results in partitioning accuracy, it can only recognize information such as vehicles and cannot determine whether an object is in motion, so it needs to be used in combination with other methods.

For the loop detection module of SLAM backend optimization, it usually includes two steps: First, finding similar positions in historical keyframes, and then using loop constraints to optimize and correct the estimated state in the pose graph. In recent years, many visual-based methods [20, 21] have been proposed, but they cannot overcome the impact of lighting changes and have poor robustness in outdoor environments. In contrast, laser-based methods can overcome defects such as lighting changes and exhibit better performance outdoors. M2DP [22] is a global 3D descriptor that projects 3D point clouds onto multiple 2D planes, generates density signatures for point clouds in each plane, and then uses the left and right singular vector values of these signatures as descriptors for the 3D point cloud. Scan Context [13] uses extended bird's-eye views of laser point clouds to calculate similarity scores to measure the distance between two scan contexts, but it does not have rotational invariance. ISC [23] proposes a loop detection method based on point cloud geometry and intensity information, and uses two-stage intensity scan contexts to detect loops. Iris [24] represents a location as a LiDAR Iris image and detects loops based on a binary signature image obtained after several Gabor filtering and thresholding operations. SSC [25] proposes a two-stage semantic ICP and semantic scan context descriptor for loop detection.

3 RB-LIO Approach

3.1 System Overview

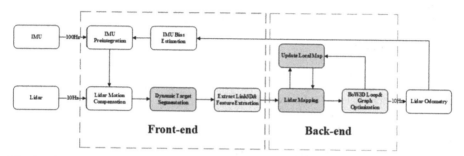

Fig. 1. The overall process of the mapping system RB-LIO is demonstrated, consisting of two parts: the front-end odometer and the back-end map optimization. The front-end IMU compensates for motion and corrects distortion in the laser point cloud, while performing dynamic object segmentation and static object feature extraction. The back-end utilizes BoW3D for loop constraint and factor graph optimization.

Figure 1 illustrates the overall framework of RB-LIO. The front-end odometer first utilizes IMU pre-integration to infer the robot's motion and correct the distortion in the laser point cloud. Then, the corrected point cloud is down-sampled, and ground normals, clusters, and PCA are computed to filter out dynamic object point clouds. Meanwhile, Link3D features are extracted from static point clouds, and plane and edge features are computed based on smoothness. The back-end optimization module incorporates loop closure constraints and factor graph optimization using BoW3D and updates the local mapping accordingly. Finally, the results are outputted to the LiDAR odometer and updated to the IMU Bias Estimation.

3.2 Dynamic Object Segmentation

The dynamic removal module is a key component of RB-LIO, as it can filter out dynamic object point clouds from the collected point cloud to satisfy the static assumption. In this module, dynamic object point clouds are filtered out for point clouds that have undergone IMU motion compensation. Ground point clouds in the environment are an important component of the static object point clouds, so ground point cloud segmentation is performed first. Algorithm 1 is used for algorithm implementation: first, point cloud data is down-sampled, and all point clouds are mapped to a three-dimensional grid space. Then, a representative point cloud is selected within a certain range to replace all point clouds in nearby areas. Next, ground normals are computed, and the point cloud is corrected to restore all point clouds to the same plane through coordinate transformation. Then, the ground plane is divided into grids, and the point clouds are segmented into ground point clouds based on the maximum relative height difference T_{re} and the maximum absolute height difference T_{ab} between the point clouds in the grid and the ground.

Algorithm 1: Ground Segmentation

Input:	Lasercloudin
Output:	Abovepoints
Define:	T_{re}: The maximum height difference in the pointcloud grid
	T_{ab}: The maximum absolute height in the point cloud grid
	Main Loop:

1	if not enable_seg:
2	return;
3	end
4	for pointcloud in Lasercloudin do
5	if visit[pointcloud]==1
6	return;
7	else
8	downsample pointcloud;
10	end
11	end
12	for pointcloud do
13	GetGndpos(pointcloud);
14	Correctpoints(Gndpos,pointscloud);
15	if pointcloud.height not in T_{re} or pointcloud.height not in T_{ab}
16	Abovepoints←pointcloud;
17	else
18	Groundpoints←pointcloud;
19	end
20	end
21	return Abovepoints;

Regarding the remaining point clouds, our algorithm, as shown in Algorithm 2, adopts a region-growing approach to separate static object point clouds, because dynamic object point clouds in urban areas are generally not very high. Thus, high point clouds are selected as seeds, and the k-d tree is searched for their neighboring points, which allows for the segmentation of static background point clouds and dynamic object point clouds.

Algorithm 2: Dynamic Object Segmentation

Input:	Abovepoints
Output:	Dynamicpoints
	Main Loop:
1	for Abovepoints do
2	if pointcloud.height>4
3	Bgpoints←pointcloud;
4	end
5	if pointcloud.height<6
6	seeds←pointcloud;
7	end
8	end
9	for seeds do
10	for seed.kdtree.radiusSearch do
11	if pointcloud not in Bgpoints or pointcloud.height<0.1
12	Bgpoints←pointcloud;
13	else
14	Dynamicpoints←pointcloud;
15	end
16	end
17	end
18	return Dynamicpoints;

3.3 Back-End Loop Closure Optimization

In this section, the LinK3D features extracted from the point cloud are updated to the BoW database. The LinK3D descriptor is represented by a 180-dimensional vector that describes the feature using neighboring point pairs around the key points. The neighborhoods around the key points are divided into 180 regions, with the first dimension being the region closest to the key point and the remaining regions arranged counterclockwise. The BoW database is stored using a hash table that stores the descriptors of point cloud frames and the IDs of the key frames, building a one-to-one mapping relationship between words and their occurrence locations. During the back-end optimization process, the database is updated in real-time and continuously searched, and an inverse document frequency (IDF) [26] mechanism is used to avoid repeatedly searching for words that appear in multiple locations. Based on the point sets $\{S_C\}$ of the current frame and $\{S_L\}$ of the matched point sets of the loop closure frame, the loop closure is calculated by minimizing the cost function, which is calculated as follows:

$$f_{c,l}\left(R_{c,l},t_{c,l}\right)=\frac{1}{2}\sum_{i=1}^{n}\left\|S_l^i-(R_{c,l}S_c^i+t_{c,l})\right\|^2 \tag{1}$$

Here, $S_c^i \in \{S_C\}$ and $S_l^i \in \{S_L\}$ represent the corresponding matched points, $R_{c,l}$ and $t_{c,l}$ and represent the rotation and translation of the $T_{c,l}$ transformation. $T_{c,l}$ is defined as follows:

$$T_{c,l}=\begin{bmatrix} R_{c,l} & t_{c,l} \\ 0^T & 1 \end{bmatrix} \tag{2}$$

Since a factor graph is used, based on the loop closure constraint result, the current state X_i is matched with candidate sub-keyframes $\{X_{m-n}, \ldots, X_m, \ldots, X_{m+n}\}$ in the BoW database. The transformation relationship is obtained and used as a loop closure factor with the IMU and odometer results for graph optimization. Feedback is provided to update the local map, and the results are outputted to the LiDAR odometer.

4 Experiments

We performed quantitative analysis of our proposed system by comparing it with A-LOAM, F-LOAM, LeGO-LOAM, LIO-SAM, and FAST-LIO2 on a laptop with an R7-5800H processor, 8 cores/16 threads, and an RTX 3060 graphics card. The methods were implemented in C + +, using Ubuntu 18.04 and ROS Melodic. The proposed method was validated on publicly available KITTI and MulRan datasets, with experiment details listed in Table 1. We also tested our method on real-world campus environment data collected using a 16-line Robosense LiDAR and 6-axis IMU mounted on the MR500 mobile robot.

4.1 Experiments on KITTI and MulRan Datasets

KITTI dataset: We conducted simulation experiments on sequences 05, 07, and 08. The dataset provides multimodal data, including RGB images, LiDAR point clouds, GPS/IMU data, and vehicle pose labels. The dataset covers a variety of driving scenarios, such as urban roads, highways, and rural roads, and also includes different weather conditions and time periods, providing rich real-world scene data.

MulRan dataset: It is a dataset aimed at urban environments provided by KAIST in Korea, including various sensors such as LiDAR, ultrasonic radar, IMU, and GPS. The dataset features designed include reverse and lane change loop closures, and scene recognition based on environmental priors. In this experiment, we selected three sequences from the Dajeon Convention Center (DCC), KAIST, and Riverside. The DCC sequence mainly includes complex situations such as narrow passages and loop closures on urban roads; the KAIST sequence contains campus scene data with a small number of dynamic targets; and the Riverside sequence has situations such as long.

Our proposed algorithm has undergone rigorous validation on the KITTI dataset, with the results firmly establishing the superiority of our approach. As demonstrated in Fig. 2, our algorithm consistently outperforms other methods in terms of generating more accurate robot motion trajectories. This achievement can be attributed to the successful integration of our specialized front-end dynamic target point cloud filtering module and our back-end loop closure optimization module, both of which contribute significantly to optimizing trajectory accuracy and precision. Further evaluation of our results was carried out using evo to measure the Root Mean Square Error (RMSE) of Absolute Trajectory Error (ATE), with the best result highlighted in bold in Table 2. Our evaluation results showed that the average error of our proposed method was 1.19m, which is markedly better than the minimum average error of 1.98 m observed among other advanced SLAM systems. This remarkable 40% accuracy improvement over other methods demonstrates that our proposed algorithm is highly effective in motion estimation and offers exceptional accuracy and precision performance.

Table 1. Details of the Experiment Sequences.

Sequences	Time(min:sec)	Distance(Km)
KITTI05	4:48	2.205
KITTI07	1:54	0.69
KITTI08	7:05	3.222
DCC01	9:13	4.912
DCC02	12:35	4.273
DCC03	12.27	5.422
KAIST01	13:41	6.124
KAIST02	14:53	5.965
KAIST03	14.22	6.249
Riverside01	9:13	6.427
Riverside02	13:35	6.613
Riverside03	17.27	7.249

Table 2. KITTI Datasets Experiment (RMSE: m)

Sequences	Method					
	A-LOAM	F-LOAM	LeGO-LOAM	LIO-SAM	FAST-LIO2	RB-LIO
KITTI05	3.171	3.594	2.699	0.879	3.602	**0.728**
KITTI07	0.510	0.560	1.037	1.385	1.689	**0.351**
KITTI08	7.951	7.809	5.074	3.686	4.949	**2.514**
Average	3.877	3.988	2.937	1.983	3.413	**1.198**

In this study, we also evaluated the performance of various SLAM systems on the MulRan dataset. Our evaluation results, as presented in Fig. 3 and Table 3., highlight the notable differences in performance between our proposed method and the LIO-SAM algorithm on the DCC, KAIST, and Riverside sequences. Despite being equipped with a loop detection module, LIO-SAM's Euclidean distance-based cycle detection module is inadequate in guaranteeing accuracy when faced with complex outdoor environments containing numerous pedestrians, vehicles, and tall buildings. In contrast, our proposed method is capable of generating more accurate trajectories with greater robustness and accuracy.

Regarding Table 3., our evaluation results demonstrate that the average absolute error of our proposed method is only 7.8m across all nine sequences of the MulRan dataset, with the minimum average absolute error of other advanced SLAM algorithms such as FAST-LIO2 being 43.4m. These findings establish that our proposed method dramatically improves accuracy by at least 82% when compared to other available algorithms. In

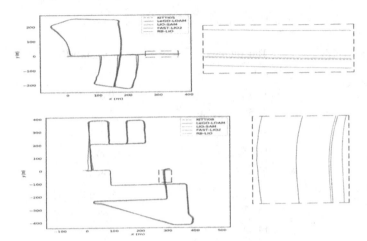

Fig. 2. Comparison results of RB-LIO 、LeGO-LOAM 、LIO-SAM and FAST-LIO2 trajectories (the purple curve is our method) on the KITTI dataset (sequences 05 and 08).

particular, our method's performance in the Riverside scene, which has fewer reference objects.

Fig. 3. RB-LIO and LIO-SAM running and trajectory comparison on the MulRan dataset (Sequences DCC02, KAIST02, and Riverside02), demonstrating that our method can effectively improve trajectory accuracy.

Table 3. MulRan Datasets Experiment (RMSE: m)

Sequences	Method					
	A-LOAM	F-LOAM	LeGO-LOAM	LIO-SAM	FAST-LIO2	RB-LIO
DCC01	39.854	38.249	88.564	36.233	26.603	**6.164**
DCC02	31.672	31.345	73.873	26.911	17.742	**3.707**
DCC03	33.376	34.156	57.419	9.119	17.305	**2.884**
KAIST01	51.863	49.843	76.902	41.912	29.905	**3.634**
KAIST02	36.657	36.657	125.564	24.474	22.308	**4.088**
KAIST03	39.846	37.865	74.159	36.892	21.658	**3.881**
Riverside01	98.678	91.516	287.233	105.158	54.214	**10.284**
Riverside02	126.368	100.193	491.877	111.795	65.752	**13.603**
Riverside03	130.828	123.182	585.215	188.014	135.212	**22.150**
Average	65.460	60.344	206.756	64.501	43.411	**7.822**

4.2 Campus Dataset Experiment

In our study, we utilized a mobile robot for the purpose of collecting information about the campus environment. The actual scene satellite map is presented in Fig. 4 (a), with multiple students positioned around the robot to maintain a safe distance during the course of the experiment. While the experiment did not feature large, moving targets such as vehicles, the presence of numerous dynamic targets for prolonged periods led to substantial "ghosting" during the mapping process. As illustrated in Fig. 4(b), the pedestrian activity during LIO-SAM's campus dataset run significantly impacted the quality of the final point cloud map, with other advanced algorithms failing to adequately address this challenge.

However, in stark contrast, our proposed method - as demonstrated in Fig. 4(c) - proved to be highly effective in terms of segmenting and filtering dynamic target point clouds, leading to a significant boost in the overall quality of the point cloud map. Indeed, the empirical results from our study provide direct evidence of the effectiveness of our dynamic target point cloud filtering method.

Overall, our study highlights the efficacy of our proposed method in improving mapping accuracy and quality in dynamic urban environments containing multiple moving targets. These findings offer valuable insight into the development of more robust SLAM systems capable of effectively handling the challenges posed by increasingly complex urban environments, paving the way for further innovation and advancement in this critical field of research.

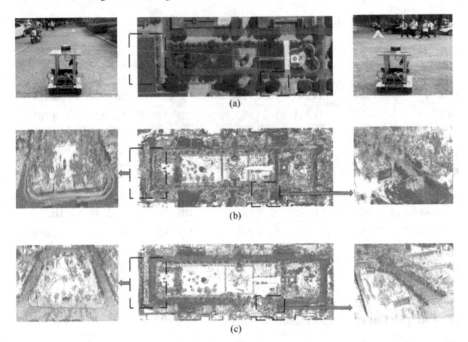

Fig. 4. (a) Satellite map of the campus dataset collection. (b) Running the campus dataset with LIO-SAM. (c) Running the campus dataset with RB-LIO.

5   Conclusion

In this paper, we introduce a novel Simultaneous Localization and Mapping (SLAM) system, RB-LIO, designed for large-scale, complex urban road environments with multi-dynamic characteristics. Our system overcomes the limitations of traditional SLAM algorithms based on static assumptions by effectively segmenting and filtering dynamic target point clouds in real-time while carrying out long-range loop detection with high accuracy. We experimentally validated and evaluated our proposed algorithm using three different datasets - KITTI, MulRan, and campus - spanning a variety of environments and rigorously benchmarked it against state-of-the-art SLAM algorithms, specifically LIO-SAM and FAST-LIO2. Our results demonstrate that the RB-LIO algorithm outperforms these advanced SLAM algorithms in terms of mapping accuracy and quality, offering a promising new direction for future research in this important area.

References

1. Qin, T., Li, P., Shen, S.: VINS-mono: a robust and versatile monocular visual-inertial state estimator. IEEE Trans. Rob. **34**(4), 1004–1020 (2018)
2. Campos, C., Elvira, R., Rodríguez, J.J.G., Montiel, J.M.M., Tardós, J.D.: ORB-SLAM3: an accurate open-source library for visual, visual–inertial, and multimap SLAM. IEEE Trans. Rob. **37**(6), 1874–1890 (2021)

3. Ye, H., Huang, H., Liu, M.: Monocular direct sparse localization in a prior 3d surfel map. In: IEEE International Conference on Robotics and Automation (ICRA), pp. 8892–8898 (2020)

4. Zhang, J., Singh. S.: LOAM: lidar odometry and mapping in real-time. In: Robotics: Science and Systems (RSS), pp. 1–9 (2014)

5. Shan, T., Englot, B.: Lightweight and ground-optimized lidar odometry and mapping on variable Terrain. In: IEEE/RSJ International Conference on Intelligent Robots and Systems (IROS), pp. 4758–4765 (2018)

6. Qin, C., Ye, H., Pranata, C.E., Han, J., Zhang, S., Liu, M.: LINS: A lidar-inertial state estimator for robust and efficient navigation. In: IEEE International Conference on Robotics and Automation (ICRA), pp. 8899–8906 (2020)

7. Shan, T., Englot, B., Meyers, D., Wang, W., Ratti, C., Rus, D.: LIO-SAM: tightly-coupled Lidar inertial odometry via smoothing and mapping. In: IEEE/RSJ International Conference on Intelligent Robots and Systems (IROS), pp. 5135–5142 (2020)

8. Xu, W., Cai, Y., He, D., Lin, J., Zhang, F.: FAST-LIO2: fast direct LiDAR-inertial odometry. IEEE Trans. Robot. **38**(4), 2053–2073 (2022)

9. Chen, X., Milioto, A., Palazzolo, E., Giguère, P., Behley, J., Stachniss, C.: SuMa++: efficient LiDAR-based semantic SLAM. In: IEEE/RSJ International Conference on Intelligent Robots and Systems (IROS), pp. 4530–4537 (2019)

10. Qian, C., Xiang, Z., Wu, Z., Sun, H.: RF-LIO: removal-first tightly-coupled lidar inertial odometry in high dynamic environments. In: IEEE/RSJ International Conference on Intelligent Robots and Systems (IROS), pp. 4421–4428 (2021)

11. Lim, H., Hwang, S., Myung, H.: ERASOR: Egocentric ratio of pseudo occupancy-based dynamic object removal for static 3D point cloud map building. IEEE Robot. Autom. Lett. **6**(2), 2272–2279 (2021)

12. Kim, G., Kim, A.: Remove, then revert: static point cloud map construction using multiresolution range images. In: IEEE/RSJ International Conference on Intelligent Robots and Systems (IROS), pp. 10758–10765 (2020)

13. Kim, G., Kim, A.: Scan context: egocentric spatial descriptor for place recognition within 3D Point cloud map. In: IEEE/RSJ International Conference on Intelligent Robots and Systems (IROS), pp. 4802–4809 (2018)

14. Cui, Y., Chen, X., Zhang, Y., Dong, J., Wu, Q., Zhu, F.: BoW3D: bag of words for real-time loop closing in 3D LiDAR SLAM. IEEE Robot. Autom. Lett. **8**(5), 2828–2835 (2023)

15. Fischler, M.A., Bolles, R.C.: Random sample consensus: a paradigm for model fitting with applications to image analysis and automated cartography. Commun. ACM **24**(6), 381–395 (1981)

16. Besl, P.J., McKay ,N.D.: Method for registration of 3-d shapes. IEEE Trans. Pattern Analy. Mach. Intell. **14**(2), 239–256 (1992)

17. Pagad, S., Agarwal, D., Narayanan, S., Rangan, K., Kim, H., Yalla, G.: Robust method for removing dynamic objects from point clouds. In: IEEE International Conference on Robotics and Automation (ICRA), pp. 10765–10711 (2020)

18. Schauer, J., Nuchter, A.: The peopleremover—removing dynamic objects from 3-d point cloud data by traversing a voxel occupancy grid. IEEE Robotics and Automation Letters. **3**(3), 1679–1686 (2018)

19. Pfreundschuh, P., Hendrikx, H.F.C., Reijgwart, V., et al.: Dynamic object aware LiDAR SLAM based on automatic generation of training data. In: IEEE International Conference on Robotics and Automation (ICRA), pp. 11641–11647 (2021)

20. Chen, Z., et al.: Deep learning features at scale for visual place recognition. In: IEEE International Conference on Robotics and Automation (ICRA), pp. 3223–3230 (2017)

21. Zaffar, M., Ehsan, S., Milford, M., et al.: CoHOG: a light-weight, compute-efficient, and training-free visual place recognition technique for changing environments. IEEE Robotics and Automation Letters. **5**(2), 1835–1842 (2020)

22. He, L., Wang, X., Zhang, H.: M2dp: a novel 3D point cloud descriptor and its application in loop closure detection. In: IEEE/RSJ International Conference on Intelligent Robots and Systems (IROS), pp. 231–237 (2016)
23. Wang, H., Wang, C., Xie, L.: Intensity scan context: coding intensity and geometry relations for loop closure detection. In: IEEE International Conference on Robotics and Automation (ICRA), pp. 2095–2101 (2020)
24. Wang, Y., Sun, Z., et al.: Lidar Iris for loop-closure detection. In: IEEE/RSJ International Conference on Intelligent Robots and Systems (IROS), pp. 5769–5775 (2020)
25. Kong, X., Yang, X., Zhai, G., et al.: Semantic graph based place recognition for 3D point clouds. In: IEEE/RSJ International Conference on Intelligent Robots and Systems (IROS), pp. 8216–8223 (2020)
26. Sivic, J., Zisserman, A.: Video google: a text retrieval approach to object matching in videos. In: Ninth IEEE International Conference on Computer Vision, p. 1470 (2003)

Object Detection with Depth Information in Road Scenes

Ruowang Liu[1], Xinbo Chen[2], and Bo Tao[3,4(✉)]

[1] Key Laboratory of Metallurgical Equipment and Control Technology, Ministry of Education, Wuhan University of Science and Technology, Wuhan, China

[2] Hubei Key Laboratory of Mechanical Transmission and Manufacturing Engineering, Wuhan University of Science and Technology, Wuhan, China

[3] Precision Manufacturing Institute, Wuhan University of Science and Technology, Wuhan, China
taoboq@wust.edu.cn, 771354876@qq.com

[4] Research Center for Biomimetic Robot and Intelligent Measurement and Control, Wuhan University of Science and Technology, Wuhan, China

Abstract. In recent years, depth estimation has witnessed significant advancements because of the development of deep learning. It's important to note that depth estimation tasks focus solely on predicting the depth of each pixel in an image and do not include object detection or object recognition. Depth estimation is the use of pixel transformations in the image to obtain distance information from each point in the scene to the camera to generate a depth map. Object detection is the process of classifying and localizing an image, given a picture, so as to identify the objects in the picture and determine their location. To overcome this limitation and integrate object detection into the depth estimation process, this paper proposes a novel self-supervised monocular depth estimation algorithm that leverages an attention mechanism. By combining object detection and depth estimation, a real-time multi-task model is designed to enable simultaneous detection and depth estimation of objects. The framework comprises four essential components: an object detection sub-network, a depth estimation sub-network, a lateral sharing unit, and an attention loss. These components work collaboratively to enhance distance estimation accuracy for objects and improve the object detection performance. Throughout experiments, it is evident that the proposed approach can effectively estimate distances to objects and enhances the accuracy of object detection.

Keywords: Attention mechanism · Depth estimation · Object detection

1 Introduction

With the continuous development of deep learning, convolutional neural networks (CNNs) have outperformed traditional algorithms in various fields such as natural language processing and computer vision. Numerous scholars and researchers have made remarkable progress in depth estimation and object detection tasks. To complement these

F. Sun et al. (Eds.): ICCSIP 2023, CCIS 1919, pp. 193–205, 2024.
https://doi.org/10.1007/978-981-99-8021-5_15

advances, this paper proposes a new method for monocular depth estimation and object detection using deep learning. The proposed algorithm combines the tasks of object detection and depth estimation by concatenating them. This is an end-to-end real-time monocular depth estimation and object detection multitasking model that uses supervised learning to continuously learn the relationship between the relative positions and distances of objects.

Traditional distance measurement algorithms have always faced limitations imposed by the environment. To overcome these limitations, researchers have increasingly shifted their focus towards predicting depth from a single image. In recent years, the continuous development of deep learning techniques has yielded fruitful research outcomes in the field of depth estimation, leading to its widespread application in domains such as 3D reconstruction [1–3], scene understanding [4, 5], and depth perception [6, 7].

In order to achieve object detection with depth information, this paper integrates the object detection task with the depth estimation task. An end-to-end real-time monocular depth estimation and object detection multi-task model is designed, enabling simultaneous object detection and distance measurement. This parallel approach ensures efficient and accurate object detection and depth estimation.

2   Related Works

2.1   Object Detection

The aim of object detection is to identify objects of interest within an image, involving two subtasks: object localization and object classification. Early object detection models relies on manual feature extractors, such as the Viola-Jones detector [8]. The introduction of convolutional neural networks and deep learning in image classification revolutionized the field of visual perception. Krizhevsky et al. introduced AlexNet, an architecture based on CNNs for image classification, which achieved remarkable performance and won the ImageNet Large-Scale Visual Recognition Challenge (ILSVRC) 2012 [9]. Subsequently, Kai-Ming He et al. proposed deep residual learning, which mitigates performance degradation by incorporating jump connections between stacked layers. These connections enable the direct flow of information from the input to the output of each block without introducing additional parameters or computational complexity to the network [10]. Addressing the issue of heavy inference computation, Wang et al. proposed CSPNet [11], which reduces repetitive gradient information in the network to reduce computational requirements.

Object detection algorithms can be categorized into two types: two-stage and single-stage, based on the approach used for extracting object detection frames. Two-stage algorithms, such as R-CNN, Fast R-CNN, and Faster R-CNN [12–14], operate sequentially and have evolved from 47 s per image to near real-time performance at approximately five frames per second. Lin et al. introduced the Feature Pyramid Network (FPN) [15], which adopts a top-down architecture and connects feature maps horizontally. Mask R-CNN [16] extends the Faster R-CNN framework by adding a parallel branch for pixel-level object instance segmentation.

This branch applies a fully connected network on region of interest (ROI) features, achieving efficient segmentation with modest computational overhead. The YOLO family of single-stage algorithms [17–20] prioritizes speed but sacrifices some accuracy compared to two-stage algorithms. Sun[21] propose an object detection algorithm for road scenes based on improved YOLOv5. Chae J [22] proposed Classification Depth Distribution Network (CaDDN) for monocular 3D object detection.

2.2 Depth Estimation

Depth estimation (DE) is a fundamental computer vision task that involves predicting depth information from one or more images. Deep learning based DE has proven to be highly efficient in various applications [23]. However, one of the key challenges in deep learning applications lies in the availability of suitable datasets for training [24, 25]. Collecting data for training can be expensive and typically involves LiDAR sensors, RGB-D cameras, or stereo vision cameras. To alleviate the dependency on training datasets, different learning strategies have been developed.

In the supervised learning approach, Li et al. [26] introduced a deep learning network incorporating conditional random fields (CRFs). They employed a two-stage network for depth estimation and refinement. Similarly, Qi et al. [27] utilized two networks to estimate depth and surface normals from a single image. Sheng et al. [28] proposed a lightweight supervised model for local-global optimization, employing a self-encoder network for depth estimation and a local-global optimization scheme to achieve a comprehensive range of scene depths.

Among the unsupervised approaches, Garg et al. [29] pioneered a promising method to learn depth in an unsupervised algorithm, eliminating the need for ground truth depth (GTD) maps. Zhou et al. [30] developed a network that simultaneously estimates depth maps and camera poses. The network takes three consecutive frames as input, and the pose CNN and depth CNN estimate the relative camera pose and depth from the first image. Chen et al. [31] tackled the channel representation problem by considering it as a frequency-based compression process, enhancing the structural perception of the scene and extracting more informative features.

In the semi-supervised learning algorithms, Kuznietsov et al. [32] proposed an SSL method that combines supervised and unsupervised loss terms during the training process.

3 Research Methods

The proposed monocular depth estimation and object detection network comprises four main components: an object detection sub-network, a depth estimation sub-network, a lateral sharing unit, and a attention loss. The overall architecture of the network is illustrated in Fig. 1.

These sub-networks leverage the shared high-dimensional features to reconstruct the depth maps, object labels, and detection bounding boxes. The depth estimation sub-network adopts an Encoder-Decoder architecture and shares knowledge with the decoder of the object detection sub-network through a lateral sharing unit. This enables

the network to make effective use of the learned features from both tasks during training, allowing for enhanced focus on the target regions. The entire training process is
supervised by an attention loss, which is a composite loss function that includes a depth
estimation loss, object detection loss, and other attention losses. This attention loss
ensures that the network receives proper guidance and optimizes both depth estimation
and object detection tasks simultaneously.

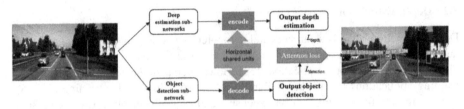

Fig. 1 Overall architecture of the monocular depth estimation and object detection model

3.1 Loss Function

The joint monocular depth estimation and object detection network is a multi-task model
that requires incorporating the training loss for object detection and depth estimation
into a unified loss function. Additionally, a depth-aware loss function is introduced to
guide the network in adaptively focusing on different regions by dynamically adjusting
the weights of each training sample, prioritizing the closer pixel samples. By combining
these three tasks, the overall training loss function is formulated as follows:

$$L_{total} = L_{det\,ect} + \beta\left(L_{depth} + L_{DA}\right) \tag{1}$$

Here, L_{detect} is object detection loss; L_{depth} is depth estimation loss; L_{DA} is depth
perception loss; β is a hyper-parameter. β was set to 0.5.

YOLOv5 uses the GIoU_Loss loss function. GIoU_Loss is a loss function distance
metric that directly satisfies the requirements of the basic loss distance function metric.
GIoU_Loss also has a strong scale invariance, the expressions are as follows:

$$L_{GIoU} = 1 - IoU + \frac{|c - b \cup b^{gt}|}{|c|} \tag{2}$$

However, when there is a two-box inclusion, GIoU_Loss degenerates into IoU_Loss
and GIoU_Loss requires many iterations to converge. Considering the shortcomings of
GIoU_Loss, CIoU_Loss is introduced.

$$L_{CIoU} = 1 - IoU + \frac{\rho^2\left(b, b^{gt}\right)}{c^2} + \alpha v \tag{3}$$

Here, α is the weight; v measures the similarity of the aspect ratio; b is the prediction
frame; b^{gt} is the centroid of the target frame; ρ is the distance using Euclidean distance;

and c the slope of the smallest enclosing frame that can contain both the prediction frame and the target frame.

The depth estimation loss consists of two components: a scale-invariant squared difference loss is used to ensure that the predicted depth values are closer to the true depth values; while horizontal and vertical gradients are calculated for the images in order to preserve similar local structure, as follows:

$$L_{\text{depth}}(D, D^*) = \frac{1}{n} \sum_i d_i^2 - \frac{1}{2n^2} \left(\sum_i d_i \right)^2 + \frac{1}{n} \sum_i [(\nabla_x d_i)^2 + (\nabla_y d_i)^2] \quad (4)$$

Here, D is the predicted depth; D^* is the true depth; d_i is the difference between the predicted depth and the true depth.

$$L_{DA} = \frac{1}{N} \sum_{i=1}^{N} (\alpha_D + \lambda_D) \cdot \ell \left(d_i, d_i^{GT} \right) \quad (5)$$

Here, N is the total number of pixels in the depth image; I is the pixel index; $\ell(\cdot)$ is the distance metric formula; d_i is the predicted depth; d_i^{GT} is the true depth; α_D is depth-aware attention parameter, used to guide the network to focus more on more distant depth regions to reduce data distribution bias.

3.2 Depth Estimation Sub-Network

The depth estimation sub-network follows an Encoder-Decoder architecture. The encoder passes the input through multiple convolutional pooling layers to extract features from the image. These features are then stitched together based on the intermediate resolution size. The stitched features are further processed through convolutional pooling, allowing for the extraction of higher-dimensional features. Additionally, the sub-network employs lateral shared units and corresponding convolutional layers from the object detection sub-network to propagate information between the tasks.

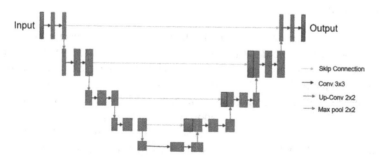

Fig. 2 Depth estimation Encoder-Decoder network

The structure of the depth estimation sub-network is illustrated in Fig. 2. Convolutional layers at three different scales facilitate the fusion of features. The fusion process combines shallow features, which capture more global and spatial information, with higher-level features that preserve finer details. This fusion enhances the network's accuracy in pixel prediction.

3.3 Object Detection Sub-Network

The object detection sub-network incorporates CSPDarknet-53 as the backbone feature extraction network. One key aspect of this network is its utilization of a residual network structure, which excludes pooling and fully connected layers. Instead, it employs scale pooling alongside local feature fusion. Figure 3 illustrates the specific structure of the object detection sub-network.

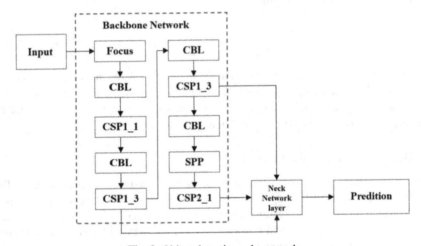

Fig. 3 Object detection sub-network

3.4 Shared Units

Since both the object detection task and the depth estimation task primarily concentrate on local features within the input image, leveraging shared feature maps can enhance the focus on object regions. However, it is crucial to strike a balance in knowledge sharing between the region-level regression task of object detection and the pixel-level regression problem of depth estimation. In this context, the bi-directional Lateral Sharing Unit (LSU) in a multi-task network proposed by Jiao et al. [33]. is adopted. The LSU facilitates automatic learning of the sharing strategy through dynamic routing, enabling information sharing through both forward and backward propagation. The structure of the LSU is depicted in Fig. 4.

LSU shares features among tasks. It provides complete sharing between two tasks, assuming that the current layer feature maps of two tasks are D_1 and S_1 respectively, the shared feature expressions are as follows:

$$LSU_{D2} = D_1 + (\phi_D \cdot D_1 + \phi_S \cdot S_1) \qquad (6)$$

$$LSU_{S_2} = S_1 + (\gamma_D \cdot D_1 + \gamma_S \cdot S_1) \tag{7}$$

Here, ϕ_D and γ_D are the parameters of feature D_1; ϕ_S and γ_S are the parameters of feature S_1; LSU_{D2} and LSU_{S2} are the shared features propagated to the subsequent layers.

There parameters are all learned during network training, thus enabling dynamic sharing between each of the two layers. Although the LSUs all share the same features, there are no restrictions on their parameters, thus allowing dynamic sharing.

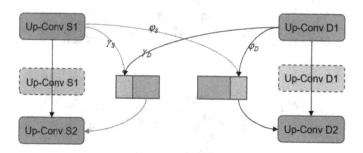

Fig. 4 LSU structure

4   Results

4.1   Experiment Environments

This paper uses the KITTI dataset, which encompasses several aspects of the autonomous driving task and includes several tasks such as 2D and 3D object detection, target segmentation, depth estimation and radar point cloud data processing. A number of scenes, including cities, residential areas, roads and schools, were the main focus of the data collection. Containing 7481 images with an image size of 1240 × 370, the dataset was randomly divided into 6000 images, 741 images and 740 images in a ratio of 8:1:1 when training the model.

During training, the training set was used for neural network training, the test set was used for weight screening during training, and the validation set was used to compare the object detection accuracy of different models. The targets to be detected are car, truck, person, tram and van. In this paper, the network model is implemented in PyTorch with 100 epochs, a batchsize of 4, an input resolution of 640 × 640 and a learning rate of 10–3. The GPU used is an NVIDIA GeForce GTX 1080Ti and the training time is 48 h.

4.2   Result Analysis

Figure 5 shows objection detection results by the object detection sub-network, identifying and predicting different pedestrians and vehicles.

Figure 6 shows the results of the monocular depth estimation, which is able to distinguish well the distance of the vehicle, presented by its colour.

Fig. 5 Object detection results

Fig. 6 Monocular depth estimation

Fig. 7 Object detection with depth information

Figure 7 shows the result of object detection and depth estimation, which can effectively label the distance information of the vehicle and pedestrian.

As shown in Table 1, these are the prediction results for the object detection sub-network, with good accuracy in the network's prediction accuracy.

As shown in Table 2, the experimental evaluations were performed on the KITTI dataset, and to extend the depth estimation range, the data segmentation approach proposed by Eigen et al. [34], was employed, enabling depth estimation up to 80m. In the depth estimation network we used absolute relative error (Abs.Rel), relative error (Sq.Rel), root mean square error (RMSE), root mean square logarithmic error (RMSE log), and threshold accuracy (δ) to compare with other literature. to reflect the effect of error with distance, the confidence of the measurement, and the deviation between the observed and true values. The results demonstrate that the model proposed in this paper enhance prediction accuracy and overall performance.

Table 1. Precision and recall of object detection sub-networks. P is the precision rate, R is the recall rate, and mAP is the mean average precision.

Model	P%	R%	mAP%
Object detection sub-network	94. 8	92. 6	96. 0

Table 2. Metrics of Depth estimation sub-network.

Method	Train	Abs Rel	Sq Rel	RMSE	RMSE log	$\delta <$ 1. 25	$\delta <$ 1. 25^2	$\delta <$ 1. 25^3
DDVO [35]	M	0. 151	1. 257	5. 583	0. 228	0. 810	0. 936	0. 974
DF-Net [36]	M	0. 150	1. 124	5. 507	0. 223	0. 806	0. 933	0. 973
Ranjan [37]	M	0. 148	1. 149	5. 464	0. 226	0. 815	0. 935	0. 973
Struct2depth [38]	M	0. 141	1. 026	5. 291	0. 215	0. 816	0. 945	0. 979
Monodepth [39]	M	0. 124	1. 388	6. 125	0. 217	0. 818	0. 929	0. 966
Monodepth2 [40]	M	0. 115	0. 903	4. 863	0. 193	0. 877	0. 959	0. 981
HR-Depth [41]	M	0. 109	0. 792	4. 632	0. 185	0. 884	0. 962	**0. 983**
Johnston [42]	M	**0. 106**	0. 861	4. 699	0. 185	0. 889	0. 962	0. 982
Ours	M	0. 108	**0. 765**	**4. 560**	**0. 185**	**0. 890**	**0. 963**	**0. 983**

Figure 8 illustrates the prediction result obtained from the joint depth estimation and object detection network. By inputting an RGB image, the network generates an object detection map that includes depth information. Initially, the object detection network locates and predicts the objects within the image. Subsequently, the brightness of the image color represents the distance between the camera and the detected objects. By comparing the predicted depth map with the ground truth depth map, objects at various distances can be accurately identified. The resulting combined object detection map, integrated with depth information, enables precise object localization and identification.

RGB image

Object Detection

Depth Estimation

Object detection map with
depth information

Fig. 8 Results of depth estimation and object detection network.

5 Conclusion

A deep learning-based approach for monocular depth estimation and object detection was proposed in this paper. It combines these two tasks to create an end-to-end real-time multi-task model. The model utilizes supervised learning methods to continuously learn the relationship between the relative position and distance of objects. The depth estimation sub-network, object detection sub-network, lateral sharing unit, and loss function are studied. The effectiveness of each module within the network model is evaluated through experiments, demonstrating improved depth estimation and detection accuracy. Additionally, a comparison is made with recently proposed algorithms, highlighting the favorable outcomes achieved in depth estimation and the feasibility of utilizing this method for pedestrian and vehicle ranging.

Acknowledgments. This project is supported by the Higher education teaching reformation project of Hubei province of China (2022231, 2022216), and the graduate teaching reformation project of Wuhan University of Science and Technology (Yjg202202).

References

1. Lertrusdachakul, I., Fougerolle, Y.D., Laligant. O.: Dynamic (de)focused projection for three-dimensional reconstruction. Optical Eng. **50**(11): 113201–113201–11 (2011)
2. Sun, M.J., Edgar, M.P., Gibson, G.M., et al.: Single-pixel three-dimensional imaging with time-based depth resolution. Nat. Commun.Commun. **7**(1), 12010 (2016)
3. Gonzalez-Romo, N.I., Hanalioglu, S., Mignucci-Jiménez, G., et al.: Anatomic depth estimation and three-dimensional reconstruction of microsurgical anatomy using monoscopic high-definition photogrammetry and machine learning. Operative Neurosur. **10**, 1227 (2022)
4. Chen, P.Y., Liu, A.H., Liu, Y.C., et al.: Towards scene understanding: Unsupervised monocular depth estimation with semantic-aware representation. In: Proceedings of the IEEE/CVF Conference on Computer Vision and Pattern Recognition, pp. 2624–2632 (2019)

5. Ren, H., El-Khamy, M., Lee, J.: Deep robust single image depth estimation neural network using scene understanding. In: CVPR Workshops, vol. 2, p. 2 (2019)
6. Aguilar, W.G., Quisaguano, F.J., Rodríguez, G.A., Alvarez, L.G., Limaico, A., Sandoval, D.S.: Convolutional neuronal networks based monocular object detection and depth perception for micro UAVs. In: Peng, Y., Kai, Y., Jiwen, L., Jiang, X. (eds.) Intelligence Science and Big Data Engineering: 8th International Conference, IScIDE 2018, Lanzhou, China, 18–19 August 2018, Revised Selected Papers, pp. 401–410. Springer International Publishing, Cham (2018). https://doi.org/10.1007/978-3-030-02698-1_35
7. Miclea, V.C., Nedevschi, S.: Monocular depth estimation with improved long-range accuracy for UAV environment perception. IEEE Trans. Geosci. Remote Sens.Geosci. Remote Sens. 60, 1–15 (2021)
8. Viola, P., Jones, M.: Rapid object detection using a boosted cascade of simple features. In: Proceedings of the 2001 IEEE Computer Society Conference on Computer Vision and Pattern Recognition, CVPR 2001, vol. 1 pp. I-I. IEEE (2001)
9. Krizhevsky, A., Sutskever, I., Hinton, G.E.: Imagenet classification with deep convolutional neural networks. In: Advances in Neural Information Processing Systems, vol. 25 (2012)
10. He, K,, Zhang, X., Ren, S., et al.: Deep residual learning for image recognition. In: Proceedings of the IEEE Conference on Computer Vision and Pattern Recognition, pp. 770–778 (2016)
11. Wang C.Y., Liao, H.Y.M., Wu, Y.H., et al.: CSPNet: a new backbone that can enhance learning capability of CNN. In: Proceedings of the IEEE/CVF Conference on Computer Vision and Pattern Recognition Workshops, pp. 390–391 (2020)
12. Girshick, R., Donahue, J,, Darrell, T., et al.: Rich feature hierarchies for accurate object detection and semantic segmentation. In: Proceedings of the IEEE Conference on Computer Vision and Pattern Recognition, pp. 580–587 (2014)
13. Girshick, R:.: Fast r-cnn. In: Proceedings of the IEEE International Conference on Computer Vision, pp. 1440–1448 (2015)
14. Ren, S., He, K., Girshick, R., et al.: Faster r-cnn: towards real-time object detection with region proposal networks. In: Advances in Neural Information Processing Systems, vol. 28 (2015)
15. Lin, T.Y, Dollár, P., Girshick, R., et al.: Feature pyramid networks for object detection. In: Proceedings of the IEEE Conference on Computer Vision and Pattern Recognition, pp. 2117–2125 (2017)
16. Hev. K., Gkioxari, G., Dollár, P., et al:. Mask r-cnn. In: Proceedings of the IEEE International Conference on Computer Vision, pp. 2961–2969 (2017)
17. Redmon, J., Divvala, S., Girshick, R., et al.: You only look once: unified, real-time object detection. In: Proceedings of the IEEE Conference on Computer Vision and Pattern Recognition, pp. 779–788 (2016)
18. Redmon, J., Farhadi, A.: YOLO9000: better, faster, stronger. In: Proceedings of the IEEE Conference on Computer Vision and Pattern Recognition, pp. 7263–7271 (2017)
19. Redmon, J,, Farhadi, A.: Yolov3: An incremental improvement. arXiv preprint arXiv:1804. 02767 (2018)
20. Bochkovskiy, A., Wang, C.Y., Liao, H.Y.M.: Yolov4: optimal speed and accuracy of object detection, vol. 2004, p. 10934 (2020)
21. Li, A., Sun, S., Zhang, Z., et al.: A multi-scale traffic object detection algorithm for road scenes based on improved YOLOv5. Electronics 12(4), 878 (2023)
22. Reading, C., Harakeh, A., Chae, J., et al.: Categorical depth distribution network for monocular 3d object detection. In: Proceedings of the IEEE/CVF Conference on Computer Vision and Pattern Recognition, pp. 8555–8564 (2021)
23. Khan, F., Salahuddin, S., Javidnia, H.: Deep learning-based monocular depth estimation methods—A state-of-the-art review. Sensors 20(8), 2272 (2020)

24. Bugby, S.L., Lees, J.E., McKnight, W.K., et al.: Stereoscopic portable hybrid gamma imaging for source depth estimation. Phys. Med. Biol. **66**(4), 045031 (2021)

25. Praveen, S.: Efficient depth estimation using sparse stereo-vision with other perception techniques. Coding Theory **111** (2020)

26. Li, B., Shen, C., Dai, Y., et al.: Depth and surface normal estimation from monocular images using regression on deep features and hierarchical crfs. In: Proceedings of the IEEE Conference on Computer Vision and Pattern Recognition, pp. 1119–1127 (2015)

27. Qi, X., Liao, R., Liu. Z., et al.: Geonet: geometric neural network for joint depth and surface normal estimation. In: Proceedings of the IEEE Conference on Computer Vision and Pattern Recognition, pp. 283–291 (2018)

28. Sheng, F., Xue, F., Chang, Y., et al.: Monocular depth distribution alignment with low computation. In: 2022 International Conference on Robotics and Automation (ICRA), pp. 6548–6555. IEEE (2022)

29. Garg, R., Bg, V.K., Carneiro, G., Unsupervised, C.N.N.: For single view depth estimation: Geometry to the rescue. In: Computer Vision–ECCV 2016, 14th European Conference, Amsterdam, The Netherlands, 11–14 October 2016, Proceedings, Part VIII 14, pp. 740-756. Springer International Publishing (2016). https://doi.org/10.1007/978-3-319-46484-8_45

30. Zhou, T., Brown, M., Snavely, N., et al.: Unsupervised learning of depth and ego-motion from video. In: Proceedings of the IEEE Conference on Computer Vision and Pattern Recognition, pp. 1851–1858 (2017)

31. Tao, B., Chen, X., Tong, X., et al.: Self-supervised monocular depth estimation based on channel attention Photonics. MDPI **9**(6), 434 (2022)

32. Kuznietsov, Y., Stuckler, J., Leibe, B.: Semi-supervised deep learning for monocular depth map prediction. In: Proceedings of the IEEE Conference on Computer Vision and Pattern Recognition, pp. 6647–6655 (2017)

33. Jiao, J., Cao, Y., Song, Y., Lau, R.: Look deeper into depth: Monocular depth estimation with semantic booster and attention-driven loss. In: Ferrari, V., Hebert, M., Sminchisescu, C., Weiss, Y. (eds.) Computer Vision – ECCV 2018: 15th European Conference, Munich, Germany, September 8-14, 2018, Proceedings, Part XV, pp. 55–71. Springer International Publishing, Cham (2018). https://doi.org/10.1007/978-3-030-01267-0_4

34. Eigen, D., Puhrsch, C., Fergus, R.: Depth map prediction from a single image using a multi-scale deep network. In: Advances in Neural Information Processing Systems 27 (2014)

35. Mahjourian, R., Wicke, M., Angelova, A.: Unsupervised learning of depth and ego-motion from monocular video using 3d geometric constraints. In: Proceedings of the IEEE Conference on Computer Vision and Pattern Recognition, pp. 5667–5675 (2018)

36. Zou, Y., Luo, Z., Huang, J.-B.: Df-net: Unsupervised joint learning of depth and flow using cross-task consistency. In: Ferrari, V., Hebert, M., Sminchisescu, C., Weiss, Y. (eds.) Computer Vision – ECCV 2018: 15th European Conference, Munich, Germany, September 8–14, 2018, Proceedings, Part V, pp. 38–55. Springer International Publishing, Cham (2018). https://doi.org/10.1007/978-3-030-01228-1_3

37. Ranjan, A., Jampani, V., Balles, L., et al.: Competitive collaboration: joint unsupervised learning of depth, camera motion, optical flow and motion segmentation. In: Proceedings of the IEEE/CVF Conference on Computer Vision and Pattern Recognition, pp. 12240–12249 (2019)

38. Casser, V., Pirk, S., Mahjourian, R., et al.: Depth prediction without the sensors: Leveraging structure for unsupervised learning from monocular videos. In: Proceedings of the AAAI Conference on Artificial Intelligence , vol. 33(01), pp. 8001–8008 (2019)

39. Godard, C., Mac Aodha, O., Brostow, G.J.: Unsupervised monocular depth estimation with left-right consistency. In: Proceedings of the IEEE Conference on Computer Vision and Pattern Recognition, pp. 270–279 (2017)

40. Godard, C., Mac Aodha, O., Firman, M., et al.: Digging into self-supervised monocular depth estimation. In: Proceedings of the IEEE/CVF International Conference on Computer Vision, pp. 3828–3838 (2019)
41. Guizilini, V., Ambrus, R., Pillai, S., et al.: 3D packing for self-supervised monocular depth estimation. In: Proceedings of the IEEE/CVF Conference on Computer Vision and Pattern Recognition, pp. 2485–2494 (2020)
42. Johnston, A., Carneiro, G.: Self-supervised monocular trained depth estimation using self-attention and discrete disparity volume. In: Proceedings of the IEEE/CVF Conference on Computer Vision and Pattern Recognition, pp. 4756–4765 (2020)

Mobilenetv2-SSD Target Detection Method Based on Multi-scale Feature Fusion

Boao Li[1,2,3], Du Jiang[1,3,4,5(✉)], Xinjie Tang[1,2,3], Ying Sun[1,3,4], and Yaoqing Weng[1,2,5]

[1] Key Laboratory of Metallurgical Equipment and Control Technology of Ministry of Education, Wuhan University of Science and Technology, Wuhan 430081, China
1786735051@qq.com, jiangdu@wust.edu.cn

[2] Research Center for Biomimetic Robot and Intelligent Measurement and Control, Wuhan University of Science and Technology, Wuhan 430081, China

[3] Hubei Key Laboratory of Mechanical Transmission and Manufacturing Engineering, Wuhan University of Science and Technology, Wuhan 430081, China

[4] Precision Manufacturing Research Institute, Wuhan University of Science and Technology, Wuhan 430081, China

[5] Hubei Longzhong Laboratory, Xiangyang 441000, Hubei, China

Abstract. Most of the deep learning networks used in target detection algorithms are very complex, which poses difficulties for edge devices with limited storage capacity and computing power, such as mobile terminals. A MobileNetv2-SSD target detection algorithm based on multi-scale feature fusion is proposed in this paper. We use MobileNetv2 to improve the SSD algorithm by replacing the original network's backbone network VGG16 with the lightweight network MobileNetv2 to perform the model streamlining. The problem of accuracy loss due to model compression is improved by the designed feature fusion module and finally tested on the dataset. The experimental results show that the mAP and FPS are 90.37% and 50FPS, respectively, and the detection accuracy is improved by 3.24% compared with the original SSD network, the detection speed is 1.9 times of the original one, and the size of the model is only 28.5M, which is only 30.5% of the original model.

Keywords: Machine Vision · Target Detection · Multi-Scale Feature Fusion · Mobilenetv2 · SSD

1 Introduction

Since the concept of robotics was first introduced in the 1960s, robotics has been a hot topic and there has been uninterrupted research related to this field [1–4]. Initially, robots were mainly used as industrial equipment to improve productivity and reduce the labor cost of enterprises. With the development of society and the advancement of technology, the various capabilities of robots have been enhanced and their intelligence has been increasing. From initially being able to perform only simple repetitive mechanical tasks, they gradually perceive the environment and understand human commands to complete corresponding tasks autonomously or semi-autonomously.

F. Sun et al. (Eds.): ICCSIP 2023, CCIS 1919, pp. 206–217, 2024.
https://doi.org/10.1007/978-981-99-8021-5_16

Computer vision gives robots the ability to do this. Classification, detection, recognition, and segmentation are the four main types of tasks that are currently dominant in computer vision. The detection task is to detect what kinds of objects are in the current environment and where each object is located. Compared to the classification and segmentation tasks, the detection task yields more specific and comprehensive information about the objects, which is more conducive to the robot's understanding of the environment it is in [5]. At the beginning of the new century, the continuous accumulation of Internet big data and the rapid increase in chip computing power have provided explosive opportunities for deep learning [6–8], and a variety of deep learning-based target detection algorithms have been proposed one after another, which has promoted the rapid development of detection algorithms. However, in practical applications, the effectiveness and stability of the algorithms are affected to varying degrees due to numerous factors such as object density, light intensity, and imaging quality, resulting in unsatisfactory detection results. In addition, the target detection model is too large for the memory of robots and the now popular mobile devices. Therefore, how to improve the detection accuracy and stability of the algorithm and simplify the complexity of the algorithm as much as possible is a research focus for target detection tasks [9, 10].

A MobileNetv2-SSD target detection algorithm based on multi-scale feature fusion is proposed in this paper. The SSD algorithm is improved using MobileNetv2 by replacing the original network's backbone network VGG16 with the lightweight network MobileNetv2 for model streamlining and improving the speed of target detection.

2 Related Work

Thanks to the increasing computing power of computers and the emergence of large-scale datasets, scholars' attention began to focus on deep learning before the idea of target detection was proposed again. Deep learning-based target detection techniques gradually replaced the traditional method of manual feature extraction and became the mainstream of target detection task research [11]. Depending on the inspection process, there are two types: Two-Stage and One-Stage.

The detection process of Two-Stage consists of generating suggestion areas and feeding classifiers, and both parts are done by different networks. The R-CNN [12] target detection network, pioneered by Girshick et al. in 2014, is the first target detection field deep learning-based target detection algorithm, and it attracted many scholars upon its appearance. In 2015, Girshick et al. proposed the Fast R-CNN [13] target detection network, which optimizes the grid structure. This network optimized the grid structure, implemented a multi-task learning approach, and synchronized target classification and candidate frame regression, which improved the accuracy while significantly improving the speed. In the same year, Kai-Ming He's team proposed the Faster R-CNN [14] target detection network, which successfully realized the end-to-end target detection network by replacing the original candidate frame generation method with the RPN network, achieving the quasi-real-time detection requirement for the first time. 2017, for the situation that the top layer of the target detection network is rich in feature semantic information, but the location information is missing, Kai-Ming He et al. proposed the FPN network [15]. Network.FPN solves the problem of detecting multi-scale targets by changing the network connections to achieve the same amount of computation while keeping the same amount of computation.

The One-Stage algorithm performs detection in the network by directly outputting the bounding box with the classification label. Joseph and Girshick et al. proposed the YOLO [16] target detection network in 2015. The most prominent advantage of this network is the high detection speed, which truly achieves real-time monitoring and solves the deep learning-based target detection network in The pain point of slow detection speed. However, the detection accuracy of this model is lower than that of the Faster R-CNN in the same period. In the same year, SSD [17] target detection network was proposed by Wei Liu et al. This network borrowed from YOLO network and RPN network, and innovatively regressed and multi-scale detection of candidate frames directly on the feature maps of multiple sizes. It makes its detection speed similar to YOLO and detection accuracy similar to Faster R-CNN, which is a target detection network with balanced performance. However, both SSD network and YOLO network have the problem of low detection accuracy for multiscale targets and small object targets, and the algorithm still has much room for improvement.

3   Mobilenetv2 Based SSD Target Detection Algorithm

3.1   MobileNetV2 Network

MobileNetV1 network in the process of using deep convolution, due to not changing the dimension of the input features, from time to time, the kernel is too small resulting in a convolution kernel parameter of 0, making the network feature extraction is only in a shallow dimension. For this reason, Google team proposed MobileNetV2 based on MobileNetV1 to solve the problems of the former. The main idea of MobileNetV2 is to use deep convolution to concatenate point convolution and introduce the inverse residual block structure, and to use a linear activation function instead of the ReLU6 activation function after point convolution.

(1) Residual unit

It was found that the direct use of shallow networks stacked into deep networks not only makes it difficult to utilize the powerful feature extraction ability of deep networks, but also causes feature loss, network degradation, and gradient disappearance, resulting in a decrease in the accuracy of the model. To solve this problem, Kaiming He's team proposed the ResNet [18] residual network in 2015. The residual network is constructed from residual units, and the core is the addition of jump mapping, i.e., the input and output are directly summed to supplement the feature information lost in the convolution process. A residual block can be represented by Eq. (1), i.e., the input of the next layer is obtained by directly adding the residual to the output of the previous layer.

$$x_{l+1} = x_l + \mathcal{F}(x_l, W_l) \tag{1}$$

The structure of the residual unit is divided into two types: regular residual unit and deep residual unit, as shown in Fig. 1. Regular residual units are for shallow networks, such as ResNet-18/34, and deep residual units are for deeper networks, such as ResNet-50/101/152. The purpose of using this approach is to reduce the number of parameters, save memory and improve the detection speed of the model.

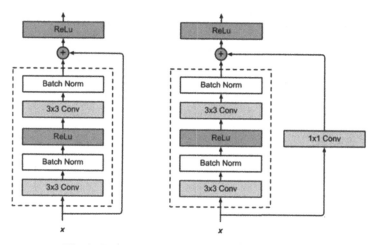

Fig. 1. Regular residual units and deep residual units

(2) Inverse residual structure.

The inverted residual structure is adapted from the residual structure of the ResNet network, and a comparison of the two is shown below:

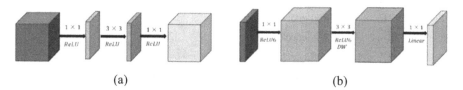

(a)   (b)

Fig. 2. Residual structure and inverse residual structure

The operation of the residual block structure is shown in Fig. 2 (a), which in general is to ascend and then descend the dimensionality of the feature matrix, specifically: firstly, the input feature matrix is descended using a 1×1 convolution kernel, then a 3×3 standard convolution kernel is used for feature extraction, and finally, a 1×1 convolution kernel is used for ascending the dimensionality. In contrast, the inverted residual block, as shown in Fig. 2 (b), first ascends and then descends the dimensionality of the feature matrix, with the difference that the middle is no longer a normal convolution but a deep convolution. In addition, the residual block structure uses the ReLU activation function, while the inverse residual block uses the ReLU6 activation function, which adds a suppression maximum to the ReLU function, and the difference between the two activation functions is shown in Fig. 3 below.

The structure of the MobilenetV2 model is shown in Table 1, where the parameter t is the expansion factor, c is the dimensionality of the feature and also the number of convolution kernels, the parameter n is the number of repetitions of the layer, and the parameter s is the step size of the first convolution.

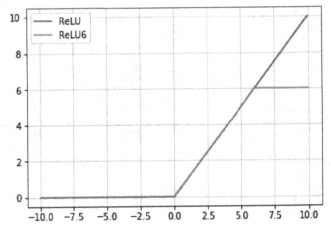

Fig. 3. ReLU function and ReLU6 function

Table 1. MobileNetv2 structure

Input	Operate	t	c	n	s
224 × 224 × 3	conv2d	–	32	1	2
112 × 112 × 32	Bottleneck	1	16	1	1
112 × 112 × 16	Bottleneck	6	24	2	2
56 × 56 × 24	Bottleneck	6	32	3	2
28 × 28 × 32	Bottleneck	6	64	4	2
14 × 14 × 64	Bottleneck	6	96	3	1
14 × 14 × 96	Bottleneck	6	160	3	2
7 × 7 × 160	Bottleneck	6	320	1	1
7 × 7 × 320	conv2d 11	–	1280	1	1
7 × 7 × 1280	Avgpool77	–	–	1	–
1 × 1 × 1280	FC	–	k	–	–

3.2 MobileNetV2-SSD

The VGG16 network model has better feature extraction capability but is too large for embedded platforms. The MobileNetv2 model, as a lightweight network designed for resource-constrained devices, is much smaller than the VGG model in terms of the number of parameters and operations, and its performance in detection accuracy is not bad compared with VGG. Table 2 shows the performance comparison between the VGG16 network and the MobileNetv2 network on the ImageNet dataset. The MobileNetv2 model has a significant advantage over the VGG model, both in terms of the size of the model and the number of operations considered.

Table 2. Comparison of VGG16 and MobileNetv2

Network	Number of convolution layers	Number of participants	MASc Operation M	Top-1
VGG16	16	15300	138.3	71.5%
MobileNetv2	21	300	3.4	74.0%

To achieve a lightweight target detection model, the SSD network is modified based on the MobileNetv2 network by replacing VGG16 in the SSD network as the backbone network using MobileNetv2 and removing the fully connected and pooling layers at the end of MobileNetv2. Four sets of inverse residual block structure convolution are added at the end of the network, using Conv14_pw_1 and Conv18 in the backbone network, and the six layers added later, Conv19_pw_2, Conv20_pw_2, Conv21_pw_2, and Conv22_pw_2, as the feature layers for target detection, whose sizes are 19×19, 10×10, 5×5, 3×3, 2×2, and 1×1. The improved lightweight network is called MNV2SSD, and its structure is shown in Fig. 4.

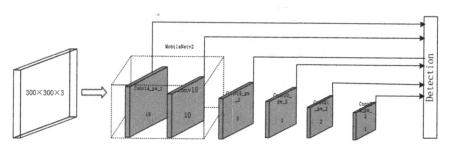

Fig. 4. MNV2SSD Structure

4 Lightweight Model Optimization Based on Feature Fusion

In the target detection model, with the stacking of convolutional and pooling layers, the detail information of the feature layers is seriously lost, and the detection of targets directly on the high-level feature layers is easy to cause the inaccurate detection of small targets or even missed detection. Deep learning-based target detection algorithms usually use pyramid structure to improve the problem of poor small target recognition, and the pyramid structure uses feature maps of different scales for prediction, i.e., multi-scale prediction, to improve the detection effect of small targets. Later on, feature fusion is even proposed, i.e., the fusion of high-level feature maps and low-level feature maps using jump connections to further improve the detection performance of the model. The feature pyramid structure can be divided into four categories, which are shown in Fig. 5.

A multi-scale feature fusion algorithm is proposed in the paper, the predicted feature layer and its adjacent layers are fused before detection. The MNV2SSD network with the

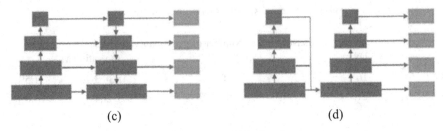

(c)   (d)

Fig. 5. Feature Pyramid Fusion Structure

addition of the fusion module is called light-SSD. Light-SSD uses fusion to enhance the complementarity between high-level feature maps and low-level feature map information, which improves the detection performance of multi-scale targets and also further promotes the utility of the model in complex scenarios. The structure of the light-SSD network is shown in Fig. 6.

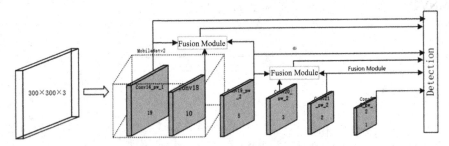

Fig. 6. Light-SSD Network Structure

The commonly used feature fusion methods are the concat operation and add operation. Among them, concat operation is to stitch two feature maps to be fused on a channel. Concat has no requirement on the dimensionality of the two feature layers, but the size should be the same, and the fused features after the concat operation should be dimensionally adjusted using convolution. For example, if the dimensions of the two feature layers to be fused are a and b, the dimension z of the feature map after the concat operation is a + b. The operation diagram is shown in Fig. 7.

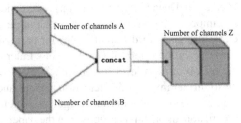

Fig. 7. Concat Operation

The add operation is to add the corresponding elements of the two feature maps to be fused, requiring their dimensions to be the same before fusion, i.e., a = b. The dimensions will not change after add fusion, and the operation is shown schematically in Fig. 8.

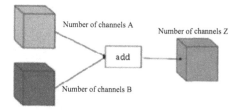

Fig. 8. Add Operation

The add operation is a simple addition of corresponding elements, which does not change the dimensionality while supplementing the amount of information on the features. In contrast, concat is the merging of channels, and the dimensionality will expand, which will easily lead to the mixing of speech information between different channels, and the computation is also higher than the add operation. Considering that the fusion in this section needs to focus on the target detection layer, the original lightweight characteristics of the network need to be preserved as much as possible. Therefore, the add method is used to fuse the feature layers of different scales, and then the convolution is used to reduce the superposition effect of fusion.

Taking the fusion of Conv14_pw_1, Conv18, and Conv19_pw_2 as an example for further details, the feature layer Conv18, which is in the middle of the three, is called the target layer, and the feature layer Conv14_pw_1, which is lower than Conv18, is called the low-level feature layer, and the feature layer Conv19_pw_2, which is higher than Conv18, is called the high-level feature layer. The add operation requires the same size of the feature layers to be fused, so the size of the target detection layer is used as the standard, and the high and low-level feature layers are resized by up-sampling and down-sampling methods, respectively. The common methods for upsampling the feature map are flash bilinear interpolation and deconvolution. Considering the more flexible way of deconvolution and the stronger ability to extract features, deconvolution is used to expand the size of the Conv19_pw_2 feature layer by upsampling operation. Commonly used downsampling methods are average pooling and maximum pooling. Average pooling tends to pool the overall information of the features, while maximum pooling takes the tendency feature texture information, so maximum pooling is chosen. To further preserve the detailed information of the original feature layer, the Convolution operation is used to extract features from the Conv14_pw_1 layer first, and then the maximum pooling is performed to reduce its size. To facilitate the training of the model at a later stage, a normalization operation is used. At this point, the processed Conv14_pw_1, Conv18, and Conv19_pw_2 layers reach the same size and dimensionality, then the three are fused by add operation, and finally the new feature map obtained by fusion is convolved using 3x3 convolution to reduce the stacking effect after feature fusion. According to the above description, the multiscale fusion module can be obtained as shown in Fig. 9, and the fusion of other target detection layers is also done in the same way.

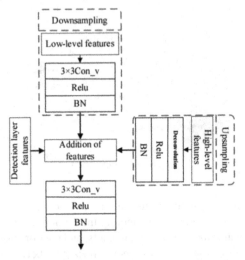

Fig. 9. Multi-Scale Feature Fusion Module

5   Experiments and Results

The experimental setup is based on the hardware configuration of CPU, NVIDIA Geforce RTX2070 GPU, Windows 10 operating system, CUDA software environment, and Tensorflow framework, as shown in Table 3.

Table 3. Experimental environment parameters

Category	Detail
Operating System	Windows11
GPU	NVIDIA GeForce RTX 2070
CPU	AMD Ryzen 7
Memory	16G
Video Memory	8G
Framework	Tensorflow1.13
Cuda with Cudnn	10.0/7.6.5

Based on the built experimental platform, the light-SSD model is trained after adding the feature fusion module, and then the light-SSD model is compared with the original SSD model and the MNV2SSD model in terms of detection performance, and the experimental results are shown in Table 4 below.

Table 4. Comparison of Results

Algorithm	mAP(%)	FPS	Model Size (MB)
SSD	87.13	26	93.2
MNV2SSD	86.94	64	21.6
light-SSD	90.37	50	28.5

As can be seen from the table, the improved light-SSD model performs significantly better than the MNV2SSD network. From the perspective of detection accuracy, the light-SSD model improves 3.43% relative to the MNV2SSD model and 3.24% higher than the original SSD model, which proves the effectiveness of the feature fusion module proposed in this section on model accuracy improvement. In terms of detection speed and model size analysis, the detection speed of light-SSD is 50 FPS, which is lower than that of MNV2SSD, which is caused by the extra computation brought by fusion, but the detection speed is still much faster than that of the original SSD network. The model size also has slightly increased, but only 30.5% of the original SSD network. In summary, the light-SSD model based on MobileNetV2 lightweight, combined with the improved feature fusion, substantially improves the detection speed of the model and reduces the memory required for the model, while ensuring the detection accuracy, achieving the purpose of this chapter to compress the SSD model. Figure 10 shows the comparison of the detection effect of three models for a test image.

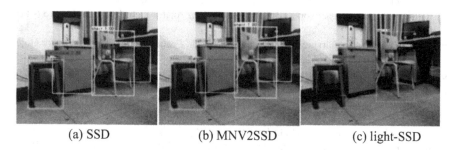

(a) SSD   (b) MNV2SSD   (c) light-SSD

Fig. 10. Comparison of Detection Results

6 Conclusion

A MobileNetv2-SSD target detection algorithm based on multi-scale feature fusion is proposed to achieve target detection network lightweight in this paper. Then the MobileNetv2 network applicable to indoor scene target detection is divided in detail, and the SSD network is modified based on MobileNetV2 for lightweighting. The number of parameters of the modified SSD algorithm is significantly reduced and the detection speed is much higher than that of the original SSD network, but the detection accuracy of the model is reduced. Then the feature fusion module is used to improve the lightweight network, and finally the constructed lightweight network has improved detection accuracy and detection speed, and the model size is reduced significantly, which achieves the goal of compressing the model by maintaining accuracy and speed as proposed in this chapter.

References

1. Raveendra, K., Vinothkanna, R.: Hybrid ant colony optimization model for image retrieval using scale-invariant feature transform local descriptor. Comput. Electr. Eng. **74**, 281–291 (2019)
2. Zhou, N., Constantinides, A.G., Huang, G., et al.: Face recognition based on an improved center symmetric local binary pattern. Neural Comput. Appl. **30**(12), 3791–3797 (2018)
3. Bilal, M., Hanif, M.: Benchmark revision for HOG-SVM pedestrian detector through reinvigorated training and evaluation methodologies. IEEE Trans. Intell. Transp. Syst. **21**(3), 1277–1287 (2020)
4. Felzenszwalb, P.F., Girshick, R.B., et al.: Object detection with discriminatively trained part-based models. IEEE Trans. Pattern Anal. Mach. Intell. **2**(47), 3–7 (2010)
5. Girshick, R.B., Jeff, D., et al.: Rich feature hierarchies for accurate object detection and semantic segmentation. CoRR, abs/1311.2524 (2013)
6. He, K.M., Zhang, X., Ren, S., Jian, S.: Spatial pyramid pooling in deep convolutional networks for visual recognition. IEEE Trans. Pattern Anal. Mach. Intell. **37**(9), 1904–1916 (2015)
7. Li, J., Liang, X., Shen, S.M., et al.: Scale-aware fast R-CNN for pedestrian detection. IEEE Trans. Multimedia **20**(4), 985–996 (2017)
8. Ren, S.Q., He, K.M., Girshick, R., et al.: Faster R-CNN: towards real-time object detection with region proposal networks. IEEE Trans. Pattern Anal. Mach. Intell. **39**(6), 1137–1149 (2015)
9. Lin, T.Y., Dollár, P., Girshick, R., Belongie, S., et al.: Feature Pyramid Networks for Object Detection. CoRR, abs/1612.03144 (2016)
10. Redmon, J., Divvala, S., Girshick, R.: You only look once: unified, real-time object detection. In: Computer Vision and Pattern Recognition, pp. 779–788. IEEE (2016)
11. Girshick, R., Donahue, J., Darrell, T., et al.: R-CNN for object detection. In: IEEE Conference (2014)
12. He, K., Zhang, X., Ren, S., et al.: Spatial pyramid pooling in deep convolutional networks for visual recognition. IEEE Trans. Pattern Anal. Mach. Intell. **37**(9), 1904–1916 (2015)
13. Girshick, R.: Fast R-CNN. In: Proceedings of the IEEE International Conference on Computer Vision, pp. 1440–1448 (2015)
14. Ren, S., He, K., Girshick, R., et al.: Faster R-CNN: towards real-time object detection with region proposal networks. In: Advances in Neural Information Processing Systems, vol. 28 (2015)
15. Lin, T.Y, Dollár, P., Girshick, R, et al.: Feature pyramid networks for object detection. In: Proceedings of the IEEE Conference on Computer Vision and Pattern Recognition, pp. 2117–2125 (2017)
16. Redmon, J., Divvala, S., Girshick, R., et al.: You only look once: unified, real-time object detection. In: Proceedings of the IEEE Conference on Computer Vision and Pattern Recognition, pp. 779–788 (2016)

17. Liu, W., Anguelov, D., Erhan, D., et al.: SSD: single shot multibox detector. In: Computer Vision–ECCV 2016: 14th European Conference, Amsterdam, The Netherlands, 11–14 October 2016, Proceedings, Part I 14. Springer International Publishing, pp. 21–37 (2016). https://doi.org/10.1007/978-3-319-46448-0_2

18. He, K., Zhang, X., Ren, S., et al.: Deep residual learning for image recognition. In: Proceedings of the IEEE Conference on Computer Vision and Pattern Recognition, pp. 770–778 (2016)

No-Reference Point Cloud Quality Assessment via Contextual Point-Wise Deep Learning Network

Xinyu Wang, Ruijun Liu, and Xiaochuan Wang[✉]

School of Computer Science and Engineering, Beijing Technology and Business University, Beijing 100041, China
wangxc@btbu.edu.cn

Abstract. For the processing of point clouds, an accurate assessment of the quality is essential. However, point cloud quality assessment has proven to be a difficult issue, especially when the pristine point clouds are unavailable. Most existing no-reference point cloud quality assessment methods adopt projection-based routes, which inevitably suffer from occlusion and misalignment, resulting in loss of information. Alternatively, this paper proposes a novel no-reference point cloud quality assessment method via a contextual point-wise deep learning network (CPW-Net). Compared with projection-based methods, it reduces information loss by learning features directly from point coordinates and attributes. In particular, CPW-Net utilizes an Offset Attention Feature Encoder (OAFE) module to extract local and contextual features. Experiment results demonstrate that the proposed method overwhelms most publicly available no-reference metrics on SJTU dataset and gains compatible performance in comparison with most full-reference methods.

Keywords: point cloud quality assessment · no-reference · attention mechanism · visual perception

1 Introduction

With the development of automatic drive and mixed reality [1–4] technologies, there is an increasing demand for realistic and immersive experiences. Point cloud, as a format of data that can accurately represent 3D scenes, thus has become an essential input source for AR and VR applications. Point cloud is composed of a large amount of discrete points, each of which consists of geometry attributes, aka 3D coordinates $< x, y, z >$ and other attributes, including color (i.e. $< R, G, B >$), normal, reflection intensity, etc. Due to the distortions introduced during the procedures from the acquisition, encoding, processing, and transmission, to the rendering of point clouds, a proper evaluation of the distorted point cloud becomes critical. Point cloud quality assessment (PCQA) tries to predict the quality of the distorted point clouds, so as to mimic the visual perception of human beings. By utilizing PCQA to guide the above mentioned procedures, the quality of the distorted PCs can be optimized to the most extent.

© The Author(s), under exclusive license to Springer Nature Singapore Pte Ltd. 2024
F. Sun et al. (Eds.): ICCSIP 2023, CCIS 1919, pp. 218–233, 2024.
https://doi.org/10.1007/978-981-99-8021-5_17

Inspired by the image quality assessment (IQA) [5, 6], current PCQA methods can be categorized into three kinds according to the information of the pristine point cloud utilized in the assessment process, namely, the full-reference (FR), the reduced-reference (RR) and the no-reference (NR) methods. The FR methods measure the quality of the distorted point cloud by comparing the variations between the pristine point cloud and the distorted one. The RR methods utilize part of the pristine point cloud to measure the quality of the distorted point cloud. However, the pristine point cloud is unavailable in most practical applications, thus limiting the use of FR and RR methods. This paper focuses on NR methods, which get rid of the pristine point cloud. Most existing NR methods [7–9] adopt the projection-based route. In particular, they first project the distorted point cloud onto the six orthogonal planes corresponding to its bounding box, obtaining multiple projection images, and then predicting the overall point cloud quality by averaging the predicted quality scores of the projection images. Consequently, these methods inevitably suffer from loss of information, i.e., occlusion and misalignment due to the orthogonal projection, which further affects the precision performance. Besides, the features extracted from the projection images can not sufficiently represent the local topology and contextual relationship of the point cloud in the 3D space.

To improve the performance of current no-reference PCQA methods, meanwhile compensating the drawbacks of projection-based routes, we alternatively propose a novel no-reference point cloud quality assessment metric by designing a Contextual Point-Wise Network (CPW-Net). Firstly, we directly learn the feature representation of point clouds in 3D space to reduce the loss of information. By doing so, the geometric and topological information in the point cloud is fully learned to better capture the detailed features in the distorted point clouds. Secondly, we introduce the attention mechanism into feature learning to better mimic the visual perception of human beings. As cited in [10], the human visual system (HVS) usually understands and interprets visual information by perceiving contextual relationships, where the attention mechanism [11] can dynamically learn the interactions between points based on their relationships and importance. To better fit the characteristics of point cloud, i.e., unordered, sparse, and irregular, we particularly use the offset attention mechanism. The offset attention mechanism [12] uses an offset between the input and the attention features instead of the attention features, allowing the network to select and adjust the region of attention more flexibly. This will be discussed in detail in Sect. 3.3. However, most of the point cloud data used for point cloud quality assessment are dense point clouds with ten thousand points or more, which is difficult for the current point-wise point cloud learning networks within limited computation resources. This causes problems for subsequent feature learning and quality prediction. Therefore, we divide the point cloud into various sub-patches for processing. Finally, a regression module is utilized to predict the overall quality score of the distorted point cloud. Consequently, the main contributions can be concluded as follows.

(1) A contextual point-wise deep learning network (CPW-Net) is proposed to implement the no-reference PCQA task. The proposed network can prevent the loss of information during data pre-processing and dimensional reduction in comparison with projection-based ones, thereby leveraging the accuracy of quality score prediction.

(2) Inspired by the human visual system, the global interaction and feature representation of the point cloud data is extracted by the offset attention mechanism. The local topological information and contextual relationships of the point set are comprehensively considered to increase the consistency between the predicted quality scores of point clouds and the human perceived quality.

(3) Experiments show that the proposed method gains superior performance on SJTU dataset in comparison with publicly available NR metrics and competitive performance on most of the FR metrics.

The rest of the paper is organized as follows. A brief review of related work is addressed in Sect. 2. The proposed contextual point-wise network is elaborated in Sect. 3. Section 4 presents the implementations and experimental results, followed by a brief conclusion in Sect. 5.

2   Related Work

2.1   FR and RR Methods

Point cloud quality assessment has been a significant research area in recent years. Most of the existing PCQA metrics belong to the FR methods. By using the pristine point cloud as the reference, the FR-PCQA approaches measure the diversity between the pristine and the distorted point cloud, which can be mapped to the quality score in corresponding to the subjective ratings.

According to the feature extraction, the FR methods can be further divided into point-wise and projection-based methods. The typical point-wise methods include p2point [13] and p2plane [14], where the offset distance of a point concerning its original coordinate and the projection error along the normal direction is considered, respectively. However, these methods only consider geometric distortions. Moreover, the properties of human visual perception are not taken into consideration. Yang [15] proposed the GraphSSIM, which evaluates the similarity between the pristine and the distorted point clouds by constructing a topological structure graph. Alexiou [16] proposed the PointSSIM by fusing four different attributes of point clouds, including geometry, normal vector, curvature, and color.

Given the relative maturity of IQAs in the 2D image domain, many scholars have attempted to convert point clouds into multi-view images by using 2D projections. After that, they can leverage the FR-IQA metrics to gain the quality scores of the projection images, and then calculate the final result with different pooling strategies. Queiroz [17] calculated the MSE and PSNR on the projected images. Meynet [18] proposed the PCQM method, where the geometric and texture features of the projected images are extracted via CNNs, respectively. The FR-PCQA methods rely heavily on high-quality pristine point clouds, which are not available in practical applications. Consequently, the application of FR-PCQA methods is restrictive. RR-PCQA also demands partial information on the pristine point cloud, thereby attracting little attention to it. Viola [19] proposed an RR-PCQA metric that utilizes the side information from the pristine point cloud via lossy compression. In practical application, the sender transmits only the key features or partial information of the original point cloud to the receiver instead of the complete data. Then the receiver uses the received features for reconstruction and then monitors the quality of the reconstructed point cloud as feedback.

2.2 NR Methods

NR-PCQA methods do not rely on any reference point cloud information and only perform quality assessments based on the individual point cloud data itself. It is more widely used but also faces greater difficulties. In particular, they rely heavily on the large subjective point cloud quality datasets for training. Currently, there are only a few NR-PCQA methods.

In a related study, Liu [7] proposed the PQA-Net adopting the projection-based route. Specifically, a simple but efficient convolutional neural network [20] was applied to extract features at different scale levels of the projected images. These features are then used to predict the distortion classes and quality scores, respectively. Zhang [21] projected point clouds from the 3D space to the feature space by computing multiple geometric and color features, including surface curvature, color consistency, and color saturation. The extracted features were then aggregated and regressed to the visual quality scores by training a support vector regression model. Yang [22] adopted the transfer learning strategy where the natural images are considered and the source domain, and the distorted point clouds are employed as the destination domain. Then, the point cloud quality is inferred adaptively by the unsupervised domain transfer. Bourbia [8] proposed a no-reference point cloud quality assessment model based on projected images via a Transformer network and saliency-based pooling strategy. Zhang [24] proposed the VQA-PC method by taking full advantage of the dynamic characteristic of point cloud data. In particular, it treated the point cloud data as a video captured by a moving camera, thereby capturing the motion, shape, and structural features by using a video feature extractor.

Since the projection of point cloud from the 3D space to the 2D space inevitably results in the loss of information, Liu [23] proposed the ResSCNN model by using sparse convolution to construct a residual network to extract features. Specifically, the distorted point cloud is transformed to the voxels firstly, and then used the sparse convolution to construct a residual network. Finally, the quality score is predicted with a regression operation.

3 Methodology

3.1 Overview

The architecture of the proposed contextual point-wise network is illustrated in Fig. 1.

As is shown in Fig. 1, our proposed CPW-Net is composed of three major components, including the segmentation sub-patches (SSP), the offset attention feature encoder (OAFE) and the quality score prediction (QSP). First, the point cloud is sent into the SSP module. It divides the point cloud into several small patches. After that, the point cloud patches are separately encoded into a new feature space through the OAFE module, which is used to characterize the semantic similarity between points. In particular,

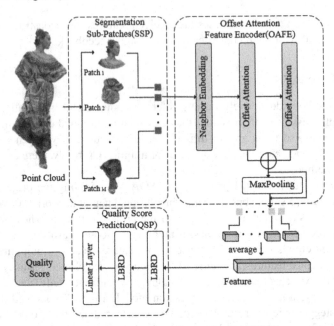

Fig. 1. The framework of the proposed CPW-Net.

the OAFE contains a neighbor embedding and two stacked offset attention modules to further capture the contextual features. Finally, the QSP module regresses the features to the quality scores.

3.2 Segmentation Sub-Patches

Given an input point cloud composed of N points, each of which is consisted of the geometric coordinates and color attributes, we can represent as follow form.

$$\mathcal{P} = \{\boldsymbol{p}_i | i = 1, 2, \ldots, N\} \in \mathbb{R}^{N \times 6}. \tag{1}$$

$$\boldsymbol{p}_i = (x_i, y_i, z_i, r_i, g_i, b_i). \tag{2}$$

where (x_i, y_i, z_i) indicates the geometric coordinates and (r_i, g_i, b_i) stands for the color attributes.

For point cloud quality assessment tasks, the most common inputs are color point clouds containing large amounts of points. For instance, the *LongDress* model in Fig. 1 contains 806806 points. However, directly processing such a large point set will not only consumes high computational memory but also prevents the network from effectively learning the features from the distorted point cloud. Therefore, we first preprocess the input point cloud data into M sub-patches P_m, where $m = 1, 2, ..., M$.

Specifically, a key point set $\{p_m\}_{m=1}^{M}$ of M points is progressively constructed by iteratively selecting the point with the maximum distance from the currently selected point using farthest point sampling (FPS) on the input point cloud. The FPS algorithm has better uniformity and coverage. It is computationally efficient and suitable for the processing of large-scale dense point cloud data. For each key point, the k-nearest neighbor (KNN) algorithm is used for sampling to obtain a patch with N points. The KNN algorithm is based on the local domain for decision-making. By choosing the appropriate k, KNN can capture subtle features, boundaries, and shape details in the point cloud. By doing so, the detailed local information of the point cloud is preserved. After that, these patches are sent into the OAFE module, respectively.

3.3 Offset Attention Feature Encoder

A. Neighbor Embedding The feature encoder (OAFE) of the network first encodes the point cloud patch into a d_e dimensional embedding feature F_e by the neighbor embedding module. The neighbor embedding module enables the neighborhood information of each point to be considered along with the single-point information. As illustrated in Fig. 2, the neighbor embedding module consists of two LBR (combining Linear, BatchNorm, and ReLU Layers) layers as well as two Sample and Group (SG) layers. In the feature aggregation process, inspired by convolutional neural networks, we employ two cascaded SG layers to gradually widen the perceptual area. In the point cloud sampling process, the SG layers use the Euclidean distance to aggregate features from the neighborhood for each point gathered by the KNN search.

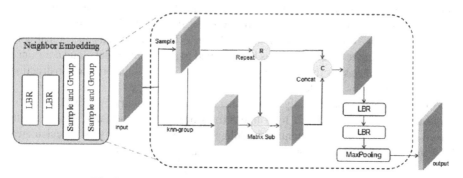

Fig. 2. The framework of the neighbor embedding module.

The specific structure of the SG layer is shown in Fig. 2. Assume the SG layer receives a point cloud P with N points and associated features as input. The result is an output consisting of an aggregated feature F_s and a sampled point cloud P_s with N_s points. The output features F_s is calculated as shown below:

$$\Delta F(p) = concat_{q \in knn(p,P)}(F(q) - F(p)). \tag{3}$$

$$\widehat{F}(p) = concat(\Delta F(p), RP(F(p), k)). \tag{4}$$

$$F_s(p) = MP(LBR(LBR(\widehat{F}(p)))). \tag{5}$$

where knn(p,P_s) denotes the k-nearest neighbor of P_s for each sampled point p $\in P_s$. F(p) is the input feature of point p. $F_s(p)$ is the output feature of sampled point p. MP is the MaxPooling operation. The operator RP(x, k) creates a matrix by iteratively repeating the vector x k times.

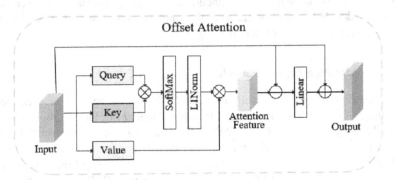

Fig. 3. The framework of offset attention module.

B. Offset Attention To make the attention module more expressive, an offset attention module that combines the Laplace operator in graph convolution with the traditional self-attention module is used. The offset attention module works by replacing the attention features with an amount between the input of the self-attention module and the attention features. The offset attention module can effectively capture the global contextual features in the point cloud. It is better suited to processing point cloud data since it also includes intrinsic substitution invariant. Figure 3 depicts the precise construction of the offset attention module.

Let Q, K, and V specifically be the query matrix, key matrix, and value matrix, respectively, that are produced by a linear transformation of the input features with regard to the traditional self-attentive module. First, the attention weights are calculated by matrix dot product using the query matrix (Q) and the key matrix (K):

$$\tilde{A} = (\tilde{\alpha})_{i,j} = Q \cdot K^T. \tag{6}$$

These weights are then normalized to yield $A = (\alpha)_{i,j}$:

$$\overline{\alpha}_{i,j} = softmax\left(\tilde{\alpha}_{i,j}\right) = \frac{\exp\left(\tilde{\alpha}_{i,j}\right)}{\sum_k \exp\left(\tilde{\alpha}_{k,j}\right)}. \tag{7}$$

$$\alpha_{i,j} = \frac{\overline{\alpha}_{i,j}}{\sum_k \overline{\alpha}_{k,j}}. \tag{8}$$

There, the softmax operation is used in the first dimension and the $l1$ norm is used to regulate the attention map in the second dimension. The attention weights are increased compared to the traditional method. Then, the attention output features $F_a = A \cdot V$ are obtained using the corresponding attention weights and value matrix (V).

Finally, the offset difference between the attention feature F_a and the input feature F_{in} is further utilized. The output feature F_{out} of the whole offset attention module is obtained through the LBR network as follows:

$$F_{out} = OA(F_{in}) = LBR(F_{in} - F_a) + F_{in}. \tag{9}$$

The output of each attention layer is concatenated. Finally, a linear transformation is performed to form a per-point feature F_o, which can be expressed as:

$$F_1 = OA^1(F_e); F_2 = OA^2(F_1). \tag{10}$$

$$F_o = concat(F_1, F_2) \cdot W_o. \tag{11}$$

The effective global feature F_g, which represents the point cloud, is then extracted by performing a pooling operation directly on the features following the offset attention layer. The pooling operation here is to concatenate the output of max-pooling and average-pooling. The point-by-point feature F_o and the global feature F_g are concatenated to obtain the final encoded feature F_P:

$$F_P = F_o + F_g = \theta_P(P_m). \tag{12}$$

where θ_P denotes Offset Attention Feature Encoder (OAFE). The encoded features of each sub-patch are averaged and fused to obtain the final point cloud features $\widetilde{F}_P$:

$$\overline{F_P} = \{F_P^m\}_{m=1}^M = \{\theta_P(P_m)\}_{m=1}^M. \tag{13}$$

$$\widetilde{F}_P = \frac{1}{M} \sum_{m=1}^{M} F_P^m. \tag{14}$$

where, F_P^m denotes the perceptually encoded feature of the m-th sub-patch P_m.

3.4 Quality Score Prediction

The quality regression module (QSP) is made up of two feedforwards neural network LBRD (combining Linear, BatchNorm, ReLU Layers, and Dropout) layers and one linear layer. The Dropout layer is used to reduce the probability of overfitting, which is set to 0.2. This module is used to map the point cloud feature vectors extracted by the OAFE module to the predicted quality scores. Then the predicted quality score Q_P can be expressed as:

$$Q_P = QSP(\widetilde{F}_P). \tag{15}$$

The least absolute value error (LAE) loss function $L_1(x) = |x|$ is not derivable at the lowest point. It may oscillate around the optimal solution and fail to converge to the minimum. The mean square error (MSE) loss function $L_2(x) = x^2$ is insensitive to outliers (meaning points far from the center) and outliers, resulting in unstable training.

Therefore, adopt Smooth $L1$, which combines the advantages of both, as the loss function, which can be expressed as:

$$SmoothL_1(x) = \begin{cases} 0.5x^2, |x| < 1 \\ |x| - 0.5, otherwise \end{cases}. \tag{16}$$

$$x = Q_P - Q_l. \tag{17}$$

where Q_l is the mean opinion score (MOS) of the input point cloud. The gradient of the loss functionto x is expressed as:

$$\frac{\partial smoothL_1(x)}{\partial x} = \begin{cases} x, |x| < 1 \\ \pm 1, otherwise \end{cases}. \tag{18}$$

It is evident that the gradient of x is less when x is small. The gradient is stopped at 1 when x is very big to guarantee that all order derivatives are continuous.

4   Experiments

In this section, we first go through the experimental setups and evaluation metrics. Then the SJTU database and the WPC database are presented separately. The performance of our CPW-Net is compared with that of previous mainstream FR, RR, and NR methods. After that, we perform an ablation study on the number of patches, neighbor points, and attention modules.

4.1   Experiment Implementation and Criteria

The Adam optimizer [25] is used for training, the weight decay is set to 1e-4, and the initial learning rate is set to 5e-5. By default, we train the model for 100 epochs. Each point cloud data is divided into $M = 10$ patches, and each patch contains $N_P = 10240$ points. The value of M is proven in the following ablation experiments. In the neighbor embedding module, we use the KNN algorithm to select $R_t = 32$ neighboring points around each sampling point.

To verify the efficiency of the suggested approach, we used three evaluation metrics commonly used in the field of image quality assessment (IQA), including Spearman Rank-Order Correlation Coefficient (SROCC), Kendall Rank-Order Correlation Coefficient (KROCC), and Pearson Linear Correlation Coefficient (PLCC).

The Spearman Rank-Order Correlation Coefficient (SROCC) is a nonparametric statistic that is used to determine the relationship between two variables. It is calculated by the formula:

$$SROCC = 1 - \frac{6\sum_i d_i^2}{N(N^2 - 1)}. \tag{19}$$

where N is the number of measured point clouds, and d_i is the magnitude difference between the ground truth MOS and the predicted score of the ith point cloud. SROCC takes values in the range of [-1,1]. Whereas 1 represents a fully positive correlation, -1 represents a perfectly negative correlation, and 0 represents no linear connection.

The Kendall Rank-Order Correlation Coefficient (KROCC) is used to measure the ranking correlation between quantitative variables. Its calculation formula is:

$$KROCC = \frac{P - Q}{P + Q + T}. \tag{20}$$

P denotes concordant pairs, Q denotes discordant pairs, and T denotes tied pairs. KROCC takes the same range of values as SROCC above. KROCC is closer to 1, meaning the ordering relationship between two variables is more consistent.

The Pearson Linear Correlation Coefficient (PLCC) is a metric for determining the strength and direction of a linear link between two variables. It is calculated as:

$$PLCC = \frac{\sum_i (Q_i - Q_m)(\widehat{Q_i} - \widehat{Q_m})}{\sqrt{\sum_i (Q_i - Q_m)^2}\sqrt{\sum_i (\widehat{Q_i} - \widehat{Q_m})^2}} \tag{21}$$

Q_i and $\widehat{Q_i}$ denote the ground truth MOS and prediction score of the ith point cloud, respectively. Q_m and $\widehat{Q_m}$ denote the mean values of the variables Q_i and $\widehat{Q_i}$, respectively. When the absolute value of PLCC approaches 1, it implies that the two variables have a stronger linear connection. Before calculating PLCC, we used a five-parameter logistic nonlinear fitting function to fit the data.

4.2 Prediction Performance on SJTU Database

The SJTU dataset [26] is a point cloud quality assessment dataset consisting of 420 point clouds. Generated by ten reference point clouds through seven distortion types at six different distortion levels. Ten reference point clouds include six human body models ('RedandBlack', 'Loot', 'LongDress', 'Hhi_ULLIWegner', 'Soldier', and 'Ricardo') and four inanimate objects ('ULB_Unicorn', 'Romanoillamp', 'Statue Klimt', 'Shiva'). The seven distortion types include four single distortions: Octree-based compression (OT), Color noise (CN), Geometry Gaussian noise (GGN), Downscaling (DS), and three compound distortions: DS + CN, DS + GGN, CN + GGN.

To the literature [9, 27], the experiments use a K-fold cross-validation strategy. The limited datasets are fully utilized for model evaluation to make the model more generalizable. Specifically, for the SJTU dataset, one set of point clouds is selected as the test set, while the remaining eight sets of point clouds are used as the training set. Nine repeats of this process are performed. And just one instance of each point cloud collection is utilized as the test set. Cross-validation is performed 9 times and the mean result is used to determine the ultimate result. The training and test sets don't contain any content that is similar. In performance comparison, we validate the methods that do not require training on the same test set and calculate their average performance.

Table 1 displays the experimental results. 'P' and 'I' stand for the point cloud and projected image modality, respectively. The best performance in the FR-PCQA method and NR-PCQA method is marked in bold. The results show that our proposed CPW-Net

Table 1. Performance comparison on the SJTU dataset.

Type	Methods	Model	PLCC↑	SROCC↑	KRCC↑	RMSE↓
FR-PCQA	MSE-p2point[13]	P	0.81	0.72	0.56	1.36
	HD-p2point[13]	P	0.77	0.71	0.54	1.44
	MSE-p2plane[14]	P	0.59	0.62	0.48	2.28
	HD-p2Plane[14]	P	0.68	0.64	0.45	2.12
	PSNR[29]	P	0.81	0.79	0.61	1.31
	PCQM[18]	P	0.88	0.86	0.70	1.08
	GraphSIM[15]	P	**0.89**	**0.87**	**0.69**	**1.03**
	PointSSIM[16]	P	0.74	0.71	0.54	1.54
RR-PCQA	PCMRR[19]	P	0.68	0.47	0.33	1.72
NR-PCQA	BRISQUE[30]	I	0.42	0.39	0.29	2.09
	NIQE[31]	I	0.24	0.13	0.10	2.26
	PQA-net[7]	I	0.85	0.83	0.63	1.07
	3D-NSS[21]	P	0.74	0.72	0.52	1.66
	ResSCNN[23]	P	0.82	0.81	0.61	1.11
	CPW-Net(Ours)	P	**0.90**	**0.87**	**0.70**	**1.03**

method outperforms all the NR-PCQA and FR-PCQA methods compared. Compared with PQA-net, the second-ranked NR-PCQA method. PLCC and SROCC improved by 0.04 (0.90 vs 0.85; 0.87 vs 0.83), and KROCC improved by 0.07 (0.70 vs 0.63). Generally, the FR-PCQA method uses the original undamaged point cloud as a reference and will perform better than the NR method. It shows that our method has some advantages in performance.

4.3 Prediction Performance on WPC Database

The Waterloo Point Cloud (WPC) dataset [28] contains 20 reference point clouds with different geometric and textural complexity, including snacks, fruits, vegetables, office supplies, containers, etc. Each reference point cloud corresponds to 37 distortion point clouds. Distortion types are: Downsampling, Gaussian noise contamination, G-PCC, and V-PCC. To facilitate the experimental comparison, we use the same training set and test set division method as PAQ-net. The training set accounts for 80% of the total, whereas the test set accounts for 20%. The test set point clouds are 'Banana', 'Cauliflower', 'Mushroom', and 'Pineapple'.

Table 2 shows the overall results of CPW-Net and the selected PCQA methods on the test set. 'P' and 'I' stand for the point cloud and projected image modality respectively. The best performance in the FR-PCQA method and NR-PCQA method is marked in bold. From the results, the performance of all methods on the WPC dataset is significantly lower compared to the results of Table 1 on the SJTU dataset. By analyzing the point cloud data in the dataset, we believe that the geometric structure of the selected point clouds for WPC is relatively simple and color limited. This creates difficulties for the model to extract distorted features. The best performing method among NR-PCQA methods is PQA-net. This method is quality assessed by extracting features from the projected image. It is more advantageous for evaluating point cloud data with a simple geometric structure. 3D-NSS is traditionally evaluated by computing statistics. Compared to deep learning methods, the computation is more complex and takes a longer time. The ResSCNN method is a deep learning method based on point clouds using sparse convolution. Its performance is slightly inferior compared to other methods. Our proposed CPW-Net method is also a deep learning method based on point clouds and outperforms ResSCNN in terms of performance. It proves that our improvements on the network are useful.

Table 2. Performance comparison with state-of-the-art approaches on the WPC.

Type	Methods	Model	PLCC↑	SROCC↑	KRCC↑	RMSE↓
FR-PCQA	MSE-p2point[13]	P	0.50	0.48	0.33	18.43
	HD-p2point[13]	P	0.37	0.36	0.25	19.73
	MSE-p2plane[14]	P	0.34	0.16	0.11	20.00
	HD-p2Plane[14]	P	0.27	0.20	0.14	20.48
	PSNR[29]	P	0.56	0.53	0.37	17.61
	PCQM[18]	P	**0.65**	**0.71**	**0.52**	**21.28**
	GraphSIM[15]	P	0.47	0.46	0.32	18.79
	PointSSIM[16]	P	0.14	0.18	0.14	21.07
RR-PCQA	PCMRR[19]	P	0.29	0.26	0.19	21.28
NR-PCQA	BRISQUE[30]	I	0.42	0.38	0.26	22.54
	NIQE[31]	I	0.39	0.39	0.26	22.55
	PQA-net[7]	I	**0.70**	**0.69**	**0.51**	**15.18**
	3D-NSS[21]	P	0.65	0.64	0.44	16.57
	ResSCNN[23]	P	0.42	0.43	0.25	23.27
	CPW-Net(Ours)	P	0.59	0.55	0.39	17.68

4.4 Ablation Study

A. Number of Patches The problem of dividing the point cloud into several patches is also needed to be explored. Too few patches will cause a loss of information and affect prediction accuracy. Too many patches will result in overlapping patches, which will lead to redundancy of extracted features. This leads to performance degradation and increased computational memory burden. Therefore, we verify the value of the number of patches M by ablation study. Four sets of experiments are set up with M = 6, 8, 10, and

12. From Table 3 results, we can get that the model prediction has the highest accuracy when M = 10 is taken.

B. Number of Neighbor Points In the neighbor embedding module, the KNN algorithm is used to aggregate the neighboring points. Improving local feature extraction capability. It has been demonstrated experimentally that combining neighborhood points to learn local features is beneficial for assessing the quality of point clouds. For the experiments, several values of k are chosen, and the results are reported in Table 4. When k = 32, the performance results are the best.

Table3. Performance results on the SJTU database by changing the number of patches.

M	PLCC	SROCC	KRCC	RMSE
6	0.6338	0.6609	0.4651	1.7800
8	0.7503	0.7267	0.5219	1.5212
10	**0.8304**	**0.8494**	**0.6378**	**1.2146**
12	0.8138	0.7878	0.5902	1.3375

Table4. Performance results on the SJTU database by changing the number of neighbor points.

k	PLCC	SROCC	KRCC	RMSE
0	0.6005	0.5374	0.3991	1.8401
8	0.8204	0.8053	0.6160	1.3158
16	0.8437	0.8122	0.6315	1.2355
32	**0.8494**	**0.8304**	**0.6378**	**1.2146**
64	0.8044	0.7548	0.5666	1.3672

Table5. Performance results on the SJTU database by changing the number of attention modules.

S	PLCC	SROCC	KRCC	RMSE
1	0.8265	0.8093	0.6280	1.2953
2	**0.8494**	**0.8304**	**0.6378**	**1.2146**
3	0.8218	0.7897	0.6137	1.3110

C. Number of Attention Modules In the offset attention feature encoder (OAFE) module, we used two stacked offset attention modules. In order to explore the contribution of multiple offset attention modules to point cloud feature extraction, we set different numbers of them for experiments separately. The performance results are shown in Table 5. It is clear that using two offset attention modules provides the greatest performance results. With two stacked offset attention modules, semantically rich and discriminative representations in each point can be learned.

4.5 Visualization Comparisons

In addition to the quantitative performance results, we also validate the visualized point clouds with the quality scores predicated by the CPW-Net method presented in this paper. The point clouds of different distortion levels with incremental Gaussian noise distortion are shown in Fig. 4. Its original reference point cloud is 'cake' in the WPC dataset, which contains 2486566 points. For these four distortion point clouds, the quality scores predicted by our model are'73.26','61.45','47.59', and'18.69'. Through human visual perception, we can clearly distinguish the variation in point cloud quality. This is the same trend as the variation of the fraction from the prediction. Therefore, the proposed CPW-Net method successfully distinguishes the distorted point cloud data with different perceived quality fractions and is consistent with real human visual perception.

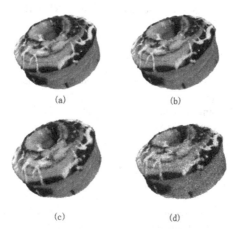

Fig. 4. Examples of perceptual quality prediction. The distortion level increases in the order of (a),(b),(c), and (d).

5   Conclusion

In this paper, we proposed a new contextual point-wise deep learning network for no-reference point cloud quality assessment. To prevent the loss of information in projection-based approaches, a point-wise deep learning network is designed to extract features directly in the point set domain. In particular, we utilize an offset attention feature encoder module to extract the local and global features concurrently. Finally, we invalidate the performance of our proposed method on the SJTU and WPC dataset, respectively. The experimental results demonstrate that the learned features directly from the point set can effectively improve the prediction performance.

In future work, we will further investigate the effect of a saliency-based pooling strategy in our network. The combination of projection-based and point-wise feature representation may also prompt the prediction performance.

Acknowledgment. This work was sponsored by the Beijing Natural Science Foundation (No. 4232020), Scientific and Technological Innovation 2030 - "New Generation Artificial Intelligence" Major Project (No. 2022ZD0119502), the National Natural Science Foundation of China (No. 62201017, No.62201018, No.62076012). The authors would like to thank the anonymous reviewers who put in efforts to help improve this paper.

References

1. Thomas, P.C., David, W.M.: Augmented reality: an application of heads-up display technology to manual manufacturing processes. In: Hawaii International Conference on System Sciences. ACM SIGCHI Bulletin, vol. 2 (1992)
2. Yuen, S.C.Y., Yaoyuneyong, G., Johnson, E.: Augmented reality: An overview and five directions for AR in education. J. Educ. Technol. Dev. Exch. (JETDE) **4**(1), 11 (2011)
3. Radianti, J., Majchrzak, T.A., Fromm, J., et al.: A systematic review of immersive virtual reality applications for higher education: design elements, lessons learned, and research agenda. Comput. Educ. **147**, 103778 (2020)
4. Slavova, Y., Mu, M.: A comparative study of the learning outcomes and experience of VR in education. In: 2018 IEEE Conference on Virtual Reality and 3D User Interfaces (VR), pp. 685–686. IEEE (2018)
5. Mohammadi, P., Ebrahimi-Moghadam, A., Shirani, S.: Subjective and objective quality assessment of image: A survey. arXiv preprint arXiv:1406.7799 (2014)
6. Wang, X., Liang, X., Yang, B., et al.: No-reference synthetic image quality assessment with convolutional neural network and local image saliency. Comput. Vis. Media **5**, 193–208 (2019)
7. Liu, Q., Yuan, H., Su, H., et al.: PQA-Net: deep no reference point cloud quality assessment via multi-view projection. IEEE Trans. Circuits Syst. Video Technol. **31**(12), 4645–4660 (2021)
8. Bourbia, S., Karine, A., Chetouani, A., et al.: No-reference point clouds quality assessment using transformer and visual saliency. In: Proceedings of the 2nd Workshop on Quality of Experience in Visual Multimedia Applications, pp. 57–62 (2022)
9. Fan, Y., Zhang, Z., Sun, W., et al.: A no-reference quality assessment metric for point cloud based on captured video sequences. In: 2022 IEEE 24th International Workshop on Multimedia Signal Processing (MMSP), pp. 1–5. IEEE (2022)
10. De Silva, V., Fernando, A., Worrall, S., et al.: Sensitivity analysis of the human visual system for depth cues in stereoscopic 3-D displays. IEEE Trans. Multimedia **13**(3), 498–506 (2011)
11. Liu, Y., Wang, W., Hu, Y., et al.: Multi-agent game abstraction via graph attention neural network. Proc. AAAI Conf. Artif. Intell. **34**(05), 7211–7218 (2020)
12. Zhu, X., Cheng, D., Zhang, Z., et al.: An empirical study of spatial attention mechanisms in deep networks. In: Proceedings of the IEEE/CVF International Conference on Computer Vision, pp. 6688–6697 (2019)
13. Mekuria, R., Li, Z., Tulvan, C., et al.: Evaluation criteria for point cloud compression. ISO/IEC MPEG 16332 (2016)
14. Tian, D., Ochimizu, H., Feng, C., et al.: Geometric distortion metrics for point cloud compression. In: 2017 IEEE International Conference on Image Processing (ICIP), pp. 3460–3464. IEEE (2017)

15. Yang, Q., Ma, Z., Xu, Y., et al.: Inferring point cloud quality via graph similarity. IEEE Trans. Pattern Anal. Mach. Intell. **44**(6), 3015–3029 (2020)
16. Alexiou, E., Ebrahimi, T.: Towards a point cloud structural similarity metric. In: 2020 IEEE International Conference on Multimedia & Expo Workshops (ICMEW), pp. 1–6 IEEE (2020)
17. De Queiroz, R.L., Chou, P.A.: Motion-compensated compression of dynamic voxelized point clouds. IEEE Trans. Image Process. **26**(8), 3886–3895 (2017)
18. Meynet, G., Nehmé, Y., Digne, J., et al.: PCQM: a full-reference quality metric for colored 3D point clouds. In: 2020 Twelfth International Conference on Quality of Multimedia Experience (QoMEX), pp. 1–6. IEEE (2020)
19. Viola, I., Cesar, P.: A reduced reference metric for visual quality evaluation of point cloud contents. IEEE Sig. Process. Lett. **27**, 1660–1664 (2020)
20. Krizhevsky, A., Sutskever, I., Hinton, G.E.: ImageNet classification with deep convolutional neural networks. Commun. ACM **60**(6), 84–90 (2017)
21. Zhang, Z., Sun, W., Min, X., et al.: No-reference quality assessment for 3D colored point cloud and mesh models. IEEE Trans. Circuits Syst. Video Technol. **32**(11), 7618–7631 (2022)
22. Yang, Q., Liu, Y., Chen, S., et al.: No-Reference Point Cloud Quality Assessment via Domain Adaptation. arXiv preprint arXiv:2112.02851 (2021)
23. Liu, Y., Yang, Q., Xu, Y., et al.: Point Cloud Quality Assessment: Dataset Construction and Learning-based No-Reference Approach. arXiv preprint arXiv:2012.11895 (2020)
24. Zhang, Z., Sun, W., Min, X., et al.: Treating Point Cloud as Moving Camera Videos: A No-Reference Quality Assessment Metric. arXiv preprint arXiv:2208.14085 (2022)
25. Kingma, D.P., Ba, J.: Adam: A method for stochastic optimization. arXiv preprint arXiv: 1412.6980 (2014)
26. Yang, Q., Chen, H., Ma, Z., et al.: Predicting the perceptual quality of point cloud: a 3D-to-2D projection-based exploration. IEEE Trans. Multimedia **23**, 3877–3891 (2020)
27. Chetouani, A., Quach, M., Valenzise, G., et al.: Deep learning-based quality assessment of 3D point clouds without reference. In: 2021 IEEE International Conference on Multimedia & Expo Workshops (ICMEW), pp. 1–6 IEEE (2021)
28. Liu, Q., Su, H., Duanmu, Z., et al.: Perceptual quality assessment of colored 3D point clouds. IEEE Trans. Vis. Comput. Graph. **29**(8), 3642–3655 (2022)
29. Torlig, E.M., Alexiou, E., Fonseca, T.A., et al.: A novel methodology for quality assessment of voxelized point clouds. In: Applications of Digital Image Processing XLI. SPIE, vol. 10752, pp. 174–190 (2018)
30. Mittal, A., Moorthy, A.K., Bovik, A.C.: No-reference image quality assessment in the spatial domain. IEEE Trans. Image Process. **21**(12), 4695–4708 (2012)
31. Mittal, A., Soundararajan, R., Bovik, A.C.: Making a "completely blind" image quality analyzer. IEEE Sig. Process. Lett. **20**(3), 209–212 (2012)

Measurement of Solder Wetting Angle Based on Image Processing and Polynomial Fitting

Xingyu Zhou and Shanzhong Liu[✉]

College of Information Engineering, Henan University of Science and Technology, Henan, China
szliu@haust.edu.cn

Abstract. The study focuses on the solder wetting image and proposes a solder wetting angle measurement method based on image processing and polynomial fitting. Specifically, the method involves using contrast limited adaptive histogram equalization, bilateral filtering, gradient computation, non-maximum suppression, Otsu's method for determining dual thresholds, dual threshold-based edge connection, and morphological processing to obtain the boundary contour of the wetted solder. By determining the left and right endpoints of the wetted solder contour, a baseline is established, with the left endpoint as the center to establish a Cartesian coordinate system. The position information of the solder contour is then converted into discrete coordinate points in the coordinate system. Therefore, the measurement problem of the wetting angle between the solder contours is transformed into the calculation of the slope of the tangent line at the intersection of the polynomial fitting curve with the coordinate axis. Experimental verification shows that the proposed method can accurately measure the wetting angle on different solders, successfully solving the issue of measuring the wetting angle during the wetting process, and improving the efficiency of wetting angle measurement.

Keywords: Wetting angle · Contour extraction · Image processing · Polynomial fitting

1 Introduction

The wetting property of lead-free solder determines whether the solder can spread and wet the substrate to form reliable solder joints. In the wetting spread experiment with lead-free solder, the wetting angle is one of the important indicators to evaluate the wetting performance of the solder. Therefore, the method of indirectly measuring the solder wetting angle through image processing is widely used by recording the wetting spread experiment with an industrial camera. In the measurement of the contact angle, a critical step is to find the contour of the solder and accurately determine the boundary points of the solder. Currently, the measurement of solder wetting angle is mainly obtained through manual analysis of wetting solder images, which is inefficient and whose accuracy depends on the operator's ability [1–4].

In recent years, researchers have achieved significant improvements in the calculation of wetting angles for materials based on image processing algorithms. Pei Zhang et al. [5]

© The Author(s), under exclusive license to Springer Nature Singapore Pte Ltd. 2024
F. Sun et al. (Eds.): ICCSIP 2023, CCIS 1919, pp. 234–245, 2024.
https://doi.org/10.1007/978-981-99-8021-5_18

proposed an automatic measurement method for droplet contact angles based on droplet boundary information. Tian Zhang et al. [6] presented a particle swarm optimization-based Canny algorithm for measuring the contact angle between droplets and substrates. Jinhui Liu et al. [7] designed a convolutional neural network super-resolution Young's contact angle image measurement system for contact angle measurement of droplets. Kunyue Zhao et al. [8] proposed an automatic contact angle measurement method based on feature point detection. Jian Li et al. [9] proposed a droplet contact angle calculation method based on the local contour of the droplet. It can be seen that the calculation of wetting angles based on image processing depends on the extraction of material edge contours. However, these methods are suitable for analyzing and calculating contact angles of droplet images with smooth surfaces and uniform lighting conditions.

Ranya Al Darwich et al. [10] proposed a contour edge extraction method for high-temperature metal droplets based on local gradient estimation, aiming to extract the contours of high-temperature metal droplets under low contrast and blurry boundaries. Chuhao Zhang et al. [11] transformed the traditional method of detecting contours by obtaining gradient value responses into acquiring large-scale connected domains that match the molten pool area, achieving accurate extraction of the contours of the molten pool area. In the solder wetting and spreading experiment, the solder dynamics are constantly changing, requiring timely adjustment of relevant parameters based on the solder state for the measurement of the solder wetting angle. Additionally, the shape of the solder and surface texture information further increase the difficulty of extracting the contour of the wetting solder in the image. Currently, there is limited research on the calculation of the solder wetting angle. This paper designs a method based on image processing and polynomial fitting to measure the wetting angle during the solder wetting process.

2 Methods and Experiments

2.1 Acquisition of Solder Images

In the paper, a high-speed camera with a horizontal angle was used to record the wetting spreading experiment of solder on a copper plate. The size of the collected images was 640×1024, and the wetting solder images collected are shown in Fig. 1(a).

Due to the small area of the solder region in the collected solder images relative to the entire image, in order to accelerate the computation speed of the algorithm for measuring the contact angle, the collected solder images were cropped to the region of interest. The cropped solder image is shown in Fig. 1(b).

Based on the characteristics of wetting solder images, a method for measuring the solder wetting angle is designed, as shown specifically in Fig. 2.

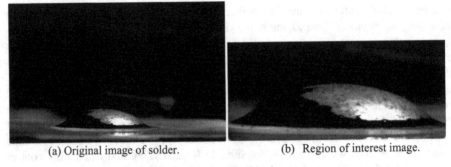

(a) Original image of solder.   (b) Region of interest image.

Fig. 1. Obtain the solder image.

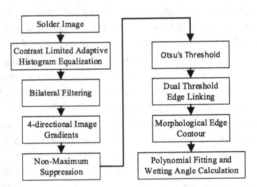

Fig. 2. Flowchart of the solder wetting angle measurement method based on image processing and polynomial fitting.

2.2   Solder Contour Extraction

To measure the wetting angle during the wetting process of the solder, it is first necessary to obtain the contour boundary of the solder. The traditional Canny edge detection method is widely used for extracting edge information, which mainly consists of four steps: smoothing filter, gradient calculation, non-maximum suppression, and double threshold edge linking [12]. The effectiveness of the traditional Canny edge detection algorithm is shown in the figure below (Fig. 3):

Fig. 3. Effect of Canny Edge Detection Overlayed on Original Image.

From the image, it can be observed that the contour edges of the solder have weak edge gradient information in certain areas, resulting in incomplete solder edge contours. The presence of rich texture information on the surface of the solder and background noise greatly interfere with determining accurate solder edge contours.

2.2.1   Contrast Limited Adaptive Histogram Equalization

To address the problem of weak edges in the wetting solder image, contrast limited adaptive histogram equalization [13] is used to enhance the image. The specific steps are as follows: First, the image is divided into several regions; second, the histogram of each region is computed; then, the histogram of each region is limited by a threshold T.

$$T = C \times \frac{N_x \times N_y}{M} \tag{1}$$

N_x and N_y represent the number of pixels in each region in the x and y directions, respectively; M represents the number of gray levels in the image; C represents the limitation coefficient.

According to the threshold T, the histogram in each region is limited. Let the total number of pixels exceeding the amplitude T be S, and the average distribution of pixels per gray level be A, then we can obtain the following:

$$S = \sum_{x=0}^{M-1} \{\max[h(x) - T], 0\} \tag{2}$$

$$A = \frac{S}{M} \tag{3}$$

$$h\prime(x) = \begin{cases} T + A & h(x) \geq T \\ h(x) + A & h(x) < T \end{cases} \tag{4}$$

In the equation, $h(x)$ represents the histogram of the image region; $h\prime(x)$ represents the histogram after image transformation; then, each sub-region's new histogram $h\prime(x)$ is sequentially subjected to equalization processing, and the final image is obtained through bilinear interpolation [14]. The processing effect of histogram equalization with the contrast limitation method is shown in Fig. 4.

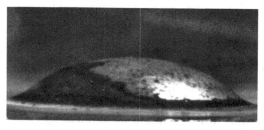

Fig. 4. The effect diagram of histogram equalization with contrast limitation.

2.2.2 Bilateral Filtering

Bilateral filtering is an improvement of Gaussian filtering and can be seen as the integration of two Gaussian filters: one calculates the weights based on the spatial proximity of image pixels, and the other calculates the weights based on the similarity of image gray values. The expression for bilateral filtering is as follows:

$$\omega_j(t) = \exp(-\frac{\|j\|^2}{2\rho^2}) \tag{5}$$

$$\phi_i(t) = \exp(-\frac{t^2}{2\sigma^2}) \tag{6}$$

$$g(i) = \eta(i)^{-1} \sum_{j \in \Omega} w(j)\phi_i(f(i-j) - f(i))f(i-j) \tag{7}$$

$$\eta(i) = \sum_{j \in \Omega} w(j)\phi_i(f(i-j) - f(i)) \tag{8}$$

In the equation, $\omega(j)$ represents the spatial filter kernel in the image, which corresponds to the weights of the corresponding image spatial pixels; $\phi_i(t)$ represents the range filter kernel in the image, which corresponds to the weights of the corresponding image range pixels; $g(i)$ represents the result of the entire filter; $f(i)$ represents the original image; and $\eta(i)$ represents the sum of weights within the filter window. The effect diagram after wetting solder bilateral filtering.

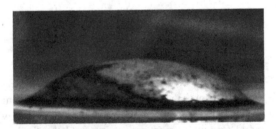

Fig. 5. The effect diagram after wetting solder bilateral filtering.

From Fig. 5, it can be observed that bilateral filtering smooths the image while preserving the contour edges of the solder; hence, bilateral filtering is chosen to smooth the solder image.

2.2.3 Image Gradient Calculation

In this paper, the extended Sobel algorithm is used to calculate the image gradient in four directions, which includes the addition of gradient templates for the 45° and 135° directions. The extended gradient templates are shown in Fig. 6.

The convolution calculation of the preprocessed wetting solder image using the gradient templates yields the gradients G_x, G_y, G_{45}, and G_{135} in the four directions.

$$\begin{bmatrix} -1 & 0 & 1 \\ -2 & 0 & 2 \\ -1 & 0 & 1 \end{bmatrix} \qquad \begin{bmatrix} -1 & -2 & -1 \\ 0 & 0 & 0 \\ 1 & 2 & 1 \end{bmatrix} \qquad \begin{bmatrix} -2 & -1 & 0 \\ -1 & 0 & 1 \\ 0 & 1 & 2 \end{bmatrix} \qquad \begin{bmatrix} 0 & 1 & 2 \\ -1 & 0 & 1 \\ -2 & -1 & 0 \end{bmatrix}$$

$$\quad\text{(a)} \qquad\qquad\qquad \text{(b)} \qquad\qquad\qquad \text{(c)} \qquad\qquad\qquad \text{(d)}$$

Fig. 6. Extended Sobel operator templates. (a) Horizontal direction. (b) Vertical direction. (c) 45° direction. (d) 135° direction.

The gradient magnitude and gradient direction angle of the wetting solder image can be expressed as:

$$G = \sqrt{G_x^2 + G_y^2 + G_{45}^2 + G_{135}^2} \tag{9}$$

$$\theta = \arctan{G_y}\big/{G_x} \tag{10}$$

In the equation, G represents the gradient magnitude of the image; G_x, G_y, G_{45}, and G_{135} respectively denote the results of four gradient templates calculated on the image. θ represents the direction angle of the image gradient. The effect diagram of the wetting solder gradient magnitude obtained through the gradient templates is shown in Fig. 7.

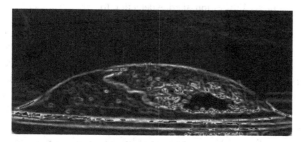

Fig. 7. The effect diagram after wetting solder bilateral filtering.

2.2.4 Extraction of Solder Contour Edges

In the previous context, we obtained the gradient magnitude and direction angle of the solder image. By comparing the pixel gradient values with the gradient values of neighboring pixels, we select the maximum value among the four directions as the edge point while suppressing the other points [13].

The Otsu method is used to determine the high and low thresholds in the Canny algorithm, as follows:

The Otsu method initially determines the threshold $l \in \{0, 1, 2, \cdots, 255\}$, divides the image into two parts L_1 and L_2 uses l. It calculates the probabilities of pixel allocation to L_1 and L_2 as P_1 and P_2, the grayscale means of L_1 and L_2 as m_1 and m_2, the average grayscale value of the image as m, and the inter-class variance of the image as σ^2.

$$\sigma^2 = P_1(m_1 - m)^2 + P_2(m_2 - m)^2 \tag{11}$$

For each threshold l in the set, the corresponding σ^2 is computed, and the threshold l corresponding to the maximum σ^2 is selected as the threshold T_{Otsu} for the Otsu algorithm.

The high threshold of the entire image is determined as $T_h = T_{Otsu}$, and the low threshold is $T_l = T_h/3$.

Based on the high and low thresholds, the pixel values of the pixels below the low threshold are set to zero, while the pixels above the high threshold are considered strong edge points, and their pixel values are marked as 255. During the traversal of the entire image, if a pixel point has other strong edge points in its 8 neighboring neighborhoods, it is retained. Otherwise, it is suppressed. The result of adaptive threshold edge detection is shown in Fig. 8.

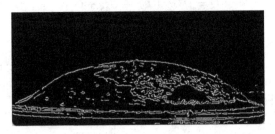

Fig. 8. Illustration of edge detection for wetting solder.

In order to extract closed and continuous contour edges from the discontinuous contour edges and the presence of internal pseudo edges in the edge detection results, a method of morphological processing using dilation and erosion is employed to obtain complete and continuous edge contours. Then, the interference of small peripheral connected domains is removed based on the judgment method of connected domain scale. After obtaining the closed contour connected domain, it is filled, and a circular structuring element with a radius of 10 pixels is established based on mathematical morphology operations, which is subsequently subjected to a closing operation with the filled connected domain to further smooth the edge of the connected domain[]. Finally, the corresponding solder contour is obtained. In the obtained solder contour, the calculation of the wetting angle is only directly related to the upper contour of the solder image. The superimposed effect of the upper contour of the image on the original image is shown in Fig. 9.

Based on the extracted wetting solder contour, the wetting angle of the solder is calculated using a polynomial fitting method. Specifically, as follows:

2.3 Calculation of the Wetting Angle of Solder

Based on the extracted wetting solder contour, the wetting angle of the solder is calculated using a polynomial fitting method. Specifically, as follows:

Firstly, due to the asymmetric nature of the solder wetting process, the wetting angle of the solder corresponds to two angles known as the left wetting angle and the right wetting angle.

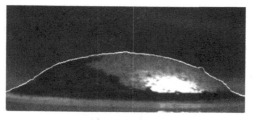

Fig. 9. Image of the extraction results of the wetting solder contour edge.

Next, based on the contour image of the solder edge, a Cartesian coordinate system is established with the bottom left pixel of the image as the origin. The contour edge information of the solder is converted into discrete data points in the coordinate system. Since each x-coordinate in the coordinate system corresponds to two y-values (upper and lower), and the calculation of the wetting angle is only related to the upper half of the contour, only the data points corresponding to the upper half of the solder contour are retained, as shown in Fig. 10(a). The left and right endpoints of the upper contour are connected to form the baseline for wetting angle determination, as shown in Fig. 10(b). To improve the measurement accuracy of the contact angle, a new Cartesian coordinate system is established with the left endpoint of the baseline as the origin, as shown in Fig. 10(c).

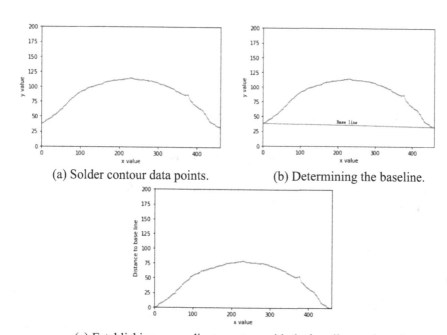

(a) Solder contour data points.   (b) Determining the baseline.

(c) Establishing a coordinate system with the baseline as the axis.

Fig. 10. Image of the data preparation process for polynomial fitting.

Polynomial curve fitting is a method based on the least squares principle to obtain the sum of squares of deviations between the fitting curve and the discrete data points [15]. It is widely used and flexible in fitting the discrete data points corresponding to the solder boundary and can be used to calculate different wetting angles of solder. Its expression is as follows:

$$y(x, \lambda) = \sum_i^M \lambda_i x^i \tag{12}$$

where M is the highest degree of the polynomial, and λ_i represents the fitting coefficients. The key to measuring the contact angle using polynomial curve fitting is to accurately fit the curve to the discrete data points corresponding to the solder contour. Then, the wetting angle of the solder is obtained by taking the derivative of the curve at the intersection point with the coordinate axis. The process is illustrated in the following diagram:

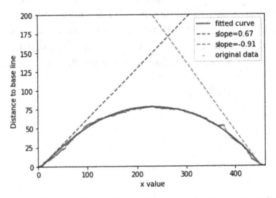

Fig. 11. The effect of fitting the wetting solder contour using a 5th order polynomial.

Figure 11 shows the result of fitting the contour edges of the wetting solder using a 5th-order polynomial. The values of the contact angle can be obtained by taking the arctan of the tangent slope at the left and right endpoints. The left contact angle is 33.63°, and the right contact angle is 42.41°.

3   Results and Discussion

To validate the effectiveness of the method proposed in this paper for measuring the wetting angle of solder, two different groups of solder, labeled A and B, were chosen for wetting spread experiments. The results obtained from measuring the wetting angle using the method presented in this paper were compared with those obtained from manual goniometer measurements.

Since solder wetting changes relatively slowly, a random selection of five consecutive images was made for groups A and B. Figure 12 shows the wetting angle of the solder on the substrate measured using a goniometer in the fifth image. As the order of polynomial

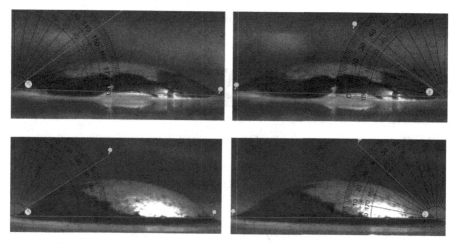

Fig. 12. Diagram illustrating the manual measurement of the wetting angle.

fitting varies, the tangent slopes of the fitting curves also differ, resulting in different measured values for the wetting angle. Different orders of polynomials were used to measure the left and right contact angles in the consecutive images, and the average value of the five images represents the respective contact angles at that time, as shown in Table 1.

Table 1. The left and right wetting angles of solder

	A		B	
	Left Angle A	Right Angle A	Left Angle B	Right Angle B
Degree2	29.09	30.15	36.24	35.99
Degree3	29.77	29.47	34.56	37.63
Degree4	36.09	35.96	36.74	39.68
Degree5	37.41	34.55	33.63	42.41
Degree6	37.95	35.16	13.13	24.82
Degree7	43.74	43.74	11.88	25.95

From Fig. 12 and Table 1, it can be seen that the method proposed in this paper achieves the best fitting results when the highest order of the polynomial is set to M = 5. The wetting angles obtained using this method are closest to the wetting angles measured manually.

To validate the feasibility of the proposed algorithm, a test was conducted on a series of consecutive solder images extracted from the collected data. The test results are shown in Fig. 13. From the figure, it can be observed that the proposed algorithm achieves excellent accuracy in the contour extraction of consecutive wetting solder images. It is suitable for measuring the wetting angle of solder in practical solder wetting spread experiments (Table 2).

| First frame | Second frame | Third frame | Fourth frame | Fifth frame |

Fig. 13. Diagram illustrating the results of testing consecutive frames of wetting solder images.

Table 2. Left and right wetting angles of consecutive frames.

	Left angle	Right angle
First frame	37.39	34.07
Second frame	37.71	34.12
Third frame	37.96	33.83
Fourth frame	37.75	33.74
Fifth frame	37.66	33.55

4   Conclusion

The article focuses on the study of solder wetting images and proposes a solder wetting angle measurement method based on image processing and polynomial fitting. In order to extract a well-located closed contour of the solder, the following steps are taken: adaptive histogram equalization with contrast limitation, bilateral filtering, gradient calculation, non-maximum suppression, adaptive dual-threshold determination using the Otsu method, edge connection using dual thresholds, and morphological processing to obtain the boundary contour of the wetting solder. The baseline is determined based on the left and right endpoints of the extracted wetting solder contour, and a Cartesian coordinate system is established with the left endpoint as the center. The position information of the solder contour is converted into discrete coordinate points in the coordinate system. The polynomial fitting method is used to fit the discrete data points in the coordinate system, and the tangent slope of the intersection between the fitting curve and the coordinate axis is calculated to obtain the solder wetting angle. Experimental verification results show that the method described in the article can accurately measure the wetting angles on different solders, successfully solving the problem of solder wetting angle measurement during the wetting process and improving the efficiency of wetting angle measurement.

Acknowledgments. This research was supported by the National Natural Science Foundation of China (U1604132).

References

1. Ismail, N., et al.: A systematic literature review: the effects of surface roughness on the wettability and formation of intermetallic compound layers in lead-free solder joints. J. Manuf. Processes **83**, 68–85 (2022)
2. Yu, W., Wang, M., Wang, F., Wang, X., Wu, B.: Study of the dynamic wetting behavior of Sn droplet impacting Cu substrate. Appl. Phys. A **128**, 646 (2022)
3. Cheng, S., Huang, C.-M., Pecht, M.: A review of lead-free solders for electronics applications. Microelectron. Reliability **75**, 77–95 (2017)
4. Jung, D.-H., Jung, J.-P.: Review of the wettability of solder with a wetting balance test for recent advanced microelectronic packaging. Crit. Rev. Solid State Mater. Sci. **44**(4), 324–343 (2018)
5. Zhang, P., Wan, Y., Zhou, Y.: A new boundary extraction algorithm and its application in contact angle measurement. J. East China Univ. Sci. Technol. (Nat. Sci. Ed.) **40**(6), 746–751 (2014)
6. Zhang, T., Tian, H., Rong, X., et al.: Application of particle swarm optimized Canny operator in high-precision contact angle measurement. J. Hebei Univ. Technol. **47**, 30–35 (2018)
7. Liu, J., Liao, F., Liang, X., et al.: Convolutional neural network-based high-resolution Young's contact angle image measurement system. Autom. Instrument. **9**, 238–324 (2022)
8. Zhao, K., Tian, H., Guo, D., et al.: Automatic contact angle measurement method based on feature point detection. J. Electron. Meas. Inst. **32**(11), 147–153 (2018)
9. Li, J., Fei, X., Wang, L., et al.: Contact angle measurement method based on local contour of droplets. Sci. Technol. Eng. **21**(24), 10134–10139 (2021)
10. Darwich, R.A., Babout, L., Strzecha, K.: An edge detection method based on local gradient estimation: application to high-temperature metallic droplet images. Appl. Sci. **12**(14), 6976 (2022). https://doi.org/10.3390/app12146976
11. Zhang, C.H., Zhao, Z., Lu, J.: Contour extraction of weld pool based on template matching using edge-oriented operator. Trans. China Weld. Inst. **43**(2), 67–74 (2022)
12. Liu, Q., Zhang, L., Li, X.: Improved Canny-based edge detection algorithm for chip image. Comput. Eng. Design **37**(11), 3063–3067 (2016)
13. Feng, X., Chen, X., Min, H., et al.: Enhancement of aerospace engine guide vane DR images based on improved CLAHE. J. Aeros. Power **37**(7), 1425–1436 (2022)
14. Wang, H., Li, R., Wang, J.: Underwater color image enhancement algorithm based on improved CLAHE. Ship Electron. Eng. **39**(11), 119–122, 141 (2019)
15. Hao, L., Wang, D., Xu, C.: Research on fitting of weld seam images based on least squares polynomial. Electron. Des. Eng. **28**(23), 173–176 (2020)

Infrared Aircraft Anti-interference Recognition Based on Feature Enhancement CenterNet

Gang Liu[✉], Hui Tian, Qifeng Si, Huixiang Chen, and Hongpeng Xu

College of Information Engineering, Henan University of Science and Technology,
Luoyang 471000, China
lg19741011@163.com

Abstract. Infrared imaging guided air to air missile is a typical infrared imaging guided weapon system. In the process of attacking targets such as fighter and helicopter, when the target discovers that it has been intercepted, it will release interference to induce the missile to deviate from its trajectory, which brings great difficulties to the missile's successful destruction of the target. By utilizing the powerful learning and representation capabilities of deep learning networks for target features, an infrared aircraft anti-interference recognition algorithm based on feature enhancement CenterNet is proposed. In order to enhance infrared aircraft features, a channel feature enhancement module is constructed. This paper applies this module to different scale feature layers of the feature extraction network and performs feature fusion through feature pyramid network. In order to reduce the impact of background and interference on aircraft and place the learning focus of feature extraction network on aircraft and its neighborhood, a mixed attention mechanism is incorporated into the backbone network. The experimental results show that the proposed method can effectively achieve anti-interference recognition of infrared aircraft.

Keywords: Infrared Aircraft · Anti-Interference Recognition · CenterNet · Feature Enhancement · Attention Mechanism

1 Introduction

Infrared imaging guidance is a guidance technology that uses image information to control aircraft to fly to the target accurately. Automatic target recognition is the process of computer automatically completing target capture and classification, and is one of the core technologies of infrared imaging guidance. The recognition rules of target recognition method based on manually designed features is predetermined. When the combat environment exceeds the predetermined rules, this method will fail. Deep learning based methods have strong self-learning and representation capabilities for target features, without the need for manual rule design, and are currently a hot topic in infrared target recognition research.

The current detection algorithms based on deep learning can mainly be divided into anchor based detection and anchor free's. The anchor based detection algorithms include two-stage algorithms and single-stage algorithms [1]. The two-stage detection

F. Sun et al. (Eds.): ICCSIP 2023, CCIS 1919, pp. 246–259, 2024.
https://doi.org/10.1007/978-981-99-8021-5_19

algorithm decomposes the target detection process into three steps: candidate region extraction, candidate region classification and candidate region coordinate correction. The mainstream algorithm for two-stage target detection is mainly based on R-CNN (Region-Convolution Neural Network) series. Zhu Dawei [2] applies R-CNN target detection framework to the field of infrared aircraft detection and verifies the feasibility of using CNN to solve such problems. Jiang Xiaowei [3] uses Faster R-CNN model to the detection of airborne infrared aircraft in the context of air defense weapon applications. The two-stage detection algorithm has high accuracy but complex model structure. The single-stage detection algorithm, also known as the detection algorithm based on regression analysis, treats the target detection problem as a regression analysis problem of target position and category information, and can directly output the detection results through a neural network model. YOLO (You Only Look Once) and SSD (Single Shot MultiBox Detector) are currently the main algorithms for the single-stage target detection. Zhao Yan [4] utilizes YOLOv3 to achieve infrared small target detection in complex environments. Chen Tieming [5] proposes an improved YOLOv3 infrared guidance target detection method by optimizing loss weights. Liu Zhiying [6] improves the multi-scale fusion strategy and realizes automatic target recognition of land cruise missiles under the guidance of TV image homing using YOLOv3. He Qian [7] uses YOLOv3 to detect stealth aircraft and decoy bombs in infrared images. Xie Jiangrong [8] improves the positioning accuracy of small infrared targets in the air by introducing semantic enhancement branches of shallow feature maps and adding prediction boxes on deep feature maps using an improved SSD detection framework. Shu Leizhi [9] achieves infrared and visible light fusion detection of ground targets using an SSD model on an unmanned aerial vehicle embedded platform. The algorithms based on anchor mechanism need to set the size, aspect ratio and other parameters of the anchor according to the learned features, so it waste computing time. Moreover, the detector is sensitive to parameters and has low detection efficiency.

The target detection algorithm based on anchor free can reduce the calculation amount and training time, and avoid the problem of sample imbalance in the training process because all the outputs of the detection network are obtained from the key point estimation without the non maximum suppression operation based on IoU (Intersection over Union). FCOS (Fully Evolutionary One Stage Object Detection) [10] allocates real boxes of different sizes to different feature maps through the regression values of targets on different feature maps, which can ensure that the targets to be regressed are more completely included in the receptive field of feature map. The main drawback of FCOS is that when the predicted pixels are far from the actual center point of target, the detection results are easily affected by the semantic overlap of overlapping targets [11]. CornerNet [12] replaces the regression bounding box by predicting the key points of target, while also predicting fine-tuning values for each corner point to slightly adjust the corner position. ExtremeNet [13] is an improvement on CornerNet. Unlike CornerNet, ExtremeNet no longer detects the upper left and lower right corners of target, but instead detects the four extreme points of target (top, bottom, left, and right). Compared with CornerNet, it is more stable, but with a large number of parameters and slow processing speed, so it cannot meet real-time applications. Furthermore, it is unable to handle targets that are collinear and have the same scale [14]. CenterNet [15], which continues the key point based detection techniques of CornerNet and ExtremeNet, directly performs convolution operations on the input image and improves the grouping post-processing operation of CornerNet. By replacing the upper left and lower right points with a center point, the network structure is simpler.

In the process of infrared imaging guided air to air missile attacking targets such as fighter and helicopter, the target will release interference when it discovers that it has been intercepted. Aircraft target recognition in interference state has great significance for the missile to successfully destroy the target. Zhang Kai [16] adds feature attention modules at the end of the backbone network to obtain the importance weight of each feature channel, then adds multi-scale dense connection modules and combines them with multi-scale feature fusion detection to achieve anti-interference recognition of infrared aircraft. Zhang Liang [17] enhances the ability of target feature extraction by combining traditional algorithms with deep learning's, maximizing the feature information of missile detection and implementing anti-interference recognition for aircraft. Gao Fan [18] proposes a lightweight convolutional structure with anchor free, adding a SkipBranch module to combine shallow information with high-level information to enhance feature expression ability, and achieving infrared target recognition through asymmetric convolution. In accordance with the character of small infrared targets, Miao Zhuang [19] designs a corresponding feature fusion network based on the spatial information and semantic information of different levels of features, and finally realizes infrared target detection.

Because all outputs of anchor free detection model are obtained from key points estimation, the non maximum suppression operation based on IoU is not required, which can reduce the amount of calculation and training time, and avoid the problem of sample imbalance in the training process. Therefore, this paper conducts research on anti-interference recognition of infrared aircraft from the perspective of CenterNet based on anchor free.

2   CenterNet

CenterNet uses three-layer deconvolution for upsampling after the backbone network to obtain higher resolution feature maps for detection, which can enhance the feature expression ability of infrared aircraft. CenterNet adopts the center point of target detection box to represent the target, predicts the center point offset, width and height of target, and obtains the actual bounding box of target. CenterNet can remove some erroneous target boxes by detecting the position of center point of target, making it more suitable for detecting small-scale targets. It has not the need for grouping processing to determine whether the center point of detection box corresponds to the same target, resulting in faster detection speed.

The obtained feature map can be used for three convolutions: (1) Heatmap prediction: Taking points with high response values as the central key points, as well as types and confidence levels of the corresponding target for each point. (2)Offset prediction: obtaining the offset of each target center point. (3)Width and height prediction: Obtaining the predicted width and height of each target, which is the size of target detection box.

The three parts predicted in CenterNet detection model correspond to three Loss function, namely, the center point prediction loss L_k, the target length and width prediction loss L_{size}, and the center point offset loss L_{offset}.

$$L_{det} = L_k + \lambda_{size} L_{size} + \lambda_{off} L_{off} \tag{1}$$

where λ_{off} and λ_{size} represent the importance weight values of bias regression and size regression, respectively.

The overall framework of CenterNet is shown in Fig. 1.

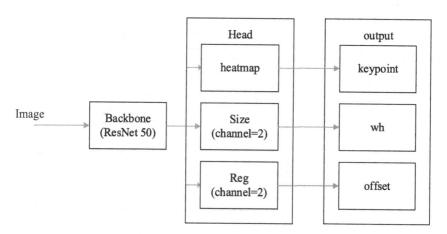

Fig. 1. The overall framework for CenterNet

3 CenterNet Infrared Aircraft Anti interference Recognition Model Based on Feature Enhancement

In response to the characteristics of weak feature information and complex background in infrared aircraft images, this paper strengthens the expression of infrared aircraft feature information by adding a feature fusion module on the basis of CenterNet, and adds an attention mechanism to enable the network to focus on target and its surrounding areas, ignoring irrelevant background information. The ability of feature extraction network to learn input image features is related to the depth of the network. The deeper the network level, the stronger the model's ability to learn complex features. ResNet can alleviate the problems of gradient vanishing and inability to fit mappings in deep neural networks through residual connections. It has a deeper network structure layer and can better learn target features. Therefore, this paper chooses ResNet50 as the backbone network of CenterNet. The overall structure of CenterNet for infrared aircraft recognition based on feature enhancement is shown in Fig. 2.

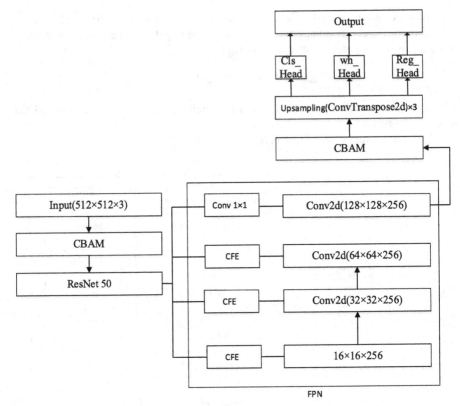

Fig. 2. The structure for CenterNet based on feature enhancement

3.1 Feature Fusion Based on Channel Feature Enhancement

In convolutional neural network, the features of each layer have different characteristics. Deep level features contain rich semantic information and are highly abstract, and shallow level features whose receptive field is small contain more details such as edges and textures. Due to the fact that CenterNet only utilizes a single effective feature layer processed by the backbone network for detection, there is not much pixel and feature information in the image when there are aircraft with small scale and long distance, and information loss may occur when compressing the resolution. In order to simultaneously utilize feature information from deep level and shallow level features, this paper uses a multi-scale feature fusion network (Feature Pyramid Network, FPN) to extract target feature information.

FPN constructs a top-down structure with horizontal connections, thereby obtaining more semantic features at all sizes and extracting candidate regions from multiple fusion feature maps of different scales. Adopting a top-down path and connection structure and combining lower resolution and higher semantic information with higher resolution and lower semantic information, the obtained feature pyramid has strong semantic information at each layer and can be quickly constructed from a single scale. By utilizing high-level features to compensate for low-level features, high-resolution and strong semantic prediction results can be obtained, which can improve the recognition accuracy of small-scale aerial targets.

Before constructing a top-down path in FPN, the input image passes through the ResNet50 backbone network to obtain target feature layer, and the depth features obtained from different convolutional layers adopt 1 × 1 convolution to achieve channel dimensionality reduction and obtain feature layers with the same number of channels, thereby reducing the computational burden of training. However, this will cause more loss of semantic information to high-level features, which will have a certain impact on the expression of high-level features, and limit FPN's ability to learn multi-scale features better.

Therefore, based on FPN, this paper designs a Channel Feature Enhancement (CFE) module to replace the original 1 × 1 convolution. In order to increase the correlation between the input feature layer C_i and the output feature layer F_i, the interdependence between the channel information of the two feature layers is modeled to reduce the loss of feature information caused by channel dimensionality reduction.

In CFE, the input feature C_i is mapped to the feature map F_i firstly by 3 × 3 convolution. Compared with 1 × 1 convolution for feature mapping, 3 × 3 convolution has a larger receptive field and more parameters, so it can perform more nonlinear transformations on the input feature map to capture the spatial features in the image better. The global feature information can be obtained by the global maximize pooling for C_i and F_i. Then, the global maximum pooling feature map's channel for C_i is transformed and multiplied by the global maximum pooling feature map for F_i to obtain a channel attention map M_i which integrates different channel information, thereby the channel feature information are enriched. The channel attention map M_i are multiplied by F_i to obtain a new feature map G_i which represents the global correlation between the input image feature map F_i and the channel attention map M_i. The output feature map F_o contains richer channel feature information, which is more conducive to the detection of infrared aircraft. The structure of Channel Feature Enhancement module is shown in Fig. 3.

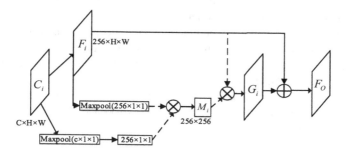

Fig. 3. The structure of Channel Feature Enhancement module

Due to the reduction of channel feature information in only C_3, C_4, and C_5 in FPN, therefore, Channel Feature Enhancement modules are added to these three horizontal connected parts. The FPN fused with CFE is shown in Fig. 4. The CFE module can help the network learn the relationship between channel features better, reduce the semantic information loss caused by FPN on high-level features, and increase the robustness of the network model to target size's change.

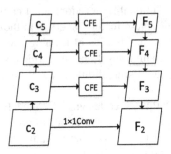

Fig. 4. The structure of FPN fused with CFE

3.2 Attention Mechanism for CenterNet

Adding an attention mechanism enables feature extracting network to focus on aircraft target and its surrounding neighborhood, ignoring irrelevant background information. Common attention mechanisms can be divided into three categories: (1) One is spatial attention, which mainly focuses on pixel regions of key information; (2) The other type is channel attention, which mainly learns features in the channel dimension to obtain the importance weight of each channel's features; (3) The third type is mixed attention, which combines spatial attention and channel attention to focus output information more on key features.

Convolutional Block Attention Module (CBAM) adjusts feature attention weights from both spatial and channel perspectives for feature maps by concatenating channel attention modules and spatial attention's. Due to having only a small number of pooling layers and fusion operations internally, without a large number of convolutional structures, the model is simple and computationally efficient. It can be combined with the original detection network structure to improve detection performance with limited parameters. Therefore, this paper chooses to add CBAM to CenterNet. The overall structure of CBAM is shown in Fig. 5.

In order to focus feature learning on levels containing more detailed information, CBAM is added to the first layer of the CenterNet backbone network and the highest resolution layer of FPN.

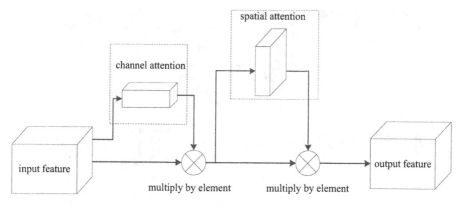

Fig. 5. The overall structure of CBAM

4   Experiment and Analysis

The experimental hardware platform is an Intel i7-8700k CPU with 3.7 GHz, 32 GB memory, and an NVIDIA GTX1080Ti GPU graphics card. The software platform is Anaconda3.5.2.0, spyder2.2.4 and python 3.5 under Win10 operation system.

4.1   DataSet

The dataset used in the experiment is LSOTB-TIR [20]. Three helicopter sequences are selected, and interference is generated based on the motion, radiation, and deployment methods according to real condition and added to the helicopter image. There are 3133 frame images, 10% of the dataset is Randomly divided for algorithm test, and the remaining dataset is divided into training set and validation set with 8:2 ratio using the cross over method. Some images of the dataset are shown in Fig. 6.

4.2   Performance Evaluation Index

This paper uses Average Precision (AP) and Mean Average Precision (mAP) to evaluate the detection performance of infrared aircraft anti-interference recognition algorithm. The AP reflects the detection effect of a single category, and its calculation formula is:

$$AP = \int_0^1 p(r)dr \qquad (2)$$

The calculation formula for precision p and recall rate r is as follows:

$$p = \frac{TP}{TP + FP} \qquad (3)$$

$$r = \frac{TP}{TP + TN} \qquad (4)$$

where *TP* represents the number of positive samples which are predicted correctly, *FP* is the number of negative samples which are predicted as positive samples, and *TN* represents the number of positive samples which are predicted as negative samples.

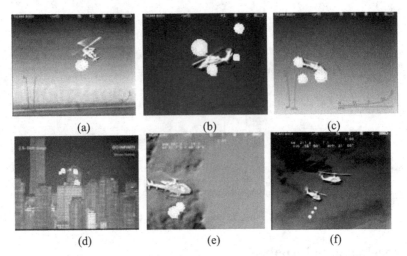

| | (a) | (b) | (c) |

| | (d) | (e) | (f) |

Fig. 6. Dataset image with interference

4.3 Ablation Experiment

ResNet50 is selected as the base network in CenterNet, and CFE and CBAM based feature fusion module are added to the ResNet50 network. The results of ablation experiments are shown in Table 1.

Table 1. Ablation experiment

	FPN	CFE	CBAM	mAP
CenterNet				89.6%
CenterNet + FPN	√			90.5%
CenterNet + CFE		√		91.13%
CenterNet + CBAM			√	88.2%
Centernet + CFE + CBAM		√	√	91.42%

According to Table 1, it can be seen that mAP of CenterNet based on feature enhancement has increased by 1.82%, compared with the original CenterNet. The training curve is shown in Fig. 7.

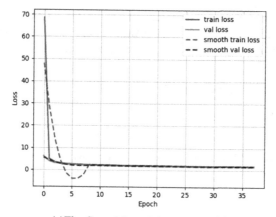

(a)The CenterNet training curves with CFE

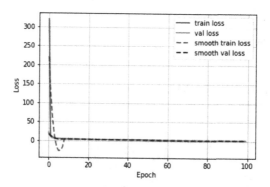

(b)The CenterNet training curves with CBAM

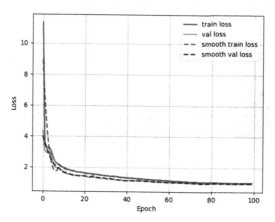

(c)The CenterNet training curves with adding CFE and CBAM

Fig. 7. The CenterNet training curves

As can be seen from Fig. 7, compared with only adding CFE module or CBAM module, CenterNet with adding CFE and CBAM has lower loss value of training curve, smaller overall oscillation range and faster rate of convergence.

4.4 Comparison of Different Algorithms

Table 2 shows the detecting results of different algorithms.

Table 2. Comparison of Different Algorithms

detection model	mAP
CornerNet	88%
RetinaNet	70.5%
FCOS	66.3%
CenterNet	89.6%
The improved CenterNet	91.42%

Figures 8, 9 and 10 show the detection results of the proposed algorithm and the other classical anchor free's.

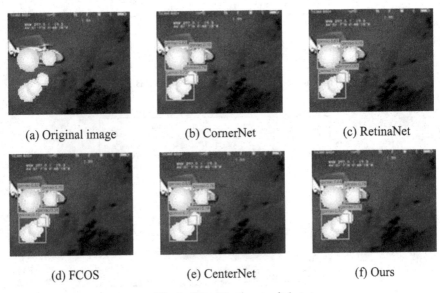

(a) Original image   (b) CornerNet   (c) RetinaNet

(d) FCOS   (e) CenterNet   (f) Ours

Fig. 8. The detection result 1

From the detection results in Fig. 8, it can be seen that other classic detection algorithms don't detect the occluded aircrafts. The original CenterNet and the CenterNet

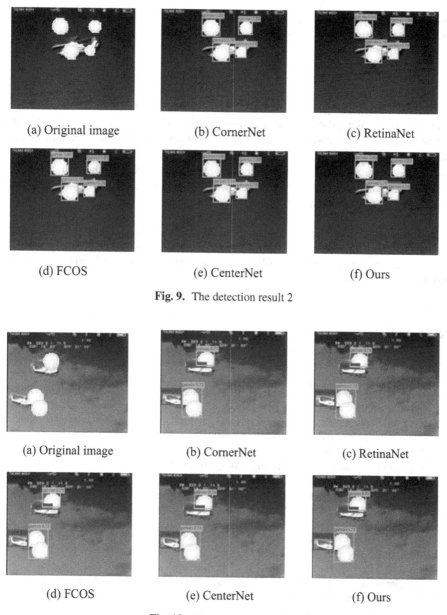

(a) Original image (b) CornerNet (c) RetinaNet

(d) FCOS (e) CenterNet (f) Ours

Fig. 9. The detection result 2

(a) Original image (b) CornerNet (c) RetinaNet

(d) FCOS (e) CenterNet (f) Ours

Fig. 10. The detection result 3

based on feature enhancement can detect the occluded aircrafts. From the detection results in Fig. 9, it can be seen that other classic detection algorithms and the original CenterNet don't detect the occluded aircrafts. The CenterNet based on feature enhancement can detect the occluded aircrafts. From the detection results in Fig. 10, it can be seen that the confidence level of aircrafts detected by the CenterNet based on feature enhancement is higher than other classic detection algorithms and the original CenterNet.

5   Conclusion

In the basis of analyzing the characteristics of the anchor free CenterNet target detection model and taking the weak feature information and complex background of aerial infrared aircraft into account, this paper designs a feature enhancement module and an attention module in order to enhance the abilities of feature extraction and complex background suppression for CenterNet. The experimental results show that the proposed CenterNet based on feature enhancement improves the anti-interference detection performance of infrared aircraft.

Acknowledgment. This work is supported jointly from Aviation Science Foundation (No. 20170142002) and Key Scientific Research Project of Colleges and Universities in Henan (No. 21A520012). The authors would like to thank the anonymous reviewers and the editor for the very instructive suggestions.

References

1. Liu, L., et al.: Deep learning for generic object detection: a survey. Int. J. Comput. Vision **128**(2), 261–318 (2020)
2. Zhu, D.: Infrared image plane target detection method based on deep learning. Xidian University (2018)
3. Jiang, X., Wang, C., Fu, Q.: Airborne infrared aircraft detection based on convolution neural network. Laser Infrared **48**(12), 1541–1546 (2018)
4. Zhao, Y., Liu, D., Zhao, L.: Infrared dim and small target detection based on YOLOv3 in complex environment. Aero Weaponry **26**(6), 29–34 (2019)
5. Chen, T., Fu, G., Li, S., Li, Y.: Typical target detection for infrared homing guidance based on YOLOv3. Laser Optoelectron. Progr. **56**(16), 161506-1–161506-8 (2019)
6. Liu, Z., Xie, C., Li, J., Sang, Y.: Land-attack missile target recognition algorithm based on improved YOLOv3. Tactical Missile Technol. **2**, 127–134 (2020)
7. He, Q.: Research on target recognition simulation technology of anti-infrared Bait. Univ. Electron. Sci. Technol. China (2019)
8. Xie, J., Li, F., Wei, H., Li, B., Shao, B.: Enhancement of single shot multibox detector for aerial infrared target detection. Acta Optica Sinica **39**(6), 0615001-1–0615001-9 (2019)
9. Shu, L.: Research on key technology of fast image fusion, object detection and tracking based on UAV. Natl. Univ. Defense Technol. (2018)
10. Tian, Z., Shen, C., Chen, H., He, T.: FCOS: fully convolutional one-stage object detection. In: 2019 IEEE/CVF International Conference on Computer Vision (ICCV), Seoul, Korea, pp. 9626–9635 (2019)
11. Li, K., Chen, Y., Liu, J., Mu, X.: Survey of deep learning-based object detection algorithms. Comput. Eng. **48**(7), 1–12 (2022)
12. Law, H., Deng, J.: Cornernet: detecting objects as paired keypoints. In: Ferrari, V., Hebert, M., Sminchisescu, C., Weiss, Y. (eds.) Computer Vision – ECCV 2018. LNCS, vol. 11218, pp. 765–781. Springer, Cham (2018). https://doi.org/10.1007/978-3-030-01264-9_45

13. Zhou, X., Zhuo, J., Krahenbuhl, P.: Bottom-up object detection by grouping extreme and center points. In: Proceedings of the IEEE Computer Society Conference on Computer Vision and Pattern Recognition (CVPR), pp. 850–859, Long Beach, CA, United States (2019)
14. Du, Z., et al.: Small object detection based on deep convolutional neural networks: a review. Comput. Sci. **49**(12), 205–218 (2022)
15. Duan, K., et al.: Centernet: keypoint triplets for object detection. In: Proceedings of the IEEE International Conference on Computer Vision (ICCV), pp. 6568–6577, Seoul, Korea (2019)
16. Zhang, K., Wang, K., Yang, X., Li, S., Wang, X.: Anti-interference recognition algorithm based on DNET for infrared aerial target. Acta Aeronautica et Astronautica Sinica **42**(2), 236–251 (2021)
17. Zhang, L., Li, S., Yang, X., Tian, X.: Research on hybrid intelligent anti-interference against air targets in complex confrontation scene. Aero Weaponry **29**(1), 22–28 (2022)
18. Gao, F., Yang, X., Lu, R., Wang, S., Gao, J., Xia, H.: Anchor-free lightweight infrared object detection method. Infrared Laser Eng. **51**(4), 135–143 (2022)
19. Miao, Z., Zhang, Y., Chen, R., Li, W.: Method for fast detection of infrared targets based on key points. Acta Optica Sinica **40**(23), 2312006-1–2312006-9 (2020)
20. Liu, Q., et al.: LSOTB-TIR: a large-scale high-diversity thermal infrared object tracking benchmark. In: Proceedings of the 28th ACM International Conference on Multimedia, pp. 3847–3856 (2020)

MHRN-ST: Go Board Recognition With Multi-stage Highlight Removal Network Based On Swin Transformer

Junxian Zhou⑩, Yunhan Lin⑩, and Huasong Min$^{(\boxtimes)}$ ⑩

Institute of Robotics and Intelligent Systems, Wuhan University of Science and Technology,
Wuhan, China
mhuasong@wust.edu.cn

Abstract. Artificial intelligence has generally surpassed humans in the game of Go, and the actual human-machine gaming environment is often more complex. In this environment, issues such as highlights, piece misplacement, and occlusions on the image can severely affect board recognition and reduce the intelligence level of the robot player. This paper proposes a multi-stage highlight removal network based on Swin Transformer, which can remove highlights on the image and recognize Go game information. Firstly, the image is processed by a multi-task detection network based on YOLOv5 to obtain highlight information. Then, the image is enhanced with the highlight information and input into the highlight removal network based on Swin Transformer for highlight removal. The output image is further processed by the detection network to obtain board information. We collected a total of 4242 images from publicly available datasets to train the detection network, which to some extent solves the problem of piece displacement. Additionally, we collected 1096 pairs of images for training the highlight removal network. Finally, the effectiveness of the proposed method was tested on a test set containing 56 images, achieving a recognition accuracy of 95.67%.

Keywords: Highlight removal · Go recognition · Go board Recognition · Swin Transformer · Neural network.

1 Introduction

Since AlphaGo [1] defeated the world champion Lee Sedol, artificial intelligence has surpassed human capabilities in the game of Go. In real-world human-machine games, the commonly used method to obtain Go board information is through manual recording, which is time-consuming and lacks accuracy guarantees. Therefore, when playing against robots, it is necessary to utilize machine-assisted methods to obtain Go board information. However, the images captured during human-machine interaction may have issues such as glare, misplacement of stones, and occlusion, as shown in Fig. 1. These problems can affect Go recognition, and current Go recognition methods still struggle to effectively address these issues. Incorrect recognition information read by the robot can impact judgment and decision-making, significantly reducing the level of intelligence during gameplay. Therefore, solving the problems that arise in Go recognition is of great significance to the study of human-machine gameplay.

F. Sun et al. (Eds.): ICCSIP 2023, CCIS 1919, pp. 260–274, 2024.
https://doi.org/10.1007/978-981-99-8021-5_20

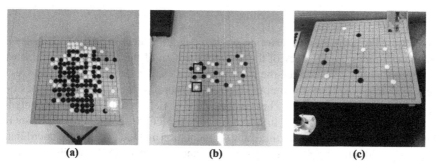

Fig. 1. (a) Go board image with highlight issues, (b) Go board image with misplacement of stones, (c) Go board image with occlusion.

2 Related work

In recent years, numerous methods have been proposed for Go recognition, and these methods can be broadly categorized into two main classes based on the tools they utilize: traditional image processing-based methods and deep learning-based methods.

2.1 Methods Based on Traditional Image Processing

As shown in Fig. 2(a), traditional image processing-based recognition methods for Go generally involve preprocessing the Go images to enhance their quality, including methods such as histogram equalization [2] and filtering. Then, the edges of the Go board are detected to obtain the four corner points of the board. In this work, Song et al. [3] used the watershed segmentation algorithm to recognize the outer boundary of the board and then constructed a reference model of the board. They extracted the complete board based on the four corners of the outer boundary using projection transformation to extract the board from a complex background. After detecting the board, the stones on the board need to be detected. Song et al. [4] first used geometric transformations and Hough transform to determine the intersection points of the board lines. They then calculated the average brightness value around each intersection point and used the K-Means algorithm for color quantization to detect the stones. In addition to the intersection point-based method, there are also template matching-based stone detection methods. Wang et al. [5], after calibrating the board, determined the type of stone based on the difference in area between small squares on different types of boards. They then calibrated consecutive images to obtain the difference image between two adjacent standard board images, and performed dilation, image masking multiplication, and erosion operations on the difference image to obtain the effective area and center coordinates of the stones. After detecting the stones, their colors can be determined using methods such as thresholding [6] or color judgment, thus obtaining all the board-related information in the image. Throughout the entire recognition process, board detection, stone detection, and stone recognition are sensitive to highlight issues, stone detection is sensitive to misplacement issues, and existing traditional image processing-based recognition methods have not addressed these problems.

2.2 Method Based on Deep Learning

As shown in Fig. 2(b), the deep learning-based recognition method first collects a dataset, which determines the accuracy of the network's output of the chessboard information. After preprocessing the dataset, the method extracts the features of the input images in the neural network. Then, the output layer of the neural network provides the position and category information of the chess pieces. Zhao et al. [7] used deep learning only for chess piece classification. They first used an edge detection algorithm to determine the chessboard position, then used a threshold segmentation method to detect the coordinates of the four calibration points on the chessboard, and calibrated them through perspective transformation. Finally, they trained a multilayer perceptron to classify the chess pieces and obtain the recognition information of the chessboard. Zhuo et al. [8] proposed an optimized CNN network to address the problem of glare. They first collected a dataset of approximately 3000 images with highlights and then trained two improved neural networks of different scales. The results detected by the two networks were fused to obtain the final recognition information. However, their method only solves partially severe highlight problems. Compared to traditional image processing methods, deep learning-based recognition methods can directly treat the chessboard corners as detection targets without the need for chessboard recognition, thus avoiding potential issues that may arise during the chessboard recognition process to some extent.

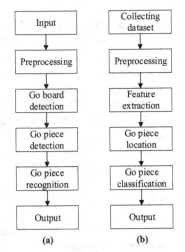

Fig. 2. (a) Process of traditional image processing-based Go recognition method, (b) Process of deep learning-based Go recognition method.

3 Methodology

3.1 Overview

In the process of collecting the dataset, to enhance the network's ability to extract features of shifted stones, we labeled the intersections of the chessboard instead of the stones themselves as the targets. As shown in Fig. 3, marking stones with different offsets as the same target helps increase the diversity of features and to some extent addresses the issue of stone shifting. To solve the problem of highlights, we attempted to remove the highlights in the image before recognizing the Go game. For this purpose, we chose a more advanced structure, the Swin Transformer [9], to remove highlight. To achieve more natural results and preserve more details and color information, we restore the highlights using the complete non-highlight image, and we apply extra weighting to the highlight regions during the restoration process. In addition, we used the YOLOv5 network [10] during the recognition process to ensure the overall accuracy of the recognition.

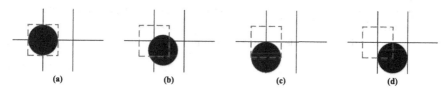

Fig. 3. Stones with different offsets: (a) the non-shifted case, (b) The piece is not far from the intersection point, (c) The piece is on a straight line, (d) The piece is completely offset and is positioned in the middle of a go board square.

MHRN-ST follows the workflow shown in Fig. 4. Firstly, we pretrain a multitask detection network (Net_D) based on YOLOv5. The glare image (Input) is first inputted into Net_D, which outputs a glare mask (Out_M). The glare image is then enhanced with the glare mask and inputted into a highlight removal network (Net_R) based on Swin Transformer. This network removes the highlight, and its output, the glare-free image (Out_R), is fed back into NetD to obtain information for board recognition ($OutD1$) and a new glare mask (Out_{M1}). The loss functions $L_{Content}$ and L_{Style} are computed based on the comparison between Out_R and the ground truth. The loss functions L_{HD} and L_{GD} are computed based on the comparison between Out_{D1}, Out_{M1}, and Out_D, Out_M. Next, we will describe the details of the network architecture and loss functions.

3.2 Specular Highlight Detection and Go Board Recognition

The YOLOv5 network has been widely used for various detection tasks. In this paper, we construct a multi-task network (Net_D) based on YOLOv5 for highlight segmentation and Go board recognition. As shown in the Stage1 part of Fig. 5., the Backbone and Neck parts of Net_D have the same structure as YOLOv5. The original image of size W × H goes through five downsampling operations in the Backbone part, resulting in a feature map of size W/32 × C/32, with the number of channels increasing from 3 to 1024. This feature map is fused with the features from the SPPF module and the Backbone in the

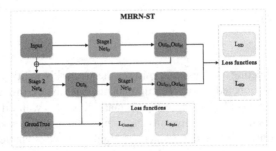

Fig. 4. Structural diagram of this paper's proposed chessboard recognition method MHRN-ST.

Neck part. Then, it is inputted into the Head parts of the two tasks. The detection head (DetectHead) is a decoupled head consisting of convolutional layers, BN layers, SiLU activation function, and an additional convolutional layer for controlling the size. The segmentation head (SegHead) consists of three upsampling blocks and an additional convolutional layer for controlling the size. Finally, the DetectHead outputs three sets of prediction boxes of different sizes, and the SegHead outputs a highlight tensor of size W × H. This information will guide the highlight removal network in performing highlight removal.

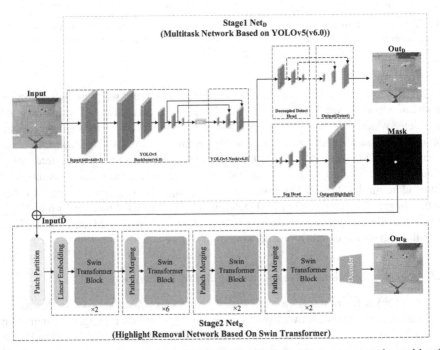

Fig. 5. The network structure details of MHRN-ST. The Stage1 part represents the multi-task detection network, while the Stage2 part represents the highlight removal network.

3.3 Specular Highlight Removal

Image restoration typically requires more contextual and semantic information. As shown in the Stage 2 part of Fig. 5, we use the Swin Transformer structure as the Backbone part of Net_R, while the decoding part consists of four upsampling layers.

Specifically, in the high-light image restoration process, the input image (Input) is different from the output mask from Net_D to obtain Input'. Input' is then subjected to patch partition operation, dividing the H × W × 3-sized image into H/4 × W/4 × 64 tensors. Subsequently, a linear embedding layer converts the tensor into a H/4 × W/4 × C feature vector. During the encoding process in Net_R, the patch merging layer divides the input into four patches and concatenates them. Each time this operation is performed, the size of the tensor is reduced by 3/4, the number of channels is doubled, and the resolution is halved. Therefore, before the Swin Transformer module calculation, a linear layer is used for expansion to maintain the tensor's resolution. As shown in Fig. 6, each Swin Transformer module consists of a layer normalization (LN) layer, a multi-head self-attention module, residual connections, and a multi-layer perceptron with non-linear Gaussian error linear units. Two different attention structures are used for joint computation in each pair of Swin Transformers, significantly enhancing the network's ability to learn contextual and global information. Throughout this process, the resolution and size of the feature tensor remain unchanged. Finally, the H × W × 3-dimensional image, after undergoing four encoding steps, is transformed into an H/16 × W/16 × 512-sized feature tensor.

After the encoding process, the tensor is passed through a convolutional layer used for dimension control to obtain the restored image (Out_R) after decoding. Finally, Out_R is input into the detection network Net_D, which outputs the chessboard recognition information (Out_D) and the highlight information (Mask'). The recognition information provides semantic information required for removing highlights, while the highlight information (M') is used in loss calculation along with the original mask (M) to enhance the network's ability to remove highlights.

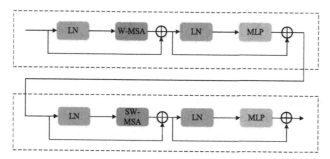

Fig. 6. A Swin Transformer Block. LN: LayerNorm layer. W-MSA: window-based multi-head self-attention module. SW-MSA: shifted window-based multi-head self-attention module.

3.4 Loss Functions

Highlight Detection. The detected networks Net$_D$ perform two detections, and the resulting M and M' respectively represent the high-gloss information that may exist in the images before and after removing highlights. Loss calculation can be performed to assess the removal capability of Net$_R$, represented as:

$$M = array(M > \delta), M' = array(M' > \delta) \tag{1}$$

$$L_{HD} = \frac{\sum_{i}^{n}(M \cap M') + \theta \sum_{i}^{n}(M' - M \cap M')}{n} \tag{2}$$

where M and M' represent the probability matrices for highlight detection, referred to as Mask and Mask' respectively. δ represents the detection threshold, which is set to 0.5 in this paper, i denotes the vector index, and n represents the total number of non-zero elements in M'. θ represents the weight, which is set to 0.2 in this paper.

Go Piece Recognition. After the completion of highlight removal, the output passes through Net$_D$ to obtain recognition information. The higher the accuracy of the recognition information, the better the ability of Net$_R$ to remove highlights. In this paper, the Go recognition loss L_{GD} refers to the loss used in YOLOv5, which includes confidence loss L_{obj}, classification loss L_{Cls}, and bounding box loss L_{BBox}:

$$L_{Obj}(P_0, P_{iou}) = BCE_{obj}^{sig}(P_0, P_{iou}) \tag{3}$$

$$L_{Cls}(c_p, c_{gt}) = BCE_{cls}^{sig}(c_p, c_{gt}) \tag{4}$$

$$L_{BBox}(b, b_{gt}) = 1 - CIOU \tag{5}$$

$$L_{GD} = \sum_{k=0}^{K}(\sum W_{Obj}L_{Obj} + \sum W_{Cls}L_{Cls} + \sum W_{BBox}L_{BBox}) \tag{6}$$

where P_0, P_{iou}, C_P, C_{gt}, b, and b_{gt} represent the predicted box confidence, IoU value between the predicted box and the label box, predicted class, true class, predicted boxes for each target, and true boxes for each target, respectively. BCE stands for binary cross-entropy loss, and sig indicates that the loss uses the sigmoid activation function. W_{obj}, W_{cls}, and W_{BBox} represent the weights used in counting the confidence loss, classification loss, and BBox loss. Here, W_{obj}, W_{cls}, and W_{BBox} are set to 0.7, 0.3, and 0.05, respectively.

Content Loss. Similar to general image restoration tasks, this paper utilizes the loss function proposed in reference [11] to supervise the generation of highlight-free images. This loss function helps reduce the texture differences between the network's predicted images and the real images.

$$L_{Content} = \alpha||I_T - I_p||_2^2 + \beta(||\nabla_x I_T - \nabla_x I_p||_1 + ||\nabla_y I_T - \nabla_y I_p||_1) \tag{7}$$

where α and β are hyperparameters representing the weights assigned to different components. Here, α is set to 0.2 and β is set to 0.4. I_T and I_P represent the ground truth highlight-free image and the predicted image, respectively. ∇x and ∇y represent the gradient values in the x and y directions of the corresponding image.

Style Loss. Style loss is commonly used in image style transfer tasks. In this paper, the style loss function proposed in reference [12] is employed, which utilizes style loss to impose constraints on both pixel and feature space.

$$\phi(I_T) = \psi(I_T)\psi(I_T)^T \tag{8}$$

$$L_{Style} = \sigma \|\phi(I_T) - \phi(I_P)\|_1 \tag{9}$$

where σ is set to 120 and ϕ represents the extraction of Gram matrices from feature tensors, while ψ represents the feature tensors obtained from the 0th, 5th, 10th, 19th, and 28th layers of the pre-trained VGG-16 network [13], I_T and I_p represent the ground truth highlight-free image and the predicted image respectively.

Net$_D$ Loss. We use the following loss function when training Net$_D$:

$$L_{YOLOHD} = BCE(P_{Pre}, P_T) \tag{10}$$

$$L_{YOLOGD} = L_{GD} \tag{11}$$

where L_{YOLOHD} represents the loss function for segmentation, BCE stands for binary cross-entropy loss, P_{Pre} denotes the predicted pixel values of an image, P_T represents the ground truth values of the image, and L_{YOLOGD} is the loss function for object detection.

Net$_R$ Loss. The total loss is represented as follows when training Net$_R$,

$$L_{Total} = \omega_1 L_{HD} + \omega_2 L_{GD} + \omega_3 L_{Content} + \omega_4 L_{Style} \tag{12}$$

where we set $\omega_1 = 1$, $\omega_2 = 1$, $\omega_3 = 100$, $\omega_4 = 0.1$.

3.5 Implementation Details

Datasets. We used a smartphone flashlight and a small flashlight as highlight light sources, shining them on different positions of the Go board and taking photos with a smartphone to obtain images with highlights. To prevent image shaking, we additionally used a smartphone holder and a Bluetooth controller to assist with the photography process. Furthermore, to approach real Go game scenarios as closely as possible, the collected Go images in this paper include different numbers of stones. The dataset in this paper is divided into two parts: Dataset$_D$ and Dataset$_R$. Dataset$_D$ consists of a total of 4242 Go images, including those from reference [8] and the ones collected in this paper, which are used to train the detection network Net$_D$. Dataset$_R$ consists of 1096 pairs of highlight images and their corresponding real images without highlights, and it is used to train the highlight removal network Net$_R$. In Dataset$_D$, we marked the intersection points of the Go board in the images to replace the marked Go stones themselves. This approach helps to some extent in addressing the issue of stone misalignment in Go images.

Training Settings. The images in the dataset of this paper are all of size 640×640. During training Net_D, We use YOLOV5s.pt to initialize the weights, with an initial learning rate of 10^{-5} and a decay rate of 1, after training for 300 epochs, we obtain the final Net_D model. During training Net_R, the initial learning rate is set to 10^{-4}, with a decay rate of 1 and a minimum learning rate of 10^{-5}, after training for 100 epochs we obtain the final Net_R model, And the Adam optimizer [14] is used in Net_R and Net_D. The whole network is deployed on a server with an NVIDIA GeForce GTX2080Ti graphics card for training.

4 Experimental Results

In this section, we first present the experimental results of MHRN-ST on the test set. We then compare the test results with those of several other methods and provide quantitative analysis to demonstrate the effectiveness of MHRN-ST.

4.1 Test Results

We select some representative images from the dataset and perform highlight removal and Go board recognition on these images. The results are shown in Fig. 7. These representative images cover various scenarios, including different shapes, different lighting intensities, and different numbers of Go stones. As shown in the figure, the proposed method in this paper can effectively detect and remove highlights in the images, and accurately recognize the state of the Go board in the images.

4.2 Comparisons

In the highlight test set, we compared the proposed method in this paper with several other Go recognition methods, including two neural network-based methods and one software-based method (YOLOv8 [15], RGGIR [8], TencentGo [16], where TencentGo is a Go software developed by Tencent that can perform recognition from photos, representing the software-based approach). Additionally, to validate the effectiveness of the data set in addressing the occlusion issue, we conducted additional comparisons between MHRN-ST and TencentGo, which does not require training.

To measure the accuracy of model recognition results, we count the number of misidentified chess pieces in the test images and calculate their average to obtain the average error rate(average error). A lower recognition error rate indicates a higher accuracy of the model's recognition. Similarly, to measure the recall rate of model recognition results, we count the number of undetected chess pieces in the test images and calculate their average to obtain the average missing rate(average missing rate). A lower average missing rate indicates a better recall rate for model recognition.

$$averageerror = \frac{\sum_{i=1}^{N} \frac{E_i}{T_i}}{N} \tag{13}$$

$$\text{average missing rate} = \frac{\sum\limits_{i=1}^{N} \frac{M_i}{T_i}}{N} \tag{14}$$

where E_i and M_i represent the total number of recognition errors and missing detections in the i-th image, N is the total number of images, and T_i is the total number of targets in the detection labels of the i-th image.

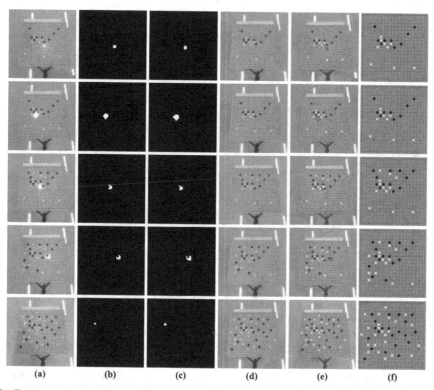

Fig. 7. Test results of the proposed method on the test set: (a) images with highlights, (b) manually created highlight detection labels, (c) highlight detection outputs, (d) diffuse real images without highlights, (e) images after the model removes highlights, (f) visualized Go board images after model recognition.

The comparative results on the high-light test set are shown in Fig. 8. Among them, the proposed method in this paper achieves the highest accuracy in the test results, reaching 95.67%. The BGGIR method performs well when the highlight is not a large area or a circular spot, but it also exhibits incorrect recognition in other cases. On the other hand, the YOLOv8 method has lower accuracy in the test set compared to the BGGIR method. It not only makes recognition errors in images with large high-light areas but also in images with weak light spots. TencentGo, as a comparative method, has the lowest accuracy. In the display images in Fig. 8, the high-light position in the third-row image is not at the intersection of the lines, making it difficult to be recognized as a chess piece. TencentGo also exhibits recognition errors in other cases. Therefore, it can be seen that the method proposed in this paper can effectively recognize high-lighted Go images.

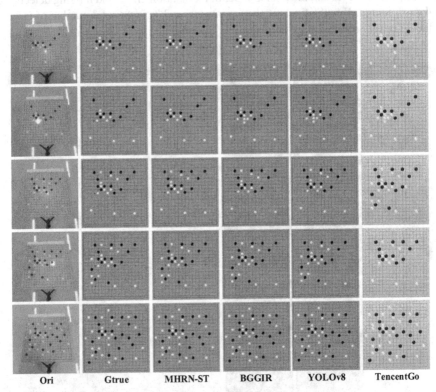

Ori   Gtrue   MHRN-ST   BGGIR   YOLOv8   TencentGo

Fig. 8. The testing results of the proposed method in this paper and several other methods on the test set are shown below. "Ori" represents the original image with highlights, "Gtrue" represents the ground truth, "MHRN-ST" represents the testing results of the method proposed in this paper, and "BGGIR," "YOLOv8," and "TencentGo" represent the testing results of the corresponding methods.

Table 1 displays two metrics for different methods shown in Fig. 8. The proposed method in this paper has the lowest recognition error rate among them. Regarding the average missing rate, there is not much difference among all the methods.

The additional offset comparison results are shown in Fig. 9. MHRN-ST is capable of addressing moderate offset situations, excluding cases where the chess pieces are completely offset. This is because these chess pieces may be located in the middle of a chessboard square or a line, far away from the intersections, making it difficult for the human eye to judge. In these images, MHRN-ST outperforms TencentGo in terms of the number of chess pieces that could not be recognized. There are some chess pieces located at the edges of the chessboard intersections that TencentGo also failed to identify.

Table 1. MHRN-ST is quantitatively compared with other methods in terms of highlight removal. The best result is indicated in bold.

Method	average error↓(%)	average missing rate↓(%)
YOLOv8 [15]	7.12	3.11
BGGIR [8]	6.41	**2.25**
TencentGo [16]	9.65	2.57
MHRN-ST	**4.33**	2.82

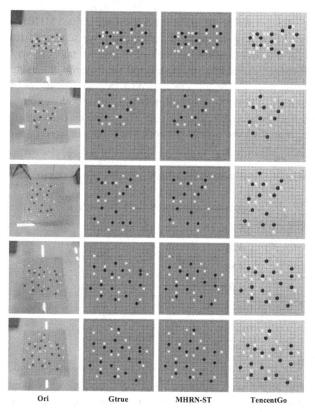

Ori   Gtrue   MHRN-ST   TencentGo

Fig. 9. The additional comparison results for the offset issue, "Ori": the original image, "Gtrue": ground truth results, "TencentGo": represent testing results obtained using TencentGo software.

Table 2 presents the results of the offset comparison experiment between MHRN-ST and TencentGo. MHRN-ST exhibits lower error rates and missing rates compared to TencentGo, indicating that MHRN-ST can to some extent address the offset issue.

Table 2. Results of the offset comparison experiment, with the best results highlighted in bold.

Method	Average error↓(%)	Average missing rate↓(%)
TencentGo [16]	3.78	8.33
MHRN-ST	**2.05**	**6.14**

4.3 Ablation Studies

To validate the effectiveness of MHRN-ST, we conducted ablation experiments on three aspects: the dataset, network architecture, and loss function. The test set was obtained from the dataset collected in this study. For the dataset, we trained MHRN-ST on publicly available datasets. Regarding the network architecture, we separately trained Net_D for recognition. As for the loss function, we trained an overall network without including L_{GD} and L_{HD}. Finally, we quantitatively analyzed the experiments using average error and average missing rate. The results are shown in Table 3. Our dataset to some extent improved the accuracy of Go recognition. Removing the high-gloss network architecture significantly reduced the recognition error rate. The additional loss functions also had a certain effect on improving the overall network's accuracy in Go recognition.

Table 3. Ablation Experiment Results Table, with the best results indicated in bold.

Method	Average error↓(%)	Average missing rate↓(%)
Without dataset	5.85	3.44
Without Net_R	9.01	3.62
Without extra loss	4.84	3.19
MHRN-ST	**4.33**	**2.82**

4.4 Limitations

For the specular highlight issue, although MHRN-ST can accurately identify most specular highlight areas and restore them by using similar colors, in extreme cases, such as when there are large areas of intense specular highlights in the image, as shown in Fig. 10, MHRN-ST may mistakenly remove the Go game information that is covered by the specular highlights, resulting in recognition errors. Regarding the offset issue, MHRN-ST is unable to recognize completely offset stones, as shown in Fig. 11(a). These stones are located far from the intersection points, making it difficult to determine their positions during recognition. As for the occlusion issue, in human-machine gameplay, the images captured by the robot may be occluded by the robot itself, as shown in Fig. 11(b). In such cases, MHRN-ST cannot recognize the occluded parts.

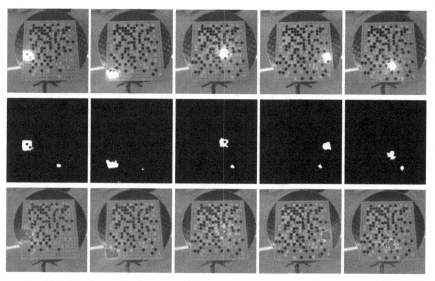

Fig. 10. The test results of this method on images with extreme highlights at different locations are shown from top to bottom, representing the original image with highlights, the detected highlights, and the restored image.

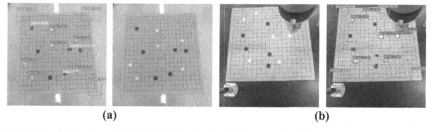

(a)   (b)

Fig. 11. The limitations of MHRN-ST in dealing with the offset and occlusion issues: (a) the offset problem, (b) the occlusion problem.

5   Conclusion

In the challenging task of Go board recognition, we collected a dataset for detecting highlights, recognizing stones, and removing highlights. We proposed a multi-stage network framework, including a multitask network for detecting highlights and recognizing stones, and a network for removing highlights. The highlight information obtained from the image input detection network serves as an auxiliary input, guiding the removal network to pay more attention to highlight areas. After removing the highlights, new highlight information and recognition information are obtained through the detection network, serving as additional loss functions to improve image restoration capability. Furthermore, MHRN-ST partially addresses the highlight and stone offset issues in Go recognition, improving the accuracy of Go recognition.

However, similar to other highlight removal methods, MHRN-ST cannot guarantee effective highlight removal and Go recognition under large-scale, high-intensity lighting conditions. Regarding occlusion issues, MHRN-ST is also unable to identify the occluded parts of the board in the image. In future research, we will create datasets based on stricter rules and employ appropriate methods to address the occlusion problem.

Acknowledgement. This work is supported by the National Natural Science Foundation of China (grant No.: 62073249) and Major Project of Hubei Province Technology Innovation (grant No.: 2019AAA071).

References

1. David, S., Aja, H., et al.: Mastering the game of Go with deep neural networks and tree search. Nature **529**, 484–489 (2016)
2. R D., Joany R.: Image enhancement by Histogram equalization. Nano. Corr. Sci. Eng., 21–30 (2015)
3. Jie, S., Miaozhong, Y.: A calibration method for the vision system of go-robot. In: Wanqing W., Lipo W. (eds.) 2019 6th International Conference on Systems and Informatics (ICSAI), Image Processing, vol.6, pp. 1157–1162. IEEE, Shanghai (2019)
4. Jie, S., Shanshan, L.: A robust algorithm for go image recognition in go game. In: 2018 IEEE 4th International Conference on Computer and Communications (ICCC), Pattern Recognition, pp. 1397–1402. IEEE, Chengdu (2018)
5. Wang, Y., Zhang, Y.: General chess piece positioning method under uneven illumination. J. Comput. Appl. **40**(12), 3490–3498 (2020)
6. Otsu, N.: A Threshold selection method from gray-level histograms. IEEE Trans. Syst. Man Cybern.Cybern. **9**(1), 62–66 (2007)
7. Zhao, X., Zhao, X.: Weiqi Recognition Method under Uneven Illumination based on Neural Networks, Software Engineering **25**(11), 1–4 (2022)
8. Zhuo, Y., Han, F., et al.: Reliable go game images recognition under strong light attack. IEEE Access **9**, 160064–160071 (2021)
9. Ze, L., Zhang, Y., et al.: Swin transformer: hierarchical vision transformer using shifted windows. In: Proceedings of the IEEE/CVF International Conference on Computer Vision (ICCV), pp. 10012–10022 (2021)
10. Joseph, R., Santosh, D.: You only look once, Unified, real-time object detection. In: Proceedings of the IEEE Conference on Computer Vision and Pattern Recognition (CVPR), pp. 779–788 (2016)
11. Kaixuan, W., Jiaolong, Y.: Single image reflection removal exploiting misaligned training data and network enhancements. In: Proceedings of the IEEE/CVF Conference on Computer Vision and Pattern Recognition (CVPR), pp. 8178–8187 (2019)
12. L. A., Ecker, A. S.: Image style transfer using convolutional neural networks. In: Proceedings of the IEEE/CVF Conference on Computer Vision and Pattern Recognition (CVPR), pp. 2414–2423 (2016)
13. Karen, S., Andrew, Z.: Very deep convolutional networks for large-scale image recognition, Computer Science (cs.CV), (2014)
14. Diederik, P., Jimmy, L.: Adam: A method for stochastic optimization, Computer Science(cs.CV) (2015)
15. Ultralytics. https://github.com/ultralytics/ultralytics
16. TencentGo. https://txwq.qq.com/

Construction of Minecraft Virtual Reality Scene Based on Voxel Point Cloud

Nuocheng Ji[1,2], Hanyang Zhuang[1(✉)], and Ming Yang[3,4,5]

[1] The University of Michigan – Shanghai Jiao Tong University Joint Institute, Shanghai Jiao Tong University, Shanghai 200240, China
zhuanghany11@sjtu.edu.cn
[2] Global Institute of Future Technology, Shanghai Jiao Tong University, Shanghai 200240, China
[3] Department of Automation, Shanghai Jiao Tong University, Shanghai 200240, China
[4] Key Laboratory of System Control and Information Processing, Ministry of Education of China, Shanghai 200240, China
[5] Shanghai Engineering Research Center of Intelligent Control and Management, Shanghai 200240, China

Abstract. Virtual Reality is an important development direction in recent years. Minecraft, a popular sandbox game, has a great potential to become a virtual reality platform for building immersive environments. Traditional methods of building virtual reality scenes rely heavily on massive human labors and require high levels of proficiency. To address these limitations, we propose an automatic, voxelated 3D modeling method with foreground and background environment segmented that can reduce modeling costs and achieve effective application in Minecraft virtual reality scenes such as virtual campuses. The proposed method leverages the use of point cloud reconstruction using a voxelization approach. A pipeline of converting point cloud to Minecraft scene is developed. Through preprocessing, segmenting, coloring, and exporting, a Minecraft virtual reality scene can be automatically generated based on voxel point cloud. Due to the noise in point cloud may cause defect during voxelization, a denoising and smoothing method using slice scanning and voxel connectivity segmentation has been implemented. It can generate building structures with clear outlines and uniform colors. And the entire process requires low computational complexity and achieves fast generation. We conducted experiments based on this method in indoor scenes, outdoor building landmarks, and complex underground scenes, and obtained results with clear structures and smooth surfaces, saving a lot of time for subsequent detailed modeling.

Keywords: 3D Modeling · Virtual Reality · Point Cloud Voxelization · Minecraft

F. Sun et al. (Eds.): ICCSIP 2023, CCIS 1919, pp. 275–291, 2024.
https://doi.org/10.1007/978-981-99-8021-5_21

1 Introduction

Virtual Reality (VR) is one of the important development directions in recent years. It is also an important core technology to realize the concepts of Metaverse and digital twins by building scenes similar to reality in virtual environments and creating immersive user experiences.

Minecraft is a well-known sandbox game with the theme of freely creating and destroying different types of blocks in a three-dimensional space filled with blocks. Minecraft has consistently topped the best-selling charts for over a decade and has become a virtual popular culture, which provides one of the most important application scenarios for virtual reality.

In December last year, we proposed the method of using Minecraft to build a virtual campus in the Metaverse scene in Virtual Campus: Voxel SJTU Exploration and Practice [3]. However, as mentioned in the paper above, in Minecraft, the traditional method of virtually reconstructing real environmental scenes relies on a large amount of manual 3D modeling work, which is time-consuming and labor-intensive, and requires high proficiency in usage. Moreover, foreground objects and background buildings often need to be separated and restored. There is currently no effective automatic modeling method for Minecraft virtual reality scenes.

In the fields of autonomous driving and architectural surveying, the main application currently is using point cloud reconstruction for automatic modeling, according to Canevese [4]. A point cloud is a dataset of three-dimensional coordinate points arranged according to a regular grid. Compared with traditional 3D models, 3D point clouds are not constrained by artificial modeling surface equations and surface continuity, and can more easily restore any complex Solid geometry, reproduce finer details and more sharp edges. However, due to the spatial disorder, color uncertainty, and noise generated during collection of 3D point clouds, they need to be processed to meet the visualization requirements of Minecraft small-scale, voxel scenes. Among them, voxelization of point clouds, which converts the representation of discrete points in 3D point clouds into the closest voxel representation, can effectively meet the above requirements, which is supported by the experiment of Hinks et al.[9].

Therefore, in response to the problems above, this paper proposes an automatic, voxelated, and segmented foreground and background environment 3D modeling method to achieve simple process, efficient operation, and popularization of virtual reality 3D scene construction in Minecraft, reduce modeling costs, and achieve effective application in Minecraft virtual reality scenes such as virtual campuses.

The main contribution of this paper is twofold:

1. Develop a pipeline to automatically generate Minecraft scene based on existing point cloud data
2. Propose an algorithm of point cloud denoising and smoothing to optimize the defects during point cloud voxelization process.

This paper is organized as follows: First, related works of this paper are summarized and analyzed; then, a methodology section is presented to show the pipeline of converting and optimizing the point cloud for Minecraft virtual reality scene; afterwards, experiments are carried out to apply the method and determine the optimal parameters;

in the end, a conclusion of this paper is drawn that this method can quickly and clearly generate voxel-based structures of buildings in virtual reality.

2 Related Works

Minecraft is closely integrated with virtual reality technology and has a wide range of applications. Rospigliosi [1] proposes that Minecraft is becoming an important application scenario for virtual reality, including education, social networking, and work. MENA Report [2] presents a method of combining Minecraft and virtual reality to assist urban design in Johannesburg. Yang et al. [3] reconstructs Shanghai Jiao Tong University in Minecraft, in which multiple virtual reality events were held. Presenting virtual reality in Minecraft is becoming a trend. However, Yang [3] points out the tediousness of the modeling process in virtual reality scene reconstruction. Thus, finding an automated modeling method from other fields may be a solution.

Reconstruction from point cloud data has been a very active area in virtual reality. Canevese [4] suggests researching new methods and tools that combine point clouds and virtual reality for 3D modeling, surpassing the simplified digital virtual reconstruction. Many methods have been proposed for automatic modeling from point cloud data (see Fig. 1):

Lafarge et al. [5] proposes a structural method for building reconstruction from single digital surface models using a library of 3D parametric blocks. However, it needs a lot of computation and lacks wall information. Poullis et al. [6] presents a complete framework for the automatic modeling from point cloud data. The models are generated based on the roof outlines. Although this will provide a clear overhead outline, it is difficult to effectively reconstruct the obstructed parts inside the building wall. Xiao et al. [7] presents a 3D reconstruction and visualization system for automatically producing clean and well-regularized texture-mapped 3D models for large indoor scenes, from ground-level photographs and 3D laser points. However, it cannot present the concave and convex surface of the wall, and the realism of the scene is limited. Han [8] proposes a systematic way to reconstruct building structures, but the main modeling work still relies on manual labor, and the point clouds are only used as reference.

Fig. 1. Results of automatic generated 3D objects [5–8]

All the methods above can realize a relatively accurate restoration of the original scene, but require a lot of computing power, and do not match Minecraft voxel scene. Voxelization, which converts the point cloud into the voxel data mesh closest to the point cloud, will be a good alternative that not only reduce the cost of computation but also facilitate the generation of Minecraft scenes (shown in Fig. 2). Hinks et al. [9] achieves results in less than 30s for data sets up to 650000 points through voxelization, demonstrating the speed and low computational consumption of voxelization. However, the voxelization method is not perfectly applied to Minecraft virtual reality scene generation currently. The voxelization of LiDAR data in Minecraft has been studied by García[10], but only the rough contour of the building has been obtained with no texture. Voxelization of ArcGIS point cloud is applied by FME [11] to Minecraft, but is only useful for the huge physical geography scene, with no high detail information, which cannot meet practical demands.

Fig. 2. Results of voxelization based automatic generated 3D objects [9–11]

Overall, voxelization approach provide a method that is very suitable for generating Minecraft virtual scenes. However, point cloud data collected using 3D modeling methods such as SLAM in real environments still has structural and color noise. There is currently limited research on how to smooth and optimize this type of noise in voxelated Minecraft scenes, which is also the focus of this paper.

3   Methodology

In this section, the methodology of the proposed point-cloud-to-Minecraft conversion pipeline is introduced. The figure below indicates the pipeline which includes three main parts: a point cloud preprocessing step is applied at the beginning to down sample the point cloud into voxels and denoise it. Afterwards, a segmentation and coloring step is utilized to the preprocessed voxel point cloud. In the end, the colorized voxels are converted to fit into the virtual reality scenario by mapping the voxels into blocks of Minecraft. The pipeline is shown below in Fig. 3.

3.1   Point Cloud Preprocessing

The preprocessing step starts from an existing point cloud. Firstly, a bounding box for the point cloud of a single building is set, so that each side of the bounding box is parallel to the wall and ground. Because the edges and corners of buildings are mostly at right angles, adjusting the bounding box faces parallel to the building faces and setting a reasonable coordinate reference system is beneficial for the subsequent voxelization of surface smoothness and aesthetics, and facilitates connectivity-based voxel cloud segmentation.

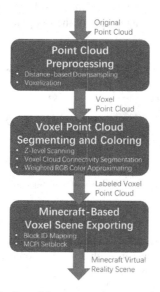

Fig. 3. Pipeline of the proposed construction method

Down sample point clouds below a certain distance threshold (such as 0.1 m) to remove outliers. In Minecraft scenes, overly dense point clouds are difficult to achieve good performance. It is necessary to preserve the shape of the point cloud while making it sparse enough to meet the performance scale of Minecraft. Therefore, apply a distance-based down sampling on point cloud data. The whole pre-process is shown below in Fig. 4.

Fig. 4. Point cloud pre-process by down sampling at a distance of 0.1 m

Then voxelization step is implemented on the preprocessed point cloud. The main idea is to voxelize the point cloud according to the preset accuracy to obtain a voxel grid. The voxelization method is as follows in Fig. 5. First, detect the cuboid bounding box of the point cloud by getting the maximums and minimums of each point's x, y and z, by calculating $x_{max} - x_{min}$, ... Then divide the bounding box into a 3D grid of equally sized voxels. The size of the voxel is defined by the parameter voxel size. If at least one point in the point cloud is in a voxel space, that voxel space is occupied; The RGB data of each voxel is taken as the average value of the midpoint of that voxel.

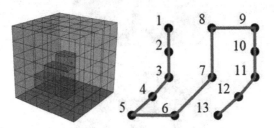

Fig. 5. Voxel grid and storage order

This step is mainly developed in the framework of Open3D. It uses a row-major order to store the voxel grid in a list, which means that the voxels are stored in a contiguous block of memory and the values in each row are stored consecutively. This order is efficient for accessing voxels in a linear fashion, but it may not be optimal for certain operations such as searching for neighboring voxels.

Therefore, in order to facilitate neighboring voxels searching, it is a good choice to create an additional hash table indexed by the (x, y, z) coordinates of voxels as reference. We first need to obtain the bounding box based on the number of voxels for the voxel grid. Here we perform the following calculation on the original point cloud:

$$B_x, B_y, B_z = \text{RoundUp}(\frac{\left[x_{max} - x_{min}, y_{max} - y_{min}, z_{max} - z_{min}\right]}{\text{voxel\_size}})$$

where B_x, B_y, B_z are the boundaries of the voxel number grid.

Build up the hash table with the length $B_x \cdot B_y \cdot B_z$. The hashed index will be $x \cdot B_z \cdot B_y + z \cdot B_y + y$ (see Fig. 6), as in Minecraft the height is expressed in axis y instead of z. All other attributes of the voxel are stored as a list in the node. This hash table would be useful for quickly finding the neighboring voxels of a certain voxel.

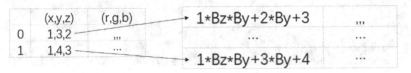

Fig. 6. Voxel grid hashing

By combining the previous row-major order voxel grid list and the voxel grid hash table together, we can achieve either fast linear or neighbor access based on different demands. The voxelized point cloud data will be stored in memory in an ordered manner, which is beneficial for reducing random memory access and increasing data processing efficiency. The ordered storage and down sampling brought by voxelization can handle point cloud data with large magnitudes. Voxelized data can efficiently use spatial convolution, which is beneficial for extracting multi-scale and multi-level local feature information. The voxelization demo is shown below in Fig. 7.

Fig. 7. Point cloud voxelization with voxel size $= 0.2$

3.2 Voxel Point Cloud Segmenting and Coloring

Point cloud coloring is easily affected by lighting and shadows, which can result in inconsistent colors on a plane with uniform colors in reality. For point clouds that contain rich information during collection, methods such as illumination compensation and reflection equalization provide feasible color optimization solutions, but this places high requirement on the scanning equipment and point cloud quality. More noteworthy is that slight difference in colors of adjacent blocks that should have the same color can create a huge sense of discord in Minecraft small-scale voxel scenes.

Therefore, it is better to use structural information to assist in coloring for Minecraft. We can perform point cloud segmentation to help color floors or walls in a same way. First, find the floors and ceilings. The floor and ceiling have a clear feature in the voxel cloud, which is that they occupy a large number of grids on the same x-y plane. So we use voxel hash table to scan the occupied grids on each z-level, taking the maximum value as the reference floor (see Fig. 8), and selecting levels that are greater than 50% of the maximum value as optional floors or ceilings.

Next, find the walls. There are two ways to fulfill this target. One way is to scan several z-levels a little above the floor or below the ceiling to obtain planar structure slices. By overlaying these planar structural slices together (see Fig. 9), we can obtain a more accurate wall contour. Then stack the contour to fill the space between the floor and the ceiling, we can get a high-quality indoor structural scene.

Another way is to use voxel cloud connectivity segmentation algorithm, clustering walls based on the property of coplanar adjacency between voxels (see Fig. 10). Start from a voxel, scan along the y and z axis to find how many voxels are connected (see Fig. 11). If the connected voxels along two axes are all above a certain number, this voxel is probably a part of the wall. Label this wall as connected.

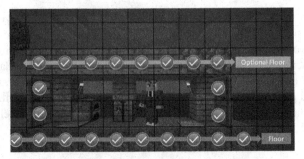

Fig. 8. Floor and ceiling selection shown in Minecraft

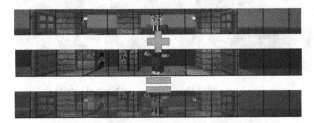

Fig. 9. Overlay slices to find the wall contour

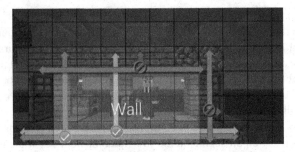

Fig. 10. Use y-z connectivity to find the wall

Slice scanning and voxel connectivity segmentation can be used in combination to improve segmentation performance. Slice scanning only segments some certain layers, which can effectively reduce computation and improve efficiency. While voxel connectivity segmentation can determine the results based on the connection relationship between pixels, thus avoiding mis-segmentation and under-segmentation.

Then we can color the segmented scene structure. In indoor scenes, such walls, floors, and ceilings often have patches of the same color. Due to the limited color quality of the point cloud mentioned above, we segment the plane and assign the same color to connected voxels with similar colors.

Here, we use the weighted RGB color difference formula to determine whether the colors are similar:

$$D(x_i \cdot y_i) = \sqrt{w_r\left(r_i - r_j\right)^2 + w_g\left(g_i - g_j\right)^2 + w_b\left(b_i - b_j\right)^2}$$

where $w_r = 3, w_g = 4, w_b = 2$.

We randomly assign a voxel as the reference voxel, and scan the y-level grid using KD Tree search on the voxel hash table to judge whether the connected voxels are closed in RGB. If so, the satisfied voxel will be labeled a new RGB of the reference voxel. If at one voxel the RGB difference is large enough, that voxel will be set as the new reference voxel, the same process above will continue until all the connected voxels are labeled (see Fig. 11). The labeled RGB will be used during the exporting-to-Minecraft process, it will be mapped to certain textures, which will be shown later.

Fig. 11. Color assignment on voxels

3.3 Minecraft Based Voxelized Scene Exporting

Export the segmented voxel cloud to Minecraft, and complete the construction of virtual reality scene.

3.3.1 Voxel Point Cloud Color Mapping

Firstly, establish a Minecraft block color dictionary. In Minecraft, each kind of block has a unique Block ID that represents its type and properties (see Fig. 12). For example, in Minecraft Java Edition 1.14, the block ID for Stone is 1, while the block ID for Grass Block is 2. Select the complete blocks in Minecraft (excluding slabs, plants, etc.) and the blocks with different texture on six faces (excluding workbenches, furnaces, etc.), and take the average RGB value of 16x16 pixel points on their surface to obtain the corresponding RGB vector of the block. Map it to the Block ID in Minecraft to establish a block color dictionary. For the example shown in Fig. 12, the RGB color vector (73, 92, 44) is mapped to 251:13, which is the Block ID of Green Concrete in Minecraft.

Mappings between RGB color and Minecraft block has been formed. For example, the voxel with RGB color of (73, 92, 44) will be mapped to a green concrete block [251, 13], and the voxel with RGB color of (78, 85, 50) will be mapped to a green terracotta

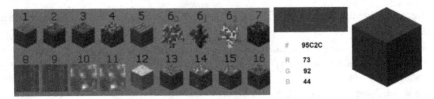

Fig. 12. Minecraft Block ID and RGB mapping

block [159, 13]. Approximating the RGB data of voxel point clouds to the Minecraft block color dictionary using the weighted RGB color difference formula, taking the RGB vector in the color dictionary closest to the voxel point RGB vector, and replacing its original RGB information with the corresponding block ID.

3.3.2 Exporting Voxel Point Cloud

Use MCPI of python, adjust the scaling ratio and origin coordinates as needed to export the voxel cloud to the scene in Minecraft. The setblock() function in MCPI can place blocks with corresponding IDs at specified (x, y, z) coordinate points.

In Minecraft, each block in the game world is stored in a three-dimensional grid of blocks called the chunk (see Fig. 13). A chunk is a 16x16x256 section of the game world that contains up to 65,536 individual blocks. Each chunk is assigned a set of X, Y, and Z coordinates that represent its position in the game world.

Fig. 13. A chunk in Minecraft (rotated)

Within each chunk, the blocks are stored as a flat array of 16-bit Block IDs, where each ID corresponds to a different type of block and its associated properties. The blocks are stored in the array in a specific order, starting from the bottom of the chunk and moving upward in vertical columns.

To place a specific block at a given coordinate, MCPI first determines which chunk the block is located in, based on its X, Y, and Z coordinates. It then uses the coordinates to calculate the index of the block's Block ID in the chunk's block array. Finally, it replaces the Block ID at that index to change the type and properties of the block.

For example, to place a block at coordinates (10, 64, 20), MCPI would first determine that this block is located in the chunk at coordinates (0, 4, 1). It would then use the coordinates to calculate the index in the chunk's block array, which would be:

$$Index = (Y \times 16 + Z) \times 16 + X = 106,498$$

To export the voxel cloud to Minecraft, select a point with an absolute coordinate in Minecraft as the origin coordinate of exporting, corresponding to (0,0,0) of the voxel cloud. Then add the coordinate vector (x,y,z) of each voxel point onto the XYZ of the origin coordinate and export using setblock(X + x, Y + y, Z + z, [Block ID]). The whole exporting process is illustrated below in Fig. 14:

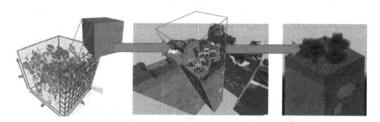

Fig. 14. Complete exporting process

4 Experiment

4.1 Experiment Conditions

The input data is an indoor office point cloud data, captured by the NavVis VLX indoor mobile mapping system in.e57 file format. 32,992,442 points, with coordinates and attributes such as color and intensity. The bounding box size (dimensions) are X = 25.3377 m, Y = 28.9057 m, Z = 5.744 m. The point cloud is shown below in Fig. 15:

Fig. 15. Original point cloud and bounding box

The processing platform used in this paper is a PC with i7-10710U CPU; the RAM is 16.0 GB. The Minecraft Version used in here is Java 1.14.3. Some of the basic parameters used are the RGB Range = 256, which is used to build the converter function from RGB attributes of each point to Minecraft Block ID; Port = 4711, which represents Minecraft RaspberryJuice Spigot server plugin's port to interface with Python; Indication Block ID: 35, 95, 159, 251, which are the Wool, Terracotta, Concrete, Stained Glass Block ID in Minecraft, each type of which has 16 different color variants, used to indicate the adjacency of voxel points.

4.2 Results and Analysis

4.2.1 Experiment Results of Preprocessing and Voxelization

We first use CloudCompare to convert.e57 to.las and change the bounding box. The original box has dimensions X = 27.49, Y = 32.20, Z = 5.74, and 32,992,442 points. Then we manually minimize the bounding box (see Fig. 16). And the box dimensions have been reduced to X = 15.06, Y = 28.50, Z = 2.68. This eliminates useless scattered outliers, and allows the bounding box to fit the main building body as closely as possible. It also reduces the number of 3D meshes and memory consumption in the following generation of hash table.

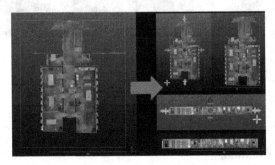

Fig. 16. Minimize the bounding box

Then Subsample the point cloud with the method of space. Set the minimum space between points as 0.1 (see Fig. 17). The points included in the box are now reduced to 71,397. This significantly reduces the memory consumption required for voxelization and export, while maintaining structural integrity. Having similar distances between points also facilitates the accuracy of subsequent grid processing.

Fig. 17. Subsample the point cloud

Then voxelize the subsampled point cloud into different sizes with different parameter v_{size}. The tested v_{size} are 1, 0.5, 0.4, 0.3, 0.2, 0.1, and the voxelization results are shown below in Fig. 18:

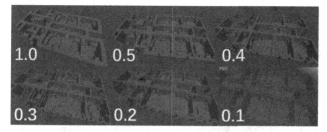

Fig. 18. Voxelization results with different v_{size}

With v_{size} gradually decreases, and the voxelization results present a more detailed scene, but when v_{size} is less than 0.1, the connectivity of voxels in its structure is significantly insufficient, resulting in a large number of gaps. It can be seen that when $v_{size} = 0.2$, voxelization results can maintain structural integrity while also maximize the details of the scene. Thus, we will use $v_{size} = 0.2$ for the following experiments. With $v_{size} = 0.2$, the boundaries of the voxel number grid are: $Bx = 76$, $By = 143$, $Bz = 14$.

4.2.2 Experiment Results of Segmentation and Coloring

First, we need to find the reference floor and the optional floors. The reference floor level is $z = 1$, with no optional floor detected. The number of voxels on each z-level and the plane of the floor is shown below in Fig. 19:

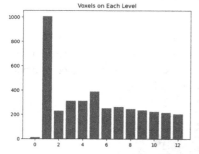 

Fig. 19. Voxels on each floor and the reference floor

Then we use two different methods to segment the walls. The first method is to slice some certain z-levels above the reference floor and overlay them together. The variable parameter used here is $h\%$, which contains percentages of the height where we can slice a good enough z-level excluding the furniture inside the room to get the contour of the wall. The following Fig. 20 shows the z-level slices with different $h\%$:

It can be seen that in order to get the clearest contour of the wall, $h\% = 0.9$ is the best choice. If we want to segment possible windows, overlay with $h\% = 0.7$. If we want to segment possible doors, overlay with $h\% = 0.5$. The image below shows the overlay of 0.9 and 0.5 slices. The yellow voxels indicate the places that on 0.7 is empty while on 0.9 is solid, which is possibly a part of a door as shown in Fig. 21:

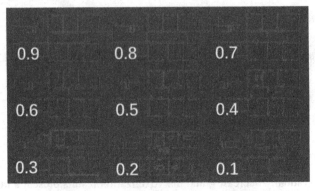

Fig. 20. Z-level slices with different h percentages

Fig. 21. Segment walls and doors by overlaying 0.9 and 0.5 slices

Another method to segment the walls is using y-z connectivity. The variable parameter used here is $connectivity_{min}$. Numbers of voxels connected to a certain voxel along an axis must be larger than $connectivity_{min}$, and then this voxel will be labeled as a part of the wall. Using $connectivity_{min} = 2$, the result is shown in Fig. 22:

Fig. 22. Segment walls using y-z connectivity > 2

Although this method can directly obtain the wall, it is not accurate in segmenting irregular sunken window parts, resulting in missing data. It is not quite useful in this scenario. But in other two examples (see Fig. 25 and 26), the results are good.

After segmenting the floors and walls, we can start to color the voxels. These are the compared results of coloring the floor. On the left, RGB colors are converted into the result of Minecraft directly using original RGB, while on the right conversion is done after segmenting and unifying the RGB. It can be seen that the influence of light and shadow has been eliminated after segmented coloring as shown in Fig. 23.

Fig. 23. Comparison of coloring results

4.2.3 Exporting Results

Then we can export the processed point cloud into Minecraft (see Fig. 24). In the entire Minecraft virtual reality scene generation process, the only manual part is adjusting the point cloud bounding box during the first preprocessing step, and all other processes are fully automated. During the voxelization and segmentation process, less than 1GB of memory was used, and the processing time was compressed to within one minute.

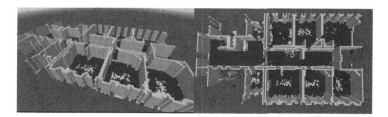

Fig. 24. Exported results in Minecraft

There are two other point cloud examples for illustration. One example is the East Gate of Shanghai Jiao Tong University (see Fig. 25). With our method, we can quickly and automatically obtain the ground, walls, and surrounding contours of the building, greatly reducing the time for subsequent manual detailed modeling.

Another example is an underground garage (see Fig. 26). The original point cloud does not contain RGB information, so we only show segmentation here. For such a complex indoor structure, it still has good ability to segment and reconstruct real-world structures.

Fig. 25. Reconstruction of East gate with our methods

Fig. 26. Segmentation of a garage with our methods

5 Conclusion

For the development of virtual reality scenes in Minecraft, this method achieves fast and convenient automatic modeling, solving the problem of traditional manual modeling being time-consuming and labor-intensive. Compared to existing automatic modeling methods, this method can meet the needs of developers while maintaining a certain degree of scene accuracy, providing another alternative to low model style. By combining software and hardware systems, it can quickly generate voxel based virtual reality building exteriors and structures.

The Voxel SJTU virtual campus is a Metaverse project initiated by me to restore Minhang Campus of Shanghai Jiao Tong University based on Minecraft. At present, the manual modeling on a block-by-block basis requires unimaginable time and effort. By studying such an automatic, voxelated, and segmented foreground and background environment 3D modeling method for virtual reality 3D scene construction in Minecraft, it is possible to generate voxel models of buildings quickly and automatically, thereby improving modeling efficiency; At the same time, clarify the three-dimensional scale to improve modeling accuracy; Provide a blueprint to assist in subsequent detailed manual modeling.

References

1. Rospigliosi, P.: Metaverse or Simulacra? Roblox, Minecraft, Meta and the turn to virtual reality for education, socialization and work. Interact. Learn. Environ. **30**(1), 1–3 (2022)
2. United States: Testing Minecraft and mixed-reality for community-led urban design in Johannesburg. (2017). MENA Report (2017)
3. Yang, Y., Ji, N., Li, A.: Virtual campus: voxel SJTU exploration and practice. China Educ. Netw. **12**, 75–77 (2022)
4. Canevese, E., De Gottardo, T.: Beyond point clouds and virtual reality: innovative methods and technologies for the protection and promotion of cultural heritage. In: International Archives of the Photogrammetry, Remote Sensing and Spatial Information Sciences, XLII-5/W1, pp. 685–691 (2017)
5. Lafarge, F., Descombes, X., Zerubia, J., Pierrot-Deseilligny, M.: Structural approach for building reconstruction from a single DSM. IEEE Trans. Pattern Anal. Mach. Intell. **32**(1), 135–147 (2010)
6. Poullis, C.: A framework for automatic modeling from point cloud data. IEEE Trans. Pattern Anal. Mach. Intell. **35**(11), 2563–2575 (2013)
7. Xiao, J., Furukawa, Y.: Reconstructing the world's museums. Int. J. Comput. Vision **110**(3), 243–258 (2014)
8. Han, D.: Research on the application of iterative reconstruction and virtual display of ancient buildings. University of Science and Technology Liaoning (2021)
9. Hinks, T., Carr, H., Truong-Hong, L., Laefer, D.: Point cloud data conversion into solid models via point-based voxelization. J. Surv. Eng. **139**(2), 72–83 (2013)
10. García-Fernández, J., Mateus, L.: Solution supporting the communication of the built heritage: semi-automatic production path to transfer semantic LIDAR data to minecraft environment. Digital Appl. Archaeol. Cult. Heritage **14**, E00112 (2019)
11. Greene, R.: Safe Software's FME 2015. GeoInformatics **18**(1), 28 (2015)
12. Lin, J., Zhang, F.: R3LIVE: a robust, real-time, RGB-colored, LiDAR-Inertial-Visual tightly-coupled state Estimation and mapping package. In: 2022 International Conference on Robotics and Automation (ICRA), pp. 10672–10678 (2022)
13. Poux, F., Billen, R.: Voxel-based 3D point cloud semantic segmentation: unsupervised geometric and relationship featuring vs deep learning methods. ISPRS Int. J. Geo Inf. **8**(5), 213 (2019)
14. Poux, F., Neuville, R., Nys, G., Billen, R.: 3D point cloud semantic modelling: integrated framework for indoor spaces and furniture. Remote Sensing (Basel, Switzerland) **10**(9), 1412 (2018)
15. Poux, F., Ponciano, J.: Self-learning ontology for instance segmentation of 3D indoor point cloud. In: International Archives of the Photogrammetry, Remote Sensing and Spatial Information Sciences, XLIII-B2-2020, pp. 309–316 (2020)
16. NavVis VLX point cloud data. https://www.navvis.com/resources/specifications/navvis-vlx-point-cloud-office

Author Index

Printed in the United States
by Baker & Taylor Publisher Services